Into Thin Places

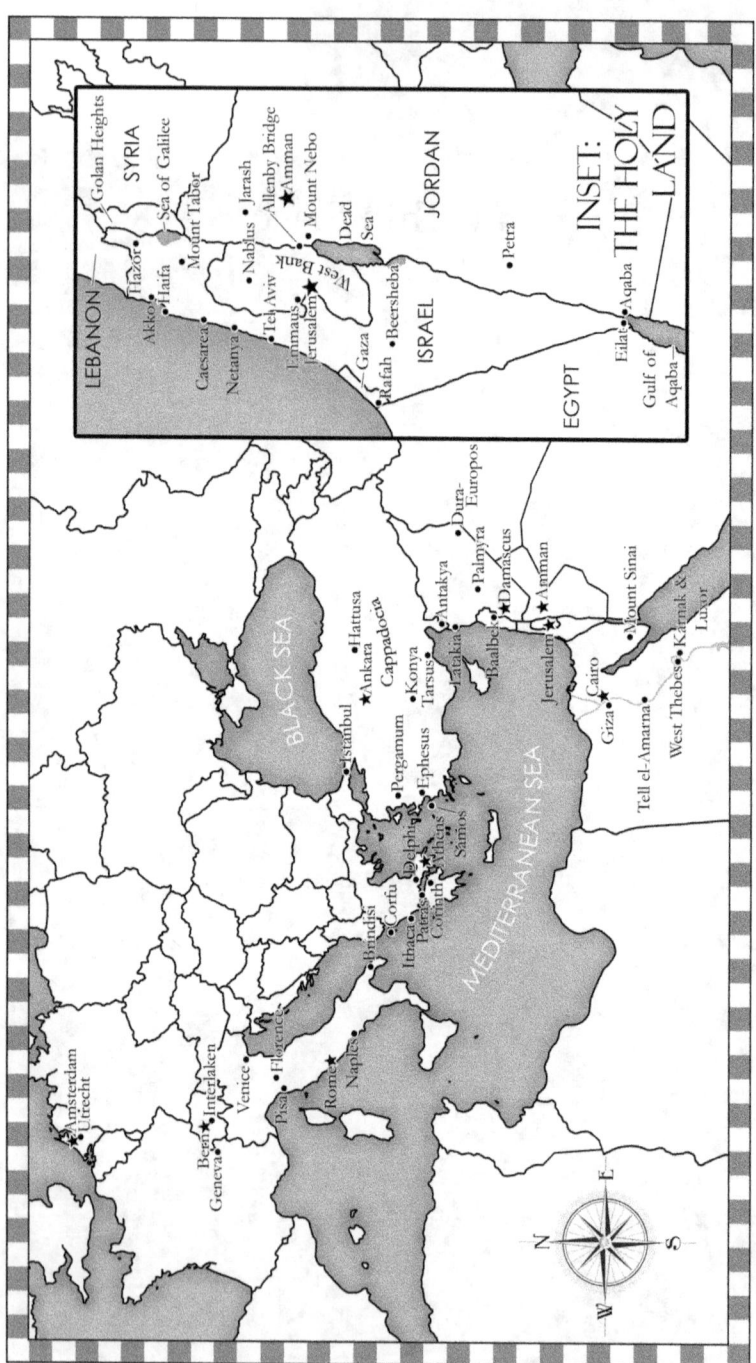

The Mediterranean World

Into Thin Places

One Man's Search for the Center

ROBERT P. VANDE KAPPELLE

RESOURCE *Publications* • Eugene, Oregon

INTO THIN PLACES
One Man's Search for the Center

Copyright © 2011 Robert P. Vande Kappelle. All rights reserved. Except for brief quotations in critical publications or reviews, no part of this book may be reproduced in any manner without prior written permission from the publisher. Write: Permissions, Wipf and Stock Publishers, 199 W. 8th Ave., Suite 3, Eugene, OR 97401.

Resource Publications
An Imprint of Wipf and Stock Publishers
199 W. 8th Ave., Suite 3
Eugene, OR 97401
www.wipfandstock.com

ISBN 13: 978-1-61097-093-8

Bible quotations, unless otherwise noted, are from the *Revised Standard Version of the Bible*, copyright © 1946, 1952, 1971 by the Division of Christian Education of the National Council of the Churches of Christ in the United States of America. Used by permission.

Illustrations used in this book were created or adapted exclusively for *Into Thin Places* by William A. ("Will") Burrows.

Cover photo taken by Daniel A. Stinson.

Manufactured in the U.S.A.

*To Susan
wife, mother, cleric:
companion through the **chronos** and **kairos**
of life's adventure.*

Life is an adventure—a spiritual adventure.

> *The fairest thing we can experience is the mysterious.*
> *It is the fundamental emotion which stands at the cradle*
> *of true art and true science.*
>
> —Albert Einstein

> Love all of God's creation, the whole and every grain of sand in it. Love every leaf, every ray of God's light. Love the animals, love the plants, love everything. If you love everything, you will perceive the divine mystery in things.
>
> —Fyodor Dostoyevsky

> We shall not cease from exploration, and the end of all our exploring will be to arrive where we started and know the place for the first time.
>
> —T. S. Eliot

> The fact that I am always searching for God, always struggling to discover the fullness of Love, always yearning for the complete truth, tells me that I already have been given a taste of God, of Love and of Truth. I can only look for something that I have, to some degree, already found. How can I search for beauty and truth unless that beauty and truth are already known to me in the depth of my heart? It seems that all of us human beings have deep inner memories of the paradise that we have lost. Maybe the word "innocence" is better than the word "paradise." We were innocent before we started feeling guilty; we were in the light before we entered the darkness; we were at home before we started to search for a home. Deep in the recesses of our minds and hearts, there lies hidden the treasure we seek. We know its preciousness, and we know that it holds the gift we most desire; a life stronger than death.
>
> —Henri Nouwen

Contents

Preface xi
Acknowledgments xiii
Introduction: Searching for the Center xv

1 The Sacred Journey 1

Journey to the Center 13

PART ONE   DEPARTURE 15

2 The Netherlands: Roots 17

3 Switzerland: Land of Wonder 27

4 Northern Italy: Venice, Florence, and Pisa 38

5 Rome: The Eternal City 51

6 Italy: Final Days 63

7 Athens: The Birthplace of Democracy 80

8 Delphi and Corinth 95

9 Ephesus: Gateway to Asia 106

10 Pergamum: The Athens of the East 119

11 Istanbul: Europe or Asia? 127

12 Anatolian Civilizations 144

13 Leaving Turkey 159

Part Two Illumination 175

14 Damascus: Crossroads of the East 177

15 Wilderness Wanderings: Jordan and the Sinai 193

16 Northern Israel, Galilee, and the West Bank 212

17 Jerusalem in Legend and History 230

18 Jerusalem: Jewish Center of the Labyrinth 243

19 Jerusalem: Christian Center of the Labyrinth 261

Part Three Return 283

20 Entering Egypt 285

21 Egypt's Monuments of Civilization 298

Epilogue: Living in the Center 312

22 Becoming a Third-phase Person 313

*Appendix A Archaeological Timeline
    of the Mediterranean World 325*

Appendix B Chronology of Roman History 330

*Appendix C Chronology of Greek History
    (including the Byzantine and Ottoman Eras) 334*

Appendix D Chronology of Anatolian History 340

*Appendix E Chronology of Canaan
    (Israel and Rest of the Holy Land 341*

Appendix F Chronology of Egypt's History 354

Appendix G Maslow's Hierarchy of Needs 358

*Appendix H John Calvin's Influence
    on the Protestant Reformation 362*

Appendix I Florence: Cradle of the Italian Renaissance 369

Appendix J The Seven Wonders of the Ancient World 374

*Appendix K The Fourteen Stations of the Cross
    (Roman Catholic Version) 375*

Appendix L   Site Plan for the Acropolis at Athens and Environs 377

Appendix M   Site Plan for the Ruins at Ephesus 378

Appendix N   Site Plan for the Archaeological Site of Hattusa (Bogazkoy) 379

Appendix O   Map of Old Jerusalem and Environs 380

Appendix P   Site Plan of the Herodian Temple Mount in Jerusalem 381

Appendix Q   Floor Plan of the Church of the Holy Sepulcher 382

Appendix R   Map of Upper Egypt (Luxor, Karnak, and the West Bank) 383

Selected Readings 385
Scripture Index 393
Subject/Name Index 396

Preface

EXPANDING ONE'S RELIGIOUS OUTLOOK, deepening one's relation to the sacred and infinite, is essential for persons to age creatively. Carl Jung, the prominent Swiss psychiatrist, emphasized that gaining a religious attitude, the kind that allows us to see our own personal lives as moving toward wholeness and our own stories as related to a larger story, is the psychological/spiritual task for one's later years: "Among all my patients in the second half of life—that is to say, over thirty-five—there has not been one whose problem in the last resort was not that of finding a religious outlook on life." If Jung was correct, then discovering one's personal way to relate to God and to speak about ultimate concerns may well be the most significant task of life.

From 1985 to 1995, I traveled extensively. Four times I headed toward a different compass point—west to the state of Washington for the start of a solo cross-country bicycle odyssey,[1] north to Scandinavia and other parts of northern Europe, south to Mexico, and twice to the Middle East. Each trip, in retrospect, was an adventure—a pilgrimage of sorts—and each experience yielded unique insights and spiritual benefits. Because these trips coincided with the start of my midlife years, life's most precarious yet promising transition, they came at a propitious time for personal growth and renewal.

This book concerns one of those journeys, a two-month sabbatical trip that started in Amsterdam and ended in Cairo. My journey—a quest for ancestral, cultural, and spiritual identity—was intentional. I mapped out an overland route, noting must-see cultural, archaeological, and religious sites along the way. My itinerary included four centers of Christianity: Geneva, known as "the Protestant Rome" and home of Reformed Christianity since 1536; Rome, the center of Catholicism; Istanbul, the historical center of Orthodoxy; and Jerusalem, spiritual

---

1. The account of this fund-raising adventure, undertaken on behalf of Habitat for Humanity, is told in *The Invisible Mountain* (Eugene, OR: Resource Publications, 2010).

home to Christians, Jews, and Muslims. Along the way I discovered additional spiritual centers as well, some quite by accident. And that sense of serendipity, of unexpected discovery, is part of every genuine pilgrimage.

As a professor of Religious Studies and an ordained college chaplain, I designed an itinerary through Europe, the Middle East, and Africa that would enable me to appreciate and better understand my roots. My objectives included (a) visiting religious and cultural centers in the region, (b) exploring archaeological sites and museums, (c) conversing with Israelis and Palestinians on matters of mutual concern, (d) gaining a perspective not ordinarily achieved in guided tours, and (e) exploring my identity to better understand its spiritual core or center.

At times I mingled with tourists and listened to tour guides. On other occasions I was accompanied by college students and other travelers who viewed me as a resource. But most of the time I traveled alone. Being on a tight budget, I arranged my own lodging in pensions or youth hostels, traveling by train, bus, and ferry instead of by plane. My two-month sojourn took me to eleven countries, where I explored hundreds of cultural and historical sites and dozens of museums. I also met some remarkable human beings.

The adventure I describe produced wonderful experiences. Travel with me in my journey across Europe and the Middle East and into history. You will be fascinated and intrigued as you encounter scoundrels, saints, and heroes. Examine places of stunning beauty and study objects of such magnetism that devout believers over time revered them as sacred. Your sojourn through these storied "realms of gold" will add clarity to your identity, challenge the way you think, and transform the way you live. As you touch history—or rather are touched by history—may you recognize your place in the Great Story and affirm your role in the ongoing metanarrative.

Acknowledgments

THIS BOOK IS THE third and final volume in an autobiographical series that combines the adventure of life with the adventure of spirituality. *Love Never Fails*, the first in the trilogy, serves as a tribute to my parents, career missionaries in Latin America. That book introduces readers to my mother and father's spiritual and cultural legacy, imparted to me, their only child, during my childhood and early adolescent years: "Christ before others, others before self, character before career, success through service, enjoying the moment—those were their priorities, this their legacy." I remain grateful for this heritage and to these "unsung heroes."

The Invisible Mountain, the second book, focuses on a period of forty-two days in the summer of 1989 when I was able to translate my dream of a cross-country cycling trip into a trek on behalf of Habitat for Humanity, utilizing adventure as a means to help disadvantaged citizens. As I cycled across the "northern tier" of the North American continent, I matured as an individual and grew spiritually by going "Homeless for Habitat."

The lessons I learned through that trip prepared me for the two-month pilgrimage related in *Into Thin Places*, a journey that began a mere three weeks after the cycling trip. The adventures related in this book were made possible by funds from a discretionary account administered by Dr. Howard J. Burnett, president of Washington and Jefferson College. I am grateful to the college for making my sabbatical trip possible and to Dr. Burnett for his support of the project. It was Dr. Burnett's life-enabling advice, imparted to graduating seniors at the annual commencement exercises, that serves as my mantra: "Life is an adventure to be lived, not a problem to be solved."

In addition, I wish to thank Mary Ann Johnson for her careful reading of my manuscript; her editorial abilities forced me to become a better writer. Will Burrows agreed to use his artistic skills to create the illustrations that appear in the appendix. Reverend Nat Roe read an early draft of the manuscript, as did Dr. Dale C. Allison Jr., Professor of New Testament Exegesis and Early Christianity at Pittsburgh Theological Seminary. Various colleagues at Washington and Jefferson College, including Dr. Daniel A. Stinson and Rabbi David C. Novitsky, agreed to read the manuscript and offered helpful advice. Others at the college provided invaluable assistance. That group includes Doree Baumgart, Claudia Sweger, and Robert Reid.

Finally, this book could not have been written without the ongoing love, advice, and support of my wife Susan, who intuited my love of adventure and helped to create a climate that turned ordinary experiences into opportunities for personal growth and renewal.

Introduction

Searching for the Center

> *The best way to keep a trail alive is to walk on it,
> because every time you walk on it, you create it again.*
>
> —Middle Eastern saying

THIN PLACES

"Thin places," a metaphor taken from Celtic spirituality, refers to places, objects, events, persons, and other phenomena that are understood as being transparent to the divine. The concept has its home in an understanding of reality that affirms at least two layers or dimensions of reality: (a) the visible world of ordinary experience and (b) the sacred, understood as the source of all things but also as a presence interpenetrating everything. In "thin places" the boundary between the two levels becomes diaphanous and permeable.[1]

As "places" of beauty, fascination, and intrigue, thin places stir the imagination; as "places" of honesty and courage, where truth and justice prevail, they call us to action and selfless service; as "places" of conviction, inspiration, and empowerment, they challenge us to transformation; as "places" of insight, wisdom, and discernment, they call us to spiritual renewal.

Thin places are paradoxical: they are places of power and weakness; they provide weal and woe, bliss and pain; they are found in crosses and cancers but also in resurrection and remission; they may be ordinary, or

---

1. Marcus Borg, "A Vision of the Christian Life," in *The Meaning of Jesus: Two Visions*, by Marcus J. Borg and N. T. Wright (San Francisco: HarperSanFrancisco, 1999), 250.

extraordinary; sometimes they delight us, other times they perplex us; they are places of wonder but also of terror. When they surround us, we are enraptured, and when they fade, we experience despair. Thin places fuel the imagination, foster risk-taking, feed the spirit, and foment human transformation. They have the ability to alter our way of thinking, transform our character, and renew our souls.

Why do they intrigue us? Why do they grip us like a vice? In his influential study, *The Idea of the Holy*, Rudolph Otto put forth the view that religious experience relies upon a deep sense of the "numinous." Coined from the Latin *numen* (holy, sacred), the term expresses a natural human response to the experience of the sacred developed prior to rational and moral notions about it. Experiencing the numinous as ultimate mystery, people feel a strong sense of awe and reverence. The holy is also *fascinans* (fascinating); it exerts an irresistible attraction because it is recognized as profoundly familiar and essential to humanity. The experience of the sacred has always involved wonder and fascination.

Thin places are liminal spaces—in-between spaces, windows, doorways, thresholds, intersections, portals, transitions—that usher us from one state or space to another. They signify boundaries, beginnings, and becomings that open the way to something new, expanding our awareness and providing unity to our reality. For Christians they encompass activities, events, persons, objects, and experiences by which the Father speaks, in which Christ is present, and through which the breath of the Spirit blows freest. Thin places are transparent to the divine because God is there: through-and-around-and-over-and-under-and-behind-and-before-and-within them.

C. S. Lewis, one of the twentieth century's foremost Christian authors, knew about "thin places." He wrote about them in the *Chronicles of Narnia*, a set of seven children's classics in which he created a land of wonder and enchantment called Narnia. Following this publication, Lewis rigorously defended the fairy tale against those who claimed that it gives a false conception of life. The fairy tale, he argued, like the myth, arouses longing for more ideal worlds but at the same time gives the real world a new depth. While Lewis's Narnia Chronicles reminds us of other works, such as the Alice-in-Wonderland-like opening of *The Lion, the Witch and the Wardrobe* or the voyage made by the *Dawn Treader*, which is akin to the voyage of Odysseus, Lewis blends Christian themes with events created from the rich world of fantasy. A dominant idea in his stories is that of an earlier time when reality was more harmonious and unified. It was Lewis's hope that upon reading these stories, children (and adults) would return to the "real world" with a new perspective, their minds opened to the possibilities of an unseen spiritual world and to the limits of merely human intellect and undeveloped imagination.

Lewis was referring to "thin places" without using the term. He knew, as children of all ages discover when they read his Narnia Chronicles or J. K. Rowling's Harry Potter books, that our world is alive with liminalities (threshold spaces between the sacred and the mundane); pictures, closets, fireplaces, train stations—any object, event, or person can open our minds to the possibilities and transport us to an unseen spiritual world.

THE CENTER

"Searching for the Center" refers to a phenomenon that is said to be universal, for it is the subject of myths and rituals found across the globe in all time periods. Joseph Campbell, the world's foremost authority on mythology until his death in 1987, labeled it the myth of the human quest. The concept can be described culturally, psychologically, and spiritually, but at its minimum, it embodies three pursuits: (1) the quest for adventure, (2) the quest for meaning, and (3) the quest for wholeness. (See chapter 1 for further discussion of these topics).

This book can be read on a number of levels. Those who are looking for an account of my travels through Europe and the Middle East will focus on chapter 2 through 21, concentrating on the travel entries that are scattered across the narrative.

Those who read the book in search of history will want to read the appendices and the various explanatory entries—cultural, historical, geographical, literary, archaeological, and religious—that introduce core persons, events, and places that helped shape Western civilization. Those who approach the story as a pilgrimage inward will appreciate the concept of the labyrinth explained in chapter 1 and will regard the book's subheadings—"Searching for the Center," "Journey to the Center," and "Living in the Center"—as pathways to spiritual health and wholeness.

Into Thin Places encourages readers to quest for the Center, to find thin places in their own journeys of discovery that are filled with extraordinary potential for insight, growth, and transformation. Chapter 1 examines questing in general, exploring the notion of the labyrinth as a unique path to the sacred. Here readers are urged to rediscover the sense of the sacred and the sanctity of space (thin places) that their predecessors found indispensable for the human quest and that pilgrims of all time utilize as requisite in their encounters with the divine.

The final segment (epilogue and chapter 22), labeled "Living in the Center," concludes the work and provides a practical dimension. Here readers can gain deeper insights into their own sacred journeys and explore how faith journeys can impact and energize them for life.

Sacred journeys should not be confused with more commonplace trips and adventures such as expeditions, tours, and vacations. As important as the latter may be for one's emotional health and wellbeing, they are primarily outward by nature. They generally have predetermined geographical destinations, as well as distinct beginnings and endings. Sacred journeys may have geographical and temporal associations, but they are largely inward journeys, and as such are not limited by space or time. They commonly result in changes of perspective and in transformations of character and emotional state. In many ways sacred journeys are atemporal because they have no discernible endings. By nature, they are beginnings. Sacred journeys prepare us for destinations that lie in eternity. The best one can hope for is to be on the way.

I believe my sabbatical trip was more than a geographical or intellectual adventure because it produced a change of perspective. I returned a citizen of the world, no longer searching for the Center but awakened to the realization that the Center lies within, that it goes wherever I go, and that it needs to be nurtured. The book's conclusion charts out the responsibilities that come with this awareness.

In narrating the account of my journey from Amsterdam to Cairo, I utilize the three classic stages that constitute every life-transforming adventure. The first stage, separation or *departure*, is described in Part I. This section narrates the journey through Holland, Switzerland, Italy, Greece, and Turkey. The middle stage—the trials and fulfillment of *illumination*—appears in Part II. This section narrates regions of the eastern and southern Mediterranean known in biblical times as Canaan. It includes my travels through Syria, Jordan, the Sinai, and Israel. The final section, the *return*, comprises Part III. This section narrates my departure from Israel and my journey through the Sinai to Egypt and back home.

1

The Sacred Journey

Mythology is the penultimate truth—penultimate because the ultimate cannot be put into words.

—Joseph Campbell

Humans search for adventure, meaning, and wholeness. And the greatest and most meaningful adventures are those that bring spiritual satisfaction, if it is true, as the biblical religions affirm, that we are made "in the image of God" and that our ultimate destination is a realm we call Heaven.

THE QUEST FOR ADVENTURE

In *The Hero with a Thousand Faces*, Joseph Campbell dwells on a particular type of myth from all time periods and found across the globe: the myth of the human quest. This classical endeavor, titled "The Hero's Adventure," symbolically addresses the stages of human realization, the trials of the transition from childhood to maturity, and the meaning of maturity. The various mythologies, whether they depict the hero as going in quest of a boon or in quest of a vision, present the same essential undertaking: individuals leave their everyday lives and travel a distance, sometimes into a depth, and sometimes up to a height. The hero leaves the ordinary world, sometimes by choice and other times by force, and undertakes a journey to the center, into a region of supernatural wonder, where he encounters fabulous forces and wins a decisive victory. Then comes a greater challenge: should the protagonist remain in his enchanted setting, thereby forsaking his former world, or should he return with a boon to benefit others? The hero does come back from this mysterious adventure, returning with the power to bestow blessings on fellow humans.

The hero's adventure, we are told, is about one's character and its potential for transformation. The path of the mythological adventure, and of all successful quests, involves a twofold venture: an inward journey to a spiritual center—a place of healing, vision, and transformation—and an outward journey toward others.

The messages of the world's great teachers—Moses, the Buddha, Christ, Muhammad—differ greatly. But their visionary journeys are much the same. All are heroes, for they leave the predictable in search of the unknown, resisting temptation to find a liberating truth. Moses is such a hero, for he ascends the mountain, meets with Yahweh on the summit of the mountain, and he comes back with Torah, a constitution for the formation of a new society. That's a typical hero act—departure, illumination (fulfillment), and return.

One might also declare that the founding of a life—your life or mine, if we live our lives authentically, instead of imitating the lives of those around us—comes from a quest as well. At birth, a lifetime of adventure beckons. A hero lies dormant within each person, awaiting a spiritual awakening, a call to departure. In order to affirm something new, one must leave the old and go in quest of the germinal idea, a seed that contains the potentiality of bringing forth that new thing.

Opportunities for transformation are present all around us. When they arise at critical moments in our lives, they are called rites of passage, conversions, revivals, or moments of awakening. What we call them is not important, but how we envision them. Not all transformational opportunities arise dramatically. Some are manifested subtly, through solitary endeavors such as meditation, fasting, confession, prayer, and Bible reading; others emerge publicly and corporately, through disciplines like worship, receiving a sacrament, or through sacrificial service to the poor and needy. The deepest opportunities arise unexpectedly, however, through the twists and turns of everyday life, including suffering, loss, and events that we think of as accidents and tragedies. Such experiences can rob us of our vitality or they can fuel the growth of our spirit and provide a powerful transformative impetus for our character.

THE QUEST FOR MEANING

Humans quest for meaning. Meaning, understood as vitality of purpose, leads to fulfillment, and the prospect of fulfillment makes life worth living. When Abraham Maslow outlined his hierarchy of needs, represented as a pyramid consisting of five levels, he placed "self-actualization" (by which he meant working toward fulfilling one's fullest potential) at the top. In Maslow's scheme, the final stage of psychological development comes when the individual feels assured that lower levels of needs—both physiological and emotional—have been satisfied. Once these are met, self-actualization drives the personality.[1]

Mythology and ritual traditionally supplied the symbols that carry the human spirit forward, energizing individuals to navigate successfully the necessary passages of their adulthood. Think of the rites of passage, those rituals associated with the vital transitions of human life, especially birth, puberty, marriage, and death. Each of these passage points frames the individual within the context of the community, serving to transform the person into the new stage of life and to integrate her or him into the community at that new spiritual level. Because passages of life are liminal—that is, they involve crossing a threshold from one state of existence to another—they are critical to the full human development of the person and also to the welfare of the community.

In the past, people quested for meaning through rites of passage; their quest was intentional, predictable, and patterned. Society demanded it, clans promoted it, and families made it happen. Although similar rites are enacted today, particularly in traditional families, modern (and postmodern) people tend to quest spontaneously, often doing so unintentionally.

To find meaning, or to connect with something deeper, some people quest through adventure, visiting exotic locations or engaging in enterprising ventures. Others quest through careers of service and devotion to others. Some apply for the Peace Corps; others participate in humanitarian efforts or campaigns to eradicate poverty or disease. Some quest through lifestyle choices such as fasting, celibacy, or vegetarianism. Others quest hedonistically, seeking meaning through pleasure, drugs, power, wealth, and materialism. Some seek meaning through disciplined acts of devotion such as prayer, Bible study, and inspirational

---

1. For information on the qualities of self-actualized individuals, see Appendix G.

reading. All such quests reenact aspects of some ancient rite of passage. When human beings stop questing, they abdicate their identity.

THE QUEST FOR WHOLENESS

Humans—indeed most living creatures—desire good health, safety, and security; taken together, these vital qualities contribute to the wholeness and wellbeing that make life supremely special. In traditional societies, the ability to apprehend the sacred was regarded as of crucial importance to health, wholeness, and wellbeing. Indeed, without this sense of the divine, people often felt that life was not worth living. Like other aesthetic experiences, the sense of the sacred needs to be cultivated. In our modern secular society, the sacred has diminished in value and in priority; left unused, it has tended to wither away.

In the past, when people tried to speak about the sacred or about their inner life, they did not express their experience in logical, discursive terms. Rather they had recourse to symbols and myths. Freud and Jung, who were the first to chart the so-called scientific quest for the soul, turned to the myths of the classical world or of religion when they tried to describe interior events. Mythology, they realized, was never designed to describe historically verifiable events. Mythology was an attempt to express inner significance or to draw attention to realities that were too elusive to be discussed in logically coherent ways. Mythology, religion scholar Karen Armstrong indicates, was an ancient form of psychology; the myths of sacred geography express truths about the interior life.[2]

One of the earliest and most ubiquitous symbols of the divine has been the concept of place. Since prehistoric times, certain places have exerted a mysterious attraction to billions of people around the world. Many cultures of antiquity recognized the existence of these sites, called "sacred," and marked their geographic locations in a variety of ways. The names of such places—Stonehenge, Machu Picchu, the Pyramids of Giza, Rome, Delphi, Mecca, Benares, Mount Sinai, Jerusalem—are familiar to us all. Such places are found across the planet in the form of sacred mountains, healing springs, oracular caverns, enchanted forest glens, ceremonial sites, monasteries, places of divine revelation, places where sages attained enlightenment, and certain cities.

---

2. Karen Armstrong, *Jerusalem: One City, Three Faiths* (New York: Ballantine, 1997), xviii.

Over time, through countless cultural expressions, people have made pilgrimages to particular sites, drawn by the magnetism of such places and by their reputation for healing and wholeness. Ancient legends, the scriptures of the world's religions, and modern-day reports tell of extraordinary experiences by people while visiting sacred sites. While contemporary science cannot explain, and therefore tends to disregard, the unusual insight and the seemingly miraculous phenomena that occur at such sites, they continue to be the most venerated and visited locations on the planet. Let's briefly examine one such site, the ancient Mayan ceremonial center at Chichén Itzá.

KUKULKAN'S PYRAMID AT CHICHÉN ITZÁ

Every year, on the first day of spring and fall, hundreds of people from all over the globe gather at Chichén Itzá to witness a mysterious ritual. On the late afternoon of the vernal and the autumnal equinoxes (March 20 and September 21), sunlight bathes the western staircase of El Castillo (known as Kukulkan's Pyramid). This causes seven isosceles triangles to form the image of a serpent's body that creeps in a combination of shadow and light down the great pyramid's ninety-one steps until it joins the huge serpent's head carved in stone at the bottom of the stairway. The symbolic descent of Kukulkan, the feathered serpent god known as Quetzalcoatl by the Aztecs and Viracocha by the Incas, signaled the most auspicious time to plant corn, the revered food staple of the Maya.

Chichén Itzá, in the Peninsula of Yucatan in Mexico, is considered one of the most magnificent archeological sites in the world, giving us a glimpse of the splendor and sophistication of an ancient Mayan metropolis ruled by the heavens. The Maya were extraordinarily good astronomers, making observations and recording the motion of the sun, the moon, and the stars. They related astronomy to many areas of everyday life. For the Maya, like most primal peoples, common chores and daily concerns, including agricultural decisions, had a religious association.

El Castillo was constructed by the Mayans around 1000 to 1200 CE, directly upon the foundations of previous temples. Built for religious and astronomical purposes, the impressive stepped pyramid has 91 steps on each side (totaling 364 steps) plus one for the platform at the top, making 365 steps, one for each day of the year. The stone edifice, which combines earthly and heavenly symbolism, was built in homage to King Kukulkan, a real person but also a mythological figure. Half god and half man, he is considered the founder of all empires in ancient America. He came from heaven to earth, and therefore is represented as a feathered serpent in all of Mexico's archaeological sites. The feathers (a symbol of the quetzal bird) represent heaven; the serpent represents earth. Kukulkan was endowed with mystical qualities: he received visitors from distant places and possessed the power to heal and to bring the dead back to life. Surprisingly, he was described by the natives as being Caucasian, with white skin, a beard, and beautiful emerald eyes. When he departed for the east, traveling the ocean on a raft of serpents, he promised his followers to return in the year that Hernán Cortés and his expedition disembarked on the shores of Veracruz to begin their conquest of Mexico.

The sanctity of a space, as affirmed at Chichén Itzá, does not happen automatically. Once a place has been experienced as sacred in some way and has proved capable of giving people access to the divine, worshippers have devoted a great deal of creative energy to helping others cultivate this sense of transcendence. The architecture of temples, churches, and mosques is symbolically important, often mapping out the inner journey that a pilgrim or worshipper must take to reach God. Liturgy and ritual also heighten this sense of sacred space.

SACRED GEOGRAPHY

Originally all cities were regarded as holy places. In the modern West, such a notion seems alien, for the city is often experienced as a godforsaken realm in which religion has an increasingly marginal role. But long before people began to map their world scientifically, they had evolved a sacred geography to define their place in the universe emotionally and spiritually. The late Romanian-American scholar Mircea Eliade, who pioneered the study of sacred space, pointed out that reverence for a holy place preceded all other speculation about the nature of the world. Just as primitive farmers sanctified the whole earth, primitive townsfolk revered the enclosure within which they lived, imagining it a sacred space, like a church, where a sacred drama was continually being enacted between themselves and their god. The city of Rome was itself a deity and was worshiped as such by its citizens. In ancient Etruria, on the Italian peninsula, each town was considered to be an image of the heavens above; like the sky, the towns were divided into sections, each of which was placed under the protection of a particular deity.

As the world grew less terrifying and more controllable, cities, like their inhabitants, became more secular. But certain cities never lost their sacred character; and some, like Mecca and Rome, even survived the extinction or eclipse of their original cult to become dedicated to a new one. Of these, the most venerated is Jerusalem. As the city conquered by David and the site of Solomon's Temple, the passion of Jesus, and the place where Muhammad ascended to heaven to converse with God, Jerusalem is revered by Jews, Christians, and Muslims alike.

Eliade summarized the properties and fundamental meaning of such places.[3] They operate as the center of the world—as the prime focus of sacred power and as the point of contact with spirits and gods. Centers such as this are often equated with a sacred cosmic mountain that permits heaven to consort with earth. The summit of the cosmic mountain is the navel of the earth, where world order is nourished by celestial power. Ceremonies performed there recapitulate the beginning of time, and the celebrant, a terrestrial officer of cosmic order, participates in the rituals of renewal. With the assistance of the gods, the ceremony makes the world habitable by invigorating its life and establishing its order in harmony with the structure and rhythm of the universe.

The devotion to a holy place or a holy city is a near-universal phenomenon. Historians of religion believe this to be one of the earliest manifestations of faith in all cultures. In *Jerusalem: One City, Three Faiths*, Karen Armstrong traces the history of how Jews, Christians, and Muslims have all laid claim to Jerusalem as their holy place. She argues that people have developed what has been called a sacred geography, which has little to do with a scientific map of the world but which charts people's interior life. Earthly cities, groves, and mountains have become symbols of this spirituality, a phenomenon so omnipresent that it seems to answer a profound human need, whatever one's belief about God or the supernatural. Mountains like Sinai and cities such as Jerusalem have become so central to the sacred geography of Jews, Christians, and Muslims, that the faithful can hardly see these sites objectively. Rather, they are bound up with self-conception, thereby providing mundane life with meaning and value.

---

3. Mircea Eliade, *Cosmos and History: The Myth of the Eternal Return* (New York: Harper & Row, 1959), 12.

THE OMPHALOS: THE NAVEL OF THE EARTH

In ancient times, inhabitants of the Greek world considered Delphi to be the center of the known world, the place where heaven and earth met. This was the place on earth where humans were closest to the gods. In mythology, Delphi was the meeting place of two eagles, released by Zeus and sent in opposite directions. Where they met indicated the *omphalos*, "the navel of the earth"; there Zeus deposited a holy stone to mark the exact spot. The stone marker is now in the Delphi Archaeological Museum.

Delphi, the home of the world famous Delphic oracle, became the most important religious center of the ancient world. Built on the slopes of Mount Parnassus, the ancient site is as awe-inspiring now as it most likely was three thousand years ago. The Oracle of Apollo at Delphi was one of the world's most intriguing and unusual establishments. Within that ancient temple-sanctuary the god Apollo spoke through a human priestess and offered inspiration and guidance to all who sought his aid. For over a thousand years, the great and less great came to consult him. Though oracular utterances at Delphi are a thing of the past, the site remains one of the world's foremost "thin places." Visitors—one million a year—still flock to Delphi in search of guidance and spiritual clarity.

When travelers visit sacred sites across the globe, they discover conceptions similar to those of Delphi, for faithful people in those regions view these places not only as sources for human nourishment and guidance but also as cosmic centers, locations where the human and divine realms intersect. Ancient Jewish lore, which influenced both Christian and Muslim beliefs, teaches that Jerusalem lies at the very center of the inhabited world, for here God created Adam. Beneath Jerusalem is the source of all sweet waters, and above it stand the throne of God and the celestial temple. And it is to Jerusalem, on the Day of Judgment, that the Garden of Eden will be transferred.

For ancient Jews, the site of the Temple in Jerusalem served as a "center" that linked heaven and earth. Built on the summit of the sacred mountain of Zion, "the Temple was a symbol of the reality that sustains the life of the cosmos. Like Jacob's ladder, it represented a bridge to the source of being, without which the fragile mundane world could not subsist."[4] In the eleventh century BCE,[5] when the Temple was erected in Jerusalem, Jews considered the inner sanctuary (the *debir* or Holy of Holies, which contained the Ark of the Covenant and the tablets of Torah) to be the dwelling of God (Yahweh) on earth.

For many Christians, the Church of the Holy Sepulcher in Jerusalem is the holiest site on earth, for what happened there—the death and resurrection of Jesus—changed the world. An early Christian tradition affirmed the Catholicon (the nave next to the Church's Rotunda) as the center of the world, and by the tenth century that spot was marked by an *omphalos*. Today a stone chalice on the Crusader floor supposedly marks the Christian center of the earth.

For primal peoples, as for ancient Greeks, Romans, and thousands of individuals across the planet today, sacred places such as Jerusalem and Delphi are "thin places," sites of wholeness, wonder, and intrigue.

THE MUSLIM TAWAF (CIRCUMAMBULATION AROUND THE KAABA)

One of the peak experiences in the life of a Muslim is the Hajj or pilgrimage to the sacred places of Islam in and around Mecca. This duty is considered one of the "five pillars" of Islam; these religious rituals or practices are fundamental to that religion because they serve to anchor human relationships with God and with other Muslims. The annual pilgrimage festival takes place in "The Month of Hajj," the last month of the Muslim year. When Muslims observe the Hajj, they perform *tawaf* or circumambulation (ritualistic movement) around the Kaaba, a large cubical structure at the center of the Meccan Grand Mosque. In one corner of the Kaaba, set within the wall, is the Black Stone, which Muslims, following the tradition of Muhammad while he was on pilgrimage, kiss or touch. The stone is believed to be a relic that has survived from ancient times. In the Qur'an the Kaaba is referred to as the "sanctuary established for humanity" (2:125) for it is regarded by Muslims as the symbol of the earliest human attempt to express a relationship with God. Hence it is the direction to which all Muslims turn in prayer.

---

4. Armstrong, *Jerusalem*, 50–51.

5. Throughout this book I will adhere to common scholarly usage, substituting BCE and CE—"Before the Common Era" and "Common Era"—for the traditional BC and AD.

Muslim pilgrims visiting the Kaaba circle it seven times, in a counterclockwise manner. This methodical pattern represents a stunning sacred geometry, for the Kaaba signifies the physical axis of the world. It is the *axis mundi*, the great wheel of the Islamic galaxy, the pole around which the believer's compass spins. When the Muslims perform *tawaf*, they believe that they are participating in a cosmic ritual, for the entire universe, which is in constant circular or elliptical rotation, is understood to be moving in the pattern of the *tawaf*. Science can be used to confirm this understanding, since the electrons of an atom revolve around its nucleus in a counterclockwise direction, as though making *tawaf*. The earth's rotations, both on its own axis and in its revolution around the sun, is also said to be counterclockwise. Indeed, the entire universe, according to Muslim cosmology, from the atom to the galaxies, is in a constant circular rotation, like a circumambulator who encircles the Kaaba in a counterclockwise direction. The Qur'an refers to the Kaaba as the "Sacred House," indicating not only that it is a place of safety and refuge for humanity, but that it represents reliable cosmological truth, serving as a pointer to the interconnectedness of all things (5:97). There is never a time when someone is not encircling the Kaaba.

The Kaaba is not merely a structure of geographical and cosmic significance; it is the symbol of the human encounter with the divine. The act of circumambulation symbolizes the belief and worship of one God, since, just as every circle has one center, so also there is only one God worthy of worship.

WALKING THE LABYRINTH TO THE CENTER

When Muslims visit Mecca, when Jews go to Jerusalem, and when Catholic Christians travel to Lourdes or Rome, it is clear that their journey means much more than mere travel. In its original and pure meaning, pilgrimage describes a religious journey to a site or set of sites that by tradition have been invested with sanctity. While a pilgrimage outwardly is a sacred journey, it is also an inner exploration of the mind, heart, and soul, and when pilgrimages incorporate sacred geometric designs such as circular and square patterns (known as medicine wheels, mandalas, or labyrinths), they are particularly powerful vehicles for healing, transformation, and renewal.

The labyrinth is found in many cultures and religions around the world. Like the Native American medicine wheel, it represents the circle of life. Its use in ceremony, for meditation, and as a place of healing is well known. Many hospitals are now providing patients and the public with a labyrinth, finding it useful in the healing of both physical and mental illness.

For Christians, the Middle Ages were a time of pilgrimage. During the early Middle Ages, pilgrims ventured to the Holy Land as a sacred journey from all over Europe. When the Crusades began, travel became very dangerous and the Church wanted to prevent a greater loss of life. Since most people could not make the grand pilgrimage to Jerusalem, considered by Christians to be both the center of the world and to represent the Kingdom of Heaven, they made pilgrimages to important cathedrals such as Canterbury, Santiago de Compostela, and Chartres. Many cathedrals built in France and Italy at that time contained a labyrinth in the floor to represent the sacred pilgrimage to Jerusalem. At Chartres, the faithful would conclude their pilgrimage by walking the labyrinth to the center, called the New Jerusalem, and then slowly retrace their steps outward to the outside world and return to their homes. Over time, the labyrinth's use became unpopular and its power came under suspicion. It was torn out or painted over in many of the church floors where it had been widely used.

Many today are rediscovering the value and the attraction of the labyrinth, and utilizing it as a path to the sacred. As one of the most talked about religious symbols in use in the West, it is also the subject of much perplexity. The labyrinth is often confused with a maze, for the word brings to mind a puzzle to be deciphered, with dead ends and no exit. But the labyrinth is not a maze: it contains a pathway that, when followed, takes one from the periphery to the center and back out again. The labyrinth's basic design—a series of concentric circles entwined in a geometric pattern—is simple. This simplicity is the first hint of its power.[6]

In Chartres Cathedral, the labyrinth remains. It is large—forty feet across—set with blue and white stones into the floor of the nave of the church. The path makes twenty-eight loops, seven in each quadrant, as it meanders to the center rosette. The stones that make up the path are not painted with the pattern: the stones are the pattern. Built around the turn of the thirteenth century, the eleven-circuit labyrinth is an intricate part of the Cathedral's grand design. The labyrinth's relationship to the

---

6. Note the figure of a medieval labyrinth on page 14.

magnificent stained glass rose window in the church's entry is also significant. If the front wall were placed flat on the floor, the entire window would exactly cover and match the size and shape of the labyrinth. The labyrinth is clearly part of the church's sacred space.

For clear reasons, the Chartres-style labyrinth is being used in many churches around the world. The labyrinth, and the three stages of the walk, is a metaphor for the spiritual life (note how these stages parallel the sequence of actions in "the hero's adventure"):

- *Purgation (releasing)*: Entering the labyrinth commences the symbolic path of purgation, of releasing and letting go. Like our pathway through life, the labyrinth contains many twists and turns.
- *Illumination (receiving)*: The labyrinth always leads you to the center, which represents illumination and opening to the divine. Seekers often receive a solution to a problem, an inspiration, a new awareness, peace, or a feeling of joy.
- *Union (returning)*: The return path provides unity to one's life, allowing pilgrims to take the walkway's benefits back into their lives.

Intention is an important part of the labyrinth journey. Pilgrims who went to the labyrinth at Chartres Cathedral in the Middle Ages went with a specific purpose. They were intentionally emulating their ancestors' walk to the Holy Land. As you read the following account of my journey to the Center, may your pilgrimage be equally intentional.

Journey to the Center

By the age of twelve, Blaise Pascal demonstrated extraordinary mathematical and scientific ability. But he was more than a mathematical genius: he was a Christian whose faith grew spasmodically before finally emerging in full maturity on November 23, 1654. On that evening he had a mystical vision that lasted two hours, which he called a "night of fire." In this powerful event—his journey to the Center—he experienced what he could only call "Fire!" He then wrote a document that he sewed into the lining of his jacket as a daily reminder of that experience. That document, known as "Pascal's Fire," reads, in part, like this: "Fire. *23rd of November 1654: From about half past ten in the evening until half past midnight, the God of Abraham, the God of Isaac, the God of Jacob, and not of the philosophers and men of science.*"

Not long after this mysterious encounter with God, Pascal began writing notes for a thorough apologetic for Christianity. However, he started to experience serious physical ailments and died at the age of thirty-nine. The notes, many of them just short phrases or paragraphs, were collected and published as the *Pensées*. Despite its fragmented nature—or perhaps partially due to it—*Pensées* forms one of the most unique and powerful defenses of the Christian faith ever written. Pascal recognized that people of his time were rejecting ancient ways and could not be approached on the basis of shared cultural beliefs or logic alone. This is why Peter Kreeft explains in *Christianity for Modern Pagans*—his guide to the *Pensées*—that Pascal is suitable "for today because he speaks to modern pagans, not to medieval Christians . . . He is the first to realize the new dechristianized, desacramentalized world and to address it."

This book, like Pascal's *Pensées*, describes a journey to the center, where "holy fire" resides. Prepare to enter the labyrinth!

Eleven-Circuit Medieval Labyrinth

Part One

Departure

TRAVEL ENTRY #1: TRAVEL AGENTS

"I'm sorry," my travel agent murmured apologetically over the phone, "but I haven't been able to pursue your request."

I was devastated. In three weeks I would embark on a two-month journey through the Middle East, and all I had was a passport. My agent had agreed to make all the necessary travel arrangements in advance, but none had been made. Bizarre excuses followed.

"This summer, while relocating my office, I temporarily moved my files to the basement. A storm stalled over the Philadelphia area and flooded my basement. But don't worry," she continued reassuringly. "I've transferred your account to another agency across the river in New Jersey, and I believe the folks there are making the arrangements you requested."

Six months earlier I had written a detailed letter to this travel agent, itemizing my sabbatical travel plans. A travel consultant in Washington, DC had recommended her as a specialist in educational tours. Initially, when I mentioned my intention to spend two months traveling alone through the Middle East, she had seemed hesitant about her role.

"My area of expertise is Southeast Asia," she admitted, noting that she generally worked with groups rather than with individuals. "However," she added, "I am interested in branching out to the Middle East, and I do have some contacts there." When I mentioned that I would be glad to provide a detailed itinerary, she agreed to work with me.

Now, a half year later, I had nothing more than the name of a new travel agent, four hundred miles from home. When I called the new agency, I learned that nothing had been done, since the staff had been awaiting further instructions before implementing my plan.

That was news to me. For the past six weeks I had cycled across the United States, raising funds for the newly formed Washington County Habitat for Humanity affiliate in southwestern Pennsylvania. I had expected that the Philadelphia agency would obtain all my required visas and would make all other overseas arrangements on my behalf.

While pedaling across the United States, I had undergone similar frustrations and setbacks and yet experienced moments of grace, particularly when my bike broke down. The next twenty-one days resulted in additional breakthroughs as I obtained a Syrian visa—the most difficult to obtain—thanks to the intercession of a former U.S. ambassador to that country, and the names of vital contacts along the way. I also obtained essentials items such as a Eurail Pass, an airline ticket to Amsterdam, and a return ticket from Cairo.

For fifty-seven days I would be traveling across Europe and the Middle East, arranging my transportation and overnight stays on site and applying for visas at border crossings where necessary. There might be hassles and delays, but I felt optimistic. Recent cycling experiences increased my confidence. For six weeks I had gone "Homeless for Habitat," leaving the comfort and security of my home to raise funds for people without adequate housing. During that time I had depended upon others for food and lodging, and I had never lacked a place to stay. The lessons I learned from that experience had increased my faith and helped prepare me for another venture into the unknown.

My sabbatical journey—my quest for the Center—would begin in Holland; exploring my genealogical roots and the land of my ancestors seemed like the obvious place to start.

2

The Netherlands: Roots

TRAVEL ENTRY #2: ARRIVAL IN HOLLAND

I WAS APPREHENSIVE WHEN I landed at Schiphol, the international airport five miles outside of Amsterdam. Although I had written to Pieter and Sien van de Kappelle, my Dutch cousins, I hadn't heard back. My arrival constituted an initial test—of my resourcefulness and adaptability to the uncertainties of the venture.

I had met Pieter and Sien once before, ten years earlier, during their brief visit to the United States, but wasn't sure I would recognize them in an airport crowd. Stepping from the plane, I looked at greeters holding signs, but none bore my name. After a walk around the reception area and a futile stop at the information booth, I headed for the baggage area in search of a bright blue backpack, my only piece of luggage. Intending to use local transportation whenever possible and knowing I would be walking much of the time, I had determined to follow two rules faithfully: travel lightly and live frugally.

My backpack contained the barest of essentials: two pairs of shorts, one pair of wash-and-wear slacks, underwear, socks, several sport shirts, toilet articles, pajamas, sneakers, a towel, a sweater, a polypropylene turtleneck, first aid items, a bathing suit, toilet paper, a lightweight rain poncho, a notebook, writing paper and envelopes, research notes, and guidebooks. I made sure to leave room for maps, brochures, and any additional guidebooks accumulated along the way.

I wore a poplin windbreaker with removable lining, its versatility ideal for the variable temperature anticipated throughout my travel. I also carried a fanny pack, which converted to an over-the-shoulder day pack, containing an inexpensive camera, several rolls of film, a diary, an insulated water bottle, and a Swiss pocket knife (allowable prior to 9/11). This small pack would be ideal for carrying food, extra water, and any other items I might need on day trips or whenever my backpack was in storage. A nylon pouch, worn around my waist, contained my most valued possessions, including my passport, travelers' checks, Eurail pass, and prescription sunglasses.

When I returned to the information booth, most of the passengers on my flight had left the terminal. As I pondered my options, Sien approached the counter. We recognized each other instantly and embraced warmly. Pieter was double parked nearby, waiting. I barely heard his apologies about the rush hour traffic, being only too happy to see him.

We headed south, toward Bilthoven, a suburb of Utrecht. Upon leaving the airport I was struck by the paradox of this tiny nation. Dutch people, modern, enterprising, and progressive in so many ways, dwelled in an idyllic locale. On both sides of the congested highway, peaceful cattle grazed beneath ancient windmills, in postcard-like surroundings. A million questions entered my mind as we drove along the picturesque setting.

Pieter politely sorted through my questions, answering one at a time. Windmills, he replied, had once been essential to Holland's survival. At one time, some ten thousand windmills dotted the nation's lowlands. Used for distributing water, draining the polders (low-lying land reclaimed from the sea and from lakes and protected by dikes), and grinding corn, they continue as an ever-present reminder of a natural, non-polluting energy source. Only about a thousand windmills remain, he explained, of which perhaps two hundred are still working, mostly for reasons of nostalgia and aesthetics. Cattle, I learned, had been kept in the Netherlands as far back as prehistoric times, giving the Netherlands a rich history of dairy production.

After a few moments, Pieter indicated that the time for sightseeing and further questions about Holland lay ahead. For the time being, we had a lot of catching-up to do. As the discussion turned to personal matters, I was impressed with Pieter and Sien's command of English. Their genuine welcome put me at ease, and I immediately felt like family, not at all the intruder I imagined myself to be.

Pieter and Sien had moved recently from a spacious older home to a charming new condominium. The place smelled of fresh paint, and a carpenter was working on shelving as we entered. In addition to home improvements, the Dutch enjoy indoor greenery. Flowers are picked or purchased regularly to adorn homes, restaurants, and businesses. Sien loved flowers and ordered a bouquet daily. Her back yard featured a landscaped garden, including a fountain. By spring, home-picked flowers would adorn Sien's kitchen table.

EXPLANATORY ENTRY #1: GENEALOGICAL INSIGHTS

A few minutes later we were seated in the living room, surrounded by maps and a genealogical chart that Pieter had constructed. He had traced the family tree through eleven generations to Abraham Janszoon ("son of Jan"), born around 1650. This ancestor had been coachman to a wealthy merchant in the Beemster-polder, once a dry lake bed but now a rich tract of land in the province of North Holland, about ten miles north of Amsterdam. Pieter's genealogical research hit a dead end prior to the mid-seventeenth century because family records (kept in church registers) had been destroyed around that time by a devastating flood.

I listened attentively as Pieter, a retired teacher, economist, and author of over a dozen books, mesmerized me with stories about my ancestors. I learned how Abraham Janszoon's son, Jan Abrahamszoon, became a millwright of the twenty-six mills in the Beemster. I was particularly intrigued by Jan Janszoon (1708–1795), who married five times and fathered fifteen children. This ancestor acquired a great deal of wealth, for each time he became a widower, he married a rich widow. His last will, filed in the provincial archives in Haarlem, discloses the extent of his vast estate.

This forebear appears to have been the first relative to add a surname to the family line, altering the traditional custom whereby sons were named after their father's first name. The widespread practice of adding a surname seems to have been encouraged by Napoleon, who established a short-lived Kingdom of Holland from 1806 to 1810, with his brother Louis as king.

Pieter believed that Jan's choice of the surname "van de Cappelle" (meaning "of the chapel") reflected one of two options: either it referred to an occupation, in this case a religious vocation, or to a location. Pieter favored the latter, for he could find no evidence that any ancestors had served as clergy. It was more likely that Jan had taken the name from a town by the name of "Cappelle," of which several existed in the Low

Countries, possibly an ancestral town famous for its central chapel or church. The spelling eventually changed to "Kappelle."

Pieter's genealogical overview provided indispensable clues to the identity I was investigating. As the story unfolded, I learned that Pieter had joined the Dutch resistance movement against Nazi Germany during World War II. When I pressed him for additional information, he started with 1940, when he was sixteen years old. That year, one week before he was to graduate from high school, Nazi Germany crossed the border and occupied Holland. The invasion was quite unexpected, for the Netherlands had been a neutral country during World War I, and the Dutch had declared their neutrality again at the outbreak of World War II. Although there was growing concern over the possibility of armed conflict, most Dutch citizens thought that Germany would again respect Dutch neutrality. However, on May 10, 1940, the Nazis launched an attack on the Netherlands and Belgium and overran most of the country quickly. Four days later, when fighting was only occurring in isolated locations, the Luftwaffe bombed the vital port city of Rotterdam, killing hundreds and leaving thousands homeless.

The Dutch resistance to the Nazi occupation developed relatively slowly, but its counterintelligence, domestic sabotage, and communications networks provided key support to Allied efforts beginning in 1944. The country's terrain, lack of wilderness, and dense population made it difficult to conceal any illicit activities, and the Netherlands was completely surrounded by German-controlled territory, offering no escape route. Discovery by the Germans of involvement in the resistance meant an immediate death sentence. Resistance took the form of small-scale, decentralized cells engaged in independent activities.

One of the riskiest activities was hiding and sheltering refugees and enemies of the Nazi regime, particularly Jewish families and draft-age youth. The Nazis deported Jewish populations to concentration camps,[1] rationed food, and withheld ration cards as punishment. They also imposed work rules which required every adult male to work in German

---

1. About one hundred and forty thousand Jews lived in the Netherlands at the beginning of the war; at the end of the war, only forty thousand Jews were alive. Of the one hundred thousand Jews that didn't hide, only one thousand survived the war. Anne Frank, who later gained world-wide fame when her diary—written while hiding from the Nazis—was found and published, died shortly before the liberation of her camp on May 5, 1945.

factories or public-works projects. As conditions became increasingly harsh and difficult, resistance grew more organized and forceful.

In 1943, on his twentieth birthday, Pieter went underground, disobeying an order to report for work duty and be sent to Germany in support of the war effort. At that time Pieter was a star soccer player, one of the nation's best. Using false papers, he joined the Dutch resistance and, on penalty of death, harassed the German occupation whenever possible. At the end of the war he met Sien and the two married in 1949. Pieter was a true patriot, and I felt honored to have such an admirable relative.

That night the entire Van de Kappelle family gathered to greet me. The small group consisted of Pieter and Sien, four of their five adult children, and their families. Chris, a son-in- law who taught English, served as interpreter. I remembered Carry and Wim, Pieter and Sien's youngest children, from their visit to the United States ten years earlier, but the others were strangers. The event was enjoyable but also awkward, for the linguistic and cultural barriers were simply too great to overcome in one evening. But when the final farewells were spoken, I knew that the future was bright with possibility. Doors existed where walls once stood. Those doors were inscribed with recognizable names, and they would open in response to discernable knocks.

TRAVEL ENTRY #3: THE BEEMSTER AND FRIESLAND

The following morning Pieter and Sien drove me to the province of North Holland so that I might see for myself where my ancestors had lived and worked, tracing their footsteps in the rich farmland known as the Beemster. A fifteen-mile drive across the Houtribdijk, one of two dikes holding back the North Sea, brought us to the Beemster and the tiny village of Kwadijk, home to several generations of Van de Kappelles and the birthplace of Pieter, my paternal grandfather. The Beemster, first polder in the Netherlands, originally was covered in peat, with a small river running through called the Bamestra (hence the name "Beemster"). Between 1150 and 1250, peat-digging lowered the level of the terrain and storm floods enlarged the river into an inland sea, with direct connection to the Zuider Zee. Around 1605, investors started to drain the Beemster lake, after which the polder became excellent farmland, making the entire project a huge economic success. The Beemster polder, considered a masterpiece of creative planning, in 1999 was declared a UNESCO World Heritage Site.

After the Beemster we visited Edam, with its picturesque canals, drawbridges, lovely old buildings, and world-famous Volendam, a fishing village popular with tourists. I requested a stop at the idyllic Broek in Waterland, birthplace of my paternal grandmother Agnes. These place names had been implanted into my mind by my father, who spoke almost reverentially of his visit to these sites as a twenty-two-year-old in 1926. On that occasion he had taken numerous pictures, which he displayed faithfully over the years. Observing these places in person further reinforced the images and bonds that subconsciously helped shape my Dutch "identity."

Following our visit to the Beemster, Piet indicated that we would continue our sightseeing in Friesland, in the northern part of the Netherlands. My maternal grandparents were Frisian, so I had been lobbying for this excursion since my arrival in Holland. As we traveled northward along the province of North Holland, we entered a region called West Friesland. This area had once been connected physically to Friesland, but when extensive flooding during the Middle Ages formed the Zuider Zee, West Friesland was separated from Friesland and was annexed by the County of Holland. Today West Friesland is physically connected to Friesland by the twenty-mile-long Afsluitdijk, the vast outer dike that divides the Ijsselmeer from the North Sea. The lengthy ride across the causeway was a bit unnerving, as the strong crosswinds pummeled our vehicle with impunity. But Pieter and Sien hardly seemed to notice. Though the forces of nature are formidable in Holland, particularly along the coast, the Dutch have learned to take everything in stride.

Time limitations prevented us from visiting Groningen, the largest city in the northern part of the Netherlands and the birthplace of my grandmother Emma Brouwers. Our destination was Sneek (pronounced "Snake" in English), the birthplace of my grandfather Allert Brouwers, and known for its Waterspoort (Water Gate), one of two remaining in Europe. After 1456, when the town received its city rights, a defensive wall was built around the city, which lay on an important trade route. To facilitate this trade, a harbor was constructed, and in 1643 the Waterspoort was erected to connect city and harbor. The gate formed part of the city walls, but later on, when the walls were demolished, the gate remained intact, each side containing a striking octagonal tower. The gate and its distinctive architectural style remain unique and have become the symbol of Sneek.

Friesland is mainly an agricultural province. The Frisians were renowned animal breeders, and the famous Frisian dairy cattle (known as Holstein) and the Frisian horse originated here. Holstein cattle, with their familiar black and white coloration, are now the most common breed of dairy cattle around the world. During the Middle Ages, Frisian horses were in great demand as war horses throughout continental Europe because their size enabled them to carry a knight in full armor. Today Frisian horses are great show horses, excelling in dressage competition and in those that require the driving of a team. Their striking appearance and mild temperament make them valuable also as circus horses and popular in the film industry.

As we drove through Friesland, I marveled at its many lakes and canals, which attract tourists and make it popular for sailing. Given this environment, I wasn't surprised to learn that the Frisians were once the major traders on the North Sea. At its peak, during the sixth and seventh centuries, the Frisian Empire dominated sea-going trade, controlling the coastal trade routes from Friesland to England, France, Scandinavia, and northwest Russia.

The region's tidy picturesque farms, mostly with identical tile-roof farmhouses and neat yards, all reinforce Holland's egalitarian image. There seems to be little economic disparity here; few are wealthy, few are poor. This charming district of the Netherlands—an attractive blend of tradition and modernity—aptly captures the Dutch mystique.

EXPLANATORY ENTRY #2: UTRECHT

Shortly after my arrival in the Netherlands, Pieter took me to Utrecht, the fourth largest and one of the oldest cities in the country. Located at the geographical center of the Netherlands, Utrecht is one of the country's major educational towns. It is famous for the Dom Tower and for lovely canals.

In the first century BCE, the boundary of imperial Rome ran along the Rhine River, through the present Netherlands. The area north and east of the Rhine was settled by Germanic tribes, who felt safe on their side of the river, trusting the river as a natural border that offered cover from retaliatory attack after their opportunistic raids into Roman territory. In order to further solidify control over this strategic border, the Romans began to build fortifications along the Rhine. In 47 CE, the Romans built a fortification that later grew to be the city of Utrecht.

Today the city's skyline is dominated by the Dom Tower (336 ft. high), the highest tower in the Netherlands. Behind it lies the remaining section of the Cathedral of Saint Martin (known as Dom cathedral), begun in 1254. The tower, originally attached to the cathedral, has been freestanding since 1674, when a hurricane caused the collapse of the church's still unfinished and insufficiently supported nave. The remains today consist of the choir, the transept, and the tower.

As I stood in the church's fifteenth-century cloister, now converted into a garden, I had the distinct impression that the scene around me captured much of the region's religious history. In 1579, the seven United Provinces of the Netherlands signed the Union of Utrecht, thereby joining forces against Spanish (and Catholic) rule. The Union of Utrecht established the Dutch Republic. The following year, this predominantly Protestant state abolished the Catholic bishoprics, including the one in Utrecht, thereby separating the Dutch population into two distinct religious groups, Roman Catholic and Protestant. During the late nineteenth and early twentieth centuries Catholics and Protestants separated into distinct sub-societies; people lived and married within their own communities, each with their own schools and universities, media, sports clubs, shops, hospitals, unions, and political parties. This intense social fragmentation, called pillarization, led to significant tension within Dutch political life.

Pillarization started to crumble in the early 1960s, due to a broad set of factors including secularization, individualism, consumerism, rising living standards, the emergence of mass media (especially television), increased social and geographical mobility, and agitation by counter-cultural movements. Like the Dom, which suffered from neglect and no longer represents a vital religious community, the Netherlands also lost its religious base and has become one of the most secular countries in Europe. Large numbers of people in the Netherlands today claim either no religion (some 42 percent of the population), or are non-practicing, nominal members of a religious group. Dutch weekly church attendance has dropped from over 80 percent in the 1950s to well below 10 percent across all churches. Like the tower, freestanding since that sixteenth-century storm and separated from its cathedral by an artificial garden,

Catholics and Protestants remain divided over man-made distinctions that erode further Christianity's vitality and wellbeing, in Europe and beyond.²

TRAVEL ENTRY #4: BIKING IN HOLLAND

After my visit to Utrecht I mounted one of Holland's ten million bicycles and joined Pieter in an exhilarating ride across flat countryside. The thirty-mile ride was taken at a brisk pace as we raced along the Loosdrechtse Plassen, an area of lakes and great natural beauty. We crossed a long causeway and pedaled back along the Vecht River (now part of the Amsterdam-Rhine Canal), passing through the town of Breukelen, for which the borough of Brooklyn in New York is named. We passed sumptuous waterfront homes, including a castle, built along the Vecht at this point as summer mansions during the seventeenth century by wealthy Amsterdam merchants. Despite the alluring landscape, this was no sightseeing excursion, for Pieter had turned the ride into a competition. Knowing that I had recently cycled across the United States and that I was in excellent physical shape, he wanted to make it clear that, as a sixty-six-year-old Dutchman (and twenty-one years my senior), he was in even better shape.

Having cycled for years in North America, often in life threatening situations, I was drawn to this peaceful nation, where cyclists are treated with respect and rewarded with safety. That ride clarified and intensified my passion for cycling: my ancestors had lived in the Netherlands, where bicycle riding is a way of life. Cycling was in my blood.

TRAVEL ENTRY #5: AMSTERDAM

On my last full day in the Netherlands, Pieter and Sien took me to Amsterdam. Founded in the twelfth century as a small fishing village on the banks of the Amstel River, Amsterdam is now the largest city in the country and one of the major commercial centers of Europe. In the seventeenth century Amsterdam was the leading financial center of the world and one of the wealthiest cities on the planet. Ships sailed from Amsterdam to the Baltic Sea, North America, Africa, Brazil, and Indonesia, and the city formed the hub of a worldwide trading network.

2. In 2004, 750 years after construction began, the collapsed portions of the Dom were temporarily rebuilt.

Amsterdam's merchants held the largest share in the Dutch East India and West India Companies, which acquired overseas possessions that formed the basis of the Dutch colonies.

Our walk through Amsterdam's impressive downtown section concluded with a meal of Rijstafel, an Indonesian specialty that recalled the days of the Dutch East India Company and Holland's colonial past. After lunch we toured Amsterdam by canal boat, the ideal way to visit, for the city is interlaced with canals, having more than Venice.

Despite its size, Holland contains over six hundred museums, and with good reason, for some of the world's most famous artists are Dutch. Earlier in the day, when I asked whether it was possible to visit the Rijksmuseum, with its magnificent collection of Dutch art, or the renowned Van Gogh Museum, Pieter responded curtly, "You did not allow enough time." He was right, of course. A visit to the Rijksmuseum, with paintings such as Rembrandt's *Night Watch*, the museum's most famous attraction, and vaunted works by Jacob van Ruysdael, Frans Hals, Johannes Vermeer, and Jan van de Cappelle, requires at least a full day to appreciate.

Understanding the Dutch people, their culture and history, provided me with rare insights into my own identity. My first days on the Continent provided a tableau of the heart as I discovered myself somehow entwined with this alluring land of windmills, canals, tulips, and cheese, and its hardworking, resilient, progressive citizens. But it was time for me to move on, for Holland was not the center.

3

Switzerland: Land of Wonder

THE GUIDEBOOKS ALL AGREE that the Bernese Alps (Berner Oberland) represent the very best of rural Switzerland: unparalleled mountain panoramas, massive glaciers, crystalline lakes, gorges and waterfalls, chic ski resorts, and emerald slopes scattered with gingerbread chalets. The region's main resort city, Interlaken, lies in green lowlands on a narrow strip of land between the twin lakes of the Brinderzee (Lake Brienz) and the Thunersee (Lake Thun). Behind them, to the south, loom craggy, forested foothills with excellent views of some of Europe's noblest peaks, most notably the Eiger, the Mönch, and the region's crowning glory, the Jungfrau.

My itinerary allowed only a four-day stay in Switzerland, half of which would be spent in Geneva, leaving only two days for the rest of the country. I had two options: to travel extensively by train, using my Eurail pass to see as much of the countryside as possible, or to spend quality time in one location. I chose the latter, based on the conviction that one powerful experience is more memorable than numerous similar ones. One area—the Jungfrau region of the Bernese Alps—stood out from the rest.

TRAVEL ENTRY #6: INTERLAKEN AND THE SWISS ALPS

From the Netherlands I traveled by train through Germany's legendary Rhineland, admiring the historic river valley and its fabled castles. By nightfall I arrived in Bern, the Swiss capital, and the fifty-minute ride to Interlaken was a blur of lights, with occasional glimpses of spectacular mountain scenery. At the train station in Interlaken I joined a group of youth headed for Balmer's, Interlaken's best lodging for travelers on a tight budget. The late-day arrival limited my accommodation to a bunk bed in a basement dormitory. But the price, around $9 a night, including breakfast and tax, made the bargain more attractive.

That night I had a decision to make concerning the following day's activities. I had come to Interlaken because it was the gateway to one of the world's most spectacular alpine areas. Months earlier, while reading *Let's Go: Europe*, a travel guide written by students at Harvard, I had come across this description of the region:

> Perhaps the most stunning ascent in this area—or in all of Switzerland—is of the Jungfraujoch (3454m/11,333ft). Trains start at Interlaken's Ostbanhof . . . While you may pay through the nose to ride this train, workers at the turn of the century paid with their lives to lay the track. The rail is chiseled out of solid mountain and goes right through the Eiger and Mönch. You'll have little to see as the train makes its way through the mountain, but two huge "windows" have been cut. The first window exposes the infamous North Face of the Eiger; the second stop offers an incredible view of the Eismeer glacier. At the summit, you'll be rewarded with a once-in-a-lifetime spectacle: a panorama stretching to the Black Forest in Germany. Included in the price are visits to the Ice Palace (a maze cut into the ice) and the Sphinx scientific station.

This depiction of the ride to Europe's highest train station, near the peak of the stunning Jungfrau, had drawn me like a magnet to Interlaken.

The following morning dawned clear and sunny, perfect for a hike in the Alps. The view from the street corner near Balmer's Hostel in Interlaken was breathtaking. Straight ahead—so close I could practically touch it—stood the world famous Jungfrau, a massive wall of granite rising ten thousand feet above the valley floor. This was the day I would experience the very best the Swiss Alps had to offer.

After contemplating the train ride up the Jungfraujoch, another option, seemingly more attractive, arose. For only a few dollars I could take Balmer's special bus to Grindelwald, at the base of the heralded north face of the Eiger. At Grindelwald I could ride Europe's longest chairlift to First, the lodge at the end of the lift, or hike one of the numerous short- and long-distance trails for which the region is known. Supplied with a lunch sack, a camera, and an ample supply of water, I decided to hike up the mountain, negotiating the 3,700-foot climb in the cool of the morning. Three hours later, when I reached First (7,113 ft), my senses were saturated with the sights, sounds, and smells of this wonderland. A foot of snow was already on the ground, although it was only October 12, more than two months before the official start of the winter season. My camera recorded the spectacle, but I knew the mental pictures would remain with me forever.

Upon returning to Grindewald and the return trip to Interlaken, I noticed that the bus from Balmer's was accompanied by a car, so I joined a small group of students who found the car more attractive than the bus. As I sat in the front, next to the driver, I overheard two young men in the back seat speaking in Spanish. Though it was obvious to me that Spanish was not their native language, I could tell from their exchange that they thought no other passenger could understand their conversation, the subject of which seemed to be several girls whom they had recently met.

After several minutes of eavesdropping, I turned around and began speaking fluently in Spanish, the language I had learned as a child in Latin America. Their surprise turned to delight when I mentioned my upbringing in Costa Rica as the son of missionary parents. They introduced themselves as Paul and Craig, who had recently completed a two-year term in Bolivia as Mormon missionaries. They were rewarding themselves with a trip through Europe before returning to their engineering studies at Brigham Young University. As they were friendly and adventuresome, we developed a deeper friendship when our paths crossed unexpectedly during the next thirty days.

That night, at Balmer's, I met Isabel, a deeply spiritual Canadian lady from Saskatchewan. Since she and I were the only over-thirty-year-olds eating at the cafeteria, I made it a point to introduce myself. When she learned that I was a professor of religion and a college chaplain, she began to pour out her life story. As a devout Catholic, she had undertaken numerous pilgrimages to Medjugorje (now in Bosnia-Herzegovina, but in 1989 the town was part of Yugoslavia), the site of regular apparitions by the Virgin Mary to six young visionaries, beginning on June 24, 1981. Each youngster had received ten secrets, messages concerning the future of the world and the necessity for prayer and repentance. When I told Isabel that I was familiar with Medjugorje and that I was contemplating stopping there on my way to Greece, she urged me to go, promising that the visit would change my life. Of course, as a Protestant, I was skeptical of Marian visionary experiences, but when Isabel provided me with names and addresses of hosts with whom I could stay, I felt I should give Medjugorje a try.[1]

On Sunday, my final day in Interlaken, I decided to observe the area's magnificent sights from a different vantage point. Early that morning I boarded a steamer that regularly crosses Lake Thun, one of the loveliest lakes in Switzerland. The early morning mist added an ethereal quality to the setting, providing glimpses of waterfalls and mountains in the distance. The trip was made even more appealing by the knowledge that the ride was essentially free—Eurail passes being valid on this and many other lake steamers in Switzerland.

Upon my return, I rented a bicycle and cycled to the town of Thun, at the northernmost tip of the lake. With its picturesque castle and quaint medieval center, Thun is one of the most original towns in Switzerland. At Thun I joined locals in a Sunday promenade along the Aare River, which flows through the city from the lake. Traditional events like these don't happen much anymore, particularly in the United States, and it may be one of the reasons why social cohesion and civic pride seem increasingly elusive. The ride fulfilled my second goal in Switzerland, to cycle in the Alps.

TRAVEL ENTRY #7: INTERLAKEN TO GENEVA

The following morning I awoke to the sound of music, pumped into each room via loudspeaker. It was Monday, and the checkout at Balmer's is 9:00 a.m., by which time all guests are required to vacate the premises for the day. The early morning serenade was followed by announcements and a summary of world news. On this day we were all in for a shock as we heard the news that the stock market in the United States had suffered a crash on Friday, the previous working day. That morning, as I boarded the train to Geneva, frightening economic scenarios rolled through my mind. To minimize whatever loss I might incur from the dollar's further devaluation, I determined to exchange dollars into Swiss francs as soon as possible.

The morning's ride through the Berner Oberland was unforgettable. The spectacular journey through some of Switzerland's finest

---

1. I was disappointed later to discover that transportation to that remote mountain village, and from there to Greece, is erratic at best, particularly for those traveling on their own. It is ironic that two years later, the region was caught in the fierce fighting that followed the breakaway republic of Croatia's quest for independence.

alpine scenery ended with a steep descent at Montreux, with its magnificent view of Lake Geneva, central Europe's largest lake. Likened to the French Riviera for the mildness of its climate, its panoramic setting, and its many palaces and Edwardian hotels, this resort town is home to numerous international festivals, including the world famous Montreux Jazz Festival, held annually in July. The ride from Montreux to Geneva followed the length of the lake, and an hour later I found myself disembarking at the Gare de Cornavin, Geneva's main train station. My first priority was to exchange money, for I knew that Geneva would be more expensive than Interlaken.

The lines at the station's currency exchange seemed unusually long and more rowdy than I had expected. This was my first time traveling alone in a major European city, and the throng caught me off guard. I felt vulnerable carrying three bags—a day pack, a fanny pack, and a heavy backpack—through this bedlam. I was still a novice at this, and I sensed that I needed a better system.

When the teller asked me to sign my traveler's checks, I lowered my day pack, which I carried over my shoulder, and placed it on the counter next to me. Long lines of travelers surged on either side of me at the exchange booths, and I was concerned that someone might snatch money or some of my valuables from my fanny pouch. Completing my transaction, I zipped my pouch and turned toward my next destination, the tourist office, where I hoped to obtain a map and some help with accommodations.

As I approached the tourist office, I realized that I had left my day pack on the counter where I had exchanged money. I immediately panicked, for in that bag were my camera, rolls of film, my diary, and my return airline ticket from Cairo to New York. But then I remembered something my wife Susan had mentioned about her experience in Switzerland sixteen years earlier: "Switzerland is such a safe country that one can leave luggage on a street corner and find it there an hour later."

That thought brought me some consolation, but only temporarily, for when I re-entered the exchange area my anxiety returned. The crowd was gone, and the counter on which I had left my pack was empty. To make matters worse, a new teller stood behind the window where I had exchanged money only minutes earlier. The cashier had no knowledge of my pack, and that's when I realized my naïveté, for I was in Geneva now and not in some safe Swiss village. And this was 1989, not the early 1970s, when Susan had visited Switzerland. Social conditions had changed dramatically since then. As I roamed the hallways, looking for some clue to the whereabouts of my pack, I became aware that the train station was a rendezvous for transients, drug addicts, and thieves. Geneva was no longer safe, and that meant that no city in Europe was safe. The sooner I learned that lesson the better, for in a few days I would be in Rome, a city notoriously rife with pickpockets and thieves.

An hour later, after exhausting my knowledge of French at the police station, I left the scene of the crime with the knowledge that I was a wiser person. I lamented the loss of my diary and even more of my camera and the undeveloped pictures of Holland, the Rhineland, and the Swiss Alps.

At the tourist office I learned that finding affordable accommodations for the night, without prior reservation, was practically impossible. The clerk called numerous establishments before informing me that one single room was available at the Evangelische Stadtmission, a German religious center about a mile away, close to Geneva's Old Town. Though the price was three times what I had paid for a dorm room at Balmer's, the privacy and location of this lone available room made it the perfect base from which to explore Geneva.

My expectations in Geneva were particularly high, for this was one of the world's true international cities. Considered the "City of Peace," Geneva houses some two hundred international organizations, including the headquarters of the World Trade Organization and of the United Nations in Europe. The world renowned Red Cross had its birth here in 1863. Geneva is also home to the World Council of Churches, the world's foremost ecumenical movement.

In 1536, John Calvin was called to Geneva to establish a "Protestant Rome." Since the founded of his academy in 1559, the city had become a renowned university and scientific center. In the sixteenth and seventeenth centuries, it served as a place of refuge for persecuted Protestants. Gradually the city developed into a major banking and industrial center famous for arts, sciences, watchmaking, and the advancement of human knowledge. A list of secular luminaries associated with the city includes Voltaire, Rousseau, and psychologist Jean Piaget.

I had less than two days to explore Geneva. My priorities included the Old Town, the headquarters of the World Council of Churches, and the United Nations complex. In addition, I hoped to obtain visas for

Jordan and Egypt and to replace the stolen airline ticked I had lost at the train station. I was able to acquire a visa for Jordan almost immediately, in a diplomatic office located only a few blocks away. The process took a mere fifteen minutes to complete. Obtaining an Egyptian visa was a bit more complicated, for it required two trips to the consular office, but on the following day I met that goal as well. Obtaining a replacement airline ticket was more challenging, for I had to find my way to the local office of the airline that had issued my ticket and there rely solely on my knowledge of French. Eventually, after paying a hefty fee, I achieved that goal as well.

It was suppertime when I checked into the Stadtmission, and as soon as the concierge learned that I was an ordained minister, she invited me to join the staff and students for dinner. The meal was followed by devotions, which were conducted in German. Despite having studied some German in college and for my doctorate, I was unable to understand more than a few words or phrases. Nevertheless, the unexpected ritual, enacted in this multicultural setting, added an authentic touch to the Reformation segment of my journey.

TRAVEL ENTRY #8: GENEVA'S OLD TOWN

All cities have their historical center, and Geneva is no exception, with its oldest buildings high upon a hill, topped by Saint-Pierre Cathedral, where Protestant reformer John Calvin preached and led in worship. The view from the church's northern tower yields incomparable panoramic views of the city and the lake.

Walking is the best way to experience Geneva's famous Vieille Ville (Old Town), less than a ten-minute walk from my residence. My late-day arrival to the old city, after most of the sites were closed, limited me to a hasty walk along the narrow, dimly-lit streets, with only a brochure for a guide. I began at the Hôtel de Ville, Geneva's town hall for five hundred years; the oldest part, Baudet Tower, dates from 1455. This historic structure witnessed some of the city's most important diplomatic events, including the meeting of the Geneva Convention, which formulated the humanitarian rules of war. The agreement, signed by sixteen countries in 1864, also marked the birth of the International Red Cross. The League of Nations also assembled here for the first time in 1920.

The peaceful stillness and the town's subdued lighting beckoned me onward. I felt inexorably drawn toward the Place St. Pierre, with its two prominent buildings: Saint-Pierre Cathedral and the Auditoire de Calvin (the first location of Calvin's academy). I had read about these influential sites in textbooks and heard about them in theology classes, for they were the birthplace of Presbyterianism, the denomination I served in an ordained capacity.[2]

Saint-Pierre Cathedral is best known as the church where John Calvin preached his inspiring sermons from 1536 to 1564; as a result, the cathedral became the guiding center of Protestantism. As was the case at Utrecht and many other places in Europe, the advent of Protestantism in the middle of the sixteenth century resulted in a Protestant takeover of the cathedral. The building was emptied of all decorative objects and the sanctuary's frescoes were whitewashed; only the stained glass windows survived the iconoclastic purge.

The Auditoire, a few steps from the entrance to the cathedral, is a thirteenth-century Gothic chapel built on a fifth-century predecessor. Calvin used the chapel to train missionaries, who spread Protestantism across Europe and beyond. His stress that Protestant refugees from across Europe should hold services in their native language continues to this day in the Auditoire (now called John Knox Chapel because Knox preached here from 1556 to 1559), currently a place of worship for the Church of Scotland, the Dutch Reformed Community, and the Waldensian Church of Italy.

TRAVEL ENTRY #9: THE PALAIS DES NATIONS AND THE ECUMENICAL CENTER

During my stay in Geneva, I made it a point to visit the Palais des Nations, the United Nations center in Europe. In 1920, when the League of Nations chose Geneva as its headquarters, it paid tribute to Switzerland as the most peaceful country in Europe.[3]

The setting of the complex, with its surrounding park and splendid views of the city, the lake, and the Alps, is magnificent. The Palais hosts

---

2. For additional information on John Calvin and his influence on Protestantism, see Appendix H.

3. In 1989 Switzerland was one of nine countries not affiliated with the United Nations. That list included the Vatican, Tonga, North and South Korea, Lichtenstein, San Marino, Monaco, and the Republic of Nauru. With the exception of the Vatican, all have since joined the United Nations. North and South Korea did so in 1991, and Switzerland joined in 2002.

some seven thousand meetings annually, with about twenty-five thousand delegates from around the world. Perhaps the most impressive stop of my guided tour was the Council Chamber, called the Spanish Room because of its superb frescoes painted by the Spanish artist J. M. Sert, which depict humanity's philosophical and social history. This room has witnessed the signing of numerous peace agreements, including the agreement signed by Iran and Iraq on August 20, 1988, ending their decade-long dispute.

Another highlight of the visit was the Assembly Hall, where distinguished and controversial speakers alike, including Pope John Paul II and Yasser Arafat, have addressed the delegates. The immense complex also includes the Rockefeller Library, one of the largest libraries in the world (with one million volumes and fifteen million documents).

Near the United Nations center, and dwarfed by its imposing structures, is the Ecumenical Center, headquarters of the World Council of Churches (with over three hundred member denominations), Lutheran World Federation, World Alliance of Reformed churches, Conference of European Churches, and several other international church offices, including representatives of Orthodoxy. The staff of the organizations based in the Ecumenical Center numbers nearly five hundred, from more than fifty countries. Such a center, and the global networks here represented, substantiates Geneva's moniker: the "Protestant Rome."

The center is renowned for its library, the world's largest ecumenical collection. The center also contains a conference hall, where World Council committees and other gatherings take place. Its main decoration is a huge tapestry, hung at the front of the auditorium. The theme is God's covenant with the world; under a vast rainbow, Jesus stands at the center, stretching his arms toward the many different churches of the world. "That all may be one," in Greek, is Jesus' prayer.

Among the many sights, for me the most important was the chapel, clearly the center's essence. Its interior design is contemporary, mostly using glass, wood, and other natural materials. Ecumenical symbolism, much of it provided through gifts and artwork from around the world, enhances the site. Entering the chapel, one walks over a pattern of waves in green and white inlaid stones, symbols of baptismal waters. On the wall above, another mosaic, given by Patriarch Athenagoras of Constantinople, tells of Christ's baptism in the Jordan. An icon on the altar depicting the Trinity is a gift of the Russian Orthodox Church. The silver and marble crosses are gifts of the Armenian Apostolic church. The Bible was offered by the United Bible Societies and the pipe organ was a gift of the Evangelical Church in Germany. The chapel serves as the focal point of the communal, worship, and reflective life of the center. Staff gathers here for weekly worship services, daily prayers, and special celebrations. The natural colors, diffused light, liturgical use of space, and abstract stained windows symbolize unity and sharing.

I ended my visit to Switzerland with a stroll along Geneva's lakefront. As Paris has its Eiffel Tower and New York its Statue of Liberty, Geneva has its Jet d'Eau. The fountain, located near Geneva's Rive Gauche (Left Bank), throws a plume of water 453 feet into the air. In the evening the fountain is illuminated by eight projectors, creating an enchanting view of the city and its waterfront.

The nearby Mont Blanc Bridge, where the Rhône River exits the lake, provides a dramatic view of Mont Blanc, Europe's highest mountain (15,774 ft), shimmering in the distance, fifty miles away. From the bridge one can also see the famous flower clock, a symbol of Geneva's watch industry. The clock's face, fifteen feet in diameter and fifty feet in circumference, is made of carefully landscaped beds of flowers, its eight-foot-long clock hand the longest in the world.

Viewing this clock in the watch-making capital of the world brought to mind a lesson from my biblical studies. The Greek language has two words for time: *chronos*, which pertains to ongoing, chronological time, and *kairos*, a reference to the momentous, life-altering quality of time. The English language hints at this distinction by differentiating between "historical" events—those that happen in time—and "historic" events— events of importance in time.[4] While most people today associate Geneva with precision timekeeping devices (with chronological time), others acknowledge Geneva's kairological impact on history. The Bible encourages readers to distinguish between events of temporal and those of eternal significance. For the Gospel writers, the words and works of Jesus are charged with kairological, life-changing potential: "Lord, to whom can we go? You have the words of eternal life" (John 6:68).

I left Geneva with a renewed commitment to the necessity of international cooperation, but it was the Ecumenical Center that made the greatest impact, for I witnessed there a genuinely caring and affirming atmosphere, which I attribute to its Third World orientation.

---

4. For a more complete discussion of the topic, see page 322.

"*Oikoumene*," the World Council's slogan, recalls the closing words of Jesus in his "high priestly prayer": "that they may become completely one . . . that the love with which you have loved me may be in them, and I in them" (John 17:23–26). The words of Jesus, "just as you did [good deeds] to one of the least of these . . . you did [them] to me" (Matthew 25:40), reminds Christians that true religion places priority on the needs of the poor, the victimized, and the marginalized, for "of such is the Kingdom of God."

That night, as I rode to Lausanne, where I would transfer to a train bound for Venice, I pondered the lessons of Geneva, particularly the theft of my pack and its valuables. Oddly, the loss of such belongings might have been beneficial, for my load was now lighter, and my concern with picture-taking ended. This change in circumstances had the potential to alter my perspective and provide greater inward focus to my journey.

Geneva, a city of humanism and enlightenment, a haven for reformers and exiles, prompted me to dedicate myself anew to those visionary values—social and spiritual—that characterized my religious and intellectual ancestors. The world stands at a crossroads today, questioning whether the role of religion is historic or historical. If Christianity is not progressive, it becomes regressive—or irrelevant. Only by remaining true to its historic core—love of God, love of neighbor, love of enemy—will it endure.

4

Northern Italy: Venice, Florence, and Pisa

Venice, an entire city built on an artificial island in the middle of a lagoon, is an architectural delight. With palaces, churches, and homes that have not changed since the sixteenth century, Venice recalls a time when it was the richest city in the world. Built on an archipelago of 118 islands, the city boasts 150 canals and 400 bridges.

Venice originated as a collection of lagoon communities founded in the mid-fifth century CE by refugees from the mainland fleeing invasions by barbarians. Because the inhabitants were at home in boats and on the water, in 811 some of them started to live on a mud bank called Rialto (the term is derived from *rivoalto*, "high shore"), in the middle of the lagoon. They started to convert this into a proper island, sinking wooden piles into the mud and constructing quays and flat areas on which to build houses. Thus the city of Venice was born. In 828 the prestige of the new city increased when two Venetian sailors stole the remains of St. Mark the Evangelist from Alexandria and eventually built a basilica to house the relics of Venice's new patron saint. By the fifteenth century Venetians were unrivalled masters of the sea.

TRAVEL ENTRY #10: GENEVA TO VENICE

I arrived at Mestre, some four miles from Venice, at the break of dawn. I was so tired and irritated that only the excitement of seeing this enchanting city for the first time kept me going. The night before, when I boarded the overnight train at Lausanne, the conductor had secured my passport and escorted me to a first class couchette, where he guaranteed me an undisturbed night's rest. He instructed me to lock the door of my compartment and to keep it locked at all times.

As soon as I fell asleep, I was awakened by a knock on the door followed by the turn of the handle, and then by a push against the door, causing the flimsy lock to give way. So much for security! I heard an apology, then silence. I secured the lock more firmly the second time around, and this time it took me longer to fall asleep. A short while later I was awakened again, this time by a loud commotion outside my compartment, followed by strong knocking and a volley of words that rang the length of the hallway. The door was forced open once again, and I faced an irate Italian customs officer and several of his aides, who demanded that I open my luggage. We stared somewhat awkwardly for a moment, I in my skivvies and they in their uniforms, before I wisely complied with their demand. The officer looked intently at my passport, which the conductor produced, for he seemed convinced that I was hiding something illegal. Having heard stories about drugs planted in tourists' bags while they were traveling overseas and about victims being sent to jail on trumped-up charges, I watched the officer and his assistants closely until their departure. I did not sleep much after that, annoyed by the conductor's ruse and the demeaning encounter with the officials.

At Mestre I transferred to a local train bound for Stazione Santa Lucia, Venice's train station. Prior to the nineteenth century, tourists could reach Venice only by boat. But then a three-mile causeway was built for a railway, which eventually was expanded to allow cars access to the northern edge of the city. Beyond those entry points, transportation within Venice remains, as in centuries past, entirely on water or on foot.

TRAVEL ENTRY #11: ST. MARK'S SQUARE

Venice has one wide canal—the Grand Canal—which forms an inverted S as it snakes its way through the city. The city also contains many smaller canals. To get around, locals use boats, including the motorized waterbuses (*vaporetti*) that ply regular routes along the major canals and between the city's islands. The classical Venetian boat is the gondola, although it is now mostly used as a tourist attraction, much like the horse-drawn carriage rides around many European cities. My destination was the center of Venice, at the far end of the Grand Canal, with its most famous site, St. Mark's Square.

Knowing that I might have difficulty locating affordable lodging in Venice—the guide books warned that rooms cost twice what they would elsewhere—I decided to check my backpack at the station's baggage depot, hoping to see the important sites in a single day and possibly return in time to catch a train to Florence.

It was 8:00 a.m., and I was enthralled as I followed the city's labyrinthine system of streets and alleys. I stopped at a small grocery store for the cheese, hard rolls, and milk that would keep me going that morning. Since October is the beginning of Venice's off-season, I was surrounded by Venetian locals, with hardly a tourist in sight. I followed my nose to the fish and vegetable markets, located in the Rialto, the oldest part of the city. Ahead stood one of Venice's most recognizable attractions, the Rialto Bridge, which for much of the history of the city was the only bridge across the Grand Canal. Lined with shops and quite steep, the bridge is constructed so that the central arch was high enough to allow warships to pass underneath.

Minutes later I entered St. Mark's Square, lined on three sides with elegant shops, hotels, and cafés and on the fourth side by the Basilica of St. Mark, an eleventh-century cathedral. The Campanile, the 324-foot bell tower of the cathedral, stands separately in the square. Next to the piazza and joining it to the lagoon is the smaller square (Piazzetta), with the Doges' Palace along one side.

Noticing a tour group in the square, with an English guide, I wandered over and attached myself to the group. The tour guide pointed toward two granite pillars standing near the water's edge. The columns represent Marco and Teodoro, Venice's two patron saints. Atop one column is a winged lion, the traditional symbol of St. Mark. In addition to his role as Evangelist—one of four authors of the New Testament Gospels—Mark is considered the first patriarch of Egypt by the Eastern Orthodox Church as well as by the Coptic Orthodox Church and thus the founder of Christianity in Africa. In 68 CE he was martyred by pagan Alexandrians who resented his efforts to turn them away from the worship of their traditional Egyptian gods. The second pillar holds a statue of St. Theodore, standing on the sacred crocodile of Egypt. During Venice's heyday, these columns constituted the official gateway to the city. Both had been brought from Constantinople after the infamous sacking of that city by Crusaders in 1204.

Along the eastern side of the Piazzetta, facing the square and the lagoon, lies the Doges' Palace, with its elegant pink and white marble façades and interior with paintings by Tintoretto and Veronese. More than just the dwelling of the Doges, the titular rulers of Venice, the palace also included various chambers where different councils of the government met. Attached to the palace is a famous prison in which Casanova, the infamous adventurer and womanizer, was incarcerated but from which he made a fantastic escape. Prisoners were sentenced in the palace and then crossed an enclosed bridge known as the "Bridge of Sighs," so called because the prison was also a place of torture and execution.

The remains of St. Mark are contained in St. Mark's Basilica, a cathedral built between 1063 and 1073 to house the relics. The five-domed basilica has a very Eastern look and is distinctly different from the Gothic cathedrals of the rest of Europe. St. Mark's is built on the plan of a Greek cross, surmounted by a bulbous dome flanked by four smaller domes placed on the arms of the cross. The basilica, the state church of the republic, also functioned as the chapel of the Doges, who attended ceremonies and made their public appearances here. Positioned across the central portal are replicas of four bronze horses (dating from the Greco-Roman period) that were looted from the hippodrome in Constantinople when the Venetians helped sack the city in 1204. By some accounts the horses had originally adorned the Arch of Trajan in the Roman Forum before they were transported to Constantinople.

While the basic structure of the basilica has been little altered, its decoration changed greatly over time. The succeeding centuries all contributed to its adornment, and seldom did a Venetian vessel return from the Orient without bringing columns, capitals, or friezes from some ancient building to add to the basilica, until the exterior gradually became covered with marbles and carvings. Over the centuries the church, enriched with the loot of conquest, became virtually a museum. The basilica's main treasure is the Pala d'Oro, an altar screen made from solid gold, encrusted with precious gems. The church is adorned with mosaics—supposedly forty-three thousand square feet of them.

The spacious interior of the building, with its multiple choir lofts, was the inspiration for the development of a Venetian polychoral style. Most notable were the uncle and nephew organists and composers Andrea Gabrieli (c. 1533–1586) and Giovanni Gabrieli (c. 1554–1612), who are often credited with the first use of instruments in sacred music in a church, as well as the development of antiphonal music. It was here that Claudio Monteverdi (1567–1643), whose compositions mark the transition from Renaissance to Baroque, performed his famous *Vespers of the Blessed Virgin*, a work that foreshadows sacred Baroque classics such as Handel's *Messiah* and J. S. Bach's *St. Matthew Passion*.

The opulence of St. Mark's left me sensually intoxicated yet spiritually empty. I had witnessed extravagant wealth before, even in ecclesiastical settings, but not to this degree. St. Mark's Basilica evoked Venetian splendor rather than divine glory. Such intermixing of the sacred and the profane would have perplexed Jesus, as it did the Reformers, who responded with iconoclastic fury. I recalled the words of Jesus concerning extravagant religiosity: "Truly I tell you, they have received their reward" (Matthew 6:2). Jesus blessed the poor, and indicated that theirs was the kingdom of God (Luke 6:20). I could find no biblical beatitude applicable to what I saw and felt in this kingdom of man.

The straight-lined simplicity of the 324-foot-high Campanile, the basilica's bell tower, makes a strong contrast with the lavish excess of the cathedral. The tower itself, the tallest in Venice, is of relatively recent construction (the original tenth-century tower collapsed in 1902). During the fifteenth century, clerics found guilty of immoral acts were suspended from the tower in wooden cages, living on bread and water for as long as a year before dying of exposure.

Although there was still much to see in Venice—including the Lido,[1] a plush resort and beach area some fifteen minutes away by boat, and the Accademia, a museum that displays a world-class collection of paintings—I decided to conclude my delightful morning with a return trip to the train station via *vaporetto*. Line 1, the local waterbus that runs along the Grand Canal, provided me with a parting view of Venice's main thoroughfare, described by the fifteenth- century French writer Philippe de Commines as "the finest street in all the world"; the two-mile canal is lined with two hundred of the world's most beautiful buildings.

My brief visit provided me with a lasting taste of this former maritime center, its throbbing pulse replaced by tourism and an uncertain battle against the ravages of tide and time.

TRAVEL ENTRY #12: FLORENTINE WONDERS AND LUMINARIES

Wednesday afternoon, as I approached Florence by train, I studied my informational packet on Tuscany with particular care. For its landscapes and its artistic legacy, Tuscany is considered the most beautiful region in Italy. Besides Florence, the region includes the must-see cities of Pisa

---

1. The word *lido* means "shore." As a barrier island, on the sea, the Lido acts as Venice's shoreline.

and Siena, and I had only thirty-six hours to spend, for I needed to arrive in Rome before the start of the weekend.

The city of Florence reached its peak between the eleventh and fifteenth centuries, when it became wealthy because of textile manufacture, trade, and banking. After several experiments with representative government, Florence was ruled by an oligarchy of wealthy aristocrats, among whom the Medici family became dominant in the fifteen century. Under the patronage of these wealthy families the arts and literature flourished as nowhere else in Europe.[2] Lorenzo de' Medici, who ruled Florence in the late fifteenth century, was perhaps the greatest patron of the arts in the history of the West.

Florence was the city of such writers as Dante, Petrarch, and Boccaccio and of artists and engineers such as Alberti, Botticelli, Brunelleschi, Cellini, Leonardo da Vinci, and Michelangelo. Because of its dominance in literature, the Florentine language became the literary language of Italy. Humanism brought new philosophical ideas and a full appreciation of classicism. In Florence, Machiavelli inaugurated the new political science, Guicciardini introduced modern historical prose, and Galileo created and developed experimental science.

In Florence, my first priority, as always when I traveled without hotel reservations, was to secure lodging. On the far side of the Arno River, only a fifteen-minute walk from the Stazione, I located Ostello Santa Monaca, an affordable youth hostel where I spent the next two nights. There I met a Norwegian named Halvor, a seasoned traveler who had visited Jordan, the Sinai, and Cairo, and who was willing to share indispensable tips on travel through the Middle East. That evening Halvor and I strolled through the moonlit city, amazed by the magnificence of the Duomo, one of the largest cathedrals in Christendom, the nearby Baptistery, and the 269-foot-high Campanile (bell tower), all standing in a rather cramped square. Halvor was more interested in finding Dante's House, reputed to be the poet's birthplace, than in viewing religious architecture, so we agreed to return to the square on the following day for a closer look.

After locating Dante's House, Halvor and I proceeded to the great Piazza della Signoria, the square that has been the center of Florentine life since before Medici times. Described as one of the most beautiful squares in the world, the piazza is a virtual open-air museum of sculpture. Here, in the heart of Florence, I first encountered scaffolding, a

---

2. For additional information on Florence and the Italian Renaissance, see Appendix I.

disappointing sight for tourists bent on touching history. Portions of the piazza, including the space chosen by Michelangelo for his exquisite statue *David*, were dug up and fenced in. The site had become an archaeological dig, for buried beneath were the remains of a medieval city sitting atop Roman ruins dating to the first century. The three-year dig was nearing its conclusion, as archaeologists were working to repave the square for the onslaught of 1990 World Cup soccer fans.

The scaffolding hid some of the magnificent sculptures in the Loggia dei Lanzi, the arcade along one side of the square. Built at the end of the fourteenth century, the loggia contains antique and Renaissance statues, including a copy of the dramatic *Rape of a Sabine Woman* (1583) by the Flemish artist Jean de Boulogne, better known as Giambologna. This impressive work was made from one imperfect block of white marble, the largest block ever transported to Florence. The gallery also contains the bronze statue of *Perseus* by Benvenuto Cellini, the most famous work in the Loggia and probably his best bronze sculpture. It shows the well-proportioned body of the mythical Greek hero holding his sword in his right hand and triumphantly holding up Medusa's decapitated head in his left. Cellini, who worked almost ten years on this bronze, met with numerous difficulties because the casting of the statue was several times unsuccessful. On the final try, Cellini is said to have fed the furnace with his household furniture and finally with his pots and pans and some two hundred pewter dishes.

At the corner of the Palazzo Vecchio, a bronze plaque marks the spot where Savonarola was executed. Savonarola, an Italian priest and leader of Florence from 1494 until his execution in 1498, was known for religious reformation, anti-Renaissance preaching, book burning, and destruction of art. He vehemently preached against what he saw as the moral degradation of the clergy. At the time the Roman Catholic Church's clergy were increasingly corrupting morality and leading a corrupt life themselves; the Papacy itself was filled with abuses and personal immorality. Savonarola's impassioned sermons in Florence brought about a reform that has never been duplicated in the history of that city. In 1497 he and his followers carried out a "Bonfire of the Vanities," going door to door collecting items associated with moral laxity and burning them all in a large pile in the Piazza della Signoria. Fine Florentine Renaissance artwork was lost in the bonfire, including paintings by Botticelli.

Florence soon tired of Savonarola and his intimidating tactics. During his Ascension Day sermon on May 4, 1497, bands of youths rioted, and the riot became a revolt. On May 13, 1497, he was excommunicated by Pope Alexander VI and a year later Alexander demanded his arrest and execution. On May 13, 1498, the day of his execution, he and some followers were taken to the Piazza della Signoria, where they were handed over to the secular authorities to be burned. Savonarola was executed in the same place where the "Bonfire of the Vanities" was lit and in the same manner that he had condemned others. As the authorities did not want Savonarola's followers to have any relics, the ashes were thrown in the Arno River.

Having viewed the famous square and the impressive statuary, Halvor and I completed our walk-through tour by crossing the unique Ponte Vecchio, viewing the shops that line Florence's oldest and most famous bridge. This fourteenth-century bridge was the only one in the city that was spared by the retreating German forces during World War II.

The following morning, Halvor and I were among the first to enter the Galleria degli Uffizi at 9:00 a.m., when it opened. The Galleria, one of the world's most famous museums, houses Italy's most important collection of paintings. Located adjacent to the Piazza della Signoria, the museum was created in 1581 on the top floor of a Renaissance palace that contained the administrative offices (*uffizi*) of the Florentine state, to safeguard collections assembled by the Medici family in the fifteenth and sixteenth centuries. The museum opened to the public in the seventeenth century, making it the world's first public gallery of modern times.

The highlight of my brief tour was the Botticelli Room, particularly its graceful paintings *The Birth of Venus* (c. 1485) and *Spring* (often known by its Italian name, *Primavera*, c. 1478), both painted by Sandro Botticelli (1445–1510). *The Birth of Venus* depicts the goddess arriving at the seashore. She has just emerged from the sea as a full grown woman, blown towards shore by the Zephyrs, symbols of spiritual passions. She is joined by one of the Horae, goddesses of the seasons, who hands her a flowered cloak. According to some commentators, the naked goddess is a symbol not of earthly but spiritual love. The anatomy of Venus and various subsidiary details—her elongated neck and her left shoulder sloping at an anatomically unlikely angle—do not display strict classical realism and like El Greco paintings, suggest spirituality. The *Primavera* depicts classical gods scantily clothed and life-size; interpreting the painting's complex philosophical symbolism requires deep knowledge of Renaissance literature and classical iconography.

The effect of both paintings is distinctly pagan, considering they were made at a time and place when most artwork depicted Roman Catholic themes. It is surprising that these canvases escaped the flames of Savonarola's bonfires, where a number of Botticelli's other "pagan" works perished. Because of Botticelli's friendship with Lorenzo de Medici and Lorenzo's power, these works were spared the disapproval of the Church.

TRAVEL ENTRY #13: PIAZZA DEL DUOMO AND THE GALLERIA DELL' ACCADEMIA

The Baptistery of St. John is clearly *the* building to see in Florence. The original Baptistery, probably the first Christian church in Florence, was built in late Roman times on the ruins of a Roman building, possibly a Roman temple dedicated to the god Mars. However, the Baptistery as we see it today is built in an octagonal Romanesque style and dates from the eleventh through the thirteenth centuries. The sanctuary is particularly famed for its three doors in gilded bronze, including the so-called "Doors of Paradise," cast between 1330 and 1452.[3]

The nearby Cathedral of Santa Maria del Fiore, known as the Duomo, was the largest in Europe when it was completed, with room for thirty thousand people. It is exceeded in size today by only four Roman Catholic cathedrals, including St. Peter's Basilica in Vatican City. Constructed over a 170-year period, the Duomo's most striking feature is its high dome, which served as the inspiration of such later domes as that of St. Peter's and even the Capitol in Washington, DC Our tour of the Duomo ended with an ascent to the cupola gallery, a climb of 463 steps; the panoramic view of Florence and the surrounding area was certainly worth the climb. Aware of our tight schedule, we proceeded down the stairway to our final destination in Florence, the Galleria dell' Accademia.

Upon entering the museum, we were surprised to find a crowd gathered around the gallery's main attraction, Michelangelo's *David*. Since it was off-season, we had timed our visit to coincide with the lunch hour, but we quickly realized that there is never an off-season when it comes to the world's most recognizable artistic statue. To appreciate the seventeen-foot statue, one must see it from every angle. The more one investigates, the more one becomes aware of the statue's disproportion, particularly in David's hands. This was intentional, we learned, a neces-

---

3. For additional information on the Piazza del Duomo and its two architectural wonders—the Baptistery and the Duomo—see pages 370–73.

sary part of the perspective the artist was attempting to achieve. The statue had been carved from a piece of marble previously utilized by two inferior artists, who had abandoned their project due to a lack of skill and a fault that lay through the block.

The sculpture is said to depict the biblical David at the moment he decides to do battle with Goliath. It came to symbolize the Florentine Republic, threatened on all sides by more powerful rival states and yet proclaiming itself morally superior to them. Instead of depicting David as victorious over a foe much larger than he, the youngster looks ready for combat. His veins bulge out of his lowered hand and the twist of his body effectively conveys the feeling that he is in motion.

Among the museum's other works stood Michelangelo's *Four Slaves*, once intended for the tomb of Pope Julius II but left "unfinished," its rough surface accentuating the attempt of the slaves to escape their bondage of stone. The finished project was to be the most prestigious commission of the sculptor's career—an eighth wonder of the world. The free-standing tomb with some forty figures was to be located in St. Peter's. However, Michelangelo was soon diverted from the monumental project—and from his first love of sculpting—to paint the ceiling of the Sistine Chapel. When Pope Julius died in 1513, his heirs asked that he be interred in a simpler tomb, one that could be completed quickly. What Michelangelo eventually called "the tragedy of the tomb" ended in 1545, when a much smaller version of the tomb was installed in the Church of St. Peter in Chains, Julius's titular church in Rome.

TRAVEL ENTRY #14: VISIT TO PISA'S CAMPO DEI MIRACOLI (FIELD OF MIRACLES)

That afternoon Halvor and I boarded the train for a fifty-mile trip to Pisa. Once a maritime republic that ranked with Genoa and Venice, today Pisa is a quiet and over-commercialized town, its old port—silted over and now six miles inland—all but forgotten. We had one goal in mind: to see—and climb—the legendary Leaning Tower, the reputed site of Galileo's famous experiments on motion.

While the Leaning Tower is the most celebrated image of the city, it is but one of several monuments in the city's Campo dei Miracoli ("Field of Miracles"), a walled area at the heart of Pisa that is recognized as one of the main centers for medieval art in the world. The site is dominated by four great religious edifices: the Duomo, the Leaning Tower, the Baptistery, and the Camposanto (a cemetery). The marble buildings, their whiteness heightened by the backdrop of the brilliant green grass, are built in a distinctive style of architecture known as wedding-cake Romanesque.

The Leaning Tower of Pisa, the crown jewel of the Campo dei Miracoli, serves as the campanile or bell-tower of the cathedral. Known in Italian as the Torre Pendente, the 183-foot tower is often considered one of the seven wonders of the modern world. Theories vary as to whether the famous sixteen-foot list is due to shifting foundations or to an amazing architectural feat. The construction of the white marble tower was performed in three stages over many years, beginning with construction of the first floor in 1173, during a period of military success and prosperity. The tower first acquired a lean after the third floor was built in 1178, due to a mere ten-foot foundation set in unstable subsoil. Construction was then halted for almost a century because the Pisans were engaged in continual battles with Genoa, Lucca, and Florence. This allowed time for the underlying soil to settle; otherwise, the tower would almost certainly have toppled. In 1272, another four floors were built at an angle to compensate for the tilt.

During the twentieth century the Italian government made various attempts to reinforce the foundation and thereby prevent collapse of the tower. However, it was considered important to retain the current tilt, due to the vital role that this element plays in promoting tourism. A multinational group of engineers, mathematicians, and historians have met to discuss stabilization methods. After over two decades of work on the subject, the tower was closed to the public in January 1990 and did not reopen until December 15, 2001. The tower has now been declared stable for another three hundred years.

My visit to Pisa in 1989 made it possible for me to climb the tower's 294 steps to the top. Knowing that the closing was just months away and that there was no guarantee when or if the building would reopen to the public again made my climb a gratifying experience.

EXPLANATORY ENTRY #3: GALILEO GALILEI'S GREATEST CHALLENGE

One cannot come to Pisa and not think of Galileo (1564–1642). His experiments with falling objects paved the way for Newton and gravity. But those experiments served a further purpose—it was in this town that Galileo first questioned the theory that the sun revolved around the earth. As yet he had no proof against the earth-centered theories espoused by Aristotle and affirmed by Ptolemy around 150 CE. Geocentrism had been the ultimate authority for centuries, and this view seemed to be supported by the Bible. Galileo's belief in heliocentrism eventually got him into trouble with the Catholic Church.

In 1610, he published *The Starry Messenger*, an account of his telescopic observations of the moons of Jupiter, using his observations to argue in favor of the Copernican theory of the universe. He dedicated the work to the young Grand Duke Cosimo de' Medici, whom he had tutored in mathematics and who had ascended the throne in 1609. In 1610 Galileo moved to Florence, where he took the position of court philosopher. Skeptics, including church authorities, continued to question his views, so he invited them to examine the skies for themselves. However, they could not see what he saw, for the implications threatened the established cosmological foundations.

His discoveries attracted widespread attention, making Galileo the most famous scientist in Europe. But they also engendered further controversy, particularly with the Catholic Church. Believing that his theory countered biblical truth, the Church threatened action. Galileo rushed to Rome to defend his Copernican views, which were clearly heretical in the eyes of the church. In Rome he appeared before Cardinal Bellarmine, the Church's chief theologian. The Cardinal advised Galileo to discontinue his research, warning him that if he persisted in his publication, he would recommend trial by the Inquisition. Galileo submitted to Bellarmine's demands, but he remained committed to heliocentrism.

In 1623, Cardinal Barberini, longtime Florentine and a friend and admirer of Galileo, became Pope Urban VIII. The following year, Galileo visited the Pope and asked for permission to continue his literary career. Urban assured him that he could write about Copernican theory as long as he treated it as a mathematical proposition. However, after the printing of his book, *Dialogue Concerning the Two Chief World Systems* (1632), Galileo was called to Rome to face the Inquisition. Galileo had constructed his book around a conversation among three characters: Salviati, who argues for the Copernican theory and presents some of Galileo's views directly; Sagredo, an intellectual layman who is initially neutral; and Simplicio, who enunciates the church's position but who comes across as a simpleton or fool. The Pope felt betrayed by the book and ordered Galileo to renounce his conclusions publicly on pain of torture or execution.

In October 1632, in the face of formal charges by the Catholic Church, Galileo prepared to face his accusers. He wrote a will prior to his departure for Rome, for not only were his science and reputation at stake, but possibly his life as well. In 1633, the sixty-nine-year-old Galileo stood alone against the Catholic Church. He was ill, frightened, and emotionally unstable. Threatened with torture, he presented a confession, but the Church did not accept it as sincere. In a moment of weakness, he signed the following statement, renouncing belief in heliocentrism: "I, Galileo, being in my seventieth year, being a prisoner and on my knees, and before your Eminences, having before my eyes the Holy Gospel, which I touch with my hands, abjure, curse, and detest the error and the heresy of the movement of the earth." But under his breath he is said to have whispered, "*E pur sì muove*" ("Nevertheless the earth *does* move").

The verdict was given on June 21, and was surprising in its severity. Galileo was no ordinary man; as the most renowned scientist of his age, he had many patrons in religious and secular circles. Despite the pronouncement of reduced guilt as regards his advocacy of the Copernican theory, the tribunal found Galileo guilty of "suspected heresy," a term that constituted an actual offense. He was sentenced to an unlimited period of imprisonment and forced to publicly recant his erroneous doctrine. Moreover, publication of the *Dialogue* was prohibited. Galileo, however, was not imprisoned in the cellars of the Inquisition. He was taken to the home of the Tuscan ambassador, and six months later returned home, where he remained under house arrest until his death.

Galileo was formally rehabilitated in 1741, when Pope Benedict XIV authorized the publication of Galileo's complete scientific works. In 1758, the general prohibition against heliocentrism was removed from the *Index of Prohibited Books*. In 1992, on the 350th anniversary of Galileo's death, Pope John Paul II gave an address on behalf of the Catholic Church in which he expressed regret for how the Galileo affair had been handled. But he did not admit that the Church was wrong to convict Galileo on a charge of heresy.

5

Rome: The Eternal City

TRAVEL ENTRY #15: ARRIVAL IN ROME

"At Termini Station, take bus #64 to the last stop before the Tiber River, then walk across the river to the North American College." The directions seemed simple enough. I had just arrived by train from Florence and was trying to get my bearings. And after my experience with robbers in Geneva, I was a bit paranoid about boarding a packed bus with all my belongings. I knew that buses in Rome were generally crowded and were frequented by pickpockets.

I was on the phone with Jim Bird, an American in Rome studying for the priesthood, and when he sensed my anxiety about locating one particular bus stop among many, he quickly modified his directions: "Cross the river, and stay on the bus past the entrance to St. Peter's Square. That's the end of the line, and I'll wait for you there."

Earlier, while planning my sabbatical trip, I knew that getting around Rome would be difficult, but I was certain that finding affordable accommodations would be even more challenging. So I had contacted a priest who served as chaplain to Catholic students at Washington and Jefferson College. He, in turn, gave me the name of Father Charles (Chuck) Christian, a fifth-year student at the Gregorian University in Rome. Although he was from the Pittsburgh area, his experience in Rome qualified him as a valuable resource. I had written to him at the North American College, his residence in Rome, and it was Jim Bird who had answered the telephone when I called from the train station. Chuck was still in class, so Jim agreed to help me get settled until Chuck returned.

As Jim and I walked toward the dormitory, we stopped at a bar for a latte, a surprisingly refreshing Italian specialty. A short distance later we came to St. Peter's Square, where I couldn't help but stare at the grandeur of St. Peter's Basilica. I stood trancelike, scarcely able to believe that I was finally in Rome, witnessing one of the religious wonders of the world. The look of awe on this Protestant's face must have given Jim some sense of satisfaction.

After a leisurely shower and lunch at the college, I joined Father Christian, recently arrived from his classes at the university, for a short midday mass, conducted in the dormitory's chapel. After the service, Chuck took me for a drive along the west bank of the Tiber River. We passed the Tempietto, the spot where, according to tradition, St. Peter was crucified. The ride south, following the ridge of the Janiculum Hill, presented us with a magnificent panoramic view, the most beautiful in Rome.

After our short drive Chuck took me to the Pensione Padri Trinitare, a small hotel that catered to pilgrims. It was run by members of a Catholic religious order, and Chuck had made a reservation on my behalf. I felt fortunate to be able to stay in this quiet neighborhood, located less than a mile from the Vatican. Best of all, I had a private bath, with a western-style toilet.

Chuck gave me a moment to register and get settled before he returned for me on a motor scooter, heading on it to the university for another class. Within minutes we were weaving through the maze of Friday afternoon traffic in downtown Rome. It was a bizarre cacophony: horns honking, vehicles swerving, and fumes so foul that many scooter drivers wore bandannas and masks over mouth and nose to avoid suffocating. Chuck had lent me a helmet, which was mandatory, but what I really needed was a face mask.

Traveling through Rome's crowded streets on a scooter made economic sense, but then I was struck by the irony of my situation: a Protestant minister clutching the clerical garb of a Catholic priest. The scene felt like an episode from television's *The Flying Nun*.

After a brief tour of the Gregorian University, Chuck dropped me off at the Trevi Fountain, made famous by the legend of "three coins in the fountain." At that point I set off on my own, eager to begin a walking tour of the Centro Storico, Rome's irregular core. I was disappointed to find the famous fountain drained and under repair, but not nearly as frustrated as when I arrived at the Pantheon, one of Rome's greatest structures, to find that it too was closed, its entrance blocked with scaffolding.

EXPLANATORY ENTRY #4: THE PANTHEON

The Romans possessed an unrivaled talent for engineering. Wherever the Romans ventured in their campaigns, they brought with them this passion for city building, borrowing architectural elements from the Greeks, particularly in their use of Doric, Ionic, and Corinthian columns, as well as the arch, a form bequeathed to the Romans by the Etruscans. And knowledge of the arch led to the vault—a broad enclosure that could reach massive proportions without internal pillars.

The Pantheon, meaning "temple of all the gods," was originally built as a temple to the seven deities of the seven planets in the state religion of ancient Rome. It is the best-preserved of all Roman buildings and one of the few ancient Roman buildings to remain intact. Arguably the most amazing structure ever built by the Romans, the current building dates from 126 CE, during the reign of the Emperor Hadrian, who served as emperor from 117 to 138. The structure is a rotunda ringed with seven recesses that may have been designed as shrines for the deities the Romans associated with the heavens—including Mars, Mercury, Venus, and Jupiter.

The magnificent domed ceiling, the largest and most daring of antiquity, is the heart of the Pantheon's design. Rising 141 feet to form a perfect hemisphere, the dome was envisioned as a symbol of the firmament. As such, it was to remain unsupported by columns or obtrusive buttressing. Through the oculus, an opening at the top of the dome, the sun's rays could penetrate to gild the marble floor below. No interior space had ever looked like this before.

EXPLANATORY ENTRY #5: THE ROMAN FORUM AND THE PALATINE

A short distance from the Pantheon, at the foot of the Capitoline Hill and just north of the Roman Forum, is the Piazza Venezia. This square, which marks the center of Rome, is dominated by an enormous marble monument to Victor Emmanuel II, first king of unified Italy (1861–1878). To the right of the memorial stands a majestic ramp, designed by Michelangelo, leading to the Campidoglio (Capitol Square) on the Capitoline Hill. Michelangelo's design of the Campidoglio effectively reversed the orientation of the Capitoline, turning Rome's civic center to face away from the pagan Roman Forum and instead in the direction of Papal Rome and the Christian church in the form of St. Peter's Basilica.

In the valley below the Campidoglio one can view the remains of the Roman Forum, the religious, political, and commercial center of ancient Rome. The ruins, excavated in the late nineteenth and twentieth centuries, have been dug to the level of the first century BCE, to the period of Julius Caesar. As I stood at the overlook, attempting to identify the principal monuments of this "boneyard of history," I knew I was standing at what two thousand years ago was the center of the then-known world.[1]

Although Rome was settled on seven hills, between them was a marshy plain that became the hub of the city. There the early inhabitants gathered to trade their wares and settle disputes. The meeting ground was eventually drained and paved, and public buildings were erected around a spacious plaza. The site served many functions over time, including the residence of kings, the place where the Senate met, and where public meetings were held. Early temples in the Forum included the Temple of Vesta, where virgins dressed in white tended the city's sacred flame. Basilicas such as the Temple of Castor and Pollux and the Temple of Saturn were also used for commercial and judicial activities. Due to the political importance of the area, numerous honorary monuments were scattered about the site. Gradually more public buildings were constructed around the square until by the end of the second century CE, no fewer than six emperors had enlarged the site with temples and additional forums.

Early in his long regime, Augustus, the first Roman emperor (27 BCE–14 CE), was named Pontifex Maximus, the head of Rome's state religion. Religion had suffered during the late republic, so Augustus launched a movement to restore Rome's old gods to their former positions of importance and ordered the rehabilitation of eighty-two temples that had fallen into disrepair. Seeing religion as a way to stimulate and focus patriotism, he likely believed that his massive building and rebuilding program was for purposes less than exclusively devotional.

About a century later, Emperor Trajan (98–117) widened the idea of what it meant to be Roman. Under his reign, the boundaries of the empire achieved their farthest reach, including Armenia and Mesopotamia. Surprisingly, the rough old soldier spent the plunder in a massive building campaign, including roads and other public works. In addition, the emperor commissioned a massive forum to accommodate

---

1. For a chronology of Roman history, consult Appendix B.

the inhabitants of Rome, now a city of one million. To create a flat plain large enough in downtown Rome, north of the Forum of Caesar, he leveled a huge section of the Quirinal Hill.

Trajan's Forum surpassed all others in size and splendor. To enter the huge public square, one passed through a basilica, the largest of its kind. In 113, the year after the forum was completed, a freestanding column known as Trajan's Column was erected in the forum's square. The structure, 125 feet high, still stands. A 650-foot-long frieze winds around the column 23 times; the carvings crowded with some two thousand five hundred figures of sailors, soldiers, statesmen, and priests, providing a valuable source of information for modern historians. In 1588, Pope Sixtus V replaced the nude statue of Trajan on top with a statue of St. Peter, which still remains.

The Roman Forum continued as the political and economic center of Rome well into the imperial period, when it was reduced to a monumental area. The Forum's most imposing monument, the Arch of Titus, was built in 81 CE by Emperor Titus to commemorate his triumphs in Palestine, particularly his destruction of Jerusalem in 70 CE. The arch was erected at the southern end of the Via Sacra, the Forum's principal roadway.

In the distance, to the right of the Arch of Titus and still visible despite nightfall, I saw the ruins of the Palatine Hill, the centermost of the seven hills of Rome and the site of the first city of Rome (c. 800 BCE). Here, according to fable, Romulus and Remus, twin sons of Mars, were suckled by a she-wolf and survived to found Rome. In classical times this hill was the place on which Rome's rich and powerful chose to live.

The Palatine also became the home of emperors. On this hill the emperor Augustus was born; his private dwelling, known as the House of Livia, still stands. The imperial palace, begun by Tiberius and enlarged by Nero, Trajan, Hadrian, and other emperors, extended across the Palatine Hill and even included the area where the Coliseum was later built. Today the entire area is enclosed and preserved as an archaeological museum.

Having absorbed as much of Rome's historic section as possible in one evening, I headed by foot toward my hotel, three miles away. Following the Tiber, I crossed at the small island called Isola Tiberina, once the center of a temple to Asclepius, the god of medicine and healing in

Greek mythology. Nearing the river, I came across the ruins of a huge theater—the Theater of Marcellus—space for which had been cleared by Julius Caesar. The project was completed by Emperor Augustus in 13 BCE, with space for twelve thousand spectators. It is the only ancient theater remaining in Rome, in a dark and gloomy section of the city that once housed the famous Jewish ghetto.

In 1555, during the Reformation, Pope Paul IV decreed that all Jews were to be segregated into their own quarters (ghettos). They were forbidden to leave their home during the night, were banned from all but the most strenuous occupations, and had to wear a distinctive badge—a yellow hat. More than four thousand seven hundred Jews lived in the seven-acre Roman Jewish ghetto that was built in the Trastevere section of the city (which remains a Jewish neighborhood to this day). Crossing Tiber Island, I remembered the Jews of Rome who were brought to this spot by the Nazis in 1943, prior to their deportation to Auschwitz. That memory lingered as I walked along the Tiber and through the bohemian areas of the Trastevere.

The following morning I awoke to a fairly typical Roman sound—the tolling of church bells. For a moment I was confused, thinking it might be Sunday, but it was Saturday. I would not be sleeping late while in Rome, for my *pensione* stood next to a church. The bells ring daily, morning and evening, calling the faithful to worship and reminding all within reach that "the chief end of man is to glorify God." The bells actually set an appropriate mood, for my schedule that day included a visit to St. Peter's Basilica and the Vatican museums.

EXPLANATORY ENTRY #6: THE VATICAN AND ITS WONDERS

For Roman Catholics, Rome is the centerpiece of their faith. And if Rome is the magnet, the Vatican is the lodestone, for it represents the oneness of the Body of Christ, indeed the oneness of God. For non-Catholics, the Vatican is also a treasure. The United Nations has declared the Vatican a World Heritage site for its extraordinary cultural importance, thus entitling it to special protection. No other country has been so designated.

In the first century CE, Vatican Hill was outside the city limits and therefore was the site of a cemetery as well as a circus (the Circus of Nero). Though Vatican Hill was not one of the famed Seven Hills of Rome, it was included within the city limits of Rome during the reign of Pope Leo IV, who between 848 and 852 expanded the city walls to protect the basilica and the Vatican, which had been looted in 846 by a raiding party of Saracen pirates.

St. Peter's Basilica, until recently the largest church in the world,[2] is the most prominent building inside Vatican City. One of the holiest sites of Christendom in the Catholic tradition and arguably Rome's most impressive sight, it is traditionally the burial site of Saint Peter, who was one of the twelve apostles of Jesus and is believed by Catholics to have been the first bishop of Rome. Although the New Testament does not mention Peter's presence or martyrdom in Rome, ancient tradition holds that his tomb is below the altar; hence many popes, starting with the earliest ones, have been buried there. Today there are over one hundred tombs located within St. Peter's Basilica, including ninety-one popes.

Emperor Constantine built the first basilica in 319. Although it was only half the size of the current church building, it was a huge structure in its day. Construction on the current basilica, erected over the old Constantinian church, began in 1450 and was completed in 1626, on the site of the Circus of Nero, where thousands of Christians suffered martyrdom. According to tradition, Peter was executed in this circus, at the base of an ancient obelisk brought by the emperor Caligula (37–41) from Heliopolis, Egypt. Close to the circus was a cemetery where martyred Christians were buried, and in this place Peter is said to have been buried.

St. Peter's Square, the huge oval that fronts the basilica, is capable of holding four hundred thousand people. It is shaped like a keyhole, symbolizing St. Peter's traditional role as keeper of the keys of the heavenly kingdom. The first impression one gains upon entering St. Peter's Basilica is one of overwhelming size. The nave, over two football fields in length, is 693 feet long, and the dome is 138 feet in diameter (thus exceeding the dome of the Pantheon by about three feet) and 435 feet high. The effect is so staggering that it takes a while to absorb the structure's sheer magnificence. The first basilica, built by Constantine, lasted over one thousand years; the task of building this much larger building took almost two hundred years and involved some of Italy's greatest Renaissance masters, including Bramante, Raphael, and Michelangelo.

---

2. It is surpassed today by the Basilica of Our Lady of Yamoussoukro in Ivory Coast, which was dedicated in 1990 by Pope John Paul II.

The basilica contains many extraordinary works of art. In the first chapel to the right as one enters from the square is St. Peter's best-known treasure, Michelangelo's famous *Pietà* (1499), carved from a single slab in less than two years. His interpretation of the *Pietà*—a depiction of the body of Jesus in the arms of his mother Mary after his crucifixion—was far different from those created by other artists. The artist decided to create a youthful, serene, and celestial Virgin Mary instead of a broken-hearted and somewhat older woman. Although the figures are quite out of proportion, owing to the difficulty of portraying a full-grown man cradled full-length in a woman's lap, the relationship of the figures appears quite natural. The statue remains safe behind its bullet-proof glass, impeccably restored after a deranged individual attacked it with an axe in 1972.

Beneath the celebrated dome, designed by Michelangelo, stands the high altar, crowned by Bernini's unrivalled bronze baldachin (canopy), its serpentine columns rising to a height of ninety-five feet. The twisted, spiraling columns were made thus because tradition had it that Solomon's temple had been supported similarly. The canopy, constructed amid much controversy, took nine years to complete—and all the bronze that could be found. Some of the metal came from as far away as Venice; some was even stripped from the portico of the Pantheon and the sides of St. Peter's cupola, all by orders of Pope Urban VIII, of the Barberini family. His practice of plundering ancient monuments provoked the celebrated quote: *Quod non fecerunt barbari, fecerunt Barberini* ("What the barbarians didn't do, Barberini did").

Behind the papal altar, in the apse of the basilica, is Bernini's most spectacular religious decoration, the *Throne of St. Peter*, a gilt-bronze cover for the *cathedra*, a medieval wooden chair said to have been the Episcopal chair used by the apostle Peter. The masterpiece is topped by a yellow window (made of finely cut alabaster), with a figure of a dove (portraying the Holy Spirit) surrounded by twelve rays (symbolizing the twelve disciples). The sunburst protruding from the window also depicts the source of Peter's authority.

As soon as one enters St. Peter's Square, one is technically within the sovereign State of the Vatican City, a country within the city of Rome. The Vatican is enclosed by thick, high walls, its gates guarded by Swiss Guards, who still wear the colorful dress uniforms designed by Michelangelo. Of approximately 109 acres, the Vatican is the smallest independent nation in the world. Though one can walk around it in about forty minutes, the Vatican nevertheless contains more art treasures than any empire. The collection of art in the Vatican museums covers nearly five miles of displays, making it impossible for a visitor to take them all in during one visit.

The Sistine Chapel, one of the great treasures in the Vatican, is also one of the most celebrated sites in the world. Named Sistine after Pope Sixtus IV, who commissioned its construction (1471–1481), the chapel's fame rests on three qualities: (1) its architecture, (2), its purpose, and (3) its decoration, frescoed throughout by the greatest Renaissance artists, including Michelangelo, whose painting of the ceiling is legendary.

The rectangular Sistine Chapel measures 134 feet long by 44 feet wide, dimensions said to have been those of the Temple of Solomon. Like the biblical Temple, a screen divides the chapel into two parts; the larger one, together with the altar, is reserved for papal religious and functionary activity, notably the conclave, at which a new pope is selected.

TRAVEL ENTRY #16: INSIDE THE SISTINE CHAPEL

By the time I found the special entrance to the Vatican museums, located part-way around the wall of the Vatican, I had only ninety minutes left before closing (2:00 p.m. during off-season). Knowing that I would return to the museum several days later, with Susan, I decided to move rapidly through the displays so that I could spend at least thirty minutes in the Sistine Chapel.

As I made my way to the famed chapel my expectations were high, for I imagined the sanctuary to be a sort of holy ground, closer to paradise and unlike any other place on earth. Upon entering, however, I felt distracted, even disappointed. Though signs at the entrance requested silence, the room was crowded, with scaffolding covering major portions of the ceiling. On the wall immediately behind me as I entered the chapel stood the celebrated *Last Judgment*, Michelangelo's amazing composition, but it too was a disappointment, dingy, dark, and obstructed by scaffolds.

My visit to the chapel coincided with a major restoration of its legendary frescoes. The first stage of restoration, on Michelangelo's lunettes, had lasted from 1980 to 1984. The work then proceeded to Michelangelo's paintings on the ceiling, among the most famous works of art ever created. That stage of restoration (1984–1989) was scheduled to be completed in December, two months after my visit. The next stage, the restoration of Michelangelo's *Last Judgment* (completed in 1994), would be followed by the final stage, the restoration of the wall frescoes (1994–1999).

After the restoration of the ceiling, it was discovered that Michelangelo's frescoes were in remarkably good condition, as the master painter had employed the best possible fresco techniques and had used a very stable and mould-resistant base, in which the plaster was mixed with volcanic ash. The restoration reveals Michelangelo to have been a masterful colorist, not only by choice, but a necessity if the frescoes were to stand out in the dark chapel, with its high, narrow windows.

It took me a while to adjust to the chapel's size and the sixty-eight-foot height of the ceiling. Gradually, however, I blocked out the distractions and began to experience the room as it was intended to be experienced, as a place of worship and meditation. Sitting down, I took a deep, cleansing breath, and arched my head upward. Within a few minutes the distractions faded and I became totally absorbed by "the most powerful painting in the world."

The ceiling's decorations are considered masterpieces because they required the combined skills of sculptor, painter, and architect. I recalled the story of how Michelangelo the sculptor had rebuffed Pope Julius II when asked by him to paint the ceiling: "It is not my trade!" Because Pope Julius had come to the papacy only a few weeks after the death of his enemy, the Borgia Pope Alexander VI, the luxuriously frescoed Borgia apartments made Julius uncomfortable. So he moved to new quarters and commissioned the brilliant Raphael to paint his new suite. This young artist, eight years younger than Michelangelo, soon developed an intense rivalry with Michelangelo. So he and other rivals of Michelangelo placed the sculptor in an impossible situation by suggesting to the Pope that he should have Michelangelo paint the vault of the chapel of Pope Sixtus IV. If the sculptor should refuse the fresco project, he could alienate the pope; if he accepted the offer, his inexperienced work with a paintbrush would be unflatteringly compared to the murals of Raphael. Later Michelangelo wrote, "All the dissensions between Pope Julius and me arose from the envy of Bramante and Raphael . . . They wanted to ruin me; and Raphael had a good reason . . . for all he had of art, he had from me."

But because Pope Julius was adamant, for three and a half years (1508–1512) the sculptor-turned-painter worked arduously atop the high scaffold, painting straight over his head. Michelangelo was originally commissioned to paint only twelve figures, the apostles. When he refused, the pope offered to allow him to paint biblical scenes of his own choice, as a compromise. On the lowest part of the ceiling he painted the ancestors of Christ. Above this he alternated male and female prophets, with Jonah over the altar. On the highest section of the ceiling he painted nine episodes from the book of Genesis. When the work was finished, it was encumbered with three hundred figures; the scenes from Genesis depicted the creation, Adam and Eve in the Garden of Eden, and the Great Flood. Despite Michelangelo's initial reluctance, the project vindicated him as a painter and became his personal triumph.

The capstone of the chapel is the painting done for the altar, Michelangelo's *Last Judgment*, a theme suggested by Pope Clement VII on his deathbed. The work is massive—sixty-six feet in height and thirty-three in width—spanning the entire wall behind the altar. It is the largest and most comprehensive scene in the world. Based loosely on Dante's *Divine Comedy*, the painting is a stunning depiction of the second coming of Christ and the apocalypse. The project took Michelangelo seven years (1535–1541) to complete. In contrast to other frescoes in the chapel, the figures in the *Last Judgment* are heavily muscled and appear somewhat tortured; the painting is fearful and was meant to instill piety and respect for God's power. When it was completed, the *Last Judgment* became the object of heavy dispute. Michelangelo was accused of immorality and obscenity for depicting figures in the nude; some of the offensive elements were subsequently covered by the artist Daniele da Volterra. Curiously, one of the figures, St. Bartholomew displaying his flayed skin, is a self-portrait by Michelangelo.

TRAVEL ENTRY #17: SATURDAY NIGHT LIVE

It was Saturday afternoon when I completed my four-hour tour of St. Peter's and the Vatican museums. I was exhausted and unable to process any additional information. It was time to heed the advice of a wise guide: "The important thing while sightseeing is to enjoy Rome. Don't try to see everything, but do take time to savor its pleasures."

After lunch I returned to my room for some rest and to arrange for next week's rendezvous with my wife Susan, who planned to join me for a few days. I learned that my room at the *pensione* would not be available beyond Tuesday, for the entire hotel had been booked by a tour group at that time. The news was the same elsewhere: other than the most expensive hotels, all lodging in Rome was booked. I recognized my indebtedness to Father Chuck for his previous assistance, but even he had exhausted his leads; I was clearly on my own now. Eventually I located a room in an ideal location, close to the *centro*'s main monuments. Though the place had fewer amenities than the *pensione* and was more expensive, at least I had a place to stay.

That afternoon I headed for the Piazza di Spagna, with its famous Spanish steps. I followed the Via del Corso, central Rome's main thoroughfare, for about a mile, and then turned on to the Via Condotti, Rome's most elegant and expensive shopping street. By the time I reached the Piazza di Spagna, at the head of Via Condotti, night had fallen. A huge crowd was gathered in the square on this Saturday evening, while hundreds sat along the 137 steps of the grand staircase. The mood was festive and the crowd diverse as people sang and conversed in numerous languages. This popular attraction, once the haunt of writers and artists such as Shelley and Byron, is called "perhaps the most magnificent flight of steps in the world." The steps were a gift from France in 1725, to pave the muddy slope to the French Church, Santa Trinità dei Monti. The square and steps are popularly called "Spanish" because the Spanish embassy to the Vatican is located on the square.

After mingling with the crowd and reveling in the upbeat atmosphere, I headed to Piazza Navona, one of Rome's finest squares. The piazza is a lively place, surrounded by open air cafés and regularly crowded with vendors, artists, and occasionally with mimes and other entertainers. Once the site of the Circus Domitianus (Domitian's stadium), the square is exceptionally long and shaped to the ruins of the racetrack. The piazza features many fine old buildings and three stunning fountains. In the center is Bernini's most spectacular fountain, the allegorical Fountain of the Rivers, erected in 1651. It features a central rocky structure that supports a Roman obelisk, an imitation of the Egyptian form. Around this structure are four giant statues representing the Nile, the Danube, the Ganges, and the Río de la Plata, each symbolizing one of the four quarters of the world. The statues are so lifelike that they appear to be gesturing.

6

Italy: Final Days

TRAVEL ENTRY #18: CASTEL SANT'ANGELO

When I awoke on Sunday, the city was quiet, its stillness accompanied by a reduction of the smog that hangs like a blanket over the city on other days of the week. Though Italians consider Sunday a day of rest, I had designed a rather aggressive schedule, starting with a visit to Castel Sant'Angelo, the imposing fortress featured in Dan Brown's novel, *Angels and Demons* (2000). According to legend, the structure received its present name in the sixth century when Pope Gregory the Great beheld atop the mausoleum the apparition of the archangel Michael, sheathing his sword as a sign of the end of the plague of 590.

The structure was built by Emperor Hadrian (117–138) as a mausoleum for himself and the succeeding Caesars of his line. Despite its location on the west bank of the Tiber, Hadrian's tomb became incorporated into the Aurelian Walls and was converted into a military fortress in 401, during the barbarian invasions. In the fourteenth century the structure was converted into a castle for use by the popes. Pope Nicholas III connected the castle to the Vatican by a long elevated passageway called the Passetto, enabling popes to take refuge in the castle when necessary. Since 1901 the castle has been used as a museum, containing among its holdings a collection of antique weapons, courtyards piled with stone cannonballs, and rooms that recall their use as papal apartments.

At the completion of my self-guided tour through the castle I boarded a bus for Piazza Venezia, intending to visit San Pietro in Vincoli (St. Peter in Chains), the church that houses Michelangelo's famous *Moses*, a statue carved for the mausoleum of Pope Julius II.

EXPLANATORY ENTRY #7: ST. PETER IN CHAINS: MICHELANGELO'S MOSES

The original proposal for the mausoleum of Pope Julius II called for a free-standing tomb of some forty figures, each corner to contain a large marble figure representing active life, contemplative life, St. Paul, and Moses. Topping the monument would be a statue of the pope, whose body would rest inside the tomb. The planned size and ambitious decoration—to be located at St. Peter's Basilica in the Vatican—would create a new standard for funerary art. However, Michelangelo was called to other projects and the project languished. Eventually a much smaller version of the tomb was installed in a far less impressive St. Peter's, named St. Peter's in Chains because the fetters of St. Peter are on display in the church's confessional.

What one sees at San Pietro in Vincoli, then, is a much scaled-down version of the artist's design. The monument is not free-standing, as originally planned, but is attached to one wall. And it is called the tomb of Pope Julius II, even though Julius's body actually rests at St. Peter's Basilica. The colossal figure of Moses, measuring 7 feet 8 ½ inches, depicts Moses with horns on his head. This anomaly is believed to be due to a mistranslation of Exodus 34:29–30 by St. Jerome in the Latin Vulgate version of the Bible. When Moses came down from Mount Sinai after receiving the Ten Commandments, the Bible says, "the skin of his face shone." *Shone* is translated from a rare Hebrew word that contains the consonants of *horn* and was so rendered in the Vulgate. As a result of this translation, Michelangelo sculpted his famous Moses with horns.

St. Peter in Chains is located near the Coliseum, along the Esquiline Hill. I had walked a long way that morning and had climbed the steep hill to the church to see the celebrated *Moses*, thereby completing my examination of the third of Michelangelo's greatest sculptures, after the *Pietà* in St. Peter's and the *David* in Florence. But Rome, ever surprising and sometimes frustrating, had both in store for me that morning, for I had arrived in time for worship.

An officer of the church was posted at the door to inform tourists that they should return another day. But I had not come this far for naught. This being Sunday, I decided to enter as a worshipper. Even a peek would be better than nothing. The official, seemingly understanding my dilemma, allowed me to enter, but only through the door of his choosing. I proceeded with caution, hoping to catch a glimpse of the statue while respecting the sanctity of the moment. Once inside, however, I found myself on the opposite side of the sanctuary from the monument, and what I could see of the statuary cause my heart to sink. Major portions of the sanctuary were boarded up, blocking the monumental project altogether. I remained seated, trying to make sense of the priest's Italian, but after about fifteen minutes of frustration, I sheepishly walked to the door and past the official. I would return later, because the statue was simply too important to miss.

From the Piazza Venezia I walked toward the Coliseum, about a mile away, following the broad Via dei Fori Imperiali, named for the imperial forums built by Julius Caesar, Augustus, Trajan, Nerva, and Vespasian to supplement the Roman Forum. By the time I reached the Coliseum, it was already past noon. The weather was perfect for enjoying this fabled landmark and its environs, so I decided to explore the amphitheater before eating my bag lunch. I would need energy to hike the vast ruins of the Palatine and the Roman Forum, both high on my list of priorities. That's when I encountered my next disappointment: the Coliseum was closed on Sundays. Because my guidebook on Italy had been stolen in Geneva, I lacked background material on Rome to forewarn me. I decided to walk around the perimeter of the arena instead, learning as much about the structure as my powers of observation would supply.

EXPLANATORY ENTRY #8: THE COLISEUM

The Coliseum's 160-foot façade consisted of four levels, three stories studded with eighty arches each and a gallery at the top added later to increase its seating capacity. The attached columns followed a decorative order: sturdy, unadorned Doric on the ground floor, more elegant Ionic next and luxuriant Corinthian on top. The entire structure was originally faced with marble and decorated with stucco; the audience sat in the shade under an ingenious system of awnings that covered the top of the building. Spectators were seated by rank, social class, and gender. The emperor had his own "court side" box. Senators were allocated choice ringside seats. The rich and well-connected had the next best seats. Male commoners sat behind them, and women were relegated to the highest tier.

The Coliseum, the largest amphitheatre ever constructed in the Roman Empire and built to seat fifty thousand spectators, was completed in 80 CE by Emperor Titus, with further modifications made during the reign of Domitian. The site chosen was a flat area on the floor of a low valley among three hills, through which ran a stream. The densely inhabited area was devastated by the great fire of Rome in 64 CE, after which Emperor Nero seized much of the area to add to his personal domain. On the site he built the grandiose Domus Aurea (Golden House), in front of which he created an artificial lake surrounded by pavilions, gardens, and porticos. A gigantic bronze statue of Nero dressed in the garb of the Roman sun god Sol was placed just outside the main palace entrance. The Coliseum, originally known as the Flavian Amphitheatre (after the dynasty of emperors that built it), was later renamed after the 120-foot Colossus of Nero, which stood nearby.

Located just east of the Roman Forum, the arena was used for gladiatorial contests and other public spectacles, including executions, reenactments of famous battles, and dramas based on classical mythology. The building was inaugurated in 80 CE with a program of games and shows that lasted one hundred days. On opening day five thousand wild animals perished in the arena while lucky ticket holders won slaves as door prizes. For nearly five hundred years Romans witnessed Christians being eaten by lions, gladiators fighting to the death, animals pitted against humans, and naval battles to the death in the arena filled with water.

The managers of the Coliseum imported animals from as far away as Africa and India. The wild beasts were kept in cages and cells directly underneath the wooden floor on which the combats occurred. To add excitement to the spectacles, trap doors were strategically hidden in the wooden floor. To the delight of the crowd, a door would spring open without warning, releasing a charging lion or other savage animal. Because the wooden floor no longer exists, the network of underground rooms and corridors is now visible to visitors.

The building ceased to be used for entertainment in the early medieval era. Severe damage was inflicted on the Coliseum by the great earthquake of 1349, causing the outer south side to collapse. Much of the tumbled stone was reused for building projects elsewhere in Rome. It was later used for such varied purposes as housing, workshops, quarters for a religious order, a fortress, a quarry, and a Christian shrine. The Coliseum still has close connections with the Catholic Church, whose pope leads a torchlit procession to the amphitheater each Good Friday.

The Coliseum has long been an iconic symbol of Imperial Rome and is one of the finest surviving examples of Roman architecture. The renowned nineteenth-century English poet Lord Byron penned this prophecy regarding the Coliseum in his *Childe Harold's Pilgrimage*: "While stands the Coliseum, Rome shall stand; When the Coliseum falls, Rome shall fall; And when Rome falls—the World."

When I arrived at the entrance to the Palatine, an area steeped in history and controversy, it was a few minutes after one o'clock. That's when I experienced yet another frustration, for a sign indicated that the gate closed at one o'clock on Sundays. I stood for a moment in utter disbelief. How could one of the world's greatest archaeological sites be closed on a Sunday afternoon? A clerk was still at the ticket counter, but I couldn't persuade him to let me in. I was exasperated, not only by this inconvenience, but also by my ignorance, for a half hour earlier I had been sitting nearby, calmly eating a sandwich, oblivious to my impending disappointment.

Unwilling to give up without a fight, I quickly walked to the exit, hoping to at least get a close-up of the famous Arch of Titus, which stood nearby. The arch commemorated Titus's victory over the Jews in 70 CE, when ten thousand rebels were slain and the temple in Jerusalem was burned. The remaining Jews were brought in a victory procession to Rome, to serve as slaves. I already knew that one side of the arch contained a bas-relief of the triumphal procession carrying Jewish spoils, including the table of showbread and the seven-branched menorah, which I had come to Rome to see for myself. But the guard paid no attention to my entreaties, although visitors were still strolling through the ruins only a few feet away.

TRAVEL ENTRY #19: THE CATACOMBS

My dismay quickly led to a decision to spend the remainder of the day in the gloomy darkness of the catacombs, at the southern edge of the city. The catacombs consist of a vast labyrinth of subterranean galleries—underground cemeteries—where the early Christians buried their dead and held memorial services and celebrations of anniversaries of Christian martyrs. In ancient times, Etruscans had buried their dead in underground chambers, so Christians, on account of their belief in the resurrection, revived the practice because they did not wish to cremate their dead. From the second century CE onwards, the first large-scale catacombs began to be carved. Originally they were located outside the boundaries of the city, because Roman law forbade burials within city limits. Catacombs were situated along the main highways leading away from the city, from the first to the third milestone. Cut into the soft volcanic rock of the Roman subsoil, these chambers were easy to dig, yet they were remarkably stable. Narrow steps connect as many as four levels, superimposed one below the other. There are forty known subterranean burial chambers in Rome; twenty-five are large catacombs and the rest are smaller.

After the bus negotiated the Porta Appia, the small opening in the ancient city walls, it continued south along the Old Appian Way, some of which is still paved with cobblestones. This road, known as the first "Roman road," was the same route that Paul used as he came to Rome. Roman tombs, catacombs, and villas line the way for several miles.

A short distance from the city walls, as one approaches the catacombs, is a chapel with the strange name of Domine, Quo Vadis? According to legend, St. Peter had a vision of Christ here. After the fire that burned Rome, when Nero persecuted the Christians, Peter was urged to leave Rome for his safety. Not far from the Porta Appia he met a traveler going towards Rome. Recognizing the man as Christ, Peter uttered the famous words: "*Domine, quo vadis*?" (Master, where are you going?) Jesus replied, "I am going to Rome to be crucified again." The vision vanished, but the divine footprints are said to remain on a paving stone.

I decided to visit Saint Callixtus's catacomb, one of the largest, with over twelve miles of underground passageways. The chambers are named for Callixtus, a canonized saint of the Catholic Church. He served as pope from 217 to 222, when he was martyred for his Christian faith. At first many desired to be buried in chambers alongside martyrs, but the practice of catacomb burial declined after 380, when Christianity was declared the official state religion. From that point, when the dead were increasingly buried in church cemeteries, the catacombs ceased to be visited, and over time were completely lost and forgotten, until rediscovered by the archaeologist Giovanni Battista de Rossi in 1849.

Contrary to popular thought, Christians did not use the catacombs as hiding places or for secret worship, for during times of persecution the catacombs were closed by Roman authorities. Christians worshipped in the catacombs because of their association with martyrs and because many early Christians were buried in the catacombs (on account of their predominantly lower-class status, since most had been slaves).

Columbarium-like niches, each containing two or three bodies wrapped in linen, were cut into the walls of the catacombs. Bodies were placed in stone sarcophagi and hermetically sealed. Today, many of the niches are empty, for over the centuries the bones of Christians were carried off to many nations for use as relics. Decorative paintings of Christian symbols such as fish, doves, and anchors still remain, however, adorning the walls.

My visit to the catacombs helped me appreciate the religious devotion of these early believers and to realize how invaluable their faithful persistence under duress proved to be for the future of western Christendom.

TRAVEL ENTRY #20: THE VATICAN GROTTOES

The State of Vatican City has no uninvited visitors. One can sign up for an escorted tour of the gardens or buy a ticket for the museums—all under the watchful eye of guards and guides. Monday morning's venture took me to the graveyard beneath St. Peter's Basilica. Commercial groups are not allowed in this area, though small groups are permitted to enter at specified times, with a knowledgeable guide. Having obtained a pass, I strode up to the Arco delle Campane (Arch of the Bells), presenting my credentials to the Swiss Guard while awaiting the guide who would lead me through the grottoes. Passing through the Square of the First Christian Martyrs, marked in the center by a spot that originally held Emperor Caligula's obelisk, I followed the guide through a side door and down the narrow stairways to the cramped passageways far beneath Christendom's most famous shrine. Unsure what I would see, I hoped it would have historical rather than mere superstitious value.

When the current basilica was built during the sixteenth and seventeenth centuries, a thirteen-foot space had been left between the pavement of the new basilica and that of Constantine's earlier structure, to preserve the church from dampness. This space constitutes the Vatican Grottoes. In 1939, shortly after the accession of Pope Pius XII, a long-standing project was begun: converting the grottoes into an underground chapel. As workers proceeded with the challenging task, removing the pavement and digging into the hard packed earth, they uncovered the remains of an old cemetery, over which Constantine had erected his basilica. They were not surprised by their find, for everyone knew that Constantine had covered the cemetery and the small shrine marking the grave of St. Peter in order to protect the ancient site from natural deterioration and from plunder.

One day the workmen came upon a brick wall; as more of the surrounding dirt was removed, the men could see that brick walls more than a foot thick defined a quadrangle some twenty feet long. This had once been a building, its roof long ago removed, and its interior filled with earth. Carefully, the excavators removed the dirt until they saw that the plastered wall had an arrangement of niches for cremation urns. They found numerous drawings before coming upon a picture of a woman drawing water from a well and doves with an olive branch. On a marble slab laid into the floor they saw the Latin words *dormit in pace*—"rests in peace." They knew this was the grave of a Christian.

As the excavations came closer to the area under the high altar, diggers encountered older graves. They then uncovered a wall painted red, at right angles to which stood another wall, with a patchwork of graffiti, mostly illegible. At a later date someone added the words "Peter within" in Latin. Beside these walls, the excavators found votive offerings, thousands of coins, and a cache of bones. This was clearly an early grave site, possibly the tomb of St. Peter and his bones, which were placed in a metal box and sealed in the pope's apartments. In 1950 Pope Pius announced that the tomb of St. Peter had been found.

At a later date the bones were examined and found to be those of several people—and of some domesticated animals as well. By reason of age and sex, none of those bones could have been Peter's. But other bones had been discovered in the graffiti wall and conserved as well. These bones were carefully analyzed in laboratories and pronounced to be those of a robust man between sixty and seventy years of age and about 5 feet 6 inches in height—a description that could fit St. Peter. The remains contained a surprising element: the feet were missing. This fact seemed to give greater credence to the possibility that the bones belonged to someone who might have been crucified upside down, after which a guard had found it easier to remove the body from the cross by simply cutting off the feet. In June 1968, the laboratory analysis led the cautious Pope Paul VI to announce: "the relics of St. Peter have been identified in a manner which we believe convincing." The pope then returned the bones to their resting place in the graffiti wall, where they remain visible behind glass. The remains may leave us uncertain of Peter's life and death, but they remind us that his remains endure not so much in a grave as in the human heart.

TRAVEL ENTRY #21: AN AUDIENCE WITH THE POPE

On Tuesday, taking a break from my tourist activities, I assumed the role of a host as I welcomed my wife Susan to Rome. For the next two days I retraced earlier steps, experiencing Rome with new questions and through another pair of eyes. The highlight was the weekly Wednesday morning public audience with Pope John Paul II. As Protestants and recent arrivals in Rome, Susan and I were fortunate to be included in this select gathering of Catholic faithful. Tickets are hard to come by, and we were indebted once again to Father Christian's intervention, for no one can enter without a ticket, which must be acquired far in advance.

Public audiences are lively, long, and jammed. In fair weather they are held in St. Peter's Square, to accommodate large crowds. But during winter or rain, as on this occasion, the site is the Paul VI Audience Hall, a modern auditorium seating nine thousand people. Four Swiss Guards opened the ceremony, marching out to take their place, halberds at the ready. They were followed by a retinue of cardinals, assistants, and lectors. Lights signaled the shining moment, the emergence of the pope. As John Paul II emerged, resplendent in white, the crowd rose as one, applauding the popular pope. After the Scripture lesson, read by six lectors in as many languages, the pope addressed the crowd, delivering a homily in six languages: French, English, Spanish, Portuguese, Polish, and Italian. At the conclusion, visiting groups were introduced, some rising quietly, others breaking into a song, chant, or cheer as their names were called. The pope acknowledged each group, spontaneously exchanging greetings in at least twelve languages. At the end of the ceremony John Paul descended the marble stairs and mingled with well-wishers, singling out the young and the infirm for special attention.

It will take some time to assess his profound legacy, which will certainly include his special relationship with youth and his concern for the disadvantaged. In 1989, when Mother Teresa of Calcutta requested a place within the Vatican, Pope John Paul responded by constructing a hospice for her Missionaries of Charity next to his Holy Office. The hospice, accommodating up to seventy-two homeless women, has kitchen facilities able to feed hundreds of men and women who enter directly from the streets of Rome.

EXPLANATORY ENTRY #9: FINAL THOUGHTS ON ROME

That night, my last night in Rome, Susan and I experienced genuine Italian hospitality at Rome's Military Club, where we joined Colonel and Mrs. Gianfranco L'Abbate, parents of a former student of mine at Washington & Jefferson College. The following day Father Christian stopped by our hotel and drove us to Fiumicino Airport, some twenty miles from Rome. I stayed with Susan until her flight was announced and then took the bus back to Termini Station, where I boarded the train for Naples and the famous ruins at Pompeii.

I left Rome feeling a love/hate relationship for the city. Like most large urban centers, Rome certainly had its unpleasant side. Its streets, noisy and polluted, went everywhere but straight. Public transportation, crowded and unsafe, contributed to the confusion. Archaeological ruins and museums were often closed and unavailable to tourists, particularly during off-season and on Sundays, and scaffolding was an ever-present irritation.

Yet Rome was worth the aggravation. Though one can find both the best and the worst of the past in Rome, much there speaks to the worst and the best of the present. As I departed this incomparable place, I took with me lasting memories: the friendship of Father Christian, the generosity of the L'Abbates, and an encounter with Pope John Paul II that allowed me to see for myself why Roman Catholics call their chief prelate "pope," from the Greek word *papas* ("patriarch," "bishop," originally "father"). The term was used for any bishop during the first centuries of the church, but John Paul was the "peoples' pope," embodying its meaning in his words, actions, and priorities. Despite past abuse of the papal office and excessive opulence in the Vatican, I couldn't help but think of the hospice within the Vatican, that house of refuge that points to the architecture of love, perhaps the Eternal City's most enduring quality.

TRAVEL ENTRY #22: IN THE SHADOW OF VESUVIUS

The city of Naples, one of the largest ports in the Mediterranean, is located in the heart of southern Italy, two hours south of Rome by train. Situated on the Bay of Naples, it is overshadowed by Mount Vesuvius, less than ten miles away. At the base of this volcano, the only active volcano on the mainland of Europe, lies the famous ancient city of Pompeii, buried during an eruption in 79 CE.

Founded by Greek colonists around 600 BCE, Naples became a summer playground for Roman emperors and aristocracy. Following the Roman period, the city was controlled by many different groups, the most splendid of which were the Bourbons, who ruled from 1734 until 1860. Using Naples as their capital, the Bourbon kings erected many of the city's most elegant structures, including the San Carlo Opera House, one of the most famous in the world.

Naples has played an important and vibrant musical role over the centuries, not just in the music of Italy, but in the general history of western European musical traditions. The vitality of Neapolitan popular music from the late nineteenth century made such songs as *O sole mio* and *Funiculì Funiculà* a permanent part of musical consciousness. Naples counts among its native sons one of the greatest tenors in the history of operatic music, Enrico Caruso (1873–1921). Though he is best known as the leading male singer at New York's Metropolitan Opera for seventeen years, he began his career in Naples and is buried there.

Modern Naples, however, sends out mixed signals. Although Naples is one of the most beautiful cities in Europe and rich in history and monuments, it is less visited than other Italian cities. Though high in violent crime, the city is known for its zest for life, its pizza (practically invented here), and its seafood.

I planned to use Naples as a base from which to explore the region. In addition to Pompeii, I hoped to visit the majestic isle of Capri, a four-mile island at the southern end of the Bay of Naples famous for its Blue Grotto. I also hoped to see the beautiful resort town of Sorrento, which in times past had attracted artists such as Goethe, Byron, Dumas, Renan, Longfellow, Nietzsche, Grieg, and Wagner. My plans were contingent upon the expiration of my Eurail Pass, seven days later. By then I wanted to be in Greece.

I spent my first night in Naples sightseeing and sampling some of its famous cuisine. After locating a room near the Piazza Garibaldi, I boarded a bus bound for Santa Lucia, Naples's waterfront district. My tourist map indicated the presence of several imposing structures in that vicinity, including a massive stone fortress known as Castel Nuovo, a thirteenth-century castle built by Charles I of Anjou.

From the rear of the castle I could see a cluster of buildings, equally ancient and impressive, including the Royal Palace, built in 1600 and later used as the official residence of Bourbon and Savoy kings, and the

San Carlo Opera House. Nearby stood another fortress, the eleventh-century Castel dell'Ovo, built on what looked like a jetty. The edifice was originally constructed on a small island, where colonists founded the original nucleus of the city in the sixth century BCE. In the first century CE a magnificent villa was erected on the site, the place where the last western Roman emperor, Romulus Augustus, was exiled in 476.

On Friday morning I boarded the local train at Stazione Circumvesuviana ("Around Vesuvius") and headed southeast toward the area known for spectacular ruins and incomparable views. Stepping from the train at Villa dei Misteri, near Pompeii, I saw two familiar figures ahead of me, Paul and Craig, the two Mormons I had met in Interlaken, Switzerland. They too had visited Venice, Florence, and Rome, but also Monaco and the French Riviera. The three of us joined forces as we attached ourselves to one or more tour groups in the area, but after a while we parted, for our interests differed. We agreed to meet on the train to Brindisi the following day, for they were staying in Naples and were also headed for Greece via ferry.

EXPLANATORY ENTRY #10: POMPEII: A CITY FROZEN IN TIME

Pompeii, strategically located near the mouth of the Sarno River, was one of two ancient cities destroyed by the catastrophic eruption of Vesuvius in 79 CE. This prosperous commercial Roman city was covered by some twenty feet of volcanic ash and preserved thus until 1748, when sporadic excavations began. Since then, its excavation has provided an extraordinarily detailed insight into life at the height of the Roman Empire, in a town located in an area where ancient Romans had their vacation villas. At the time of the eruption, Pompeii had reached its high point in society as many Romans frequently vacationed there. It is the only ancient town of which the whole topographic structure is known precisely as it was, with no later modifications or additions. The eruption, which claimed all of Pompeii's twenty thousand inhabitants, killed many of its victims by poisonous fumes before engulfing them in ash. Some died in their sleep, others with agonizing looks on their faces. Archaeologists and other specialists were able to preserve many of those poses for posterity.

The wealth of Pompeii's ruins lies in the architecture and the large number of well-preserved frescoes, which provide evidence of even the smallest detail of everyday Roman life, frozen at the moment it was buried. Because of the remarkably preserved remains, some observers consider Pompeii to be *the* most important archaeological site in the world. Here one can see the actual former layout of the entire city, including temples, forums, an amphitheater (the oldest yet discovered),[1] public baths, and a palestra (a public gymnasium). The streets of Pompeii are narrow, with chariot ruts still visible in the cobblestones and sidewalks raised above the streets, allowing water and sewage runoff.

Pompeii, together with its better preserved sister city, Herculaneum, was a thriving commercial town and a resort for the rich. It was the pleasure abode of the Roman aristocracy, who introduced luxury, vices, and corruption. Patrician villas, such as the nearby Villa dei Misteri, are richly decorated with frescoes. Of special interest to visitors are the House of the Faun, one of the largest and most luxurious examples of a first-century residence, where a mosaic of Alexander the Great was found, and the richly decorated House of the Vettii, typical of the homes of prosperous merchants. Other places of interest include the Lupanare (brothel), bakeries, shops, and factories.

The city of Pompeii was found to be full of art, frescoes, symbols, and inscriptions regarded as pornographic. Even many recovered household items had a sexual theme. The ubiquity of such imagery and items indicates that the sexual mores of the ancient Roman culture of the time were much more liberal than most present-day cultures, although much of what might seem to us to be erotic imagery was in fact fertility-imagery, designed to bring good luck.

The ruins also teach us a great deal about the nature and role of civic religion. At the time of its destruction, public life centered in the forum, a long open rectangle in the southwestern part of town. At the north end of the forum stood the Temple of Jupiter, the town's chief temple. A colonnade screened other nearby structures, including the Temple of Apollo, a public market, a rectangular basilica (used as a law court), and a number of other commercial, religious, and civic buildings.

The religion of Pompeii forms a rich tapestry. Chief among the gods worshipped in the Roman state religion was Jupiter Optimus Maximus ("Jupiter the Best and Greatest"). His consort was Juno, and in council

---

1. Pompeii boasts the Roman Empire's oldest preserved stone amphitheater, built shortly after the founding of the Roman colony in 80 BCE; the Coliseum in Rome, for example, was built more than 150 years later.

he had the help of Minerva, Mercury, Vulcan, Neptune, Venus (patron goddess of Pompeii), and others, numbering twelve altogether. Although Roman mythology sprang from Greek tradition—Jupiter, for example, was the Roman counterpart of the Greek Zeus—Roman gods were not merely the same gods with different names. Only Apollo had the same name and identity in both Greece and Rome. Public worship rested in the hands of priests, prominent citizens elected or appointed to perform the proper ceremonies and rituals on behalf of the community. At home the father of the family fulfilled the same office, offering daily prayers and gifts at the household shrine, within which were displayed figures of the traditional gods and other divinities honored by the family.

Emphasis on fertility and reproduction, an aspect of primitive religion, continued into Roman times. Wreaths of fruit and horns of plenty commonly appeared as decorative themes. Phallic images appeared on street corners and statues, as well as in the entrances to shops and houses, not in an erotic sense but as symbols of wellbeing and economic success.

Worship of the ruler as divine, long a practice of Eastern religions, did not reach Italy until the time of Augustus, the adopted son of Julius Caesar. After assuming the reins of government, Augustus had the murdered Caesar declared divine and thus became the son and successor of a god. Cults in honor of Augustus's position as head of the Roman state soon sprang up all over Italy. Each succeeding emperor was similarly honored because establishing cults to the Caesars demonstrated loyalty and might reasonably attract the emperor's favor.

Whereas traditional Roman religion sought to influence the higher powers through obeisance and other ritual observance, mystery religions put worshippers into a more direct relationship with the sources of divine power. Worshippers went through some form of initiation, during which a "mystery" was revealed, granting promise of divine favor in this life and in the afterlife. Pompeian mystery cults included those devoted to Isis, Dionysus, the Great Mother (Cybele), Attis, Mithras, and Sabazios, all having originated in Asia Minor, Syria, or Egypt.

In Pompeii, the most popular of the foreign gods was Isis, worshipped together with her consort Serapis (Osiris). Significantly, only the Temple of Isis, of all the temples in Pompeii, was completely restored after an earlier earthquake in 62 CE.

In a town with prosperity so closely linked to the wine trade, it is not surprising that many revered Dionysus, god of wine. Symbols of

Dionysiac worship were depicted so frequently in Pompeian art that they seem to be chiefly decorative motifs. Mythology, too, was a major source of inspiration. Paintings of scenes from Greek myths like the *Rape of Europa* and *Theseus and the Minotaur* decorated the interiors of Pompeian houses.

My cursory examination of Pompeii's instructive ruins ended with a late lunch. I took one last glance in the direction of Vesuvius, its looming crater scarcely visible through the thick haze, and pondered how generations of upper classes had nonchalantly purchased lots and built lavish homes in this beautiful locale, risking the potential devastation that loomed nearby. I thought of modern Californians who build homes near fault lines and on the slopes of hills where mudslides and forest fires regularly cause irreparable loss. As Jesus cautioned his followers, each of us must examine our lives, whether we are building on a secure or a faulty foundation.

TRAVEL ENTRY #23: SORRENTO AND THE ISLE OF CAPRI

Boarding the Circumvesuvian once again, I rode it to Sorrento—the end of the line. Sorrento, renowned for its fresh air and brilliant peninsular landscape, lies on a terrace of limestone rock 1,650 feet above sea level. Its sea-cliff setting and luxury hotels make it a popular tourist destination. On a clear day, a walk through the quiet resort town provides magnificent views of Vesuvius and the Bay of Naples, with its lovely green and white islands. From Sorrento visitors can take the famed "Amalfi drive," considered one of the most scenic drives in Europe. This narrow coastal road that connects Sorrento to the resort town of Amalfi,[2] on the other side of the Sorrentine Peninsula, threads around the high cliffs above the Mediterranean. Sorrento's ferry boats and hydrofoils provide service to Naples and Amalfi as well as to the islands of Capri and Ischia.

At Sorrento I decided to return to Naples by way of Capri. The nearby island, a popular resort for two thousand years, is considered one of Italy's loveliest locations. The Emperor Augustus purchased the island and his successor, Tiberius, lived there from 27 to 37 CE, govern-

---

2. Amalfi was one of Italy's first independent city-states. In the Middle Ages it was a maritime republic rivaling Genoa, Venice, and Pisa. Amalfi was a populous city until 1343, when a tsunami destroyed a large part of the lower town; its harbor is of little importance today. Like Sorrento, Amalfi's sea-cliff setting makes it a popular tourist destination.

ing Rome from his Villa Jovis, now one of the best preserved Roman villas in Italy. The eight-mile trip was shortened considerably by the rapid hydrofoil, which travels at a rate of forty-two miles per hour.

Capri, with its quaint villages, stunning scenery, and exceptional natural beauty, has a mountainous landscape. The steep, jagged coastline is penetrated by fascinating grottoes—sixty-five of them, including the outstanding Blue Grotto—and flanked by imposing rocks, above all the famous Faraglioni, now the symbol of Capri. Visited by intellectuals and artists from the nineteenth century onwards, Capri today is a favorite destination for tourists. Gracie Fields, an English singer and comedian who became one of the greatest stars of both cinema and theater, had a villa on the island and popularized two songs about Capri: *The Isle of Capri* and *Come Back to Sorrento*.

My schedule prevented me from visiting Capri's famed tourist haunts, but I had sufficient time to stroll along the Marina Piccola (Small Harbor) and ascend the steep hillside to the city of Capri, with its lovely view of the port and the Gulf of Salerno's enchanting blue water. The remarkable day ended with a seventeen-mile hydrofoil ride across the bay to Naples.

TRAVEL ENTRY #24: THE TRAIN RIDE TO BRINDISI

The trip to Brindisi, unlike earlier train rides in Italy, seemed interminable, but was made tolerable by the companionship of an Australian couple traveling, like myself, in first class. Eurail holders over the age of twenty-six are entitled to first-class travel, whereas younger travelers are eligible for the more affordable Youthpass, which restricts them to second-class.

After a visit with Paul and Craig in second class, I returned to the nearly empty first class and the privacy of my own compartment. A short while later Mike, the Australian chap, stopped and invited me to join him and his wife for a visit. This rollicking couple had many stories to tell, not only of their native Australia, but also accounts from fellow travelers, one of which involved a horrifying tale about two teenage girls they had met in Spain. The girls had been to Morocco, and were traveling overnight by train through Spain when they heard a knock on their compartment door. The train was between stops, and they had drawn the curtains to gain privacy, so they could not see who was knocking. They opened the door, tentatively, only to have a man force his way in, and before they could react, sprayed both with a chemical, which rendered them unconscious. By the time they regained their senses the assailant had rifled through their possessions and left the train.

Though such events are rare, it is frightening to think how unsafe travel can be when thieves, possibly driven by drug habits, become bolder and more technologically sophisticated. Of course, the threat to travelers in the post 9/11 era is immeasurably greater. I recalled my own experience on the Italian border, when the conductor had warned me to bolt the door and not to open it for any reason. My own misfortunes, even the loss of my bag in Geneva, paled by comparison to the trauma and the sense of helplessness those girls suffered that night.

As the Australian couple continued their story, the conductor appeared, asking for tickets. My companions seemed nervous as their Eurail pass was scrutinized; a bit later they confessed that they had tampered with their card because it had expired. They had erased the original termination date and replaced it with a new date, matching the ink on their card. I returned to my seat soon thereafter, not wanting to be party to their dishonesty and wondering whether they had sought my company to distract the conductor.

The day's ride ended at Brindisi, a major port on the Adriatic, in southeastern Italy. There I rejoined Paul and Craig and Steve, their temporary Australian traveling companion. We had two hours of free time before boarding the international ferry for Greece. During the tourist season, passengers are advised to allow an entire day for that procedure, particularly if they haven't purchased a ticket.

Following dinner we walked to the spot where two Roman columns mark the end of the Appian Way, the oldest and most important Roman highway. Begun in 312 BCE by Appius Claudius, for whom it was named, the road was built to link Rome with the military center of Capua. From there it was extended to Tarentum (Taranto) and Brindisi. For two hundred years, during the period known as the Pax Romana (19 BCE–181 CE), Rome's great highways made it possible for the empire to subjugate conquered people and expand the empire, while maintaining peace within its borders. The highway system that resulted from the original Appian Way became a two-way street, paving the way for cultural intrusion from the East. A vast number of religions, including Judaism, Christianity, and many mystery religions, expanded and flourished across the empire in the early centuries of the Common Era.

7

Athens: The Birthplace of Democracy

TRAVEL ENTRY #25: FROM BRINDISI TO PATRAS

By ferry, the trip from Brindisi to Patras takes about eighteen hours, with stops on the island of Corfu, in the Ionian Sea, and at Igoumenitsa, on the Greek mainland.[1] The fare is free for Eurail pass holders on boats operated by Adriatic Lines and Hellenic Mediterranean, but those who select this option are relegated to the deck area. Seats and Pullman berths cost extra, and there are always hidden costs, such as port taxes and, during high season, supplemental charges. I was able to share the cost of a four-bed berth with Paul, Craig, and Steve.

Around 6:00 a.m. the ferry's giant engines began their powerful counterthrusts, indicating our arrival at Corfu. Though it seemed as if I had just fallen asleep, the ship's shuddering awakened me so sufficiently that I slipped on some clothes and made my way to the deck. Knowing that we were only a few miles from the southern coast of Albania, I went to the rear of the vessel, hoping to catch a glimpse of that forbidden land. For forty years the paranoid dictator Enver Hoxha had allowed few foreigners to enter and no Albanians to leave. Cut off from the rest of the world, Albania had a reputation for being one of the strangest of countries. Following the great shakeup brought about by the Soviet collapse, combined with the death of Prime Minister Hoxha in 1985, Albania gradually abandoned its Communist alignment. In 2006, Albania signed an agreement with the European Union, and together with Croatia and Macedonia, received an invitation to join NATO in 2008.

---

1. The Ionian Sea, and its seven major islands off the west coast of Greece, should not be confused with Ionia, an area in ancient Greece that today comprises the southwestern coastal region of Turkey.

As we sailed south along the Ionian Sea, I spent much of the day enjoying the ship's leisurely atmosphere. Although the ferry was no cruise ship, the Greek coastal scenery was lovely and the calm waters relaxing. Arriving by ship to this ancient maritime nation, renowned for its shipbuilding and sailing, and seeing it for the first time through the pristine morning mist, added to its allure.

EXPLANATORY ENTRY #11: THE GREEK HERITAGE

Greece—home of heroes and Olympian deities, of world-class statesmen, philosophers, playwrights, historians, authors, architects, sculptors, orators, and theologians; home of the Olympics, birthplace of democracy, mother of Hellenism—was perhaps the most influential of western civilizations.

Bold and brutal, arrogant but enlightened, the ancient Greeks—or Hellenes as they called themselves—are often overshadowed by later Roman achievements. Yet they deserve much credit for developing the world's first classical civilization.[2] The Hellenes, unlike any other people of their age, exhibited a wide-ranging, clear-minded curiosity about all creation: the gods, nature, and particularly themselves. No other society had such a keen awareness of individual worth or such a belief in what humans could accomplish. "Wonders are many," wrote Sophocles, "and none is more wonderful than man."

Passionate, proud, and self-reliant, the Greeks were infused with a vitality of spirit that defied all odds. At the same time, they could be the most rational of people. Individual pride, abundant energy, mental agility—such was the rare combination of traits that made up the unique Hellenic psyche. In the sixth and fifth centuries BCE, those qualities would carry the Greeks to unprecedented heights, producing the most remarkable civilization the world had yet witnessed. Athenian statesmen would transform the art of political organization. Greek generals would win extraordinary victories. Greek poets, architects, and sculptors would open up new avenues into the human consciousness. And Greek inquiry into science and philosophy would change the very structure of human thought.

---

2. For a chronology of Greek history, including the Byzantine Empire, consult Appendix C.

At one point we passed the Greek island of Ithaca, home to Odysseus (known as Ulysses in Latin), the principal hero in Homer's *Odyssey* and a central character in the *Iliad*. Renowned for his guile and resourcefulness, Odysseus is most famous for the ten years it took him to return home after the Trojan War. No figure is more recurrent in Western literature and no text occupies as central a position in the Western imagination as this.

The vast collection of stories contained in the epics of Homer and his successors were engraved in the heart and mind of every Greek. In the familiar tales of the *Iliad* and the *Odyssey* lived every kind of character; their adventures and dilemmas mirrored every human situation. Homer has been used by innumerable writers, who often interpret his characters and their actions in very different ways. Later Greek playwrights—Aeschylus, Sophocles, Euripides—interpreted these characters and situations for their audiences to reveal to them the human condition. How do mortal men and women stand in relation to the immortal gods? What choices about the patterns of existence do humans have? What are the consequences of choice? How might people understand the ambiguity of the world and live with the fact that it is both evil and good, both kind and cruel? The tragic poets explored all of these questions in their plays.

The Greeks in general regard Homer's epics as the highest cultural achievement of their people, the defining moment in Greek culture that set the basic Greek character in stone. Throughout antiquity, both in Greece and Rome, everything tended to be compared to these two works; events in history made sense when put in the light of the events narrated in these works. Despite all the evolution and permutations through the centuries following their composition, these epics remain the focal point of Greek values and the Greek worldview.

TRAVEL ENTRY #26: FROM PATRAS TO ATHENS

My deck-side reverie came to a sudden halt the moment we disembarked at Patras. Dubbed as Greece's "Gate to the West," Patras is a commercial hub in the northern Peloponnese, 135 miles west of Athens. A brisk walk brought me to the city's dismal railroad station, where I encountered the alarming scene of a platform jammed with people, far too many, I thought, for one train to accommodate. Families milled about, clan-like, claiming auspicious turf which they might use to their advantage once the train arrived.

As the train approached the platform, the crowd surged forward, and I found myself struggling for survival as people began pushing and shoving toward cars already filled with passengers. I had encountered this madness on Rome's crowded buses, but this was worse, for conditions deteriorated further during the five-hour ride to Athens as travelers along the route made desperate attempts to board our train, the final one of the weekend.

The scene on board the sluggish train was chaotic, quite a contrast to the pleasurable train rides I had experienced up to that point. Every aisle and entryway, indeed every conceivable bit of space, was jammed with bodies and belongings. But the worst part was the cigarette smoke, pungent and acrid, billowing through every crack and crevice of the train's surface and penetrating every bodily orifice. Greeks love to smoke, and no one seemed to care whether this is offensive. Earlier, when the train arrived, I had made my way toward what I believed was a first-class car, but as the crowd got out of control, my priority was simply to get on board. By the time I found myself in a smoking car, it was too late to relocate. My sole consolation was the thought that possible all cars were equally smoke-filled.

The situation, I later discovered, was atypical. Sunday evening trains, though often filled, were rarely this crowded. The day before had been a national holiday in Greece and an unusually large number of people were returning from their extended weekend. In addition, Greek national elections were less than two weeks away, and this event led to severe disruptions in travel patterns, as entire families traveled to their home of origin to vote. Greece, after all, is the birthplace of democracy, and Greeks, proud of that heritage, take every opportunity to relish it.

On the train I watched in fascination as animated groups gathered randomly, generally clustered around one or two highly opinionated individuals. Though I couldn't understand what they were saying, it was obvious that the subject was politics. From time to time the decibel level rose markedly as individuals took exception to a currently espoused viewpoint. Witnessing this spectacle made the ride bearable and helped the time pass more quickly.

As we approached Athens, perhaps an hour away from our destination, I noticed a change of atmosphere. Youthful entrepreneurs began boarding the train with flyers in hand, hoping to attract customers to their venues. These hotel hawkers represented the numerous inexpensive hotels in Athens competing for the diminishing tourist trade during the off-season. Tourists, aware of their good fortune, banded together to maximize their leverage in this bidding war. Craig, Paul, Steve, and I managed to obtain a good rate for a quad in a hotel close to Omonia Square, one of the city's main squares. The hotel was situated in an ideal location, within walking distance of the Acropolis and the National Archaeological Museum.

TRAVEL ENTRY #27:
GETTING MY BEARINGS IN ATHENS

In Athens I was more concerned with location than with comfort, for I had little time for sleeping, there being so much to see in the next few days. By 6:00 a.m. the city's inhabitants started pouring into the city streets below my window, and the commotion came straight through the hotel's meager soundproofing. Having less than a week to spend in Greece, I had to plan each day carefully. Two sites on the mainland—Athens and Delphi—were essential, as was a trip to the Aegean islands.

I used my first morning to get my bearings and walk the streets of Athens. I headed toward Syntagma Square (Constitution Square), perhaps the most famous square in all of Greece. It seems that every major event in modern Greece has been mourned, celebrated, or protested here. It has been the site of massive political rallies as well as holiday concerts and festivals. On one side stands the Greek Parliament building, completed in 1838 as the royal palace for the newly established Kingdom of Greece (1834). Every hour the Changing of the Guard ceremony is conducted in front of the Tomb of the Unknown Soldier on the area between the parliament and the square.

A walk down Amalias Avenue took me into the cool and relaxing National Gardens, a large oasis in this surging metropolis. At one end of the park, across a wide boulevard, I located the huge marble Panathenian Stadium, built for the first modern Olympic Games in 1896, on an athletic site that reportedly was used as early as the time of Lycurgus (336–330 BCE). In 131 BCE Herod Atticus built here a marble stadium with a capacity of some fifty thousand spectators. The building was eventually abandoned and the marble used to construct other edifices. In 1894, when Athens undertook to host the revival of the Olympic

Games, the stadium was rebuilt in the horseshoe form that was found at the 1873 excavation.

As I joined local joggers in a relaxed lap around the track, imagining the stands full of spectators and myself a participant in the ancient athletic competition, the heat of the day and the sight of the famed Acropolis brought me back to reality. I walked past the ruins of the massive Temple of Olympian Zeus, said to be the largest temple in ancient Greece during the Hellenistic and Roman periods. Although construction had begun in the sixth century BCE, it took until the reign of Emperor Hadrian in 130 CE—seven hundred years later—to complete. Only 15 of its 104 Corinthian columns remain, but at 56 feet high and 5.5 feet in diameter at their base, they still show how massive the original temple must have been.

I had enough time left that day to visit the city's two most famous archaeological sites: the Agora—the market, civic center, and meeting place of ancient Athenian community life—and the Acropolis, Athens' religious and cultural center. Upon arriving at the Agora, I found it closed for repairs. As I had learned in Italy, renovations of tourist attractions generally take place during the off-season, when tourist revenue is down. This trip was teaching me a great deal about how to cope with frustration and disappointment. Though the archaeological site was closed, I noticed a marvelously preserved Greek building standing by itself at the far western side of the site. Known as the Temple of Hephaestus (449 BCE), it is the best-preserved ancient Greek temple in the world. Unlike the Parthenon, its illustrious neighbor, the Temple of Hephaestus has all its columns, pediments, and even most of its original roof intact. The structure owes its survival to its conversion to a Christian Church in the seventh century CE. Later, during the centuries of Ottoman rule in Greece, the temple became the principal Greek Orthodox church in Athens. The site gets much less tourist traffic than does the Acropolis and is a welcome spot in an area that once served as the blacksmith's agora, appropriately so since Hephaestus was the god of blacksmiths.

EXPLANATORY ENTRY #12: THE AREOPAGUS (MARS' HILL)

West of the Acropolis stands a natural outcrop called Mars' Hill, the ancient meeting place of the Council of Areopagus (the Greek name for Mars is Ares; hence Areopagus means "hill of Ares" or "Mars' Hill"), the most ancient and venerable of all the Athenian courts. It consisted of all persons who had held the office of archon and who were therefore members of the council for life (unless expelled for misconduct). The council, which continued to exist even under the Roman emperors, held its meetings on the summit of the rock.

The spot is memorable because it is here where St. Paul delivered his memorable address to the men of Athens (Acts 17:22–31). As a biblical scholar, I was fascinated by the New Testament account of Paul's trip to Athens during his second missionary journey, when the apostle "disputed daily" in the Agora. In speaking with the Athenian philosophers, Paul began from the Greek view of God as creator, benefactor, and invisible presence within the universe, talking of the universal human search for God, who is "not far from each one of us." In the process he referred to statements made by the Greek poets Epimenides and Aratus (Acts 17:28). Paul was not particularly concerned with condemning the traditional spirituality of his hearers, but rather with using it as an opening to present his own message. Having observed an altar "to the unknown god," Paul identified Jesus with this unknown deity, and proceeded to explain the gospel from this perspective. Because his message was given a mixed reception, Athens was not one of the cities where Paul established a Christian community.

Nevertheless, this narrative plays a central part in the book of Acts, for while other stories give a somewhat triumphalist view of the gospel, this one reminds its readers that even Paul's mission work was not guaranteed instant success. More importantly, it also provides a model for contextualizing the Christian message in cultures where the salvation history of the Old Testament story is unknown. In doing so, Paul is shown to affirm the spiritual starting points of his audience and seems prepared to journey alongside them, while at the same time challenging them to see things from the new perspective of belief in Jesus.

EXPLORATORY ENTRY #13: THE ACROPOLIS AND THE AGE OF PERICLES

With the successful defeat of the Persian military and naval might at Salamis and Plataea (480 and 479 BCE), Athens' star was on the rise. One-sixth of the revenue from the Delian League[3] was set aside for the

---

3. The Delian League was an association of Greek city-states in the fifth century

goddess Athena and was used to adorn the capital with magnificent temples, theaters, gymnasiums, and other public buildings. The principal figure behind this ambitious program was Pericles, under whose guidance Athens reached its pinnacle. Pericles had such a profound influence on Athenian society that Thucydides, his contemporary historian, acclaimed him as "the first citizen of Athens." The period during which he led Athens, roughly from 461 to 429 BCE, is sometimes known as the "Age of Pericles." In addition to promoting literature and the arts, Pericles started an ambitious project that built most of the surviving structures on the Acropolis (including the Parthenon). This project beautified the city, exhibited its glory, and gave work to the people, thereby enhancing Athens' reputation as the educational and cultural center of the ancient Greek world.

One of Pericles's first priorities was to rebuild the public areas of Athens, large sections of which still bore the ravages of Persian occupation. Enlisting the finest architects of the day and tapping the resources of the Delian League, Pericles erected court buildings, colonnaded marketplaces, theaters for the city's drama festivals, and gymnasiums where Athenian youngsters could harden their bodies and stretch their minds in philosophical debate.

On the Acropolis, a 230-foot-high plateau overlooking Athens, Pericles built a complex of temples that ranked among the wonders of the ancient world, the greatest of these being the Parthenon, which dominates the hill's highest crest.[4] Designed by the architects Ictinus and Callicrates, and dedicated to the goddess Athena, it took fourteen years to construct and embellish. The project so drained Delian League funds that even a few Athenians complained. But the magnificent Parthenon was the epitome of restraint and proportion, with a kind of strength tempered by grace that caught the very essence of the Athenian spirit. The sculptor Phidias carved its marble friezes and created its gilded, forty-foot-statue of Athena in a style of dignified naturalism that has never been surpassed.

At the Acropolis the ancient Athenians laid the foundations for Western civilization, with its towering achievements in philosophy, literature, drama, art, and architecture, and the city grew around the base

---

BCE. It was headed by Athens and later became the Athenian Empire. In 454 BCE, the treasury of the league was moved from the island of Delos to Athens.

4. For a site plan of the Athenian Acropolis, see Appendix L.

of the steep, flat-topped hill. Today all that remains of ancient Athens is on the Acropolis or around its base, making its summit perhaps Western civilization's single-most appropriate symbol.

The Parthenon, located on the south side of the Acropolis, was dedicated to the goddess Athena, the city's patron. Constructed solely of marble, with no mortar, the Parthenon is rectangular in shape—228 feet long, 101.4 feet wide and 63 feet high—and occupies about one sixth of the hilltop. Some of its dimensions form the golden rectangle, expressing the golden ratio praised by Pythagoras in the previous century.

Despite having lost most of its decorative features over the years, whether through destruction or by plunder, the Parthenon contains an intriguing feature apparent only to the informed observer: no straight line or absolute perpendicular exists in the entire building. To counteract natural optical distortion, whereby the eye tends to make horizontal lines appear to sag at the center, the architects used curved lines. Columns tilt inward yet swell two-fifths of the way up, in order to look straight. Corner columns are slightly thicker than middle ones and metopes (sculptured marble panels beneath the pediments) vary in size to look square from below. The effect of these subtle curves is to make the temple appear more symmetrical than it actually is. The temple enjoys the reputation of being the most perfect Doric temple ever built. Even in antiquity, its architectural refinements were legendary.

On the upper external part of the main temple wall is the famous frieze (524 feet of uninterrupted reliefs) showing the Panathenaean procession, the magnificent festival of the Athenians.[5] The frieze includes ninety-two metopes, each side of the building having a different subject. The east metopes, situated above the main entrance, depict the final stages of the cosmogonic battle between the Olympian gods and the Giants. Those on the southern wall present the Battle of the Lapiths and Centaurs, in which the mythological Athenian king Theseus took part.

---

5. The Panathenaea, celebrated in honor of Athena each year in the summer (roughly July, the first month of the Athenian calendar), with a more solemn festival every four years (the "Great Panathenaea"), was one of the most important festivals of Athens, rivaling the Olympian Games in popularity. The Great Panathenaea included sports events and musical contests and was the occasion of a large gathering in Athens of people from all parts of Greece, especially from Athens' colonies. During the festival, a procession moved through Athens up to the Acropolis and into the Parthenon (as depicted in the frieze on the inside of the Parthenon). There, a vast robe of woven wool was ceremoniously placed on Phidias's statue of Athena.

The subject of the west metopes is the legendary invasion of Athens by the Amazons, while those on the north depict scenes of the Trojan War. Though little remains of these decorations, the largest part of what is left of the frieze is currently housed in the British Museum in London, because in 1806, Thomas Bruce, seventh Earl of Elgin, removed some of the sculptures and took them to England. An ongoing dispute concerns whether these sculptures, now known as the Elgin Marbles or Parthenon Marbles, should be returned to Greece.

Though visitors are not currently permitted to enter the Parthenon, due to the fragility of its ruins, there was never much to see within, for the inside was devoid of decoration from its inception. The main temple, entered from the east side, contained but a solitary cult statue of Athena. Fashioned by Phidias of wood, the forty-foot statue was covered with gold and ivory, gold representing clothing and ivory representing flesh. During the Byzantine period the statue was taken to Constantinople and later was destroyed accidentally in a fire, possibly during the sack of the city during the Fourth Crusade in 1204.

Over the years the Parthenon, like the Acropolis, was subjected to contrasting religious and political usage. The edict of Theodosius II (429), which abolished the Olympian religion, forcibly Christianized the temples on the Acropolis. The Parthenon, a temple to Athena for nine hundred years, for the next thousand years served as a Christian church, dedicated to the Virgin Mary. In 1460, after the Turkish conquest, it was converted into a mosque. The structure suffered its greatest disaster in 1687, when Venetian forces attacked the Turks, who were using the Acropolis as a fortress. Turkish gunpowder inside the building was ignited by Venetian bombardment, the resultant explosion severely damaging the Parthenon and its sculptures. The Turks remained in possession of the Acropolis until 1833, when the area was taken over by the Greeks. Restoration began almost immediately, for the Acropolis is to Greece what Masada has become to Israel—a national monument.

On the north side of the Acropolis stands the Erechtheum, an ancient Greek temple notable for its unique, two-level design. The temple, enclosing five shrines and two sacred precincts, was erected to honor the fables concerning the beginning of Athens. On the south side of the temple is the famous "porch of the maidens," with six female figures (caryatids) as supporting columns. One of the caryatids, removed by Lord Elgin in order to decorate his Scottish mansion, was later sold to the British Museum. Nowadays the five original caryatids are displayed in helium-filled glass cases in the Acropolis Museum and are replaced *in situ* by exact replicas.

South of the platform that forms the top of the Acropolis are the remains of an outdoor theater called the Theater of Dionysus and the now partially reconstructed Theater of Herod Atticus. The south slope of the Acropolis played a significant role in the artistic, spiritual, and religious activity of ancient Athens. Important public buildings were erected in the area, including two temples dedicated to Dionysus, dating back to the sixth century BCE.

The most important monument on the south slope is undoubtedly the Theater of Dionysus, dedicated to Dionysus, the god of drama and wine (among other things). The theater held seventeen thousand spectators, making it an ideal location for ancient Athens' biggest theatrical celebration, the Dionysia. It was the first stone theater ever built—cut into the cliff face of the Acropolis—and the birthplace of Greek tragedy. During the fifth century the theater housed competitions among Sophocles, Euripides, Aristophanes, and Aeschylus. To the east of the Theater of Dionysus is the Odeon (from the Greek word *ode*, meaning "song") of Pericles, a public building built by Pericles in 445 BCE and initially dedicated to musical performances. It hosted musical contests during the yearly festival of the Panathenaea. West of the Theater of Dionysus, on the hillside, was once the Sanctuary of Asclepius (known as the Asclepion), also dating to the fifth century BCE. In it were the temples of the gods Asclepius and Hygeia, where the sick came to be healed.

Various buildings were added to this area during Hellenistic and Roman times, including the Stoa of Eumenes, attributed to Eumenes II, the king of Pergamum (197–159 BCE). The stoa was built as a shelter for theater-goers along the road that runs around the bottom of the Acropolis.[6] The Odeon of Herod Atticus, a stone theater located to the west of the Stoa of Eumenes, was built in 161 CE by the famous Athenian Herod Atticus in memory of his wife Regilla. Originally a steep-sloped amphitheater seating around five thousand people, the semi-circular

---

6. A similar stoa was constructed in the Athenian Agora by Attalos II (159–138 BCE), king of Pergamum and successor to Eumenes. Considered the most important find at the Agora, the stoa was built by Attalos in gratitude to the city of Athens, where he had studied as a youth.

venue was used for music concerts. The theater, restored in the 1950s with marble, is now used for the theatrical, musical, and dance events of the annual Athens Festival, which runs from June through September.

Near the Acropolis is the Philopappus Hill, the highest summit in the south of Athens. This hill, dedicated in ancient times to the Muses, the nine goddesses presiding over the arts and sciences, was known as the Hill of the Muses. The traditional prison of Socrates—where he drank the hemlock—is said to be located on one of its slopes.

That night Paul, Craig, and I returned to the Acropolis to explore the hill's northern face. The area was marked off limits, which intrigued us further. Although we weren't sure whether the signage was due to repairs, the onset of darkness, or to some permanent condition, we decided to investigate for ourselves. This face of the hill, the steepest, contained no visible monuments, only stairways, tunnels, and caves. We were intrigued by these forbidden passageways, but the descending darkness and the fear of arrest kept us on the path. Suddenly, bright lights appeared, illuminating the hill's west side and summit. We feared that we had tripped some hidden alarm and that we might find ourselves, like Socrates, in an Athenian jail. At that moment we heard the sound of loudspeakers from nearby Pnyx Hill and realized that the Sound and Light show had begun. We emerged from the darkness undetected, with a sense of relief.

TRAVEL ENTRY #28: THE NATIONAL ARCHAEOLOGICAL MUSEUM OF ATHENS

The following morning my companions arose early and departed for Piraeus, the port city of Athens, heading eastward toward Israel and Jordan. I spent my final morning in Athens at the National Archaeological Museum, one of the world's most magnificent displays of antiquities. The museum is a huge building, containing dozens of rooms filled with staggering numbers of sculptures, striking geometric and red figure pottery, frescoes, and the famous Antikythera Mechanism, one of the most interesting pieces of ancient technology, used possibly as an astronomical and calendar calculator. It was discovered in 1900 by a sponge diver who spotted the wreck of a cargo ship off the Greek island of Antikythera. Dating from the second or first century BCE, it is a most complex mechanism, incorporating dozens of gear-wheels as well as inscriptions related to the zodiac and the months. This ancient computing device antedates by two thousand years the inventions of Charles Babbage, who originated the idea of a programmable computer in 1822, viewed by experts as the earliest prototype of modern computers. The chance finding of the device demonstrates the sophisticated level of ancient wisdom and leaves us wondering what other technological marvels still await discovery.

Among all its exhibits, the one that gives the museum its special character is the collection of monumental sculptures, for it was in the art of sculpture that the ancient Greeks excelled more than any other civilization. My favorites were *The Artemision Bronze*, a magnificent bronze statue of Poseidon/Zeus (fifth century BCE) and the *Boy Jockey and Horse* (second century BCE), both recovered from the sea off Cape Artemision. The figure of Poseidon, rendered with tremendous power, holds the trident, which he is about to fling. It is this movement that gives the statue its force and appeal. The figure of the bronze horse and the diminutive jockey boy are also remarkable. The boy's face, constricted with tension, is a supreme example of realism, comparable only to that of the striking horse's body and head.

In addition to sculpture, I was intrigued by the museum's vast collection of ceramic vases, carefully painted with geometric designs or mythological themes. Nowhere can the progressive development of the early stages in the art of ceramics be more usefully examined than in the National Museum.

Toward the end of the eighth century BCE a profound change took place in the Greek world, when the new currents were strongly reflected in the sphere of art, particularly ceramic art. Greek artists discovered that the essence of the Greek world could best be expressed in terms of mythology; therefore, the number of painted themes derived from that source expanded at an ever-increasing rate. Mythology became a limitless source from which artists drew their inspiration, and for the first time the myths themselves were provided with eloquent and tangible forms.

Another attraction of the museum is its collection of frescoes from the island of Thera (the modern island of Santorini, located sixty-nine miles north of the island of Crete in the Aegean Sea). The Thera frescoes are among the most striking of the Minoan civilization, an advanced culture that flourished on the Mediterranean island of Crete from 2700 to 1450 BCE. Thera was destroyed by a tremendous volcanic eruption sometime in the fifteenth century BCE. Like the destruction of Pompeii, which resulted in the preservation of much of the city's artwork, the sudden devastation of Thera accounted for the survival of many of the city's frescoes. The first frescoes to be uncovered and restored by archaeologists reveal lavish and charming artwork, so attractive that it clearly seems to be the work of the most skilled and inspired painters of Minoan Crete.

The destruction of Thera reminds some of the legend of Atlantis, in which Plato described an advanced society, perhaps the Minoans, living on the island of Atlantis. According to his story, the island sank beneath the sea after a great catastrophe. Although the existence of a place such as Atlantis is greatly disputed, the eruption that destroyed Thera would certainly qualify in magnitude, being one of the most powerful in the past ten thousand years. Many scholars view this eruption as a major contributor to the fall of the Minoan civilization.

The other event that contributed to the demise of the Minoan civilization was the rise of the Mycenaean civilization. The term "Mycenaean" applies to the art and culture of Greece from 1600 to 1100 BCE and derives from the site of Mycenae in the Peloponnese, where once stood a great Mycenaean fortified palace. Mycenae is celebrated by Homer as the seat of King Agamemnon, who led the Greeks in the Trojan War.

In modern archaeology, the site first gained renown through German archaeologist Heinrich Schliemann's excavations in the mid-1870s, which brought to light objects whose opulence and antiquity seemed to correspond to Homer's description of Agamemnon's palace. The extraordinary material wealth deposited in the shaft graves at Mycenae (c. 1550 BCE) attests to a powerful elite society that flourished in the subsequent four centuries. Not only did the Mycenaeans defeat the Minoans, but according to legend, they twice defeated Troy, a powerful city-state that rivaled Mycenae's power. Because its only evidence is the *Iliad* and other texts replete with mythology, the existence of Troy and the Trojan War is uncertain.

After examining the museum's remarkable exhibit of Mycenaean art, I concluded that the finest artifacts in the collection were not those found by Schliemann in Mycenae but rather two gold-embossed cups found in a tomb near Sparta. One of the cups depicts an idyllic scene of shepherds with cattle, the other the capture of a bull in a net that has been spread between two trees. Dated to the late sixteenth or early fifteenth century BCE, these exquisite cups are masterpieces of Mycenaean gold-work. They are unique because of their creator's technical skill, certainly; moreover, the sensitivity of the artist's approach to the theme, combined with the admirable composition, the power of expression, and well-calculated filling up of the space, raise this work to the highest level of artistic achievement.

8

Delphi and Corinth

IT IS SAID THAT after the Acropolis of Athens, Delphi provides the most powerful and lasting impression in Greece. Located 125 miles from Athens, Delphi is by far the most popular day trip out of Athens.

Like so many pilgrims and travelers across the ages, commoners and celebrities alike, I too felt drawn to this sacred site, the home of the world famous Delphic oracle. Built on the slopes of Mount Parnassus, the ancient site sits on the edge of a cliff, overlooking the Gulf of Corinth and a valley filled with olive and cypress trees. Despite the abundance of tourists and tourism-oriented businesses, Delphi remains a remarkable place.

Delphi is more than just another collection of ruins in a country full of them. In ancient times it was considered the center of the known world, the place on earth where individuals were closest to the gods. At Delphi's ancient temple-sanctuary the god Apollo spoke through a Pythia, or human priestess, and offered advice to all who sought his aid. Pythagoras went there, and stayed to train a Pythia to serve as voice of the god. Herodotus also went there to record what was said. Plutarch served as priest of Apollo for many years. The great lawgivers Lycurgus and Solon obtained suggestions for laws that made their city-states models of justice and freedom. Oedipus, king of Thebes, consulted the Pythia as did Alexander the Great. In 336 BCE Alexander came to the oracle before setting out to conquer the world. "My son," the oracle said, "thou art invincible." Croesus, king of Lydia, sent envoys, as did innumerable worthies of the Greek, Roman, and Christian world.

The majority of questions asked of Apollo concerned personal affairs, though some, from statesmen, sought legal guidance or sanction to build a temple, found a city, establish a colony, declare war, or make peace. Answers could be straightforward, but if the stakes were high and the question difficult, the Pythia might resort to divine doubletalk. The most famous ambiguous answer was that given to Croesus, who in 546 BCE asked whether he should go to war to thwart the rising power of Cyrus, king of Persia. The Pythia's answer, as reduced to hexameter verse by the priests, was: "Crossing the River Halys [the river that marked the boundary between the two kingdoms], Croesus will destroy a great empire." Croesus, blinded by ambition, attacked Persia and unwittingly fulfilled the prophecy, for the kingdom he destroyed was his own.

The best known Delphic injunction: GNOTHI SEAUTON ("Know Thyself") was carved into the lintel at the Temple of Apollo. On a superficial level, the command could be taken to mean that one should know one's own strength and rely on one's own judgment. Others, finding deeper meaning in these words, took the "self" to mean the higher self, the true Self. To know oneself in this sense was to know all.

Whether one believes in the channeling of gods or spirits is an individual matter, but even the most skeptical person realizes that something special went on at Delphi for thousands of years. Today tourists travel regularly to Delphi, even though the god is silent and few believe, as the ancients did, that divinities communicate with mortals.

TRAVEL ENTRY #29:
VOYAGE TO THE CENTER OF THE EARTH

My best advice to those going from Athens to Delphi is to avoid the bus. Though the distance is short, the trip can take up to three and a half hours by bus. Having one day left on my Eurail pass, I saw an opportunity to save both time and money by taking the train to Livadia. Since the train did not go to Delphi, I would transfer there to a bus for the remaining twenty-eight miles. The plan looked good on paper.

The train ride proved enjoyable—at least by previous experience in Greece—for there were only a few other passengers in the smoke-free railroad car, but my arrival and that of the bus were poorly coordinated. To save time during the lengthy layover at Livadia, I ate an early supper. The bus finally arrived, but after a twenty-minute ride, the driver pulled over at a roadside restaurant and the passengers disembarked for dinner. The rest stop lasted an hour, and my only consolation was a conversation with a fellow traveler about the region's folklore.

Delphi and Corinth

The dinner stop was close to a famous crossroads known in antiquity as the Triple Way, a foreboding spot at the start of the long, narrow valley leading to Delphi. It was there, according to legend and as described by Sophocles in *Oedipus Rex*, that the youthful Oedipus, returning on foot from Delphi, met his father Laius, the king of nearby Thebes. There is no evidence in the text to suggest that either man knew the status of the other, for Oedipus had been brought up in Corinth and had not seen his parents since his birth. The latter struck Oedipus with his whip in order to make room for his chariot. Oedipus, although living in self imposed exile, still considered himself to be of royal blood; therefore any offense, especially by some old man and his servants, was cause for a serious reprimand. In the case of Oedipus, this meant murder. By today's standards, the entire episode amounts to a grisly incident of road rage. After this incident Oedipus returned to his native town of Thebes, where he answered the deadly riddle of the Sphinx that held the town in fear.

In Greek mythology, the Sphinx sat outside of Thebes and asked a riddle of all travelers who passed by. If the traveler failed to solve the riddle, then the Sphinx killed him/her. But if the traveler answered the riddle correctly, then the Sphinx would destroy herself. Oedipus solved the riddle and the Sphinx kept her promise. The riddle was: "What goes on four legs in the morning, on two legs at noon, and on three legs in the evening?" The solution: "A man, who crawls on all fours as a baby, walks on two legs as an adult, and walks with a cane in old age."

Having already murdered his father, Oedipus thus ascended the throne and unwittingly married his mother, thereby fulfilling the prophecy that had caused his parents to abandon him at birth.

Though I arrived late in Delphi, I had no trouble finding lodging at the International Youth Hostel. The following morning I arose early, determined to make the most of my time, for I intended to return to Athens later that day and continue to Corinth, fifty miles beyond.

Delphi is magnificent for the view it commands. The sight, whether from the ruins of the nearby sanctuary of Apollo or from the town itself, clinging in terraced fashion over a deep gorge, is unusually striking. The natural setting, the glimpse of Mount Parnassus, the gorge below that opens into a lush plain and ends in the aquamarine waters of the nearby Gulf of Corinth, all contributes to its allure. The site had also been chosen for the smoking crack in the earth that it straddled, which made the oracle deliver riddles. Quite possibly the sanctuary's carefully chosen location, placed high along the gorge's northern face, was Delphi's greatest attraction. All day long, from sunrise until sunset, the sun (symbol of Apollo) parades along the ravine, its light reflecting from the marbled monuments.[1]

The entrance to the site, continuing up the slope almost to the temple itself, contains the ruins of numerous temples and treasuries. These were built by various Greek city-states to commemorate victories and to thank the oracle for advice, which was so important to those victories. The most impressive is the now-restored Athenian Treasury, built to commemorate the Athenians' victory at the battle of Marathon. The Athenians had previously been advised by the oracle to put their faith in their "wooden walls;" by taking this advice to mean their navy, they won the famous battle at Salamis.

As Delphi grew in wealth, it developed into an independent state governed by aristocrats. It became the center of a twelve-member federation called the Amphictyonia, which unified the small city-states like a League of Nations. As a result of these treasuries, through the protection of the Amphictyonic League, Delphi came to function as the de-facto central bank of ancient Greece. The abuse of these treasuries by Philip of Macedon and his son Alexander the Great and the later sacking of the treasuries led to the eclipse of Greek civilization and the eventual growth of Rome.

Upon entering the main gate, modern visitors follow the narrow Sacred Way, passing the ruins of treasuries and monuments that commemorate great events. In antiquity, those who wished to consult the oracle had to follow an elaborate procedure. They had to wash in the nearby Castalian Spring and pay fees in the temple. If they were found worthy to proceed, they would sacrifice an animal. From the behavior of the beast (whether it trembled when sprinkled with cold water, for instance) attempts were made to gauge the attitude of the deity. If the

---

1. Apollo is one of the most important and many-sided of the Olympian deities. As the patron of Delphi (Pythian Apollo), Apollo was an oracular god. As the leader of the Muses and director of their choir, he is a god of music and poetry. He was also the god of medicine and healing (mediated through his son Asclepius). In Hellenistic times, especially during the third century BCE, as Apollo Helios he became identified with the sun.

sacrificial signs were favorable, then the petitioners descended into the depths of the temple, where the voice of the Pythia could be heard.

In addition to the sanctuary ruins, several additional sites at Delphi are worth seeing, such as the fourth-century BCE amphitheater that can seat up to five thousand spectators. The theater was restored during Roman times and remains well preserved. Its location, overlooking the sanctuary with a stunning view of the gorge, is impressive. Here ancient tragedies are occasionally produced in the late afternoon, when the surroundings are most splendid. Sophocles's *Oedipus Rex*, for instance, is so timed that when Oedipus gouges out his eyes, the sun's glow is fading, turning the enclosing hills a dull gray.

Still higher up, near the slope's summit, are the ruins of a large stadium, the best preserved in Greece. Famous for its chariot races, it could seat over six thousand spectators. It is here where the Pythian Games were held. The games, second in importance only to the Olympics, were held at the beginning of September of every fourth year, two years before and two years after those at Olympia. In addition to track and field events, the games also included the performance of a sacred drama, a musical competition, and a chariot race. On a lower terrace, near the Castalian Spring, lie the ruins of the gymnasium, a complex of athletic facilities that served as a training ground and meeting-place for athletes participating in the games.

About a half-mile to the east of the sanctuary, below the gymnasium complex, is the Temple of Athena known as Marmaria (the Marbles), supposedly because of the abundance of ancient marble stones lying nearby. This archaic temple, the first sight of ancient Delphi seen by travelers from Athens, was destroyed in the fifth century BCE by a rockfall. It was replaced by a second temple, constructed in the fourth century on a spot less susceptible to avalanches. Between the two sites lies the famous Tholos, a small Doric temple some sixteen yards in diameter, whose rotunda once featured an outer ring of twenty Doric columns in a perfect circle and an inner ring of ten Corinthian columns. Now only three stand. The partly restored building is one of the most beloved in Greece.

I concluded my visit to Delphi with a tour of the museum, ending with the museum's most famous exhibit, the life-size bronze statue of the *Charioteer*, one of the most celebrated pieces of ancient art in the world. The sculpture, crafted by an unknown artist in 479 BCE, was donated by Gelon, a well-known patron of chariot racing, in commemoration of a victory at the Pythian Games. This magnificent bronze, fashioned at the height of the classical period, illustrates a quality much celebrated by ancient Greeks: restraint under pressure.

I will always remember Delphi as captured by the Charioteer's timeless pose. At few other ancient sites do legend and reality, monuments and scenery, harmonize so completely. Few other places feel so completely isolated from the everyday world yet, at the same time, the very center of things that matter—the navel of the earth, as the ancients believed.

TRAVEL ENTRY #30: HIKING THE ACROCORINTH

At the crack of dawn, after a nighttime arrival from Delphi, I stood at the bus stop in New Corinth, awaiting the local bus that would take me to the site of ancient Corinth, several miles away. I came to climb the summit of Acrocorinth, the rocky mount that once served as the acropolis of Corinth. The steep Acrocorinth, rising fifteen hundred feet above the old city, is worth climbing for its superb view of the Saronic and Corinthian gulfs to the east and north, framed by the mountains of the Peloponnese and the Greek mainland.

My grueling climb, punctuated by numerous hairpin turns, was temporarily halted by a chance meeting with a flock of sheep slowly descending the slopes and spilling out across the narrow roadway. I watched in fascination as the shepherd demonstrated his control over the flock. His technique, inherited unchanged since biblical times, required the implementation of two coordinated elements: a small dog to patrol the fringes of the flock, keeping strays close, and more importantly, the selection of leaders from the flock, communicating with them by name and reminding them, through voice intonation, of their responsibility to keep the others in line.

At one time a temple stood at the highest point of Acrocorinth, dedicated to Aphrodite (Roman Venus), goddess of love, fertility, and beauty. Her cult, of eastern origin, has been identified with the Phoenician goddess Astarte (the biblical Asherah, whose worship is linked to that of Baal and zealously condemned in the Bible).[2] The ancient geographer Strabo once claimed that a thousand sacred prostitutes

---

2. See, for example, 1 Kings 16:32–33; 18:19; 2 Kings 21:3; Deuteronomy 12:3; 16:21–22.

served Aphrodite's temple at Corinth. Though the Acrocorinth had been well fortified in pre-Christian times, during the Middle Ages it became a fortress town. Strengthened and enlarged by Byzantines, Crusaders, Venetians, and Turks, the two miles of walls enclosing sixty acres of the summit are the most imposing medieval monument in all of Greece.

The ninety-minute climb brought me to the summit of the Acrocorinth. It was still early, about 10:00 a.m., and no one seemed to be around—no tourists, no vehicles, and no guards. So I was startled when a shaggy American stepped from behind some bushes, supporting a fully-loaded bicycle. He had spent the night among the ruins of the abandoned site, watching the sun rise from his private mountain aerie. Envying his youthful freedom and vigor, I felt an immediate bond with this carefree youngster cycling around the world.

On my way down the mountain I was overtaken by a garbage truck that had come to collect trash from a restaurant near the top. When I stuck out my hand to thumb a ride, I was pleased to see the vehicle stop. Climbing into the front seat, I found myself wedged between the driver and the garbage collector. The aroma was pungent. As we inched down the hairpin turns, I thought of Strabo's claim and wondered whether soldiers, sailors, and merchants had really negotiated the difficult climb long ago, not for aesthetic or religious reasons but to satisfy their carnal lust.

EXPLANATORY ESSAY #14: CORINTH IN NEW TESTAMENT TIMES

In the fifth century BCE, Corinth was one of the three major powers in Greece and therefore one of the participants in warfare against Persia, both on land and sea. After the Persian defeat, Corinth came into frequent conflict with Athens as an ally of Sparta in the Peloponnesian League. In 431 BCE, one of the precipitating factors leading to the Peloponnesian War was the trade rivalry between Corinth and Athens. After the Peloponnesian War, Corinth and Thebes grew dissatisfied with the hegemony of Sparta and started the Corinthian War (395–387 BCE), which further weakened the city-states of the Peloponnese. This weakness allowed for the subsequent invasion of the Macedonians and the conquests of Alexander the Great.

In the third century BCE, the city became the center of the Achaean League, a confederation of Greek city-states on the northern coast of the Peloponnese; its position of prominence led to its complete destruction by Rome in 146 BCE. The site remained uninhabited until the founding of a Roman colony by order of Julius Caesar in 44 BCE. Later that year, Caesar was assassinated, but the reconstruction continued and was completed under Emperor Augustus.

Under the Romans, Corinth became the seat of government for Achaia (southern Greece). Caesar had introduced a project for the reconstruction of destroyed cities, which he intended to colonize with veteran soldiers and landless subjects from the great Roman cities. That plan went into effect at Corinth. In addition to the Roman settlers, a number of emancipated Greeks from Rome were given land in Corinth or encouraged to settle there. Traders and sailors from the East—especially from Egypt—also came to settle in Corinth. In the first century CE, Corinth had a large population and was the wealthiest and most important commercial city in Greece.

Corinth's strategic location at the lower end of the narrow isthmus connecting the Peloponnese to mainland Greece virtually assured its role as an economic and political power in the Mediterranean world. Ancient Corinth had two harbors, one on each of its coasts—Cenchrea, on the Saronic Gulf (an arm of the Aegean Sea), and Lechaion, on the Gulf of Corinth (an arm of the Ionian Sea)—and therefore provided easy access to the Aegean Sea on the east and the Adriatic Sea on the west.

Though the Romans had opened up extensive seagoing trade routes and navigational methods were well advanced, ancient sailors still preferred to travel close to the coastline whenever they could, so Corinth took advantage of this preference to establish itself as one of the foremost centers of trade and transportation. There was no canal across the isthmus then, as there is today. It was a perilous journey around Cape Malea, the southern tip of the Peloponnesus, and mariners found it more desirable to transfer their cargo across the four-mile neck of land at Corinth than to face Malea's treacherous winds. Smaller boats were taken bodily out of the water and hauled across the isthmus by a vast number of slaves, initially on roller-like skids and later by a wheeled device. The famous road over which the Corinthians hauled ships is called the Diolkos (from the Greek verb *dielko*, meaning "to haul across").

A canal had been envisioned by Periander as early as the sixth century BCE, but the technology for its construction was lacking. At the time, some also believed that Poseidon, god of the sea, opposed joining the Aegean and the Adriatic, so Periander created the Diolkos instead. In ensuing years, others dreamed of constructing a canal, because it saved two hundred miles of sailing around the Peloponnesus, but it was Nero who actually attempted the task in 66 CE. Included in his workforce were six thousand young Jewish slaves recently captured by Vespasian in Galilee, where the Jewish war had begun. His attempt was soon abandoned on the belief that if the seas where connected, the more northerly Adriatic, mistakenly thought to be higher, would flood the more southern Aegean. In 1881 a French company took up the work where Nero's crew had stopped, completing the canal in 1893. Cut through solid rock, the current canal is 4½ miles long, 75 feet wide, and 250 feet at its deepest point.

Little remains of the ancient city of Corinth. Ruined arches and entryways to shops on what was once the agora call on the tourist's imagination to see the gleaming buildings that once occupied this site. A paved portion of the Lechaion road, the chief roadway to the northern port, still remains. The ruins of public and private buildings on either side of the road provide a comprehensive picture of this once prosperous capital of Roman Greece.

One of the things that characterized Corinth in the first century, when Paul visited the city, was the diverse nature of its society. Its position as an important seaport on one of the busiest routes in the Mediterranean ensured this. Corinth commanded the traffic of both the eastern and western seas and was a city filled with sailors, merchants, adventurers, and refugees. On the streets of Corinth, people of many different ethnic origins and religious convictions mingled naturally, making the city a microcosm of the life of the entire empire. As a staging post for sailors, it was also home to one of the largest numbers of prostitutes anywhere in the empire, making its name notorious for immorality. That the city became a byword for immorality is indicated by the expression "to live like a Corinthian." One contemporary author describes Corinth in Paul's day thus: "Corinth was the Vanity Fair of ancient Greece: a sailor's favorite port, a prodigal's paradise, a policeman's nightmare, and a preacher's graveyard."

It is easy to see why the apostle Paul chose Corinth as headquarters for his Christian mission to the West. The city was young and dynamic, a mix of dislocated individuals seeking to shed their former low status by achieving social honor and material success. Paul was not intimidated by a bustling cosmopolitan city without a dominant religious or intellectual tradition, for Corinth shared many characteristics with Tarsus, his home town, and with Syrian Antioch, his home church city.

Paul clearly recognized the strategic importance of Corinth, staying there for eighteen months toward the end of his second missionary journey. His visit came at a significant time for mission work. In 49 CE the Jews were expelled from Rome, and a sizeable number migrated to Corinth. When Paul stayed in Corinth, he met with Jewish refugees from Rome, seeking out two of them, Aquila and Prisca, because they were tentmakers like him. Working together as business and religious associates, Aquila and Prisca became key leaders of the young Christian church at Corinth. It is estimated that some two hundred Christian converts were in Corinth at the time of Paul's ministry among them. They lived in large households and worshiped in house churches that reflected the city's diverse make-up.

TRAVEL ENTRY #31: CROSSING THE AEGEAN TO TURKEY

Later that day, as I crossed the Corinthian canal for the third time, I was able to view the rock-hewn creation from atop the 250-foot-high railroad bridge. Time prevented me from exploring other treasures in the Peloponnesus, including significant sites such as Mycenae, Epidaurus, and Olympia, home of the most famous of all Panhellenic contests. The allure of Greece's Aegean islands proved greater than that of the Peloponnesus.

Though scheduling difficulties prevented me from sailing for Crete, Santorini, Rhodes, or any number of other island destinations, early the next morning I stood at the docks of Piraeus ready to board the *Samena*, scheduled to depart for the island of Samos, the main transit point to the ancient site of Ephesus, on the Turkish coast. The fourteen-hour ride to touristy Samos Town (Vathy), the deep-water port of the island of Samos, was punctuated by views of spectacular Aegean scenery. I passed the Cyclades Islands—Delos, Mykonos, Naxos—each with its own history and personality, but none rivaled the sight of Poseidon's temple at Cape Sounion, the last point on the mainland of Attica, where ancient mariners prayed for safe passage on the storm-swept sea.

The ferry was crowded, but carried few tourists. Greek elections were approaching and that signaled inconvenience and limited travel for visitors. For a period of three days, tourists were banned from domestic flights and most ferry reservations were restricted to Greek citizens, many of whom were traveling to their ancestral homes to vote. In Greece, elections take precedence over all other routines. What, after all, could be more important in the birthplace of democracy than an election, an opportunity to unite passion with reason?

The ferry landed in Samos Town at 10:00 p.m., two hours off schedule. The late arrival meant that I might have trouble booking early passage to Turkey. As soon as I disembarked, I pursued a tip and went to the office of Samos Tour, near the end of the dock, hoping for help with continued passage. Though Samos closely adjoins Turkey, from which it is separated by a strait one mile wide, finding transportation to the Turkish mainland proved to be challenging. Relations between Greece and Turkey were strained, even hostile, and during the off-season there was no reliable transit between Samos and Kusadasi, the Turkish port of entry. I expected lots of red tape, but when a Dutch agent examined my credentials and saw the Dutch name on my passport, she gave my application top priority. I was happy to learn that I could book passage with a charter group scheduled to depart for Kusadasi early the following morning.

Numerous other travelers were waiting at the dock the next day, including some who had made repeated attempts to leave the island, yet I was the only one allowed to continue. The boat I had boarded was chartered by a group of German Catholics, visiting sites associated with the travels of St. Paul, and it was as a member of this group of pilgrims that I negotiated the troubled political waters separating the Greek Scylla from the Turkish Charybdis.

9

Ephesus: Gateway to Asia

EXPLANATORY ENTRY #15: INTRODUCTION TO TURKEY (ASIA MINOR)

As strong winds buffeted our tiny craft nearing the shore of Turkey, I pondered the region's turbulent history. As early as the eleventh century BCE, Turkey's Aegean coast (known to ancient Greeks as Ionia) was colonized by tribes speaking the Ionic dialect of Greek. They retained their distinctive dialect, also spoken in Athens, and became renowned for their contributions to science, philosophy, poetry, and architecture. It was from such cities as Pergamum, Smyrna, Miletus, and Ephesus that the sparks of scientific methodology and inquiry leaped across the Aegean Sea to the Greek mainland, thereby igniting human thought in the West. Since that time, Turkey (known by Romans as Asia Minor) has continued to function as a bridge between Europe and Asia, shifting back and forth between Western and Eastern cultures. In the eleventh century CE, the Seljuk Turks swept across this region from the East, gradually chipping away at the Byzantine Empire, the last remnant of Roman rule, and its religious base, Christianity.

The most recent empire to rule Turkey was the Ottoman, from the fifteenth century CE to the end of World War I. Following the war, Turkey was modernized by the extraordinary Mustafa Kemal, who is revered by the people of Turkey as Ataturk ("Father of the Nation") and is now known by that surname. He came to power in 1923, declared Turkey a republic, and by way of modernization, closed down all religious schools, abolished the Caliphate, westernized the alphabet, and laid the foundation for a democratic political system. Had it not been for his efforts in the 1920s, the coastline today would most certainly belong to Greece.

TRAVEL ENTRY #32: KUSADASI, GATEWAY TO EPHESUS

As we came within sight of the Turkish mainland, the boat's captain ordered the crew to lower the Greek flag and raise the Turkish flag. Though this is expected and even mandatory at times, on account of strong anti-Greek sentiment, the practice is contrary to international maritime law, which requires all vessels to display the flag of their country of registration. This gesture made it clear that we were in another country, but it also warned that we were entering another world. We had crossed from Europe to Asia. My sabbatical journey, now at its midpoint, had reached a watershed as well. Half had been spent in Europe; the rest would be spent in Asia and Africa.

Border crossings in the Middle East are generally an adventure. Though the bureaucratic red tape can be frustrating and time-consuming, the hassles and delays provide the tolerant traveler with valuable perspective. Because I was attached to a tour group, my passage from Greece to Turkey was the easiest of all my border crossings in the Middle East. As the tour group waited, I was allowed to proceed alone, thereby crossing the border without delay.

When I walked out into the streets of Kusadasi, I knew immediately that I was in a different country. Turks were calmer, more polite, and less passionate than the Greeks I had met. Greeks were antagonistic towards each other but more in awe of tourists. Turks, more formal, had rules of engagement, and also seemed to like each other better. Though Turkey shared a border with seven countries, Turks were less paranoid and certainly less xenophobic than their Greek counterparts. Greece was Christian by culture; Turkey was Muslim, one of the few moderate Muslim countries in the world. By contrast with the Europe I had left behind, Turks were friendly and hospitable. Merchants greeted me with smiling faces and friendly shouts while inviting me to join them for tea. That pattern repeated itself endlessly, proving that Turks are adept at the ancient Asian virtue of hospitality.

Kusadasi is an ideal base for visiting four of Turkey's most historic sites. Of the four, three lie to the south: Priene, an ancient Greek holy city with one of Turkey's best preserved theaters; Miletus, birthplace of philosophy and the site of another superbly preserved theater; and Didyma, home of the famed sanctuary of Apollo, the third largest religious structure in the ancient world and renowned for its esteemed oracle, second only to that at Delphi. The fourth was Ephesus, with its incomparable ruins. My schedule allowed time to visit only one, and that left me little choice. I headed for Ephesus.

After a ten-mile bus ride, I arrived at the village of Selcuk, only a mile from the ruins of ancient Ephesus. Whenever I arrived in a new town, my foremost priorities were eating a good meal and finding clean, affordable lodging. On some occasions enterprising youngsters took the initiative, waiting at bus stops and train stations for travelers to arrive. At Selcuk, when I followed one of them, it turned out to be a great decision. The youngster led me through the town's bustling marketplace, dodging shoppers, vendors, and stalls piled high with fruit, vegetables, and other staples of Turkish life. It seemed as if the entire population had come to shop at the market on a Saturday morning.

The boy took me to his home a few blocks away, where for several dollars a night I slept in a private bedroom, with a bath and shower nearby and breakfast included. Because the residence was new and clean, I was surprised to find a squat toilet in the modern bathroom. Although the family could have installed a more contemporary appliance, they preferred something traditional. The word "modern" is defined in widely different ways around the world.

After a brief meet-and-greet session with members of the family, I followed the youngster back to the center of town for an afternoon of sightseeing.

EXPLORATORY ENTRY #16: ANATOLIA: LAND OF MOTHER GODDESSES

Anatolia, the ancient Greek name for Turkey, means "east" or "the place where the sun rises." The Turkish form, Anadolu, though it is derived from the Greek, has its own appropriate meaning: "full of mothers" or "land of mothers." Anadolu is an appropriate name for the region, not only because the seeds of modern civilization were first sown here, but also because they were first sown by women. Anatolia is one of the regions where the transition from hunting to agricultural production was first realized, and the societies that first realized this transition were matriarchal. Anatolia is also regarded as "the land of mother goddesses" because the mother goddess made her first appearance here.

Over the years, the mother goddess of Anatolia, representing fertility and abundance, was known by many different names. Cybele, called Magna Mater by the Romans, was the name given to the great Phrygian mother goddess from Central Anatolia. Though her cult was closely associated with vegetation, it is through her frenzied worship and by the orgiastic practices of her priests that she is best remembered. Her priestesses led the people in wild ceremonies with music, drumming, dancing, and drink. The worship of Cybele spread from inland areas of Anatolia and Syria to the Aegean coast. Ephesus, one of the major trading centers of the area, was devoted to Cybele as early as the tenth century BCE. Devotion to Cybele spread to Crete and other Aegean islands, and to mainland Greece, where it was closely associated with, and apparently resembled, the cult of Dionysus, whom Cybele is said to have initiated; she was particularly welcomed at Athens.

The goddess was introduced to Rome in 203 BCE, on the advice of a passage in the Sibylline Books—Sibyl being the Latinized version of the name Cybele—interpreted to mean that if a statue of Cybele was brought to Rome, victory would follow. The Sibylline Books were a collection of oracular utterances consulted at momentous crises through the history of the republic and the empire. Only fragments have survived, the rest being lost or deliberately destroyed. A fortunate combination of circumstances that followed the cult's introduction, particularly victory by Rome over Hannibal in the Second Punic War, led to her admittance to state worship. Thereafter she became the goddess of victory for the Roman Empire.

Though at first the cult of Cybele was viewed with suspicion, by the first century CE her worship became one of the most favored sects. Many Roman emperors worshipped her as the most eminent goddess of Rome, and she was a favorite object of worship by Emperor Julian the Apostate, who regarded her as the "mother of Zeus and his wife." One emperor, Elagabalus, emasculated himself out of devotion to the goddess. Not coincidentally, when a Christian basilica was built over the site of a temple to Cybele, it was dedicated as the Basilica di Santa Maria Maggiore, thereby substituting—or equating—the Mother Goddess with the Virgin Mary.

The last and one of the most important of the Anatolian goddesses was Artemis Ephesia. The Ephesus goddess Artemis, sometimes called Diana, is not the same figure as the Artemis worshiped in Greece. The Greek Artemis is the goddess of the hunt, whereas the Ephesus Artemis was a goddess of fertility and was often pictured as draped with eggs, or multiple breasts, symbols of fertility, from her waist to her shoulders.

The Ephesus Museum in Selcuk displays two famous statues of Artemis, one known as "the Great Artemis" and the other as "the Beautiful Artemis," because the latter was made from better quality marble. Both sculptures, discovered in the ruins at Ephesus, are dated to the first century CE. These intriguing statues portray the complex goddess in her dual role as fertility goddess and mistress of wild beasts. In both cases Artemis is depicted with animals on either side of her head, as well as on her arms, chest, and skirt, including rams, goats, stags, bulls, sphinxes, griffins, and bees. The chest of the goddess is also embellished with the signs of the zodiac. As mother goddess, she is the "Source of All."

In hundreds of inscriptions from antiquity, Artemis is described in glowing terms as founder, savior, commander, guide, advisor, legislator, and queen; as victorious, invincible, powerful, and inviolate; and as one who listens to prayers. She is also described as protector of pregnant women and as guardian of sailors, which may explain why the worship of Artemis spread from Egypt and Carthage to the coasts of Italy and France, encompassing almost the entire Mediterranean area. The wealth and variety of adornments on statues of Artemis reflect her omnipotence as Mother Goddess.

An interesting literary and historical conclusion to the story of the mother goddess and the end of matriarchal civilization in Anatolia may be found in the Trojan War. There is ample evidence that the Trojans were matriarchal, or at least that their women enjoyed freedom and a respected status in society. The daughters of King Priam, we are told, lived with their husbands in their father's palace. Sons-in-law moving in with their wives' families are phenomena peculiar to matriarchal societies, for in patriarchal societies the norm is for women to join their husband's household.

According to some interpreters, the Trojan War may be regarded as the death blow to matriarchal civilization in Anatolia. In that war, two women, representative of the combatants, symbolize the two societies, one Asiatic and the other European. Beautiful Helen—daughter of the Asian mother goddess Leto, who caused the outbreak of the war—has been identified symbolically with Artemis, and Athena with the invading Achaeans from the Greek mainland. In view of the fact that the Asian Artemis (embodied in Helen) represented nature and agriculture, while Athena represented war, wisdom, and the arts, the victory of the Achaeans may also be interpreted as the victory of arts and crafts and therefore a victory of economic and political diversification over hunting and agriculture.

EXPLORATORY ENTRY #17: THE FOUNDING OF EPHESUS AND THE TEMPLE OF ARTEMIS

In classical times, Ephesus was one of the cities of the Ionian Greeks in Asia Minor, where the Cayster River flows into the Aegean Sea. Later, during the Roman Empire, Ephesus became the capital of the province of Asia, which covered the western part of Asia Minor. The city was distinguished not only for the Temple of Artemis (Diana) but also for its library and for its theater, which held twenty-four thousand spectators. In the year 100 CE, the population of Ephesus may have reached a population of some five hundred thousand inhabitants, making it the largest city in Roman Asia and one of the largest cities of the day. The city, an important center of Christianity, hosted the Third Ecumenical Council in 431. Although sacked by the Goths in 263 CE, Ephesus remained the most important city of the Byzantine Empire after Constantinople in the fifth and sixth centuries.

So what happened to this great city that turned it from a busy port to an abandoned ruin? And what happened to its great temple, once located by the sea but now found three miles inland?

The most famous attraction in the ancient city of Ephesus was the great Temple of Artemis (known as the Artemision), one of the outstanding buildings of antiquity. "I have seen the walls and Hanging Gardens of ancient Babylon," wrote Philo of Byzantium, "the statue of Olympian Zeus, the Colossus of Rhodes, the mighty work of the high Pyramids and the tomb of Mausolus. But when I saw the temple at Ephesus rising to the clouds, all these other wonders were put in the shade." Numbered among the Seven Wonders of the Ancient World, the temple was second in size only to one other building, the Temple of Hera on the island of Samos. Destroyed and rebuilt seven times, in its greatest phase the temple measured 425 by 220 feet, making it four times larger than the Parthenon. The marble roof was supported by 127 pillars 60 feet high. This forest of columns, like the pine forests suitable to the worship of Cybele, created an ideal setting for the multi-breasted statue of the Ephesian mother goddess housed within.

The Artemision served a variety of functions, including as a marketplace and a center of banking. As a popular site of pilgrimage in antiquity, it was served by hundreds of priests, priestesses, and guards. The temple also enjoyed certain privileges, such as granting the right of asylum to anyone seeking immunity. Many people, including a large number of criminals, came to the sacred area surrounding the temple in search of refuge. The precincts were also served by a great many artisans who manufactured and sold images of Artemis as lucky charms to the endless stream of visitors.

The site was sacred long before a temple was here. During the earliest human occupation of the site, people worshipped a goddess that ruled over sexuality and childbirth. In time the deity began to acquire human features, as worshippers merged primitive paganism with their belief in the Greek goddess Artemis, the nurturer of life and protector of nature. The temple at Ephesus spoke of the deep reverence for the mother goddess.

The first shrine to the goddess Artemis, probably built around 800 BCE on a marshy strip near the mouth of the Cayster River, was destroyed and rebuilt several times over the next few hundred years. By 600 BCE, when the city of Ephesus had become a major port of trade, an architect named Chersiphron was engaged to build a new large temple. This temple didn't last long. In 550 BCE, King Croesus of Lydia conquered Ephesus and the other Greek cities of Asia Minor. During the fighting, the temple was destroyed. Croesus proved himself a gracious winner, though, by contributing generously to the building of a new temple.

Marshy ground was selected once again, as a precaution against future earthquakes. The new structure was massive—the size of a football field. The Artemision stood within a beautiful deep bay, positioned so that it could be seen from five or more miles at sea. The temple became a tourist attraction, visited by merchants, kings, and sightseers from such faraway places as India, Persia, and Spain. Accumulating a vast treasure trove of precious metals and exotic jewelry, its splendor also attracted many worshippers, including the wealthy king Croesus, who was granted a line of credit by the local priest.

The marble temple was the pride of Ephesus until 356 BCE, when it came to a fiery end. Though the fire may have been started by priests attempting to steal the treasures kept in the temple, a stronger possibility is that it was destroyed by lightning during a thunderstorm. Once the fire reached the roof, the conflagration was so intense that even the marble melted.

For the devotees of Artemis, the question remained: why didn't the goddess protect her temple? According to Plutarch, the famous Greek historian, the answer given was that she was busy elsewhere. The night of the fire was the same night that Alexander the Great was born. Because the goddess had to preside over his birth in distant Macedonia, she was unavailable in Asia Minor, leaving the temple unprotected.

Faced with the destruction of their beloved shrine, the followers of Artemis performed an amazing act of devotion. Within a century of the destruction, they rebuilt the vast marble temple, to exactly the same specifications as its predecessor but different from it in that it was built on a platform, designed to protect the building from the dampness of the marshland on which it was constructed. This version of the temple was placed on the list of the Seven Wonders of the Ancient World.[1]

According to Pliny, construction took 120 years, though some experts suspect it may have taken only half that time. Ephesus was one of the greatest cities in Asia Minor at this point and no expense was spared. The Ephesians built the temple themselves, assisted by Scopas and Praxiteles, the most famous sculptors of the day. That temple would stand for six hundred years, as long as the belief in Artemis continued. But with the decline of the Roman Empire, invading Gauls plundered the temple in 262 CE and destroyed the building. The treasure was taken out by sea, and as fate would have it, the vessels all sank and the treasure was lost forever. They still lie in the depths of the Aegean—a fortune waiting to be found.

When the Roman Emperor Constantine rebuilt much of Ephesus a century later, he declined to restore the temple because he had become a Christian and had little interest in pagan temples. By the end of the fourth century, when most pagan temples were either torn down or converted into Christian churches, the Temple of Artemis followed suit. In 406, after its conversion to Christian use, the temple was razed.

Despite Constantine's efforts, Ephesus declined in its importance as a crossroads of trade. The bay where ships had docked disappeared as silt from the river filled it, until what was left of the city was miles from the sea, and many of the inhabitants left the swampy lowland to live in the surrounding hills. Those who remained used the ruins of the temple as a

---

1. For a discussion of this list, see Appendix J.

source of building materials. Many of the fine sculptures were pounded into powder to make lime for wall plaster.

Upon the orders of the Byzantine Emperor Justinian (527–565), columns from the razed temple were carried to Istanbul and used in the construction of Hagia Sophia, the greatest early Christian church. Fragments of the great altar and some of the columns may be seen today in museums in London and Vienna.

TRAVEL ENTRY #33:
VIEWING THE FABULOUS RUINS OF EPHESUS

The most compelling reason to visit Kusadasi and its environs is to see the ruins of Ephesus. The site, which extends over two thousand acres, is the most impressive ancient ruins from the Roman period.[2]

My first stop was the site of the Artemision. Since only one of the seven wonders—the Pyramid of Khufu (Cheops) in Egypt—has survived the ravages of time, I had no idea what remained of the Artemision, if anything. When I arrived at the site, I was not sure it was the correct place, for before me stood a marshy field. A single column and scanty fragments strewn on the ground are all that remain of the Seventh Wonder of the World. The marble column is home to storks that nest atop its summit. Stripped of its splendor, the temple's lone sentinel is the sole reminder of the long-lost glory buried deep beneath the alluvial plain. The site's haunting silence left much to the imagination.

A fifteen-minute stroll along the broad, tree-lined walkway brought me to the ancient city's north gate, one of two main entrances to the archaeological ruins. This road, which once connected the city with the Temple of Artemis, was considered the Sacred Way. Known today as Marble Road, because portions are paved with large marble slabs, this was the main road of the city. To my left I saw the ruins of a second century CE gymnasium and beyond that a horseshoe-shaped stadium, built during the Hellenistic era but vandalized by Christian zealots after Christianity became the official state religion.

The archaeological site of Ephesus, considered one of the great outdoor museums of the world, is vast. It is only partially excavated, but what is visible gives some idea of its original splendor, the names of the various buildings and monuments evocative of its former life. The Great

---

2. For a site plan of the ruins of Ephesus, see Appendix M.

Theater is huge and positioned to dominate the view down Arcadian Street (Harbor Street) leading to the harbor, long since silted up. The remarkable Library of Celsus, whose façade has been fully restored, once held nearly twelve thousand scrolls. Other edifices excavated include the Odeon, the Temple of Hermes, the Temple of Domitian, and the State Agora, a large rectangular esplanade, comparable to what we might call a city square. During ancient times the square would have been full of life, with small shops and people everywhere. Around the Agora were the most important buildings of the city, including the city hall, fountains, temples, and baths. Ephesus also had several major bath complexes and one of the most advanced aqueduct systems in the ancient world, with multiple aqueducts of various sizes to supply different areas of the city.

Ephesus was located on a busy sea traffic lane and it was prepared to meet, along with the needs of its immense population, the needs of an endless stream of sailors and merchants, together with a vast multitude of pilgrims to the sacred precincts of Artemis. The street from the harbor to the great amphitheater served as the entryway to Anatolia. Viewed from another perspective, all roads from Anatolia ended here. Harbor Street represented the crossroads of the world, the intersection of Asia and Europe. Here East met West. Covered porticoes lined both sides of the street, their floors paved with mosaics. Built in the first century BCE, the street was regal, for in addition to its pedestrian traffic it also served as the entryway for emperors, proconsuls, and other famous personalities.

The ruins of Ephesus that line the Marble Road are much more extensive than I had imagined. Across from the theater are the remains of the famous Commercial Agora. This great public area, the heart of Ephesus's business life, was originally floored in marble and surrounded by a colonnade and shops. The Sacred Way ends here, with the Library of Celsus and the monumental Gate of Augustus to the right (west) and Curetes Street heading east up the slope.

Curetes Street, once the most important street in Ephesus, led to a complex of public buildings, aqueducts, fountains, baths, monuments, and imperial temples, dominated by the State Agora, a semi-sacred area where political and religious meetings were held under the supervision of the state. In Paul's day this was the center of civic life, with government offices and imperial shrines surrounding it. In the center of the square was the Temple of Augustus, to the west the ruins of a temple venerating the emperor Domitian. Incorporating the temples and shrines of the imperial cult into the civic space of the city shows how inseparable were religion and politics and how religious observance promoted allegiance to the empire.

TRAVEL ENTRY #34: PURCHASING A TURKISH RUG

I left the site of the ruins knowing that I had made the most of my one afternoon in Ephesus. The following day being Sunday, I had scheduled an early departure for Bergama, site of another fabulous archaeological site. But this was Saturday, and I pondered my options for the evening as I walked back to Selcuk. My thoughts were interrupted by the voice of a young man calling to me in English from a pick-up truck parked near the tree-lined walkway. Having been on my feet all day, I found it difficult to reject his offer for a ride into town. As we rode together I learned that the gracious stranger was from Australia, and that he worked for a carpet shop owned by Australians. He invited me to the shop for some tea, and since I had intended to shop for a carpet anyway, I decided to investigate. Carpet selling is big business in Turkey, and its citizens do whatever it takes to make a profitable sale.

I found a dozen prospective buyers, like me, already in the shop when I arrived. Rugs of various shapes and colors were displayed, piled one atop another in the middle of the room. I was glad others were present, for as a novice I appreciated the opportunity to sit back and learn from the questions and reactions of those who preceded me. I decided to visit several shops, perhaps even in different towns, before showing an interest in a particular carpet. I wasn't sure yet what color or style I preferred and had to learn how to bargain effectively. After completing my initiation, I browsed in various other shops as well, where the obligatory tea sipping led to discussions on philosophy and religion. My knowledge of Islam endeared me immediately to vendors and the wider circle of acquaintances that frequent such places.

On my way back to my room, as I was walking along a deserted street, a voice called out to me in broken English from across the street: "American, come and visit me. I need to practice speaking your language." The bright teenager had been asked to mind a small carpet shop, and he was obviously bored by his job and the lack of companionship. On the promise that the conversation would not involve the sale of carpets, I agreed to the invitation.

It was I, however, who brought up the subject of carpets, asking technical questions that the youngster was unable to answer. "Wait here," he said as he scurried off into the darkness. Several minutes later he returned with his older brother Ali, a university student who was paying for his education by running a larger shop nearby. His family owned three co-ops in partnership with the government, and that meant that the shop could ship carpets anywhere in the world, duty free. The price included free shipping.

I found myself immersed in a detailed conversation with Ali, who explained that rug designs were often clues to the region in Turkey where they were manufactured. All of the rugs in his shop, he emphasized, were made by hand, utilizing natural dyes taken from plants and animals. White colors, for example, were made from tobacco plants; dark blue from eggplant; and light blue, a combination of saffron and indigo. Most of the rugs in his shops were made of wool, though some were wool and cotton blend and others were made of silk.

Armed with this knowledge, I asked to see specific samples. After examining a large selection, I eventually came across a 4 x 6 foot rug that had both the style and color I preferred. When I learned that a rug this size took about seven months to make, I felt prepared to begin the bargaining process.

"What is your best price?" I asked.

"$850," he answered. I laughed, indicating that the price was outrageous.

"$550, but only if you send me a pair of Reebok sneakers from the United States," he replied, with a perfectly serious look. Apparently a pair of Reeboks was a luxury in Turkey, practically unaffordable to this social climber.

My look of disapproval began to raise his ire. "$450 plus Reeboks," he continued. My silence seemed to annoy him.

"All right, then, $350 and no Reeboks," he concluded, informing me that the store had just opened and that I would receive this handmade rug at a bargain because the first customer is always a sign of good luck in Turkey.

The bargaining was over and we shook hands. I was the proud owner of a double knotted 100 percent wool Turkish rug, its medallion design featuring contrasting light brown and blue colors. The pattern indicated that the rug was made in eastern Turkey, possibly by Kurds.

I was assured that the rug would be sent duty free, at the shop's expense, and that it would arrive at its destination within ten days. My disbelief was confirmed when I learned that four weeks later the rug still had not arrived in the United States. I had purchased the rug by credit card and months later, after my official complaint, a package arrived at my home, without explanation or apology. So much for good luck!

10

Pergamum: The Athens of the East

TRAVEL ENTRY #35: FROM SELCUK TO BERGAMA

THE ROAD TO BERGAMA (ancient Pergamum) passes through Izmir, Turkey's third-largest city. Izmir was once known as Smyrna, and, like Pergamum and Ephesus, was among the seven Christian churches addressed in the book of Revelation. It is here that Polycarp, bishop of Smyrna, was martyred in 155 CE. Located some eighty miles north of Selcuk, Izmir is also known as the birthplace of Homer. Under the Romans the city became one of the three most important cities of western Asia, together with Pergamum and Ephesus. When Ephesus finally lost its harbor in Byzantine times, Smyrna, located at the head of a thirty-mile long gulf, remained the only large port in the region. During the Middle Ages Smyrna was the last of the Christian cities in Asia Minor to hold out against the Muslim Turks, falling finally in 1424.

I arrived in Bergama, a city of twenty-five thousand, shortly after noon and immediately purchased a bus ticket for an overnight ride to Istanbul, scheduled for eleven o'clock that night. I wasn't sure how much sightseeing awaited me in Pergamum, but an afternoon and evening seemed sufficient to view the ruins of the ancient acropolis (known as Pergamon to the Greeks and as Pergamum to the Romans) and perhaps to sample some of the town's atmosphere. For a small fee the manager of a cafeteria near the bus station agreed to store my backpack while I toured the ruins.

Since I didn't have time to look for a tourist office, I simply followed the store manager's suggestion and took a taxi to the summit of the acropolis. I was glad for the advice, for during the next few hours I would expend a great deal of energy, covering an archaeological area of four square miles. Emerging from the taxi, I beheld a magnificent spectacle. I felt like a diamond cutter trembling at the gaze of a priceless, multifaceted gem, for each view provided greater allure. Aided by a manual, I began my self-guided tour.

EXPLANATORY ENTRY #18: ANCIENT PERGAMUM

The site, sixteen miles from the Aegean coast, is isolated and not favorably situated. It consists of a fertile meadow with an eagle's nest-like natural acropolis (1,100 feet in height) at its center. Before the invasion by the Persians in 540 BCE, Pergamum was a small city under the rule of the Lydians. It did not become important, however, until the Hellenistic age.

Upon the death of Alexander the Great in 323 BC, his empire was divided among his generals. Western Anatolia came under the control of General Lysimachus, who turned Pegamum into a military base under the leadership of Philetairos, a trusted diligent officer. Lysimachus favored him so highly that he entrusted to him for safekeeping three thousand pieces of gold, his share of Alexander the Great's treasury. Philetairos promptly allied himself with another of Alexander's generals, Seleucus, king of Syria, thereby appropriating the treasure and laying the foundations of Pergamene independence and prosperity. Both conditions were aided by Pergamum's strategic location between the zones of influence of Syria in the east and Macedonia in the west. In their balancing act between the two, the kings of Pergamum later enlisted the power of Rome, to which the last king of Pergamum, Attalos III, eventually bequeathed his kingdom in 133 BCE. Pergamum continued to prosper and develop, first as the capital and then as the second city of the Roman province of Asia, after Ephesus.

Between 281 and 263 BCE, Philetairos ruled the city, using the treasure to construct a city of impressive beauty. Five monarchs, known as the Attalid dynasty, ruled Pergamum after Philetairos. Under these kings, the city became a center of arts and science, possessing a strong and disciplined army and a rich treasury.

The reign of Eumenes II (197–159) was the golden age of Pergamum. The reputation of Pergamene poets, philosophers, scientists, and scholars rivaled that of Athens and Alexandria. Eumenes II, called the "Pericles of Pergamum," expanded and fortified the city, enlarging the library and the Temple of Zeus as well other monuments and buildings on the acropolis. The Lower Agora and the Grand Gymnasium were also built at this time. A mile away, on the plain below the acropolis, the famous Asclepion was enlarged, making it capable of serving the many patients that arrived from all over the Mediterranean. The Asclepion eventually became the most famous hospital in the world. During the following century the city expanded rapidly on the plain at the foot of the acropolis, attaining a population estimated at two hundred thousand.

In Hellenistic times, the Attalids made Pergamum one of the most important and beautiful of all Greek cities. King Attalos I (241–197 BCE) determined to make his capital city "the Athens of Asia Minor" with a massive building project. A prosperous economy made it possible for Attalos and his successors to employ some of the finest architects in the Hellenistic world. The monumental structures that rose on the acropolis of Pergamum were believed by many to be superior to those of Athens itself.

The acropolis is one of the most outstanding examples of city planning in that period. In addition to the massive royal palace, the buildings included the Temple to Athena, which housed an impressive art collection, and a library that was second in size only to the library of Alexandria in Egypt. A huge amphitheater sloped down to the Stoa, a column-lined promenade that looked out over the plain below.

The Pergamene kings built the city upon leveled natural terraces, never altering the land in any significant way. Each king aided the city's growth by adding new buildings. By the second century BCE the city consisted of two sections: the Upper City, at the summit, and the Lower City, half-way down and at the foot of the acropolis. The main street, which started at the foot of the hill in the south, wound up to the peak by following the lie of the terraces.

The city was administered and defended by the Upper City, which included a garrison and arsenals at the northernmost point, royal palaces in the east, and the religious buildings and theater in the west. The main street, which ran through the center of the city, separated the religious buildings from the administrative and military buildings. The Upper City spread out around the theater, the city's most spectacular site.

The summit of the acropolis was carefully selected for the royal palaces. Five water cisterns as well as the arsenal were also placed at the summit. On the second level, below the summit, stood the Temple of Athena, the Library, and the Temple of Trajan. On the third level from the summit stood the Zeus altar and the Theater, the steepest amphitheater in the world. The fourth and lowest terrace included the Agora, the Gymnasium, and the Temple of Demeter. All of these buildings extended from south to north and faced west. The people lived in the Lower City, which included the fourth terrace with its public facilities.

Three monumental theaters were built in Pergamum at different times. The most important theater, the only one now excavated, is the one built into the steep face of the hill in the Hellenistic period. Built to accommodate ten thousand spectators, the theater is exceptionally high, with seventy-eight rows of seats. Spread out like a fan above the theater are three of the city's most impressive monumental structures: the Temple of Trajan, the Temple of Athena, and the Altar of Zeus. Facing the setting sun and located on the most attractive site on the acropolis, each structure could be seen from any spot of the Lower City spread across the plain during Roman times.

The famous Pergamene library, built by Eumenes II, was located nearby. The library, like its counterpart in Ephesus, had a large reading room on the east end, enabling readers to take advantage of the morning light. Wooden shelves surrounded the salon on three sides. As in most libraries built in antiquity, the side walls were double-layered with a space between to protect the books from humidity.

The typical book in the classical period was in the form of a scroll made from a long strip of papyrus about a foot wide, rolled around a stick. The kings of Pergamum overcame the inconvenience and awkwardness of the scroll by inventing a form known as a codex, what we know today as the paged book. The Attalids, for whom book collecting was almost a mania, eventually compiled a collection totaling two hundred thousand volumes. The greatest competitor of the Pergamum library was the library in Alexandria. According to an ancient writer, when relations between Pergamum and Alexandria deteriorated, the Egyptian king Ptolemy stopped exportation of papyrus, found almost exclusively in Egypt. The king of Pergamum thereupon resorted to the use of skins, as the Ionians had done long before; and from this "Pergamene paper" came the word "parchment." When the troops of Julius Caesar burned down the great library in Alexandria, Mark Antony consoled Cleopatra by shipping the entire collection of books from Pergamum to Alexandria.

The Altar of Zeus is the most important monument on the acropolis dating from the Hellenistic period. It was built in 190 BCE, during the city's golden age, in gratitude to Zeus and as a memorial of the victory against the Galatians. The white marble altar stood on a podium nearly twenty feet high, on a foundation of walls 120 feet by 112 feet in size. The most interesting feature of the horseshoe-shaped structure was the 400-foot-long frieze along the outer wall, considered the ancient world's most beautiful example of Hellenistic sculpture. The main theme depicted on the frieze is the victory of the Olympian gods against giants (Gigantomachy) and forces of the underworld. Since the giants were considered the sons of the Mother Earth (Gaia), their defeat depicts the final triumph by Zeus over Gaia, seen as the end of the matriarchal epoch and the establishment of a patriarchal order and culture.

By depicting the victory of the Greek gods over the giants, the altar symbolically celebrated the triumph of the city of Pergamum in the newly conquered lands of Anatolia and proclaimed the city as the legitimate continuation of the Greek civilization, a second Athens far from mainland Greece. One can also understand the Gigantomachy to designate a conflict between the rational behavior represented by the gods and the savage immoderate nature represented by the giants.

Today all that remains of the original Altar of Zeus are its foundations. Byzantine conquerors tore down the altar in the eighth century CE and used the marble as building material for a wall. Slabs from the frieze remained embedded in the wall for a thousand years until 1871, when they were discovered by Karl Humann, the German engineer in charge of constructing a railroad from Istanbul to Izmir. That year, when Humann first saw a fragment of the frieze brought to him by one of his workers, marks the beginning of the period of excavations in Pergamum. A year later the fragment was taken to Berlin and identified by the curator of the museum there as important. In 1877, after permission to excavate was granted by the Ottoman administration, excavations began at the Altar of Zeus, where the fragment had been discovered.

The fragile political condition of the Ottomans, including numerous uprisings as well as a war with Russia, increased the influence of the Germans over the Ottoman Empire. An agreement in 1878 added to German archaeological rights in Turkey, including a financial transaction that allowed all finds relating to the Pergamum altar to go to Berlin. Visitors today can go to the Pergamum Museum in Berlin and view the reconstructed altar. A vast gallery holds a U-shaped classical building enclosing a flight of marble steps and topped by double rows of Ionic columns. On the base of this structure and continuing around the walls of the vast gallery runs the extraordinary marble frieze carved in high relief and measuring 7½ feet high and 390 feet long. A large array of figures, in amazingly good shape, portrays the mythical battle symbolizing the victory of civilization over barbarism.

It has been suggested that this Altar of Zeus is the "throne of Satan" mentioned in the letter to Pergamum in the Book of Revelation: "I know where you dwell, where Satan's throne is" (2:13). "Satan's throne," however, may have been less a reference to this altar than to the city of Pergamum itself, the seat of Roman authority in the area. Some scholars interpret this scripture as a reference to emperor worship, depicted by the nearby Temple of Trajan.

One of the most important ruins at Pergamum is the Asclepion, named in honor of Asclepius, a son of Apollo, and god of healing and medicine. In accordance with a hygienic tradition, it was built outside the city, on a small plateau lying about a mile away.

The earliest temple of Asclepius was built in Pergamum as early as the fourth century BCE, though most of the remains visible today date to the second century CE. A sacred road, called Via Tecton, traversed the lower city and ended at a wide forecourt with a gated entryway. The columned road was one-half mile long and sixty feet wide. It was here that the sick gathered from far and near to be healed. The gate controlled access to the sanctuary, like a doctor's waiting room. To the right, a large, square-shaped building was the emperor's quarters, which also served as a library. The circular building on the left of the entrance was the Temple of Asclepius. It resembled the Pantheon in Rome, built twenty years earlier. To the left of the temple is the therapy building, constructed later than the temple and also cylindrical in shape. The two-storied building had niches for beds, where patients prayed until they fell asleep.

This Asclepion was one of the main medical centers of antiquity. Galen (130–200 CE), the most famous physician of antiquity after Hippocrates of Cos (fifth century BCE), was born at Pergamum and practiced in the Asclepion. Aelius Aristides, orator, hypochondriac, and chronic invalid, stayed here for thirteen years around the middle of the second century CE, receiving treatment and writing about it. Though treatment focused on three elements—diet, hot and cold baths, and exercise—the Asclepion encouraged many of today's holistic healing techniques, including massage, auto-suggestion, and herbal remedies.

Sleeping in the sanctuary and having dreams analyzed was part of the cure, as were mud and hot baths, sport, reading, and theater.

Therapy began even before one entered the Asclepion. The sick usually walked barefoot down the sacred road to the center, envisioning each step as initiating the therapy that carried them from death toward life. The outside portal contained a hopeful maxim: "Here only death is forbidden entrance." Inside, priests used techniques based on suggestion to cure illness. After bathing in the pool's sacred waters, a drugged patient would be carried along a subterranean tunnel to a therapy building, equipped with speaking tubes through which priest-doctors would whisper advice. An obese patient, for example would awaken in the morning convinced that the god himself had prescribed more exercise and less food. A large theater and library provided recreation for the patients. Concerts and plays were part of the prescribed treatment as well.

The Asclepion was not only a place for the sick but also a spa, a religious sanctuary, and an intellectual center. Three pools in front of the theater were used for bathing. Water from the sacred spring still flows today. Analysis of the water demonstrates that it contains sufficient radioactivity to be effective in treatment. The 270-foot-long tunnel that extends from the sacred fountain to the therapy building was kept very still and dimly lit. Water from the spring ran down the steps into the tunnel, its trickling sound enhancing the mystical atmosphere.

TRAVEL ENTRY #36: QUITE A SCARE

I received quite a scare when I returned from my self-guided tour. As I walked through Bergama, two teenagers joined me, both anxious to try out their limited knowledge of English and each looking for some adventure that quiet Sunday evening. When we approached the bus station, I noticed that the shop where I had stored my backpack was closed. The doors were locked, the lights turned off, and inside, leaning against the back wall, stood my pack. My heart began to race as I pondered my options. I had already purchased a ticket for an overnight ride to Istanbul, and the bus was scheduled to leave within the hour. I wondered how I might contact the manager. A few people around the bus station called him "a bad man" and said he could not be trusted.

One of the boys told me to follow him and after walking a few blocks we arrived at the police station. Turks, it seems, are afraid of the police, and in situations of harassment or fraud, they generally side with foreigners. My companion's intervention led to a quick response. Luckily I had requested a receipt for storing my pack, which I showed to the police. Within minutes I was in the back seat of a police car, heading for the bus station. By then, a light was on in the cafeteria and the manager, roused by phone or by courier, had hurried back to the shop, reopening it to avoid an incident.

The problem was undoubtedly caused by miscommunication, for the shopkeeper may have expected me to return after a brief visit, whereas I had assumed that the shop was open indefinitely, due to its proximity to the bus depot. A friendly lad had helped me avoid a potentially ugly incident and I was happy to proceed on schedule.

11

Istanbul: Europe or Asia?

AT 6:00 A.M., MY eyes heavy from the restless sleep of a nine-hour overnight bus ride, I peered out the window at the fabled skyline of Istanbul. The bus was crossing the Bosporus Bridge, a vital suspension bridge that connects the Asian section of Istanbul with the better known European side. Istanbul, the only city situated in two continents, lies at the crossing of the east-west land route from Asia to Europe and the north-south sea route from the Black Sea to the Mediterranean. It straddles the Bosporus Strait, the strategic nineteen-mile-long waterway that connects the Black Sea to the Sea of Marmara, and through the Dardanelles to the Aegean.

Istanbul! The name conjures enchantment and intrigue. Arguably the center of the planet, for more than two thousand five hundred years the site has stood—sometimes as bridge, sometimes as barrier—between conflicting surges of religion, culture, and imperial power. For most of those years the city was one of the most coveted in the world.

The old, walled city of Istanbul stands on seven hills of a triangular peninsula surrounded by "the three seas": the Golden Horn, the Bosporus, and the Sea of Marmara. The Golden Horn, a slender four-mile-long gulf, divides the historic city from newer sections to the north. The broad Bosporus, from half a mile to five miles wide, divides European Istanbul from Asian Istanbul, one third of the population residing on the Asian side. The ancient city's location astride the main crossroads of world commerce was ideal. Its one landward side, well protected by nearly impregnable walls, was easily defendable. From the fourth century CE the city was regarded as the center of the old world and for one thousand six hundred years it served as capital of three successive empires: Roman, Byzantine, and Ottoman. During that period over 120 emperors and sultans reigned from Istanbul.

EXPLANATORY ENTRY #19: CONSTANTINOPLE: THE ERA OF CONSTANTINE THE GREAT

Geographical advantage alone does not make great cities. Despite the incomparable excellence of its site, the city of Byzantium-Constantinople-Istanbul had to wait for centuries until the emergence of the right historical conditions and the personal choice of one man, Constantine, turned it almost overnight into a world center.[1]

Constantine was one of those rulers who changed the world. After overcoming the army of the rival emperor, Licinius, in 324, Constantine became sole ruler over the entire Roman Empire. Six weeks later he went to Byzantium and traced the boundaries of a much-enlarged city, tripling the size of Byzantium. The city would serve as the capital of the eastern empire and be named New Rome. Like Rome, the city had seven hills, but unlike its predecessor, the city and its empire would be founded upon the Christian religion. To mark the distinction, Constantine changed the name to Constantinople and officially dedicated the city to the Virgin Mary.

Constantine's choice of capital had profound effects upon the ancient Greek and Roman worlds. It displaced the power center of the Roman Empire, moving it eastward, and achieved the first lasting unification of Greece. Culturally, Constantinople fostered a fusion of Oriental and Occidental custom, art, and architecture. The religion was Christian, the organization Roman, and the language and outlook Greek. The concept of the divine right of kings, rulers who were defenders of the faith—as opposed to the king as divine himself—evolved here. As the centuries passed, Constantinople, seat of empire, was to become as important as the empire itself.

When Constantine died in 337, the city was half built and contained a bulging population. But it had a big problem. Though surrounded by water, there was no source of drinkable water within the city precincts. The solution—building an aqueduct system far larger than Rome's—required one of the greatest engineering feats of ancient times, for water had to be brought from a greater distance than anywhere else in the classical Mediterranean world. The task fell to an ambitious emperor named Valens (364–378), who constructed a system four hundred

---

1. For a chronology of Greek history, including that of Byzantium/Constantinople/Istanbul from antiquity to the present, consult Appendix C.

miles in length, including a vast array of tunnels and bridges, equal to a combination of all the Roman Empire's previous aqueducts.

Bringing water into the city solved one problem but created another: water storage. Because vacant land in Constantinople was scarce, engineers solved the problem by creating an underground storage system more elaborate than any other in the ancient world. They dug more than 150 subterranean cisterns, supported by massive columns, in the troughs between the city's hills. The ingenious plan provided flat building surfaces upon which new structures could be built. The solution came just in time, for by the end of the fifth century the population of Constantinople neared five hundred thousand, a far greater number than any other city in Western Europe.

In addition to its political and economic impact, the city also played an important ecclesiastical role. The first six ecumenical church councils were convened in or near Constantinople. In 381 it became the seat of a patriarch who was second only to the bishop of Rome. To this day, the patriarch of Constantinople continues as the nominal head of the Eastern Orthodox Church.

Under Justinian I (527–565), Constantinople enjoyed a period of unparalleled prosperity. The world's most important trade routes passed through the city. Protected by the strongest, most sophisticated system of city walls ever built, it sat like a vault within a bank, the richest city in the world. Justinian was an energetic and conscientious administrator who took a direct interest in the smallest details of responsibility, yet was capable of grand and sweeping concepts. Within two years after becoming emperor, he established a number of juridical commissions charged with emending, recodifying, and imposing an orderly system upon all previous Roman law. The result was the famed Corpus Juris Civilis, which would in future ages become the model for the legal system of nearly every European nation.

Justinian had a gift for surrounding himself with the most capable people of his day—administrators, lawyers, architects, generals, and not least, his wife Theodora. A former burlesque dancer, she was an improbable consort. But she was beautiful, wily, and intelligent. On his accession to the Roman Imperial throne in 527, Justinian made her co-ruler, thereby sending shock waves through the Byzantine aristocracy. It appears they ruled the empire as equals, a decision that proved wise, for she showed a notable talent for governance.

Justinian fashioned a legacy built upon restoring the glory of bygone Rome. He sent armies to reconquer lost territories, and at home went on a construction spree, supported by massive taxation. In January 532, Justinian faced a great crisis in his city, caused by rioting at a chariot race. About thirty thousand rioters were reportedly killed. The Nika riots or Nika Revolt was the most violence Constantinople had ever seen to that point, with nearly half the city being burned or destroyed and thousands of people dead. As the capital lay in ruins, Justinian saw an opportunity to cement his legacy forever. From the ruins of Constantinople would rise one of the world's most magnificent churches: the church of the Holy Wisdom, or Hagia Sophia. A triumph of skill and an inspiring monument to Constantine's faith, the church was the largest religious structure of its time.

The first Hagia Sophia had been erected in 360 CE, during the reign of Constantius II, son of the great Constantine. The wooden building was destroyed by fire in 404, and then rebuilt. When it burned again during the Nika riots, Justinian hired a physicist, Isidore of Miletus, and a mathematician, Anthemius of Tralles as architects and placed on them two demands: to build as quickly as possible and to erect a structure unlike any other on earth. Construction began six weeks after the riots. Justinian's basilica was at once the culminating architectural achievement of late antiquity and the first masterpiece of Byzantine architecture. The design was revolutionary in concept and unprecedented in scale. Utilizing a workforce of ten thousand, the building rose far faster than any other on that scale. Justinian's architects were able to construct a gigantic dome that appeared to hover in midair. The dome rose 184 feet, thirty feet higher than the Statue of Liberty, and created a nave that measured 229 feet by 245 feet, a massive open space.

The completed church was a masterpiece of Byzantine art, its halls embellished with gold mosaics, tapestries, and polished marble, porphyry, and ivory. By day, light filtered through the unbroken arcade of arched windows in the massive dome, and at night the interior glowed with the flickering light of hundreds of oil lamps in elaborate chandeliers.

From the outset of his reign, Justinian set out to restore the Roman Empire to its ancient glories. The last Roman (Western) emperor had abdicated the western throne in 476. For years the empire's borders had been receding. Vandals ruled North Africa; the Franks held sway in Gaul and the Visigoths in Spain; Britain, abandoned long ago by the Romans, was now under assault by the Germanic Saxons, and Italy, the cradle of Roman civilization, was in the hands of the Ostrogoths. Despite Justinian's efforts to intervene in the Italian peninsula, the countryside was devastated by years of war, leaving its great cities—Rome, Naples, and Milan—all but deserted. In 565, the old emperor died, and within three years the Lombards, Germanic warriors who had helped Justinian put down the Ostrogoths, began the push that would enable them to become the rulers of northern Italy.

Although Constantinople would survive and experience a second golden age in the centuries to come, the eastern empire was also threatened as the sixth century drew to a close. In the Balkans, Avars, Bulgars, and Slavs roamed the land. And in 570 CE a boy named Muhammad was born in the city of Mecca, giving birth to a militant new faith.

The Latin invasion of Constantinople in 1204, during the course of the Fourth Crusade, is a dismal chapter in the history of the city. The battle-ready crusader army had little problem conquering the city. On Good Friday, April 9, 1204, the crusaders sacked the city and immediately began robbing it of its treasures. The looting, which went on for years, included such holy places as churches and monasteries. The period of Latin rule (1204–1261) proved to be the most disastrous in the history of Constantinople. The city was stripped of everything valuable and did not regain its prosperity until after its eventual conquest by the Ottomans in 1453.

Like Mecca, Istanbul was once forbidden to foreigners—unless they were accompanied by one of the Sultan's janissary guards. It was this fabled city that I had come to see. Within the span of a mere two days, I intended to visit sites located on the city's seven hills, including world-famous mosques, museums, Topkapi Palace, the Greek Patriarchal Church, and of course, Hagia Sophia. I also hoped to visit the Great Covered Bazaar and sample Turkish culinary specialties.

A three-mile ride by *dolmus* (shared taxi; *dolma* means "stuffed," and that is the usual sensation) brought me from the Topkapi Bus Terminal, just beyond the city walls, to Sultanahmet Square. This district, close to Hagia Sophia (the Turkish name is Ayasofya), is the historical, cultural, and tourist center. A clerk in the tourist office suggested that I try the

Interyouth Hostel, across the street from Hagia Sophia and a five-minute walk from Topkapi Palace and the Blue Mosque.

EXPLANATORY ENTRY #20: SELECTED ATTRACTIONS

Topkapi Palace

One of Istanbul's greatest attractions is the sultan's *seraglio* (Topkapi Saray or Palace), enclosed behind a fortified wall at the eastern tip of the peninsula. The commanding site, originally occupied by the acropolis of classical Byzantium, so impressed Mehmed II, the conqueror of Constantinople, that he built a palace there, overlooking the confluence of the Bosporus, the Sea of Marmara, and the Golden Horn. The Byzantine emperors, with their palace a little to the south, on the site now partly occupied by the Blue Mosque, had contented themselves with only a view of the Sea of Marmara.

Topkapi Palace was not a single edifice but a collection of buildings grouped around a series of courtyards. Though primarily the residence of the reigning sultan, Topkapi also served as the center of government, housing the state mint, the archives, and the highest university of the realm. Inside its walls there gradually grew an elegant compound of pavilions, summer houses, audience rooms, residences, libraries, bath houses, kitchens, stables, and barracks. Over the centuries sultans added to the architectural extravagance, until the palace contained four courtyards and five thousand residents, many of them concubines and eunuchs, served by some twenty thousand slaves.

During the course of the Ottoman Empire, thirty-six sultans came to the throne. From the sixteenth century onward, sultans also bore the title of Caliph, the religious head of the Islamic world. For four hundred years this place of mystery and romance remained the center of Ottoman rule. Today, after fifty years of restoration, the palace has been transformed into a museum of incomparable beauty, exhibiting priceless artifacts and works of art.

Topkapi Palace, a vast complex of buildings surrounded by three miles of walls, is an ideal place to begin one's tour of the old city. Its four courtyards are connected with one another by monumental doors. The first and outermost court was once used by the Janissaries—members of the sultan's elite guard. The actual entrance to the Topkapi Palace site is the Gate of Salutation, through which one enters the second court, originally used primarily for the business of government. During certain state ceremonies, attended by as many as five thousand people, absolute silence prevailed. When the sultan was present, the imperial throne was placed in front of the third gate—the Gate of Felicity—and all those present would stand facing him with their hands tied before them in a gesture of submission.

The third courtyard was the private court of the sultans. Surrounding this court were the palace university, which trained candidates for positions of responsibility in the government's vast empire; the throne room, served by hand-picked deaf-mutes for security reasons; the sultan's treasury, consisting of four rooms filled with jewels; and the sanctuary of Holy Islamic relics. The Treasury holds some of the most famous and spectacular jewels in the world, including the eighty-four-carat Spoonmaker diamond—reputed to have been found by a pauper and traded for three wooden spoons—and the famous Topkapi Dagger. In 1747, the Sultan had this dagger made for Nadir Shah of Persia, but the Shah was assassinated before the emissary had left the Ottoman Empire's boundaries and so the sultan retained it. There are three large emeralds in the hilt and the sheath is worked with diamonds and enamel. This dagger was the subject of the film *Topkapi*. Visitors are generally not aware that the Topkapi treasury is mostly false. Though the Turks insist, for patriotic reasons, that the egg-sized emeralds and other jewels on the daggers and swords are real, the original jewels were pilfered years ago.

The Holy Islamic relics in the Pavilion of the Holy Mantle were brought from Egypt in the sixteenth century. These relics served in part as the symbols of the caliphate, which passed to the Ottoman sultans with the conquest of Egypt. They consist of personal articles of the prophet Muhammad, including his staff, his mantle, his teeth, his beard, his sword and other relics that are known as the Sacred Trusts. These include swords belonging to the first four caliphs and one of the oldest manuscript copies of the Qur'an. Muslims consider this collection of relics as holy, the repository of a supernatural power that strengthened the might of Ottoman warriors.

The fourth courtyard, overlooking the Sea of Marmara, was more a private garden of the sultan. It was dotted with small, elegant summer houses, pavilions, and pools scattered among lovely gardens. In one such pavilion, known as the Golden Cage, the closest relatives of the reigning sultan lived—under virtual house arrest. The custom, a benevolent variation to the older custom of murdering all possible rivals to the throne, helped maintain the status quo.

The most visited section of the palace is the Harem, a maze of nearly four hundred rooms grouped around the sultan's private quarters, of which forty have been restored and are available for viewing by the public. Here the sultan could enjoy the company of his concubines uninterrupted by his household staff or ministers of state. Concubines were hand-picked from the most beautiful and healthy girls of various races or were given to the sultan as gifts. Admitted to the harem at an early age, these girls were educated and trained under the strictest discipline and according to clearly defined ranks and positions. At the bottom were the novices, and above them a series of grades—the privileged ones, the favored, the fortunates—through which a young woman could rise according to her attractions and ability. If a fortunate bore the sultan a child, she earned the title of princess.

There was a down side to the question of succession, however, since only one son could inherit the throne. In the race for the sultanate, there could be only one winner; the losers faced instant execution. The administration of the harem was supervised by a woman called the mistress of the household, but the supreme ruler was the princess mother, the mother of the reigning sultan. During the reign of a weak sultan, members of the harem often indulged in power plays and intrigue.

Hagia Sophia (Ayasofya)

When the Turks took possession of Constantinople, they covered the summit of the seven hills with domes and minarets, changing forever the character of the city. Like their predecessors, the new rulers loved the city and spent much of their treasure on its embellishment. Twenty-five churches, the largest legacy from the capital of the vanquished Byzantine Empire, were converted to mosques, constituting a significant number of the 450 mosques in Istanbul.

The largest of these churches, Hagia Sophia, since converted to a museum, is still considered one of the great buildings of the world. Its dome, one of the most magnificent in the world, was also the world's largest until the dome of St. Peter's was built in Rome one thousand years later. The current structure, dating from 537 CE, was converted into a mosque in 1453 and became a museum in 1935. Hagia Sophia owes its survival not only to the care taken by Turks to preserve it as a place of worship, but also to the fact that Muslim ritual requires a minimum of alteration, beyond the removal of images and the addition of a prayer niche and pulpit.

Upon entering the nave, one is immediately struck by the structure's vastness, augmented by the seemingly preternatural lighting. The huge dome, appearing to hang unsupported from the sky, is particularly impressive. The vastness was intentional, for Justinian and his architects aimed to exceed the Temple of Solomon in grandeur. The darkness, which adds both gloom and mystery to the interior, is partly the product of history. Windows have been blocked, gleaming gold and silver removed, and mosaics and other decorations whitewashed, causing shafts of light to exaggerate the effects and ravages of time.

The building contains over one hundred columns of different shapes and sizes dating back to antiquity and brought from ruins across the empire to be used in the construction of Hagia Sophia. Eight of the largest green marble columns came from the Temple of Artemis in Ephesus; eight red porphyry columns—two in each bay—were brought from the Temple of Jupiter at Baalbek, Lebanon, while some of the columns in the second story are from Troy. The deep-grooved marble shafts create a beautiful interplay of shadow and light. The walls and floors are highly colorful as well, decorated with striking marble. The circular mosaic pattern on the floor beneath the dome is original from Justinian's time and marks the coronation spot of the Byzantine emperors.

The Blue Mosque and the Suleymaniye Mosque

Across from Hagia Sophia, next to the site of the ancient hippodrome, stands the mosque of Sultan Ahmed. Built in 1616, nearly 1,100 years after the construction of the Hagia Sophia church, this royal mosque was clearly built to outdo its Justinian rival. Known to foreigners as the Blue Mosque, the building is as grand and beautiful a monument to Ottoman Islam as Hagia Sophia is to Byzantine Christianity. The mosque was deliberately sited to face Hagia Sophia. Since the architect was unable to construct a bigger dome than Hagia Sophia's, he made the mosque splendid by the perfect proportion of domes, semidomes, and minarets. The mosque became known in the west as the Blue Mosque because of the deep blue tiles that adorn the interior. The Sultan Ahmed Mosque is the only one in Turkey with six minarets. When the number of minarets was revealed, the Sultan was criticized for presumption, since this was the same number as at the sacred mosque in Mecca. Ahmed therefore avoided religious controversy by supplying the money and the workers necessary to erect a seventh minaret at the Mecca mosque.

If the Blue Mosque, built by a pupil of the architect Sinan, is Istanbul's most beautiful, the largest and most dignified is the Suleymaniye Mosque, built by Sinan himself, the greatest of all Turkish architects. Located on Istanbul's third hill, overlooking the Golden Horn, it is the mosque dearest to Turkish hearts. Among its outbuildings, the mosque includes both the mausoleum of Sultan Suleiman the Magnificent (1520–1566), the most celebrated of all Ottoman rulers, and the less ostentatious tomb of imperial architect Sinan, the key figure in Suleiman's vast building enterprise.

EXPLANATORY ENTRY #21: ISTANBUL ARCHAEOLOGICAL MUSEUM

One of the goals of my sabbatical trip was to visit museums and sites associated with the archaeology and religion of the Middle East, and the Istanbul Archaeological Museum is among the most prominent museums in the world. Housed in three buildings just inside the first court of Topkapi Palace, the museum has an excellent collection of Greek and Roman artifacts, including finds from Ephesus and Troy. Near the entrance is a statue of a lion representing the only piece salvaged from the British archaeologists of the Mausoleum of Halicarnassus, one of the Seven Wonders of the Ancient World. The museum also displays works of Sumerian, Assyrian, and other Near-Eastern civilizations and is said to have the second largest collection of cuneiform inscriptions. One tablet contains the Treaty of Kadesh, the earliest known peace treaty, concluded between the Hittites and Egyptians in 1269 BCE, around the time of Moses and the Exodus. Written in Akkadian, the international language of the day, the treaty represents an alliance against the "Sea Peoples," displaced Europeans—including the biblical Philistines—who defeated the Hittites and ended their six-hundred-year rule in the Anatolian Middle East.

The museum features several additional items associated with the biblical period. Among the most important are the Siloam Inscription from Hezekiah's Tunnel in Jerusalem, erected to commemorate the completion of the 1,750-foot-long tunnel around the year 710 BCE, and the Gezer Calendar, a small tablet dating to 925 BCE, inscribed in a paleo-Hebraic script. It was discovered in excavations of the city of Gezer, thirty miles northwest of Jerusalem, in the early 1900s. The calendar describes monthly or bi-monthly periods and attributes to each a duty such as harvest, planting or tending specific crops. The "calendar" appears to be a "school boy's exercise" and is one of the earliest examples of Hebrew writing. One of the most spectacular displays features a glazed-tile relief of a bull and dragon from the famous Ishtar Gate of ancient Babylon. The figures on these gates date to the period of Nebuchadnezzar II (604–562 BC), conqueror of Jerusalem. They represent animals sacred to the gods Hadad and Marduk.

The museum houses over one million objects, the most extraordinary of which are the monumental sarcophagi from the Royal Necropolis of Sidon (ancient Syria) that date as far back as the fourth century BCE. The most famous is the "Alexander Sarcophagus," covered with astonishingly advanced carvings of battles and the life of Alexander the Great, discovered in 1887 and once believed to have been that of the emperor himself. Though Alexander died in Babylon, he was not buried in the nearest royal tomb at Sidon, as some have alleged, but rather in Alexandria, Egypt, where his body was entombed in a golden coffin. The Alexander Sarcophagus is now thought to have been intended for the body of Sidon's last king, Abdalonymous, who was appointed by Alexander in 332 BCE. The sarcophagus is stunning, both in its artwork and its state of preservation. Archaeologists consider the Alexander Sarcophagus one of the most important creations of antiquity ever to be excavated. Indeed, this work of art is said to have inspired the construction of the museum it now adorns.

EXPLANATORY ENTRY #22:
BYZANTINE CHRISTIAN LEGACY

During my sabbatical travels, in addition to visiting museums and sites associated with the world of the Bible, I also targeted sites associated with the Catholic, Protestant, and Orthodox branches of Christianity. This entry provides theological and historical background on Eastern Orthodoxy, of central interest during my Istanbul stay.

Based on total numbers of adherents, Eastern Orthodoxy is the second largest Christian communion in the world after the Roman Catholic Church and the third largest grouping if Protestantism is counted as a whole. The most common estimate of the number of Eastern Orthodox Christians worldwide is nearly three hundred million.

The designation "Eastern" in the title initially seems confusing, since this branch of Christendom exists in countries across the globe. The term indicates the geographical and cultural center of gravity for Orthodox Christianity. After the expansion of Islam in the seventh century, Orthodoxy's center of gravity shifted northward to the countries of Eastern Europe where—in the Balkans and Russia—it continues to be the dominant Christian church. Orthodox cultural legacy also comes from the East. As the Christianity of the Greek-speaking half of the Roman Empire, it evolved a form of Christian life, theology, and worship that distinguished it from the Latin West and from the religious traditions of the Church of Rome from which it was formally separated in 1054.

The term "Orthodoxy" refers to continuity with the ancient churches of the East, the Greek-speaking churches of the Apostle Paul's ministry. To be Orthodox, therefore, is to hold "right" (*orthos*) "belief" (*doxa*), but Orthodox Christians are quick to observe that "orthodox" also means "right praise or worship," and any who have witnessed the Orthodox liturgy know that it is for Orthodoxy a distinctive sign of its identity, the basic form its religious experience takes, and a symbol of unity among its churches.

Because in many ways the Eastern Church stands midway between Roman Catholicism and Protestantism, it is more difficult to identify features within it that are clearly distinctive, but if we were to select two, the first would be its corporate view of the Church. Although all Christians accept the doctrine that they are members of one Body, the Eastern Church seems to take this notion more seriously than either Roman Catholicism or Protestantism. For Orthodox Christians, each believer is said to be working out his or her salvation in conjunction with the rest of the Church, not individually. The Russian branch of Orthodoxy has a saying to this effect: "One can be damned alone, but saved only with others." And Orthodoxy goes further. "Not only is the destiny of the individual bound up with the entire Church; it is responsible for helping to sanctify the entire world of nature and history. The welfare of everything in creation is affected to some degree by what each individual Christian contributes to or detracts from it."[2]

The other distinctive feature concerns administration. Whereas the administration of the Roman Church is hierarchical, the Eastern Church

---

2. Huston Smith, *The World's Religions* (San Francisco: HarperSanFrancisco, 1991), 354.

is more participatory, grounding more of its decisions in the laity. The clergy has its domain, the administration of the sacraments, but effective ecclesiastical authority is decentralized, and the line that separates clergy from the laity is thin. Priests need not be celibate. Even the titular or honorary head of the Eastern Church, the Patriarch of Constantinople, is no more that "first among equals," and the laity is known as the "royal priesthood."[3]

In 1453, when Constantinople fell to the Ottomans, the city was almost deserted. Mehmed II began to repopulate it with inhabitants from other conquered areas, including Greeks from the Aegean and the Greek mainland. The patriarchate was retained but moved in 1568 to its present location on the slope of Istanbul's fifth hill, in Saint George's Church in the Fener (originally Phanar) quarter, overlooking the Golden Horn.

According to Muslim belief, Christians as well as Jews are considered "People of the Book," meaning that their religion is seen as partly true but incomplete. Theoretically, People of the Book who lived under Muslim rule deserved consideration and freedom of worship, providing they submitted to the dominion of the caliphate and the Muslim political administration and paid taxes. But any Christian mission or proselytism among Muslims was considered a capital crime. In practice, however, Christians were reduced to a subject status; they were the *Rum millet*, the "Roman nation" conquered by Islam but enjoying certain privileges.

In 1454, the sultan allowed the election of a new patriarch, empowering him as head of the entire Christian *millet*, with the right to administer, tax, and exercise justice over all the Christians of the Ottoman Empire. Under the new system, the patriarch of Constantinople saw his jurisdiction and formal rights extended, both geographically and substantially.

The defeat of the Ottomans during World War I radically changed the structure of the Orthodox world. As a result of the Greco-Turkish War—a series of military events occurring during the partitioning of the Ottoman Empire after World War I (1919-1922)—the entire Greek population of Asia Minor was transferred to Greece. Nevertheless, a small Greek population currently remains in Istanbul. Despite drastic pressures over the past five centuries, there remains a consensus within the Orthodox Church that Constantinople's primacy of honor should continue as a symbol and instrument of church unity and cooperation.

3. Ibid., 354–55.

TRAVEL ENTRY #37: ISTANBUL'S FENER DISTRICT

The Kariye Museum

Following my tour of the buildings and monuments of the Sultanahmet district, I boarded a bus headed for the northwest corner of the old city. There, on one of the city's numerous hills, lies the Church of St. Savior in Chora, a tiny dirt-colored building now called the Kariye Museum. First a Byzantine church, then a mosque, and finally a museum, the ancient structure is considered the most interesting church after Hagia Sophia in Istanbul. The church is renowned for its fourteenth-century frescoes and mosaics, considered the most beautiful product of Byzantine Renaissance art in the world. The Kariye mosaics are wonderfully supple and human, and the millions of tiny tiles have the effect of brush strokes.

When I finally arrived, I was disappointed to learn that the museum closed at 4:30 p.m. I had only about a half hour to explore the site. After purchasing the lone remaining copy of the beautifully illustrated visitor's guide, replete with full color plates, I set about viewing as many of the mosaics as time allowed. Though the building had been used as a mosque for over four hundred years, many of the mosaics were preserved, as in the Hagia Sophia, by being plastered with whitewash; others were covered with wooden partitions and shown only on occasion to Christian visitors. Beginning in 1860, the priceless mosaics were repaired and restored. In 1948 the Byzantine Institute of America restored the sanctuary; the building opened as a museum ten years later.

The artwork, grouped in two cycles along the outer and inner narthex (vestibule), depicts episodes from the life of Christ and the life of the Virgin Mary; in a side chapel, a third cycle depicts saints, the Church, and the Day of Judgment. Taken collectively, the uncovered frescoes and mosaics represent, both in brilliance of color as well as in design, a culmination of late Byzantine art. More importantly, they are considered a portent, perhaps even the birth pang, of western art.

Searching for Saint George's Church

Forced to leave the Kariye Museum sooner than expected, I used the remaining hours of daylight pursuing a sabbatical goal: locating Saint George's Church, home of the Greek Orthodox Patriarchal Church. My search for the church turned into quite an adventure, for the only city map

Istanbul: Europe or Asia? 141

I possessed was imprecise; rough lines sketched the broad avenues and dots denoted historical sites and tourist attractions. Aware that I should head in a northeasterly direction, I eventually came across an imposing structure near the top slope of a hill that looked like an educational or religious facility. It was after 5:00 p.m. and no one was around, but the front door was open. I decided to look inside but could find no clear evidence of the building's use, other than a few pictures of young people on the walls of the classroom. The only writing I found indicated that the room was used by Greek-speaking students, a clue that I was on the right track. Eventually a custodian appeared and on seeing an intruder in the building he became angry and tried to frighten me away with loud shouts. But I had not come this far to be so easily dissuaded. Though we could not communicate verbally, I tried to convey to him my status as professor and clergyman and the nature of my search. Eventually, upon learning that the building was a private school, I guessed that the seat of the patriarchate was nearby.

My persistence paid off. The custodian took me outside and motioned for me to follow. After a ten-minute walk we came to the wall of a compound and continued until we arrived at a gate. A short conversation between my escort and the guard ended in an animated gesture by the guard and the closing of the gate. The hour was late and if I wanted to visit, I would have to return the following day. I thanked my reluctant companion for his help as he left for home.

Once again I was disheartened, for I knew I could not return. Here I stood, as close to the home of Eastern Orthodoxy as I might ever be, but the lateness of the hour prevented me from completing my quest to visit the three centers of Christianity. A wall separated me from my goal, much as invisible walls stand between Christians, preventing the unity of the "Body of Christ." As darkness fell, I followed the wall along the base of the hill toward the more familiar surroundings of Sultanahmet. After a short distance I noticed in the wall an opening, which led into the Orthodox compound. Thus, under cover of darkness, I made my way to the central square, and then to the door of St. George's Church.

The church, originally part of the convent of St. George before it became the seat of the Patriarch around 1600, is outwardly unimpressive, but its interior is lavishly decorated. The structure had sustained major damage throughout its history, including a fire in 1941, and for political reasons was not fully restored until 1991, two years after my visit. Its most precious objects, saved from successive fires, are the patriarchal throne (believed to date from the fifth century), some rare mosaic icons, and relics of Saints Gregory the Theologian and John Chrysostom.

In the twentieth century, with the fall of the Ottomans and the rise of modern Turkish nationalism, most of the Greek Orthodox population of Istanbul emigrated, leaving the patriarch in the anomalous position of a leader without a flock, at least locally. Today the Church of St George serves mainly as the symbolic center of the Ecumenical Patriarchate and as a center of pilgrimage for Orthodox Christians from Greece and other Orthodox countries. All that's left is a compound of nine buildings occupying less than an acre of property. Though I found the church locked, I felt I had reached a significant milestone in my sojourn.

Fifteen minutes later, while walking along the city's twisting alleyways, I entered a factory by mistake. The entrance looked like a regular road, but as soon as I entered the premises an employee standing by a doorway yelled out a warning. A crowd gathered as the worker, perhaps a guard, began demanding an apology for my error. Fearing that the incident could escalate into something ugly, I remained calm and thought to ask directions to the nearby Fatih Mosque (Mosque of the Conqueror), named after Mehmed II. With that question the mood changed dramatically. Suddenly everyone seemed supportive, for devout Muslims are required to honor the wishes of a non-Muslim to visit a mosque. Within minutes I was walking briskly up the summit of yet another of Istanbul's hills, following an escort toward the mosque.

TRAVEL ENTRY #38: FINAL MOMENTS IN ISTANBUL

The following day, as I walked through a hotel lobby, I heard the sound of familiar voices behind me. Turning around, I beheld Paul and Craig, my Mormon friends. A combination of events had prevented them from sailing to Israel or Egypt so they had given up their goal of visiting Israel and Jordan and had returned to Athens, where they boarded a train for Istanbul.

After catching up on the events of the past week, we decided to remain together until my departure for Ankara later that evening. Our sightseeing began with a tour of nearby Hagia Sophia; looking at the magnificent structure and its priceless artwork through the eyes of inquisitive college students preparing for careers in engineering heightened my appreciation of the site. Later, on our way to the Suleymaniye Mosque, we stopped at one of Istanbul's best-known landmarks, the Covered Bazaar, the oldest and largest covered marketplace in the world. The market is a giant labyrinth with about sixty streets and four thousand shops, cafés, and restaurants. In the past, the bazaar was the business and crafts center of the city where members of various guilds clustered in specified locations. However, during the nineteenth and twentieth centuries, the bazaar lost much of its status as the major business center of Istanbul. Nowadays it appeals mostly to tourists and those interested in Turkish handicrafts, but that still includes up to four hundred thousand shoppers daily.

Following a lavish meal at a popular Turkish restaurant—made additionally attractive by the affordable price of $3 per person—I bid a final farewell to my young traveling companions and headed toward the ferry that would transport me back to Asia.

12

Anatolian Civilizations

TRAVEL ENTRY #39: ARRIVAL IN ANKARA

By day the Bosporus strait is delightful; by night, its charm is even more alluring. Magnificent palaces, ancient seaside homes and mosques along its shores, as well as the two fortresses facing one another at its narrowest point, make the Bosporus a major tourist attraction.

The railway station at Haydarpasa, on the Asian side of Istanbul, is the point of departure for Anatolian travel. Although it is faster to travel to Ankara by bus, the overnight train seemed more attractive, particularly when I compared it to the nine-hour bus ride that had brought me to Istanbul two days earlier. I was in for another disappointment, however, for no sleeping compartments were available. The train trip proved to be as arduous and unpleasant as the overnight bus ride had been. The seats were uncomfortable and each car was crammed with passengers and luggage. The problem was compounded by malfunctioning heaters, forcing passengers to choose between searing heat and cold air blowing from opened windows. Sleep was fitful and rest nearly impossible. The interminable ride ended early the next morning.

Even though I was still in Turkey, Ankara proved to be far different from Istanbul. As I walked to the tourist office, a half mile from the train station, I paused to admire the parks and sports complexes, the carefully planned open spaces and broad avenues. People around me—students, bureaucrats, businessmen—all seemed more professional and moved more deliberately than did their counterparts elsewhere in Turkey.

At the tourist office I ran into a serious communication problem, for though the staff was friendly and helpful, no one spoke English. After attempts in several languages, we finally agreed on French, though no one spoke it fluently. I left with a helpful map, intended for German-speaking tourists, and a good sense of the bus schedules I needed to master in order to visit sites in central Turkey. I eventually located a suitable hotel room, close to the archaeological museum, and was relieved to finally remove my backpack, made much heavier over the past two weeks by the growing number of guidebooks and memorabilia I had collected.

According to legend, Ankara was founded by Phrygians in the eighth century BCE. Phrygian tradition names King Midas as the founder, but Pausanias (a Greek geographer of the second century CE) mentions that the city was actually far older, in line with artifacts discovered in the city, which reveal that it was inhabited in the second millennium BCE, during the period of Hittite rule. The city significantly grew in size and importance under the Phrygians and experienced a large growth in population following the mass migration from Gordion, the capital of Phrygia, after an earthquake severely damaged that city in 400 BCE.

In 278 BCE, the city, along with the rest of central Anatolia, was occupied by the Celtic race of Galatians, who were the first to make Ankara one of their main tribal centers. The Celtic element—a warrior aristocracy that ruled over Phrygian-speaking peasants—was probably relatively small in number, though the Celtic language (a language closely related to Welsh and Gaelic) continued to be spoken in Galatia for many centuries. It was to the inhabitants of this province, or at least to those Christians dwelling in the southern sections of this region, that Paul wrote the biblical Epistle to the Galatians. Phrygian rule was succeeded by Lydian and later by Persian rule, which lasted until the Persian defeat at the hands of Alexander the Great, who conquered the city in 333 BCE. The site was subsequently captured by the Romans. During the Middle Ages, until its capture by Seljuk Turks in 1227, Ankara was a main center of Christianity. In the early 1920s, Kemal Ataturk planned and directed the Turkish war of Independence from Ankara, and in 1923 the city became the capital of the new republic.

EXPLANATORY ENTRY #23:
ANATOLIAN CULTURAL TIMELINE

I had not come to Ankara to see the capital of Turkey. Nor had I come to view its ruins or historical monuments. What attracted me here was the extraordinary collection of antiquities in the Anatolian Civilizations Museum. The city's central location also makes it a convenient base for exploring the plateau's historic sites, particularly the ruins of Hattusa, the ancient capital of the Hittites 125 miles to the east, and those of Gordion, fifty miles to the west of Ankara.

Travelers interested in archaeology and antiquity will want to visit the Anatolian Civilizations Museum, which has a rich and beautifully arranged collection exhibited in a restored Ottoman covered bazaar. Its collection of Hittite art is the best in the world. In addition to large statues and reliefs of gods, kings, lions, and hunting scenes, there are small objects of superb craftsmanship: metal stags, bulls, goddess figurines, ceramic vessels, ivories, jewels, seals, and vessels made of glass. The museum houses a collection of artifacts that covers all of Anatolian history, from prehistoric to Roman times.[1]

The finds from the Paleolithic Age (500,000–15,000 BCE) indicate that Anatolia was densely populated throughout the entire period. At Karain Cave, eighteen miles northwest of Antalya, all phases of the Paleolithic are represented without interruption. The finest exhibits of the Paleolithic Age in the museum, including stone and bone tools, among them awls, needles, and ornaments, come from Karain.

The Neolithic period (9000–5500 BCE) is generally considered as the beginning of civilization. It was during this period that communities and villages emerged in Anatolia and across the Middle East. The most highly developed Neolithic center in Anatolia is a town named Catal Huyuk (*hoyuk* means *tel* or artificial mound), located thirty-two miles southeast of Konya. Excavations have uncovered construction levels belonging to a period between 6800 and 5700 BCE. In these levels all the houses were built according to a fixed pattern and plan, each with a large living room, a storage room, and a kitchen. Most houses were built with a flat roof that provided working space where the inhabitants prepared their winter food. Interestingly, houses did not have a door

---

1. For a detailed archaeological timeline of the entire Mediterranean world, including that of Anatolia, consult Appendix A.

but were entered through openings in the roofs reached with wooden ladders. After entering, residents pulled the ladder down into the house for safety. The main distinguishing features of these houses are the wall paintings and the bulls-head emblems on the walls. Most of these decorations are believed to have had cult associations, since bulls' heads were often a symbol of deity.

The people of Catal Huyuk buried their dead under the floors of their houses. Before being buried, the bodies of the dead were left out in the open so that birds could devour their flesh. The skeletons, in the fetal position, were then placed in burial jars. The most common explanation for burying the dead in this position is that it was a preparation for rebirth. But another possibility, in light of primal people's belief that birth was a result of death, could be that the dead were buried below the houses in this fashion as a means of enhancing the fertility of women. It is important to note that of the hundreds of skeletons found at Catal Huyuk, none show any evidence of having met a violent death. This implies that its inhabitants were a peaceful people.

Numerous finds from Catal Huyuk are exhibited at the museum in Ankara. The museum features frescoes, burial jars, hand-made pottery, necklaces made from stones and sea shells, obsidian mirrors, cosmetic articles, pottery, and textiles; indeed, the earliest known surviving textile was found in Catal Huyuk. Wall paintings depict people dressed in animal skins as well as in textiles made of wool, animal hair, or plant fibers. The finds from Catal Huyuk indicate that its inhabitants were skilled in crafts. There is also much to suggest that Catal Huyuk's society was matriarchal. Women played a more active role than men in agriculture, weaving, and the manufacture of wooden and metal artifacts, so evident at this site.

One of the most significant exhibits at the museum is the baked clay figure of the mother goddess with a halo, giving birth to a child. The bloated woman, squatting at the point of birth, is flanked by two leopards. This figure is one of the oldest known pieces of sculpture. Dating to the first half of the sixth millennium BCE, it might well be the earliest statuette of the Mother Goddess. There are clearly features here that make the figurine a prototype for later representations of Cybele and Artemis.

During the Chalcolithic Age (5500–3000 BCE), a considerable increase occurred in the number of towns in Anatolia. Several important advances occurred during this period. The Mother Goddess is clearly the primary deity, and many figurines of this goddess are now used in their religious rituals. The burials that were within the houses during the Neolithic period now take place outside the towns. The discovery of copper led to the development of trade between local and remote towns, with a network of trading centers where they exchanged commodities. The need for record-keeping resulted in the development of writing. Anatolia, the leader in urban development and civilization during the Neolithic period, lost its position towards the end of Chalcolithic Period, in part because Mesopotamia and Egypt had invented writing about one thousand years earlier and therefore reached a higher level of civilization.

By the start of the Early Bronze Age (3000–2000 BCE), the inhabitants of Anatolia learned how to make bronze by mixing copper and tin. From this alloy, together with copper, gold, silver, and electron (an alloy of gold and silver), they made all their weapons, ornaments, and utensils. During this period metallurgy becomes as prominent as agriculture. Evidence for the growth of trade is seen in the distribution of goods over a large area. A center that bears witness to the high level of civilization reached during this period is Alaca Huyuk, in north central Anatolia near Bogazkoy (modern Bogazkale). Its rich tombs, belonging to the kings of Hatti, display evidence of highly developed burial rituals and of a high level of metalworking. Although Anatolia was densely populated during the Bronze Age, a uniform culture was not achieved over the entire area. Because of its location, Anatolia became colonized during this period by cultures from Greece, the Balkans, and by Assyrians from Mesopotamia.

After a long period of decline, Asia Minor reached a high level of civilization again in the Middle Bronze Age (2000–1550 BCE), at which time this region became a world leader in art, urban planning, sculpture, and pottery. The ancient sites of this period indicate that many of the towns were fortified for defense purposes, evidence that there was a struggle for power between local states and tribes. The significant increase in production and surplus of metal products made possible the export of such items to other communities and kingdoms in the area. Transportation was enhanced by the invention of four-wheel carts drawn by oxen.

In 1960 BCE the Old Assyrian State, located in northern Mesopotamia, established a sophisticated trading system with Anatolia. Trade with Assyria initiated an era known as the Assyrian Colonies Period, the start of which marks the beginning of the Middle Bronze Age in Anatolia. Under the initiative of the Assyrian merchants, who lived peaceably among their Anatolian hosts, a series of markets, called *karums*, were established outside the cities where the local rulers lived. Assyrian merchants employed donkey caravans in their travels across Syria, often crossing the Taurus Mountains through the Cilician Gates (a pass northwest of the modern city of Adana) and continuing to Kultepe (near modern Kayseri), where the central *karum* was located. It was here that the earliest documents in Anatolia have been uncovered, some twenty thousand tablets in all. Essentially economic records, the documents were kept on rectangular clay tablets written upon with a specially shaped stylus using the cuneiform script in the language of Old Assyria.

The two major items imported by the Anatolians were tin and textiles, whereas the principal items of export were goods made of gold and silver. Tin, possibly mined as far away as Afghanistan, was the trade item that made Assyria most indispensable to Anatolia. In return for the payment of taxes, tolls, and rent, the Assyrian merchants acquired security for their markets and goods and safety on the main roads. This activity of trade, exchange, and profit made the Middle Bronze Age one of the first international periods in history.

The Assyrian Colonies period is a most significant period in Anatolian history. During this age two critical advances took place: written records appear in Anatolia, and pottery is now commonly produced on the potter's wheel, instead of being handmade. These advances coincided with the emergence of the Hittites, the first great power to unify Anatolia. This group probably contributed more to the early evolution of Anatolia than any other. The art of this period is well represented in the Ankara museum. Its collection includes pottery seals, figurines of the fertility goddesses, and mould-made lead figurines of gods and divine families.

EXPLANATORY ENTRY #24: THE HITTITE LEGACY

The synthesizing power that Anatolia has always exerted is evident among the Hittites, who immigrated from the Balkans, crossing either the Bosporus or the Dardanelles, the route of numerous historic invaders such as later Phrygians, Bithynians, and Galatians. The names of the Hittite gods were Semitic, reflecting the strong cultural influences reaching into the peninsula from the great civilizations of Mesopotamia. At the same time, the language of the Hittites reveals that they were one of the Indo-European migrant groups that began moving into the Near East around 3000 BCE, creating much of Western civilization. The Hittite Empire, which at its height controlled central Anatolia, northwestern Syria, and Mesopotamia down to Babylon, lasted from roughly 1680 BCE to about 1180 BCE. After 1180 BCE, the Hittite polity disintegrated into several independent city-states, some of which survived as late as 700 BCE.[2]

According to written records, Anitta, king of Kanesh (Kultepe), established the Hittite kingdom in the last phases of the Assyrian Colonies Age (c. 1750 BCE) by uniting the Hittites then living in different Hittite city states. Over the course of the next three centuries, the ambitious Hittites gradually imposed their rule over the inhabitants of Anatolia, who called their land Hatti (the lands of the Halys River and its tributaries in central Anatolia), from which came the name Hittites. Around 1660, after the disappearance of the Assyrian trading colonies from Anatolia, the Hittites moved their capital from Kanesh to Hattusa, a citadel that stood on a storm-swept plateau three thousand feet above sea level.

The Old Hittite Kingdom peaked around the time of Mursili I (1620–1595), whose sack of Babylon in 1595 brought to an end the Babylonian dynasty established by the renowned Amorite king, Hammurabi. But Mursili's lengthy campaign strained the resources of Hatti and left the capital in a state of near-anarchy. Mursili was assassinated shortly after his return home, and the Hittite Empire was plunged into chaos.

Under ensuing rulers, the Hittites regained their dominance and created an empire that became one of the three most powerful states in the Near East, together with Egypt and Babylon. By 1300, the Hittites were bordering on the Egyptian sphere of influence, leading to the inconclusive military engagement with Pharaoh Ramses II at the battle of Kadesh in 1274. Although his own inscriptions proclaimed victory, it seems more likely that Ramses was turned back at Kadesh by the Hittite king Muwatalli II (1295–1272), successor to Mursilis II. This battle, believed to be the largest chariot battle ever fought (involving five thousand chariots and over nine thousand foot soldiers), took place in the fifth year of Ramses (c. 1274 BCE by the most commonly used chronology).

---

2. For an abbreviated chronology of Anatolian history, consult Appendix D.

Some years later, in response to increasing Assyrian encroachments along the frontier, Hattusili III (1265–1235) concluded a peace and alliance with Ramses, presenting his daughter in marriage to the Pharaoh. The Treaty of Kadesh, one of the oldest completely surviving treaties in history, fixed their mutual boundaries in Canaan, and was signed in the twenty-first year of Ramses (c. 1258 BCE).

One innovation that can be credited to Hittite rulers is the practice of conducting treaties and alliances with neighboring states; the Hittites were among the earliest known pioneers in the art of international politics and diplomacy. Hittite treaties are known as "suzerainty treaties" because they are treaties between unequal parties, the suzerain and the vassal. The Hittites made it clear that they were the suzerain and that as the superior party it was they who specified the terms to the vassal, who owed them allegiance. The terms of such treaties provided certain benefits to the vassal, including protection. It is clear that a primary intent of such treaties was the formation of a military alliance, as well as a means of preserving the peace within the empire. Hittite suzerainty treaties have been preserved in abundance, and can be taken as illustrative of a highly developed form known throughout the ancient Near East.

Biblical scholars have found a direct correlation between elements in the Hittite treaty pattern and the Decalogue (Mosaic Covenant) in Exodus 19–24. The influence of these secular treaties may be seen in other passages and books of the Bible, including the entire book of Deuteronomy, which seems to follow the Hittite treaty pattern. It is conceivable that Moses became acquainted with this treaty form in Egypt, which had a long history of encounter and political negotiation with the Hittites.

The last known Hittite king, Suppiluliuma II (1207–1178), managed to win some victories, including a naval battle against raiders known as the Sea Peoples off the coast of Cyprus. But it was too late. The Sea Peoples had already begun their push down the Mediterranean coastline, starting from the Aegean and continuing all the way to southern Canaan—taking Cilicia and Cyprus away from the Hittites en route and cutting off their coveted trade routes. This left the Hittite homelands vulnerable to attack from all directions. Early in the twelfth century (c. 1200 BCE), in the wake of the Aegean migrations that brought the Sea Peoples into Canaan, the Hittite records became silent.

Phrygians arrived in Anatolia from southeastern Europe around that time, burning Hattusa to the ground. Other cities that had been part of the Hittite Empire—Troy, Miletus, Tarsus, Alaca Huyuk, Alisar, Carchemish, Alalakh, Ugarit, Qatna, and Qadesh among them—also came to a violent end. The Hittite Empire thus vanished from the historical record, and all memory of the Hittites was lost for centuries.

When the Hittite empire collapsed early in the twelfth century, a number of kingdoms rose and flourished in Anatolia, among them Lydia, whose wealth was proverbial (the Lydians were the first people to mint coins), and Phrygia, whose native headgear oddly became a world emblem of freedom (the Phrygian bonnet still rests on the head of Marianne, the lady who symbolizes the French Republic on its coins and bills). Anatolia's new kingdoms were rather small in size, their small scale shown by the most famous of them all, the kingdom of Troy in northwest Anatolia. The proud capital, popularized and made grandiose by the *Aeneid* of the Roman poet Vergil and the *Iliad* of Homer, was not, alas, an imperial city, but merely a walled village of some seven acres.

The Hellenistic kingdoms that followed Alexander the Great's conquest of Anatolia in the fourth century BCE eventually fell to the inexorable advances of Rome, which united the countries of the Mediterranean basin, including all of Anatolia, into one super state. In the Greco-Roman period Anatolia became one peaceful state for the first time in its history. Only Rome, supreme on land and sea, could control the plateaus, the interior valleys, and the complicated coastline of Anatolia.

TRAVEL ENTRY #40: A VISIT TO THE ARCHAEOLOGICAL RUINS OF HATTUSA

I left the Anatolia Civilizations Museum with a better understanding of history and a deeper appreciation for the region's culture, but also with a strong desire to visit Hattusa, the remote capital of an empire that for hundreds of years vied with Egypt for control of the fertile lands of Mesopotamia. At the bus station I acquired schedules for the following day, hoping to travel to Hattusa and view the archaeological site all in one day. To do so required an early morning departure, for round-trip travel alone would take at least seven hours. Because *Let's Go: Europe 1989* indicated that "Travel in Turkey is a budget traveler's dream," I hoped to confirm the statement's veracity. Bus companies in Turkey are private, so they offer competitive rates and are quick, efficient, and surprisingly modern.

The next morning, traveling with only a small day pack, an adequate supply of water, a packed lunch, and a guidebook, I returned to the bus station, my gateway to Hattusa. I purchased a ticket and quickly made my way to the appropriate gate, having arrived barely five minutes before the scheduled departure time. Upon reaching the gate, I was alarmed to find the spot vacant and no passengers waiting to board. This taught me a valuable lesson: in Turkey, buses don't leave on schedule; they leave when they are full. The lesson left a bitter taste in my mouth.

At 8:45 a.m. I boarded a bus bound for Samsun, a city on the Black Sea. Three hours later we arrived at Sungurlu, where I switched to a *dolmus* heading for the tiny town of Bogazkale, a short distance from the sprawling ruins.

EXPLANATORY ENTRY #25: AN OVERVIEW OF THE HITTITE CAPITAL

Scholars have wondered how the Hittites ruled a vast empire from such a remote place. The capital's setting and central location certainly had something to do with its selection, but no doubt it was the natural advantages of the site—plentiful water and protective terrain—that kept the dynasty there. Two small rivers flow together just north of the site, creating a rocky plateau whose point faces north. Each stream had cut deeply into the limestone rock, creating gorge-like valleys. The large area bordered by the two valleys was the site of the ancient city. The terrain occupied by Hattusa dips dramatically downward from south to north, about a thousand feet over a total length of 1.3 miles. Though the uneven terrain posed difficulties for the planners of the city—the large area is cut up into valleys, slopes, terraces, rocks, and plateaus—its location between two valleys was well suited for fortification, since the natural slopes and rocky outcroppings could easily be made part of the defense system.[3]

The Lower City

Though there is evidence that the site was occupied during the first half of the third millennium, by 2000 BCE two sites were settled in the city. Both maintained their importance during the site's occupation. One is Buyukkale ("Great Fortress"), the high rocky acropolis known as the Citadel, and the other is the area near the western edge of the lower city,

---

3. For a site plan of Hattusa, see Appendix N.

about six hundred yards from the western slope of the acropolis, where the ruins of the Great Temple are located.

Around 1600 BCE, when the site became the capital of a Hittite dynasty, the residential area included at least two temples. The Great Temple, situated below the acropolis in the northern, lower city, served as the empire's cult center. It is the largest and best preserved monument of the Hittite period known to us today. This massive temple (125 by 165 feet) is larger than any other religious complex in the Near East at this time. The temple compound included the temple itself, storerooms surrounding it, and a large group of outlying buildings. At the back of the sanctuary two sacred rooms (called *cellas*) were discovered, where statues of the two principle Hittite deities, the Storm God (or Weather God) and the Sun Goddess, were kept.

From the nearly ten thousand tablets found at Hattusa, it is obvious that the king and queen participated in an elaborate religious ritual, serving in the capacity of priest and priestess to the enormous Hittite pantheon. The tablets, or archives, primarily ritualistic in nature, served as a vast reference library for the king. Some tablets were found on the acropolis, near the palace, and others were discovered in a storage area within the temple. Though some of the material is historical and legal, the vast majority consists of prescriptions for festivals, which undoubtedly occupied much of the king's time.

The Upper City

During the Imperial Period (c. 1400–1200) the city was extended toward the south, thereby tripling its size to an area of 450 acres. An elaborate section of walls was constructed during the reign of Suppiluliuma I (1358–1323) to protect this part of the city, known as the Upper City. The inclusion of the southern hills strengthened the fortification system considerably, especially the sophisticated construction of the highest section, much of which remains visible today. Here a deep moat and a high earth rampart known as Yerkapi (meaning "gate in the ground"), 50 feet high and 250 feet thick at the base, supported the wall of the city at its most vulnerable area. A 235-foot-long corbelled postern (tunnel) was built through the rampart at this point. This tunnel, which connected the interior of the city with the outside, remains intact today and is a major tourist attraction. Until now twelve such tunnels under the fortification walls of Hattusa are known, although this is the only postern that one can actually walk through today. The function of these posterns remains open to interpretation. They may have been used as sally ports, through which one could run outside the city and attack the besieging enemy from the rear.

For strategic purposes a paved glacis (a stone plastered defensive slope) covered the outer slope, making climbing to the foot of the walls more difficult and protecting the fortifications against erosion. The paved rampart must have been erected primarily as an architectural monument, a manifestation of the city's might and/or religious significance. From afar the high ridge with its crown of city walls and towers would have gleamed white, an impressive landmark to travelers and guests approaching from the south. Enemy forces would not likely have chosen to storm the city at this point when only a short distance to the right or left the wall was considerably lower.

Built into the main wall immediately above the postern is a tower with a gateway that connects the main wall with the lower outer wall. It is called the Sphinx Gate today because four large sphinxes, two on the outer and two on the inner portals, adorned the gate in antiquity. Apparently this section of the wall merited particular attention, requiring individual protection by these mythological creatures. Sphinxes, heterogeneous creatures with a human head and the body of a lion, the Hittites are believed to have adopted from Egypt, where the sphinx represented a king. The soft facial contours of Hittite sphinxes, however, suggest that they represent females.

At the ends of the straight line of the high southern fortifications are two grand gates with sculptural decorations: the King's Gate in the southeast and the Lion Gate in the southwest. The Lion Gate takes its name from the two sculptured lions whose heads, breasts, and feet were cut out of the exterior of the huge blocks lining the passageway. Lions were popular figures of protection and ornament at doorways throughout the ancient Near East, and Hattusa was no exception; lions guarded not only this gate, but several temple entrances and the portals to the Royal Palace as well. All were most vividly depicted, their teeth clenched, their tongues hanging from their mouths, and their wide eyes alert and threatening.

The Buyukkale citadel, like the King's Gate, is situated on the east side of the city, overlooking the gorge. The acropolis, a plateau 275 yards long by 140 yards wide, was the main seat of the great Hittite kings until the city's destruction shortly after 1200 BCE. What can be seen today are the ruins of the royal citadel and palace area from that date. The interior of the citadel consists of a number of separate buildings differing in size and importance.

Several buildings at Buyukkale contained archives of clay tablets. These archives have played a most important role in our knowledge of Hittite history. The hundreds of tablets that had been stored on wooden shelves here include not only contracts and official documents but also oracular prophecies, instructions in cult practice, folklore, collections of legal decisions, and historical texts as well. Among the texts was the famous Treaty of Kadesh.

The Rock Sanctuary of Yazilikaya

In the thirteenth century BCE, during a phase of intense rebuilding and refortification, the famous rock sanctuary known as Yazilikaya ("The Inscribed Rock") was completed. The open-air temple, located about a mile northeast of Hattusa, is connected to the capital by a ceremonial path. The natural rock shrine may well have been a place of worship for hundreds or thousands of years before the rise of Hittite power. There, in front of the natural cluster of rocks, the Hittites built a free-standing gateway, a vestibule with door and stairs, a court, and a sanctuary.

The principal interest at Yazilikaya lies not in the fallen temple structures but in the figures of deities carved on the rock walls of the two natural chambers, the carved reliefs representing what has been called "the Sistine Chapel of Hittite religious art." The gallery of reliefs depicts the entire Hittite pantheon, together with their protégé, King Tudhaliya IV (1235–1209), during whose reign the sanctuary was completed. The figures in the larger rock chamber (Chamber A) give the impression of two processions, one of male and the other of female deities, advancing on either side toward the rear wall, where the principal gods and goddesses meet one another at the focal point of the chamber. The male gods face forward, whereas the goddesses are shown in side view. The deities' names are often inscribed over their heads. The leading deities (the "family of the Weather God") who meet in the main scene portrayed on the rear wall of the Main Gallery are followed on either side by deities of lesser rank. The pantheon is led by Teshub, the thunder or storm god (Weather God). Behind Teshub are two unknown gods, followed in descending rank by Ea (god of water), Shaushga (goddess of war), Kirshub (moon god), the Sun God, and at the end of the procession several mountain gods and a group of identical deities known as "the Twelve."

Processing toward them is a line of deities led by Hepat, the earth goddess and wife of Teshub. Standing on a panther, which in turn rests upon two mountains, she is followed by a group of goddesses that includes Shaushga (Ishtar) again, this time as goddess of love. The Hittites are known to have been syncretistic in their religious beliefs, borrowing forty-six gods from the neighboring Hurrians alone.

Scholars have interpreted the carvings in the first chamber (Chamber A) as a cosmic narrative depicting the sacred marriage between Teshub (heaven) and Hepat (earth). All of the other gods shown on the chamber's walls have convened to witness and ratify this ritual matrimonial bond. In this way the Hittites assembled the legion of gods to assure the world's seasonal cycles of birth, death, and rebirth. Yazilikaya, then, was a fertile center of cosmic renewal. It is believed that Chamber A served as the site of the Spring Festival, which marked the beginning of the New Year and lasted for many days.

A crack in the natural rock, widened artificially, leads to the Small Gallery (Chamber B), which introduces the themes of death and the underworld into Yazilikaya's program. The entrance to the gallery is protected by two demons, appearing as winged creatures with a lion's head and a human body, raising their paws in a ferocious manner. Three niches cut into the rock probably held crematory urns. On the west wall is a relief of "the Twelve," gods marching in single file to the right, similar to the twelve depicted in Chamber A. "The Twelve," joined by the Sword God, were gods of the afterlife. The figures in Chamber B may well have been deities playing a major role in the Hittite mortuary rites that took place here. Since no remains of Hittite kings have been found, it is believed they were cremated. Chamber B may well have been a funerary chamber. Taken together, the images of Chambers A and B present a continuous cycle of marriage, death, and rebirth.

But Yazilikaya is more than just a cosmic narrative depicting the renewal of creation. Archaeastronomer E. C. Krupp has interpreted the carvings in Chamber A as a site associated with the continuity of the Hittite royal line. Yazilikaya may well have been used for an *akitu* ceremony—which involved a ritual mating of king and queen. Such a ceremony had deep roots in the Near East, where as early as 3500 BCE, a similar sacred marriage was performed in Sumeria as a seasonal ceremony of renewal. The ritual was also enacted by Babylonian rulers and their consorts in the early second millennium, during the New Year festivals celebrated at the vernal equinox. Yazilikaya was very likely the stage for similar religious rituals, ensuring continuity and growth.

It is curious that an imperial civilization at the height of its power and stability elected to house a national shrine on a hillside above the capital in a small complex of natural enclosures open to the sky. The Hittites were perfectly capable of engineering massive public works; they built great temples, palaces, and walls at Hattusa. But the power and beauty of the spot must have been overwhelming. The choice to carve their shrine on natural rock was deliberate and is no doubt partly explained by the desire to operate ritually in an environment that echoes the mountaintop territory of the high gods. As a locus for the creation and ritual renewal of power, Yazilikaya was a junction of worlds where the realms of heaven, earth, and the underworld met in images of marriage, continuity, royal succession, and death. The cosmic mountain, procreative nature, and the gods—all these converged at Yazilikaya. Charged with mystery and majesty, under eternal sky and above fertile earth, the Yazilikaya shrine was the sacred *omphalos* of the Hittite Empire.

The archaeological site of Hattusa is so vast that unless one has a good deal of time and stamina, it should be seen by car, following the road that connects the archaeological area. The site's immensity was amplified by the realization that I was the only tourist in sight. I felt like the lone survivor of a nuclear holocaust, witnessing the gutted debris of a lost civilization. I left this Anatolian Olympus convinced that I had witnessed one of our planet's foremost thin places. With a heavy heart I returned to the village of Bogazkale in time to catch the departing hourly *dolmus* for Sungurlu to return to Ankara in time for a brief night's rest and an early morning departure for the lunar-like region known in classical times as Cappadocia.

13

Leaving Turkey

"The best thing about Ankara is leaving it," the Turkish poet Yahya Kemal used to say in the early days, when the capital still approximated its original conception of a neat garden city in the middle of the Anatolian plateau. Whether one agrees with this perspective or not, leaving Ankara to explore the surrounding plateau, that most Turkish part of Turkey, is still to be highly recommended. Among the sites on that plateau, the most interesting is Cappadocia, an ancient region about 185 miles southeast of Ankara. Cappadocia derived its name from the Persian Katpatuka, meaning the "land of fine horses." Because horses were bred in this mountainous area as early as the second millennium BCE, it eventually became a tradition to pay tribute with horses.

In Cappadocia, an area defined by a triangle formed by the city of Nevsehir and the smaller towns of Avanor and Urgup, beautifully eroded volcanic formations create a bizarre landscape of cone-shaped pinnacles and "fairy chimneys" clustered in valleys and along ridges. When Christians first came to this region in the sixth century, they carved houses, churches, and entire cities out of the soft volcanic rock, mostly in sites located between two major volcanic massifs. The greatest concentration of rock-cut churches and monasteries carved out of the soft volcanic tuff lie in the valley of Goreme, whose lava formations owe their existence to the activity of Mount Erciyes (12,500 feet), a once-active volcano near Kayseri (Caesarea), the capital of historic Cappadocia.

When Christian monasticism developed in this region, following the teaching of the fourth-century church father, St. Basil the Great of Caesarea, monks began carving out their cells in the soft rock face, as local peasants had certainly done before them. These cells were often grouped around chapels or churches in cenobitical (communal) monasteries. Many of these dwellings are now available to tourists for overnight occupation. During my stay in Goreme I arranged to stay in one of these rooms, carved from one of the town's numerous rock cones. It was a pleasant but eerie sensation to sleep in a rock enclosure, imitating the solitary example set by generations of monastic predecessors.

Cappadocia, always exposed to attacks from the east, was a no-man's land from the seventh to the ninth centuries CE, during the Arab-Byzantine wars. But peace, together with a renewed interest in monasticism, returned to the region in the ninth century, with the revival of Byzantine power. Most of the Cappadocian rock churches belong to this period. According to the chronicles of a tenth-century monk who lived in the area, about 360 churches and monasteries existed in the region of Goreme alone. During the eleventh century, following the decisive defeat of the Byzantine armies at the battle of Manzikert in 1071, in the arid wastelands of eastern Turkey, Turkish tribes known as Seljuks expanded into Anatolia. With this victory, the whole of Anatolia lay open to Turkish settlement. Waves of Christians fled before the onrush, seeking protection and shelter in and around Goreme.

EXPLORATORY ENTRY #26: SAINT GEORGE AND THE DRAGON

Goreme is an ideal place to stay in Cappadocia because of its proximity to the Open Air Museum, the most impressive concentration of sights in the region and one of the most famous sites in central Turkey. The museum consists of a circular cluster of seven churches plus a monastery, dining rooms, and other communal chambers, all cut from the soft rock. The churches are decorated with remarkable frescoes, spanning most of the Byzantine era. Christian monks and others inhabited the region until the formation of the modern Turkish Republic in the twentieth century, when all Anatolian Christians were traded to Greece and other neighboring countries for Muslims living there.

Of all the churches, the Yilanli (Serpent) Church is the most fascinating, for its frescoes are highly symbolic and filled with lore. The church is so named because one of its scenes depicts two warrior saints, George and Theodore, facing one another on horseback. St. George riding a white horse and St. Theodore a red one are both seen spearing a serpent or dragon, which writhes under their horses' hooves. The most famous of these saints was Saint George, whose festival was introduced to England by the Crusaders.

Little is known about the life of St. George, but he is believed to have been a soldier of noble birth, of Cappadocian origin, who was executed under Emperor Diocletian for refusing to renounce the Christian faith. In the fourteenth century, during the reign of Edward III, St. George was elevated to the role of patron saint of England, as he already was of Portugal, Aragon, Catalan, Georgia, and Lithuania. Saint Theodore, also a soldier and a dedicated Christian, is said to have set fire to a temple of the mother goddess, for which crime he was tortured and then roasted to death in an oven. From this meager information one may conclude that the story of their killing a serpent represents their determination to die rather than abandon their faith.

In antiquity, however, serpents seem to have represented feminine powers and female sexuality. Ancient Mesopotamians worshipped serpents, for among Akkadians the word "priest" meant "serpent lover." In the Aegean region, people worshipped serpents as well as mother goddesses. The Greek goddess Demeter is frequently depicted holding serpents in her hands, and the hair of Medusa, whose face carved in relief was placed over temple doors for protection, was formed of writhing serpents.

The killing of serpents or dragons is a theme that occurs regularly in pre-Christian religions or in stories of the creation. The god or hero who performs the killing in these stories is male, and may be interpreted as symbolizing male supremacy. By killing the serpent, gods and male heroes won control over regenerative processes such as water sources and harvests as well as control over the ultimate symbol of abundance and fertility—the mother goddess. In the earliest known epic written in the English language, Beowulf kills three beings: Grendel, who has threatened the Danish throne, his mother, and a serpent. Here the association between female dominance and the symbol of a dragon or serpent is clearly evident.

In the Serpent Church at Goreme, the opposite wall from the two warrior saints slaying the dragon contains a most unusual fresco, depicting three additional saints. The figure on the left is Saint Onophrius, a man with long white hair and a beard. Next to him is Saint Thomas, in a benedictory pose, and St. Basil, bearing the Scriptures. Surprisingly, the body of Onophrius, depicted naked, is that of a young girl. According to local legend, Onophrius was a beautiful girl, pursued by men and compelled to sin repeatedly. Moved by her repentance and her pleas to be saved from future sin, God is said to have given her the face of an old man.

If the real Onophrius was a saint who lived in Egypt in the fourth and fifth centuries, this figure represents something different. Some see in this depiction yet another example of the transition from a matriarchal to a patriarchal society. According to this interpretation, Saint Onophrius has become the epitome of the mother goddess who has become masculinized.

TRAVEL ENTRY #41: CYCLING IN TURKEY

That night, having explored the Goreme Open Air Museum and some of the nearby rock-cut dwellings, I walked across town to an English-speaking restaurant. The town was mostly deserted by 7:30 p.m., not so much because of the hour but on account of the time of the year. The peaks of some of the mountains in the Taurus range were already snow-covered. Soon it would be winter, hardly a time for tourists.

Several travelers were at the restaurant that night, including an interracial Dutch couple with a toddler—I had the impression they were educated transients, staying at one site until something better turned up—and a male cyclist, traveling with a female companion across Anatolia by bicycle. Early in summer, when the two cyclists had departed from Istanbul, they had set as their destination the summit of the 7,000-foot-high Nemrut Dagi, the most heavily visited spot in eastern Turkey. They would not make their goal that year, however, for the site still lay some 250 miles to the east, and the female cyclist had been fighting a nagging virus or infection that had so weakened her that she was unable to join us for dinner. Although I admired their dream of crossing Turkey by bicycle and sympathized with them in their dilemma, I did not envy their predicament. Cycling across Turkey, especially the eastern half, is asking for trouble. The lack of sanitary conditions, the withering summer heat, eating unfamiliar food and drinking questionable water, all these sap the cyclist's energy, weaken resolve, and ultimately bring an unseasoned novice to defeat. The editors of *Let's Go: Europe* speak of eastern Turkey as "the final frontier of the budget traveler" and issue a warning that must be heeded: "As you travel eastward in Turkey, there's a point at which things change. The line where you turn from traveler to swashbuckler begins somewhere near Cappadocia."

EXPLORATORY ENTRY #27: TURKISH MIGRATIONS INTO CENTRAL ANATOLIA—THE SELJUK TURKS

The history of the Seljuks, the first Turks to conquer and unify Anatolia, is fascinating. In the seventh and eighth centuries, as Muslim Arabs were fanning out from Arabia, the Turkish people outside the Great Wall of China began moving west. Like the Huns who preceded them or the Mongols who came after them, the Turkish nomads were influenced by the cultures of the west. The single most important event to take place on their westward journey was the conversion of the Seljuk Turks to Islam. This conversion occurred during the ninth and tenth centuries, while the Turks were still beyond the Oxus River (in a region north of Afghanistan ruled by the Abbasid caliphate in Persia). The zeal with which the Seljuk family embraced the Sunni branch of Islam in the long run proved as momentous for the future of the Middle East as the conversion of Clovis and his Franks to Christian Europe. In 1056, a grandson of Seljuk was granted the title of Sultan (an Arabic word meaning "one with authority") by the Abbasid caliph, marking the beginning of a shift of power in the Muslim world.

In the late summer of 1071, news of an unprecedented disaster began to reach the rulers of Western Christendom. The Seljuk Turks had defeated the emperor of Byzantium in a battle at Manzikert, within the Byzantine heartland of central Anatolia. The Christian forces were in disarray, and worse, the emperor himself, heir of the Caesars, had been taken captive. On that fateful day the Byzantine Empire forfeited its historic position as the eastern bulwark of Christendom and as guarantor of the pilgrimage route to Jerusalem.

Almost as startling was the fact that these Muslim invaders were not members of the Arab people, whose conquests had dismayed Europe since the seventh century. They were Seljuk Turks—nomadic horsemen who had erupted out of the steppes of central Asia barely fifty years earlier and subjugated present-day Iran and Iraq in little more than a single generation. Within twenty years of their triumph at Manzikert, these mounted bowmen would rule an empire that stretched from the Mediterranean to the edges of India, embracing and unifying most of the Muslim territories of Asia. By 1100, the Seljuks had gained control of much of Anatolia, beginning the Turkification of that vast region. In a few years the Seljuks had reached the outposts of Constantinople.

The rise of the Seljuks proved a traumatic shock for Christendom. The Turkish warriors inflicted on Byzantium a defeat from which it never fully recovered. In the wake of their victory, they would settle Asia Minor and thereby open up a corridor for the later Ottoman invasion of Europe. The threat to the eastern empire in turn galvanized the Latin West into mounting the great counteroffensive of the Crusades.

During the brilliant rule of Sultan Ala al-din Kay-Qubad I (Keykubat), who ruled from 1220–1237, most of what is now Turkey was united in a tolerant, pluralistic kingdom. Under Kay-Qubad, Anatolia knew stability for the first time in centuries, with communications as secure as they had been under the Roman Empire. Caravansaries, or inns, were established along the main routes, each about eighteen miles apart, the distance a laden camel could cover in nine hours. Caravansaries were not only inns, but were also strong fortifications. As places of refuge, they were capable while under attack of supporting a caravan for long periods.

Seljuk prosperity made possible the establishment of a benevolent state in Anatolia. Schools, endowed hospitals—where free treatment was available to the poor—orphanages, and poorhouses made the thirteenth century not only the Golden Age in Seljuk rule but also a period in Islamic history when charitable precepts became rules of action.

The single greatest figure produced by this tolerant, benevolent civilization was Jalal al-Din Rumi (1207–1273), a Muslim poet and mystic. Rumi, whose surname derives from *Rum* ("Roman")—the name given to Anatolia in Seljuk times because the region had been part of the eastern Roman Empire—was brought to Anatolia from Afghanistan, the place of his birth. His father was a distinguished theologian with an interest in Sufism, the mystic path of Islam. In order to escape the approaching Mongol invaders, the family traveled widely throughout the Middle East until they settled in Konya (biblical Iconium), the capital of the Seljuk state in Anatolia and the most celebrated Muslim city of the Anatolian plateau.

Rumi's story is fascinating. He was a scholar of Islamic law until the day that a man in rags approached him. "What's this?" the man asked Rumi, pointing to his law books.

"You wouldn't understand," Rumi responded dismissively.

The man fixed Rumi with a steely gaze, waved his arm, and set the books on fire. Then he waved his arm again, and the books appeared unharmed.

"You wouldn't understand," he said, and disappeared. The man was Shams of Tabriz, and in that moment Rumi made the decision to give up his law career and follow the mystical path of love and spirituality that Shams embodied—the Sufi path.

Rumi is renowned today for his famous love poetry, some of the world's finest. Rumi's surname Mevlana ("Our Master"), as he is known to modern Turks, testifies to his role as a spiritual guide. Mevlana believed that spiritual perfection and union with the divine could take place through ecstatic dance. He therefore founded an order of Mevlevi (Whirling) Dervishes, who drew their inspiration from his writings and example and who were led by his direct descendants. Today, however, following the banning of all dervish orders by Ataturk, the dervishes dance only periodically. They perform the rite each December in Konya to commemorate the "wedding night" of Rumi, the occasion of his death and joining with his Beloved (God). The spellbinding worship service is intended to convey the dervish's love of God, humankind, and all creation.

At an appropriate moment in the Whirling Prayer ceremony, the dervishes drop their black cloaks to reveal white costumes fitted to the torso, but with long, flowing skirts. The dropping of the cloak symbolizes the casting off of falsehood and the revelation of truth. Each dervish places his arms on his chest to symbolize his belief in the oneness of God, called "the One." Bowing, he kisses the hand of the Sheikh Efendi (spiritual leader) and seeks permission to enter the prayer wheel. As he enters, each dervish slowly unfurls his arms, his right hand reaching up to heaven to receive its blessings, the left hand down to communicate them to earth. The dervishes complete four whirling sessions of approximately fifteen minutes each, whirling counter-clockwise and resting briefly between sessions. The Sheikh Efendi joins in the final session, turning slowly. Like the Muslims performing *tawaf* in Mecca, the Whirling Dervishes believe they too are participating in a cosmic ritual, experiencing the intuitive reality acknowledged by mystics throughout the ages: "God is an intelligent sphere whose center is everywhere and whose circumference is nowhere."[1]

Shortly after Rumi's lifetime, the Seljuk state disappeared from history, suffering a crushing defeat at the hands of yet other invaders from the east, the Mongols. But by then, the Turkish presence in Asia Minor was firmly entrenched. The Turkish peoples were never to leave the

---

1. Alain de Lille, twelfth-century theologian (borrowed from a Hermetic statement).

Anatolian plateau they had occupied after the victory at Manzikert. It was the battle that created Turkey. The passage of the Mongols prepared Anatolia for further Turkish migrations and the next phase in its history, the five hundred years of Ottoman rule.

TRAVEL ENTRY #42: FROM TURKEY TO SYRIA

Previously, while in Istanbul, I had pondered my options concerning places to see in Turkey. I hoped to visit Ankara and the Hittite capital of Hattusa, but my plans were vague after that. Visiting Damascus, Syria, was a certainty, but I was unsure how to get there. A direct flight from Ankara to Damascus made a lot of sense at that point, due to the uncertainties implicit in overland travel. But after reaching Ankara and finding bus transportation to be both pleasant and convenient, I decided to complete my crossing of Anatolia by land, taking in as much of the setting as possible. In the process, I hoped to follow in the footsteps of the apostle Paul, tracing his travels through southern Turkey where possible.

When I boarded the bus at Goreme, I headed for Antakya (biblical Antioch), part of Syria in biblical times but now in Turkey, near the Syrian border. As usual, traveling by bus in Turkey brought me into contact with friendly locals and with knowledgeable international travelers, all of whom seemed to like Americans. Invariably, someone on board knew enough English to strike up a conversation and answer my endless flow of questions. Around noon, the bus stopped at a restaurant high in the Taurus Mountains. We were approaching the famous mountain pass known as the Cilician Gates, which connects the Anatolian plateau with the Cilician plain. Over the centuries, armies, merchants, and travelers such as Saint Paul the missionary had crossed this strategic pass. The location, with its snowcapped mountain view, was a memorable one.

The rapid descent down the narrow pass brought us to the major coastal highway. We were on the outskirts of Tarsus, the ancient capital of the Roman province of Cilicia and the birthplace of Paul. Tarsus was an important university city in antiquity, ranking alongside Alexandria and Athens as a center of learning. It was to Tarsus that Barnabas, an early Christian leader, had come, looking for the recently-converted Saul of Tarsus, and from there the two went to Antioch, the "cradle of Gentile Christianity," where Christianity acquired its name (Acts 11:25–26). Antioch became Christianity's missionary base, for it was from its port of Seleucia that Paul set sail, together with Barnabas, on the first of his three missionary journeys (Acts 13:1–4).[2]

At the juncture with the coastal highway the bus turned east, away from Tarsus, and we headed for Adana, now the principal city in the region and Turkey's fourth largest metropolis. The city goes back to the Hittites, who established a base there and made this frontier their point of contact with Semitic civilizations east of the Mediterranean Sea. Eventually the Persians ruled the region, until their king Darius was defeated in 333 BCE by Alexander the Great at Issus, close to present-day Iskenderun. At the Battle at Issus, the invading troops of the young Alexander of Macedonia, though outnumbered roughly four to one, defeated the army led by Darius III in the great battle for supremacy in Asia.

Throughout ensuing history, this frontier region continued to serve as a battlefield for the unending armies and empires that met at its crossroads, including Kurds, Arabs, Armenians, French, and Turks. With the defeat of the Ottoman Empire at the end of World War I, the large Armenian minority joined the French occupation forces. Turkish resistance immediately developed in the Taurus Mountains, forcing the French and Armenians to withdraw to Syria and Lebanon. In 1939, the French completed their withdrawal by ceding the region of Hatay (including the port of Iskenderun and the city of Antakya, long a part of Syria) to the Republic of Turkey. This annexation, still a bitter pill for Syria, is the source of ongoing border tensions and bad blood between the two countries.

The ride along the Mediterranean's rugged northeastern coastline was spectacular and truly memorable. Crossing the steep mountains, which rose sharply from the coast, added a dramatic sense of adventure to the long day's journey. When I arrived in Antakya, I felt certain that modern powers had erred in ceding this region to Turkey. Antakya's geographical isolation, cut off from the north and south by high mountains, combined with its predominantly Arab population, strongly reinforced the region's connection with Syria. Terrain and tradition surely should trump the mere vagaries of political history.

Despite Antakya's historic importance, there is not much for the tourist to see. The remains include a Roman bridge, restored Hellenistic

---

2. Biblical scholars point out that the author of the book of Acts shifts from Saul (his Jewish birth name) to Paul (a Hellenistic name) in 13:9, as Paul moves into predominantly Hellenistic territory.

walls (whose length of more than twenty miles suggests the immensity of the metropolis they once enclosed), splendid Roman mosaics preserved in the archaeological museum, and the Crusaders' Church of St. Peter, leading to the cave where the first Christians are said to have met and where the term "Christian" was first coined. My schedule prevented me from seeing any of these sites, however, for the bus to Haleb (Aleppo), Syria, was scheduled to depart within an hour of my arrival, and it made more sense to maintain momentum by crossing the border and spending the night in Syria.

After a quick supper, I returned to the bus station in Antakya, knowing that the last bus of the day would be departing for Syria shortly. Expecting the bus to be full, I arrived with time to spare. When I boarded the bus, I was surprised to find only one other passenger. A few minutes later, the other passenger left his seat to join me at the front of the bus, informing me in broken English that he and I would be the only passengers. My companion introduced himself as Ismat al-Hasan. He was a Syrian businessman from Damascus, where he had been promised direct passage to Haleb, Syria, for important business the following day. We remained in the bus for at least an hour, waiting for the driver to arrive. He finally showed up at dusk, around 7:00 p.m.

My thoughts raced ahead, strategizing about the stop in Syria. "With a bit of luck," I thought, "we should cross the border and arrive at Haleb by ten o'clock." I hoped Ismat could help me find a room at that hour of the night. The first sign of trouble occurred when the driver tried starting the engine. The motor seemed sluggish, as if the timing was off. When the bus finally left the station, an annoying sound came from the engine, but I either blocked it from my mind or the sound may simply have stopped. The bus deviated from its normal route as the driver took us through a residential area, negotiating the sharp turns and narrow roads with great difficulty. After a while the driver stopped the bus and stepped from the vehicle to enter a home, presumably his own. It was an odd start for an international trip, but then again, this was the Middle East, and it was apparent that the bus was not on a regularly scheduled run.

The driver returned after a few minutes, and we seemed to be on our way. A glance at the map indicated that the Cilvegozu border crossing was about thirty-five to forty miles away, and I anticipated a quick trip. But the bus was heading for a different crossing, as I later discovered. The road was unusually narrow as it wound across extremely uneven mountainous terrain. The huge Mercedes bus crept up the steep, torturous grades, only to pick up momentum as it careened around endless hairpin turns.

We continued in this manner for over an hour, passing only a handful of vehicles and no other buses. I couldn't understand how such a road could lead to a major border crossing. Later I learned that few travelers entered Syria that way, the recommended point of entry being through Gaziantep, further east, where one finds the best bus connections to the Middle East.

Soon we encountered Turkish military patrols, and eventually a roadblock. As two guards entered the bus, I recalled stories of armed bandits and guerrillas roaming freely in the backwoods of Colombia, where I once lived, and how they boarded buses and robbed the passengers while dressed in military disguise. These soldiers seemed to be on official business, however, for after a search of the bus and a look into our luggage, they waived us through. The bus continued for some distance at a slow pace and eventually brought us to the Yayladagi border crossing, the most remote in the region. For some unexplainable reason the bus driver had taken us on a perilous, roundabout route to an out-of-the-way crossing rather than the direct route to Haleb. I glanced at my watch, and noticed that we had been on the road over two hours. And we were still in Turkey.

At the border, Ismat and I were instructed to exit the bus and walk to the small Turkish customs building, where we surrendered our passports to a waiting official. After our credentials were examined, we were told to wait. Eventually our bus driver entered and was ushered into an adjoining room. Soon we heard loud talking and then Ismat was called into the room. After a few minutes of heated conversation, punctuated by yelling, Ismat appeared, angry and visibly shaken. He informed me that his documents and mine were in order, but that the bus had to return to Antakya. Because of Ismat's poor English, I could not fully understand the nature of the problem, but I sensed that we had no choice at that hour but to turn back. The thought of retracing the tedious and treacherous route in the dark seemed unacceptable, but I felt I had no other choice, for the other side of the border was just as dark and desolate as the Turkish side. Crossing the border under those conditions seemed more dangerous than returning to Antakya.

Around 9:30 p.m. we left for Antakya, but after only a few miles of travel the bus broke down. Ismat and I stayed inside while the driver gathered some tools and attempted a repair. After a while Ismat and I went to check on him, but one look at his grimy face and burnt, oil-slickened hands told me the repairs required parts and mechanical expertise not currently available. I returned to the bus prepared to spend the night when I heard voices outside and noticed a third person approaching, holding a small lantern.

"Come," Ismat said, indicating that we were to follow the newcomer. I reached for my backpack but Ismat motioned that I was to leave it behind. When he saw my reluctance to do so, he informed me that we were going to spend the night in a nearby farmhouse and that the driver would stay with the bus and luggage, insuring its safety. I grabbed a small bag with my toilet articles and walked out into the night, guided only by that one small light.

The old man had seen the breakdown from his home several hundred yards away and had come to offer assistance. Ismat told me that the farmer said he would be honored if we would accept his invitation to stay at his home overnight, even though we were strangers and posed a risk to his family.

The house was located about fifty yards from the road, on a gradual ascent. The front yard and the path leading up to the house were quite muddy, as it was the rainy season, and there was no sidewalk or lawn. Despite the primitive surroundings, the house was of recent vintage, constructed of cement blocks on a cement slab. We left our muddy shoes on the front stoop and entered a large living room. A handful of children, ranging from primary school age to young adulthood, were there to greet us, along with the farmer's wife. I was surprised to see a television in the room, evidence that the long arm of modern technology reached even the most remote regions of this developing nation. Two pillow-covered beds against the far wall of the room doubled as couches. The room functioned as a family room, living room, and master bedroom.

A while later, the oldest sibling brought a large silver tray into the room, loaded with an array of Middle Eastern food, including pita bread, vegetable dips, candied apples, dates, and other fruit, accompanied by a silver tea service. The tray was placed on the rug where Ismat and I joined the farmer for dinner. The other family members refused to eat with us, though the quantity of food greatly exceeded what three persons could eat. The children pressed close as we ate, chattering incessantly. Ismat served as translator. Though his native language was Arabic, he tried his best to translate Turkish into English. It turned out that some of the older members of the family also spoke Arabic, which endeared them to Ismat and made his task manageable. The meal was extravagant, though I found some of the fruit excessively sweet and the rest quite bitter. Since we had no silverware, I used the pita bread as a scoop, imitating Ismat and diminishing my awkwardness.

Following dinner we watched a television show broadcast from Syria and then resumed our conversation. The family had eight children, I learned, though not all were at home. One was in the army, and this undoubtedly accounted for some of the home's modern features. The area was impoverished and the inhabitants mostly peasants who survived through scratch farming and growing tobacco.

One object—a huge gold coin—riveted my attention since our arrival. It hung from the farmer's wife like a medallion, and I decided to ask its meaning. The lady explained that it was her bride's dowry, an heirloom passed from generation to generation, which in the Muslim world accompanies the wife as her permanent possession and insures financial independence in case of misfortune or divorce. I learned that the coin—worth one million Turkish Lira ($630 at the current rate of exchange)—was quite valuable. To a westerner that may not seem like a lot of money but to that lady, rearing eight children on a desolate tobacco farm, it was a fortune.

Around midnight, the family bade us goodnight. The old man took me to the door and pointed to a set of mud-clogged slippers on the porch outside. I was to use them on my trip to the bathroom, an outhouse in the middle of the muddy yard. Built on a cement slab, it featured a squat toilet and a bucket for flushing. Barnyard animals roamed the area, and I determined that one trip to the privy would suffice my needs that night.

Upon my return, Ismat indicated that he and I were to sleep in the master bedroom, each in our own bed. When I started to protest, Ismat told me in clear terms that rejecting the family's generosity would be an insult. Clean linens were not part of the bargain, but a warm comforter was provided to ward off the cool mountain air. I slept well that night, but the cups of tea sipped before bedtime required the indignity of a second trip to the toilet.

The next morning I awoke early to the sound of food sizzling over a hot stove. Ismat told me that a mechanic had arrived to fix our bus and that we would soon be returning to Antakya—but not before we partook of a sumptuous breakfast. Within a few minutes a large tray was brought into the living room, loaded with heaping portions of chunk-size home-fried potatoes, pita bread, and leftovers from the previous night's dinner. Eating on the floor seemed more natural the second time around. The children crowded around us as they had the previous night and I regretted having to depart.

The unexpected setback epitomized what traveling by land on a shoestring was all about. I wanted to repay the family for their kindness and generosity but Ismat told me that our hosts had refused to accept any money. I looked through my pack for some token I could leave as a gift, but I came up empty. When I reached into my wallet I located several stamps from the United States and other countries I had visited, and it was these tokens of international communication and goodwill that I placed into the hands of the younger children. The small gifts were a sign of my gratitude, but they also represented the understanding that each person has something to give and something to receive from others.

As we approached our bus I could hear the engine running. Another bus was parked nearby, with the required mechanical part, and soon Ismat and I were on the road again, headed back to Antakya. At one point, as we neared the crest of a hill, the driver shifted to a lower gear and the bus stalled. The driver shifted into reverse and recklessly allowed the bus to drift down the steep incline so as to build enough speed to jump-start the engine. The road turned sharply to the left before continuing its steep descent. Unable to jump-start the bus, the driver simply increased its downward speed, bringing the unwieldy vehicle to the edge of the precipice on either side. As I examined the narrow, undulating road, the same one we had traveled in the pitch black night before and were now attempting to negotiate in reverse, I grasped the seat with both hands and began to pray. Ismat's reaction seemed to be the same. The road was a series of steep drops and ascents, with constant switchbacks and not a single protective guard rail. Eventually, after stalling and restarting several times, the bus driver pulled over so that Ismat and I could board the second bus, which had been trailing ours, and thus we returned to Antakya.

At the bus station, Ismat and I parted ways, for he had to travel directly to Haleb, whereas I boarded a bus bound for Damascus. As we sat together at a restaurant before our departure, he gave me a telephone number in Damascus where I could reach him, and we agreed to meet in a few days, our mishap having bound us together in profound ways.

Before Ismat left, I finally learned the real reason for our roundabout route to Haleb, and why we had been turned back at the border. We had been detained and our bus had been denied entrance because in the baggage compartment it carried a large empty gas container to purchase gas in Syria. In Turkey there is a gas surtax of $2 per liter, whereas in Syria gas is much cheaper, because the cost is subsidized by the government and there is no tax. Because the bus trip was an illegal attempt to obtain gas, that explained why the driver had taken a late night trip across the remote border, which he perceived to be a safer place to cross into Syria.

EXPLORATORY ENTRY #28: FINAL THOUGHTS ON LEAVING ANATOLIA

Through the centuries, Anatolia has witnessed in dramatic fashion the continuing struggle between paganism and monotheism. Mother goddesses, sky deities, all have vied for allegiance in this region. Empires—Hittite, Assyrian, Persian, Hellenistic, Roman, Armenian, Byzantine, Seljuk, and Ottoman—have come and gone. Some of the greatest leaders of early Christianity, including Peter, John, and Paul, spent their mature years in Asia Minor, building the religion that would hold Europe in its grip for the next fifteen hundred years. Two millennia earlier, paganism and monotheism met in northwestern Mesopotamia, near the current Syrian border. It was from this region that Abraham went on his way to the land of promise, and it was to this region that the Hebrew patriarch, Jacob, came in search of a bride. The moral consciousness of the West was born of these adventures and struggles, much as our modern world has been fashioned by the subsequent clash between the great monotheistic religions of Christianity and Islam.

The decline of Anatolia in late Ottoman times and its geographical isolation have tended to obscure the region's central role in the history of Western civilization. For the adventurous traveler, Turkey represents a goldmine, inexpensive by European standards and filled with archaeological treasures and remarkably hospitable people. Of all the places I visited on my sabbatical journey across the Mediterranean world, Turkey was the most surprising and the most enjoyable. It is here, in this beautiful and promising land, that the West can rediscover long-lost roots and much of its vitality.

By far the most sophisticated society in the Middle East, the Muslim nation of Turkey is caught in a vicious vice grip. In its pursuit of Ataturk's ideals, Turkey has attempted to westernize. In the process, it has become a vital member of NATO and is now seeking inclusion in the European Union (EU). By so doing, however, it has increased the tension with its neighboring countries as well as within its own society. To the west it finds Greece an enemy, impeding its entrance into the EU, while the Muslim countries on its eastern flank push for Turkey to be a part of that world. Within its borders are insurgent and fundamentalist groups, pulling the country in different directions simultaneously. "Why do you want to go to Syria?" Turks asked in disbelief when they heard of my plans to visit that country. Even my best answers were received with disdain.

Part Two

Illumination

WHEN I LEFT TURKEY, I was entering the Levant (the traditional name for the eastern Mediterranean world), known in the Bible as Canaan and in Christian liturgy as the "Promised Land." The term "Canaanite" requires some explanation, for it is used broadly of that group of Semitic peoples who during the Bronze Age occupied most of what is today Syria, Lebanon, Jordan, and Israel. The Canaanites were never organized politically, but their relatively independent city-states, including Ugarit, Byblos, Tyre, Sidon, Shechem, and Jerusalem, had a common language and culture called Canaanite.

This phase of my journey—crossing into Canaan—heightened my expectation, for it brought me increasingly closer to the geographical and spiritual center of my pilgrimage. I felt like a traveler through time, identifying with Abraham, Jacob, and countless pilgrims who migrated along the trade routes of the Fertile Crescent, entering this holy land in search of an identity, an encounter with the divine, and a promise of hope.

14

Damascus: Crossroads of the East

TRAVEL ENTRY #43: NORTHERN SYRIA

THE THIRD TIME WAS a charm, for the trip to the border crossing at Yayladagi, my third across this rollercoaster terrain, proved to be uneventful. I was pleased to see seven passengers on the bus for this scheduled ride, but I became concerned to learn that several of the passengers were from Libya. It had only been a few years since President Reagan had ordered the bombing of Tripoli, Libya's capital, in an attempt to marginalize Libya's leader Colonel Muammar al Qaddafi and to retaliate for the killing of several American servicemen in Germany by a bombing attributed to Libyan extremists. Fortunately, the young men kept to themselves in the mostly empty bus and since we spoke no common language, I remained out of harm's way.

Though I had cleared customs the night before, it still took two hours for the eight of us to cross the border into Syria. Matters proceed slowly in the Middle East, where religion, politics, and social distinctions dictate extreme caution, particularly when traveling by public transportation. Before entering Syria I had to fill out numerous forms, declare currency, and exchange $100 into Syrian currency at 50 percent of the official rate, in essence, returning fifty cents on the dollar. Syrian officials scrutinize all currency exchange, especially dollar transactions, for there is a strong black market in this nation, and everyone wants dollars. The exchange rate at the border was eleven Syrian pounds to the dollar, whereas the black market rate was forty-five pounds, more than double the official rate and four times the border rate.

EXPLORATORY ENTRY #29: THE UGARITIC HERITAGE

Less than twenty miles from the Turkish border crossing at Yayladagi, as the bus negotiated the mountainous descent that connects the border with Latakia, Syria's major seaport, we passed the ancient port of Ugarit. The site, once the greatest city in the entire Mediterranean, had been excavated only a scant sixty years earlier. Ugarit is one of the oldest sites in the world, dating back to 6000 BCE. The city was destroyed by an invasion of the Sea Peoples shortly after 1200 BCE and was discovered in 1928 by a Syrian farmer whose plow tip accidentally uncovered a tomb. After the farmer sold the findings to an antiquities dealer, news of the discovery leaked out, and before long a government official was sent to inspect the tomb. His report that a great city once stood at the site led to the decision to excavate. Sure enough, under the farmer's field spread the ruins of an ancient harbor town. Archaeologists eventually moved three-quarters of a mile inland to a huge mound overlooking the harbor. The tell (the archaeological site) spread over an area of fifty acres.

Ugarit, now called Ras Shamra, was one of the major Canaanite city-states dotting the eastern Mediterranean region during the second millennium BCE. During the excavations conducted at Ugarit after 1929, thousands of texts have been uncovered, indicating that this was a polyglot and cosmopolitan port and a major international center of commerce. The clay tablets include diplomatic and legal records, lists of gods, mythological texts, lexicons, and dictionaries of word equivalents in the various languages used in the city. Among the most important finds was a tablet on which was inscribed the world's oldest complete alphabet (now on display in the National Museum at Damascus), with an order much the same as that of Western alphabets.

At Ugarit, two temples were discovered, one to Dagon, the god of grain, and the other to his son Baal. Much of the literature from Ugarit is mythological and concerns the gods of Canaan such as Baal, the storm god and the patron god of Ugarit, and El, head of the Ugaritic pantheon, whom the Bible identifies with God (Yahweh/Elohim). Three female deities appear regularly in the literature, including Anat (the warrior goddess and Baal's sister and wife), Asherah (El's consort and hence the mother of the gods), and Astarte, sometimes identified with Asherah. Baal's adversary is Mot (Death), who personifies the forces of sterility, famine, and summer drought. Though Mot is king of the underworld, his domain on earth is the desert.

The Bible contains many direct references—generally hostile—to Canaanite religious practice and ideology, but there are also numerous striking literary parallels between the Hebrew Bible and the Ugaritic tablets, suggesting that the mythological tradition served as a literary background upon which biblical authors relied for poetic imagery. With the discovery of Ugarit and its thousands of texts, scholars now have an extensive and primary source for the study of Canaanite religion. At the same time, this literature can deepen our understanding of the Hebrew Scriptures, for "the Ugaritic tablets are the best available witness to the background from which the religion of Israel emerged, and to the Canaanite beliefs that it shared, adopted, compromised with, and sometimes rejected."[1] Though this literature lies closer to the Hebrew Bible than any other does, it never attained the ethical and moral heights reached in the Bible. Common and widespread practices in the Canaanite world were frequently the subject of biblical prohibitions (Deuteronomy 23:17-18 and Leviticus 18:24).

TRAVEL ENTRY #44: VIEWING REGIONAL TENSIONS THROUGH SYRIAN EYES

When we left Latakia, the bus continued in a southerly direction, following the Mediterranean coastline to a spot close to the border with Lebanon, at which point we headed east and followed the border toward the city of Homs.

As I rode the 200-mile stretch between Latakia and Damascus, I was in high spirits, content to have finally reached this historic land and to be nearing the ancient city of Damascus, touted as the oldest continually inhabited city in the world. I had always wanted to visit Syria, but I knew that at any moment political tensions in the Middle East might prevent such a visit. Four years earlier, when I visited Israel with a tour group, I had traveled through the Golan Heights, a region of Syria occupied by Israeli forces since the June war of 1967. The roads on the way to the deserted city of Quneitra were mined with defused explosives, and Israeli artillery positions were fixed in the hills behind us, pointing toward Damascus, thirty miles away. That was as close to Syria as I had gotten at the time, and I had hoped to return some day and stand on the other side of the border.

---

1. *Stories from Ancient Canaan*, edited and translated by Michael David Coogan (Philadelphia: Westminster, 1978), 19.

When the bus stopped at Homs, Syria's third largest city, it became obvious that Syria was a nation on constant military alert, due in part to its strong military presence in nearby Lebanon. It seemed as if every other person in the city's commercial sector was dressed in drab, olive-green fatigues. Once again I feared for my safety, particularly when soldiers boarded the bus and mingled with the passengers. Many of the soldiers were students in their late adolescent years, studying in this university city while serving in units akin to our National Guard.

Some of the younger soldiers spotted me among the other passengers and approached me in order to strike up a conversation. I was pleased that they were learning English and seemed interested to meet an American, for soldiers in Muslim countries of the Middle East are often taught that the United States is their principal enemy. Former American President Jimmy Carter, in a book on the Middle East, quotes then-President Hafez al-Assad as having said in 1984: "The United States does not have an independent opinion or an American policy in this region. The United States implements the policy that is decided by Israel."[2] Regional cooperation during the Persian Gulf War of 1991, when the state of Israel refrained from retaliating against Iraqi Scud missile attacks, plus additional events such as the fall of the Soviet Union and peace negotiations in 1992 between Israel and her Arab neighbors offered a change in perspective and held out new prospects for peace in the region, at a time when the restoration of annexed territories and the Palestinian quest for a homeland seemed promising. Such issues, unfortunately, remain unresolved.

Though my conversation with some of the more intellectually oriented student-soldiers touched upon the subject of international politics and American policies towards Israel and other Middle Eastern nations, the atmosphere remained cordial and respectful. Syrians, along with many other residents of the Middle East, argue that the source of many problems in the region was a decision made by the colonial powers of Great Britain and France, who, following World War I, subdivided the area without regard to natural boundaries, ethnic identity, or tribal unity.

When I arrived in Damascus, it was past 10:00 p.m. The express bus, bound for Amman, Jordan, did not stop at a bus station or in a central part of the city, as I had expected, but at a remote corner on the outskirts of town. My only information concerning budget accommoda-

---

2. Jimmy Carter, *The Blood of Abraham* (Boston: Houghton Mifflin, 1986), 81.

tions in Damascus was the name of an international youth hostel located somewhere in the city, but that seemed hardly sufficient in a major city like Damascus, with a population of 1.3 million. I flagged a taxi, a dilapidated Oldsmobile of 1950s vintage, handing the driver a slip of paper with the name of the hostel. After driving around for fifteen minutes, the driver stopped to make inquiries. Eventually he stopped to place a telephone call, at which point he learned that the hostel was closed for the winter.

Syria is off the beaten path to most tourists, especially for those traveling alone. One of the reasons is its location, but another reason is the requirement that visitors pay in dollars (or their equivalent) at better hotels, meaning that the $100 exchange at the border or at the airport could not be used for lodging. I was determined to find a cheaper alternative, but had no way to communicate my intention to the driver.

After driving through the city's downtown section for a while, including stopping at several hotels, where there were no vacancies, the taxi driver returned with a big smile on his face. He had located a triple room, and I could pay in Syrian pounds. Even though so much space seemed excessive, for the reasonable rate of $14 per night, I could have it all to myself. The location was only one block from the bazaars and a short walking distance from the city's most famous Muslim and Christian sites. I looked at the driver and returned his smile, placing into his hand a generous tip. "*Shokran gazilan*" ("thank you very much"), I said, using one of the few Arabic phrases at my disposal. The hour-long ride had cost me a mere $3.00.

EXPLANATORY ENTRY #30: DAMASCUS—AN HISTORICAL OVERVIEW

Legend connects Damascus with the Garden of Eden. While that may be a stretch, Syria's capital claims an existence antedating by three thousand years the journey of Abraham, Sarah, and Lot, who passed through the city and surely stopped en route to the Promised Land. The city's permanence may be attributed to its location in a natural bowl 2,300 feet above sea level, at the edge of one of the earth's most fertile oases.

Like a harbor for the great Syrian Desert, Damascus has beckoned desert peoples for millennia. The city and its surrounding plain owe their life and prosperity to the legendary Abana and Pharpar rivers of biblical fame (2 Kings 5:12). Known today as the Barada and Awaj, these rivers provide water in abundance for the agricultural crops of the region. The Barada River runs through the center of the city, spreading fan-like into seven branches, each subdividing into the many streams that distribute water to the houses, gardens, orchards, and vineyards of Damascus before sinking into the desert sands east of the city. The Awaj rises from the foothills of Mount Hermon and flows through the orchard country south of Damascus.

Archaeological excavations demonstrate that Damascus has been inhabited as early as 8000 to 10,000 BCE. As one of the earliest centers of human civilization, this region saw constant strife between its relatively prosperous inhabitants and invaders from the north and east. It was here that the ancient Egyptians first confronted the peoples of the great Euphrates River basin. In this region national boundaries changed constantly, reflecting the interests and ambitions of civilizations spawned by Babylonians, Amorites, Egyptians, Hittites, Assyrians, Israelites, Persians, Greeks, Arabs, Crusaders, Mongols, and Turks.

By the tenth century BCE, as David and Solomon were establishing a dynasty in nearby Israel, Damascus had become the capital of the Arameans, Semitic nomads who arrived from the Arabian Peninsula. It was the Arameans who first established the water distribution system of Damascus by constructing canals and tunnels that maximized the efficiency of the Barada River. The same network, later improved by the Romans and the Umayyads, still forms the basis of the water system of the old part of Damascus.

The principal deity of the Arameans was the Syrian god Hadad (Baal), the West Semitic god of storms, thunder, and rain. His attributes were identical to those of Adad of the Assyro-Babylonian pantheon, to the Anatolian storm-god Teshub, the Egyptian god Seth, the Greek god Zeus, and the Roman god Jupiter. The Temple of Hadad is believed to have been built on the site now occupied by the Umayyad Mosque, located in the heart of the old city.

The great mosque, which ranks next in sanctity to the mosques of Mecca, Medina, and Jerusalem, is the oldest and most venerated building in Damascus. It represents three epochs in history and the three religions that successively possessed the city: Greco-Roman paganism, Christianity, and Islam. In the fourth century CE, after Constantine embraced Christianity, the temple was reconstructed into an immense church, dedicated around 375 to John the Baptist, whose head, according to tradition, is buried here. After the Muslims captured Damascus in 634 and made it the capital of the Umayyad dynasty and the seat of the caliphate (661–750), the building was remodeled into the magnificent mosque one sees today.

TRAVEL ENTRY #45: MEMORIES OF DAMASCUS

The first morning in Damascus I awakened to a rather common nuisance in a third-world city stretched to its limits. At 7:00 a.m., as I was about to shower, the electricity suddenly went out in my room. Thinking a fuse had blown, I called the front desk, only to learn that the entire district surrounding the hotel was without power.

"Every morning, during hours of peak usage, a different section of Damascus loses power," I was told. "Tomorrow will be fine."

I showered and got dressed in the dark, figuring that a day's inconvenience would simply be part of my "Damascus experience," much as the apostle Paul had been in the dark, without sight, for three days while he was in Damascus (Acts 9:9). The following morning, however, the same thing happened, only this time I was in the shower when the power went off. I did not stay in Damascus long enough to experience a third day of darkness.

One of the joys in Damascus involves stopping at one of the city's squares for a refreshing fruit drink, mixed to order and blended from fresh fruit. During my travels in the Middle East, I always sought to maintain a proper balance between culinary precaution—drinking anything other than bottled water or hot tea was an invitation to trouble—and indulgence. My decisions for the past thirty-five days had either been wise or fortuitous, for I had yet to experience a single bout of gastric discomfort or even a hint of sickness on the trip.

In addition to the old city, with its bazaars and historic sites, a principal attraction is the city's National Museum, one of the world's outstanding museums. Its exhibits are grouped according to four collections, featuring (1) Syro-Oriental antiquities, (2) Syrian antiquities from the Greek, Roman, and Byzantine periods, (3) Arab and Muslim art, and (4) modern and contemporary art. My interest in the biblical period led me to focus on exhibits from the first and second collections, particularly the exhibits from excavations at Mari (destroyed c. 1700 BCE),

Ugarit (destroyed c. 1200 BCE), Dura-Europos (destroyed in 256 CE), and Palmyra (sacked in 272 CE).[3]

One of the first objects I noticed as I entered the museum was a small tablet, one-and-one-half centimeters in height, inscribed with the world's oldest known alphabet. The fourteenth-century BCE tablet, prominently displayed among the antiquities found at Ugarit, featured an alphabet consisting of thirty symbols. It became the basis for the twenty-two-letter alphabet used later by the Phoenicians and Hebrews and adopted by Greeks and all other phonetic languages, including the fixed order of letters from which the English alphabet is ultimately derived. The invention of the alphabet had stupendous advantages over the earlier Sumerian and Egyptian systems, which required mastery of thousands of symbols. Its simplicity represented a giant step toward democratization, for it could be learned by anyone, not just by the upper classes.

The material remains from the port city of Ugarit, including its archives and pottery, give evidence of a cosmopolitan city with numerous foreign contacts. They indicate that much trade and commercial activity took place between Ugarit and sites in Mesopotamia and Egypt as well as with the Minoan and Mycenaean civilizations to the west. An ivory carving on display dates to c. 1200 BCE, when the city was destroyed by Sea Peoples from the Aegean basin heading through Anatolia and south toward Egypt. One tribe—the Philistines—settled in the area known today as the Gaza Strip. For 150 years, until their eventual conquest by the Israelite king David, they were the dominant military presence in Palestine.

Eight civilizations have been uncovered at Mari (known as Tell Hariri in Arabic), an archaeological site located on the right bank of the Euphrates River in eastern Syria, about ten miles from the border with Iraq and some 325 miles from Damascus. The most important find at Mari was a collection of over twenty thousand cuneiform clay tablets, mainly political and economic documents, found in the archives of the palace. The tablets contain numerous cultural parallels to the Old Testament background and shed invaluable light on Israelite tribal society, its structures, organization, and institutions. For example, they mention the Habiru, often seen as forerunners—sociologically if not

---

3. For a chronology of Canaan (including Israel and the entire Holy Land), consult Appendix E.

ethnically—of the Hebrews. They also mention Ur and Haran, cities associated with the biblical patriarch Abraham.

The earliest definite references to Near Eastern divination and prophecy are found in some twenty-five Mari texts. From them we learn that the diviner-prophets of Mari acted largely as spontaneous mouthpieces of deities in behavior that consisted of ecstatic trances, dreams, and the like. This material reminds us of the biblical stories of Balaam, "seer of the gods," said to come from upper Syria. According to the narrative in Numbers 22–24, Balaam was both prophet and diviner. He was hired by Balak, king of Moab, to curse the Israelites by means of divination, but after God spoke through the mouth of Balaam's donkey, the seer could only bless Israel. Divination at Mari reveals a consciousness of prophetic mission among West Semitic tribes in a period predating Israelite prophecy by centuries.

Dura-Europos, located fifteen miles northwest of Mari, was also on the right bank of the Euphrates. Judging from its religious buildings, throughout history the city contained a mixed population. Architectural remains include Greek and Oriental temples, a mithraeum for Roman soldiers, a small Christian chapel, and its most celebrated remain, the world's oldest preserved synagogue. Discovered in 1932, the synagogue was found in a remarkable state of preservation, as noted by E. R. Goodenough and Michael Avi-Yonah in the *Encyclopedia Judaica*:

> [The synagogue] lay just inside the city wall and when the inhabitants, judged expendable by the shrinking Roman Empire, attempted to strengthen the wall against the advancing Sassanid army, they tore off the roofs of the buildings just behind the wall and filled them with sand from the desert. The synagogue was accordingly as securely buried and protected as Pompeii. The paintings [on the synagogue walls], completed only some five years before the city fell, emerged from the sand nearly as fresh as when painted.

The synagogue, with its controversial wall paintings, has been transferred to the Damascus Museum, where it can be seen only by request.[4] I had studied this synagogue and its unique Jewish art during my graduate studies and it was this exhibit in particular that had brought me to the National Museum. The hall that houses the reconstructed syna-

---

4. A copy of the Dura-Europos prayer-room, including the wall paintings, has been reconstructed at Yale University in New Haven, Connecticut.

gogue is kept closed and dark as a means of preserving the paintings and their brilliant colors. Visitors are allowed entrance for only a few minutes before they are ushered out by an attendant.

Despite the brilliance of the colors and the paintings' remarkable state of preservation, it was another feature, the portrayal of human forms, executed according to Hellenistic standards, which made the paintings famous—and controversial. Jewish artistic standards, as Muslim, have long been guided by the injunctions of the Second Commandment (Exodus 20:4), prohibiting animal and human representations. From a social as well as religious standpoint, it is significant that in the third century CE a Jewish community did not hesitate to decorate the walls of a synagogue with the human form, utilizing pagan (Greek and Persian) figures, forms, and symbols. Though the Dura specimen is the only such to have been preserved from that period, it is probable that this type of decoration was commonplace in synagogues of the period. Such influence is also evident in later synagogues in Galilee. When the sixth-century CE mosaic of the Galilean Bet Alfa synagogue was first discovered in 1928, it created a sensation, for the mosaics vividly depicted such pagan cosmological themes as the signs of the zodiac, the four seasons, and the chariot of Helios, the sun god.

The museum hall that houses the Dura-Europos synagogue closely duplicates the dimensions of the original prayer room, forty-five by twenty-five feet, with the ceiling about twenty-three feet in height. Originally, the room had been oriented for worship toward Jerusalem with a niche—presumably for the Torah scroll—in the center of the wall. Around the niche were eighteen paintings of biblical scenes, arranged in variously proportioned rectangles, separated by borders of grapevine patterns. The panel above the niche—clearly the most important design in the room—contained paintings of a *menorah*, an *etrog*, and a *lulav* (traditional Jewish symbols), the temple façade, and a crudely drawn scene of the sacrifice of Isaac.

The ceiling of the prayer room, unfortunately no longer intact, seems originally to have been made of squares and decorated with painted tiles. The many preserved tiles show a large number of fertility symbols, including bunches of grapes and grain and many representations of the ubiquitous goddess of the eastern Mediterranean: Cybele-Demeter-Persephone. Other ceiling tiles depict birds, fish, gazelles, and centaurs. Paintings along the bottom row of the room show masks and harnessed felines, of the kind generally associated with Dionysus and other deities, including Cybele.

It is thought that the synagogue was used in part as an instructional display to educate and teach the history and laws of the religion. Others think that this synagogue was painted in order to compete with the many other religions practiced in Dura Europos. In either case, the discovery of this synagogue, with its Jewish-Hellenistic art style, is of primary importance not only from the social and religious standpoint but also for the history of art.

My five minutes of wonderment were over before I could digest the initial impression. Moderate skills in Middle Eastern diplomacy enabled me to double the length of my visit, but after ten minutes (and my refusal to extend such privileges by the customary use of *baksheesh*, a form of tipping), I returned to the museum's more conventional environment.

The Palmyra exhibit indicated that the ancient city of Palmyra, one of the largest ancient ruins in the world, is also one of the most important archaeological sites in Syria. Despite its remote location—on the northern edge of the Syrian Desert, midway between Damascus and Mari—the site is a popular tourist attraction. Because of its strategic location, the oasis city was an indispensable stop along the Silk Road, the caravan route connecting the Mediterranean world with Mesopotamia, Egypt, and China. During the first century CE, the Romans built a temple to the god Bel (associated with the Babylonian god Marduk), making this temple the most impressive ruin at Palmyra. Only seven of the original 390 columns remain, supporting a portion of the ceiling decorated with the seven planets and encircled by the twelve signs of the zodiac. The city ruins, consisting of gigantic temples and colonnades surrounded by endless desert, make Palmyra's setting one of unrivaled beauty.

I hadn't been in the National Museum more than two minutes when a youngster about sixteen years of age approached me and asked if he could guide me through the museum. He introduced himself as Mohammad. Tall, bright, and handsome, he spoke with confidence, despite having a malformed right arm and hand. He knew the museum intimately, he said, as well as the archaeology and history of Syria, and he wanted only to accompany me so that he might practice his English. I was a bit wary at first, but it soon became clear that his intentions were sincere.

After a few minutes I realized that his loquaciousness and my desire for autonomy were incompatible. I thanked him for his kind offer, but he seemed to pay no heed to my rejection. I tried ignoring him, and then dealt with him curtly, but he responded almost naively to my gruffness. It seemed apparent that he desired friendship and simply wanted so much to converse in English that nothing I did or said could dissuade him. For the next hour he appeared regularly, sharing pearls of wisdom. At one point I informed him that I had been studying Arabic, whereupon he became even more devoted to me. As a concluding conciliatory gesture, he offered to exchange addresses with me and I consented, hoping by this means to brush him away, for my time in the museum and in Syria was extremely limited.

Later on, upon returning to the United States, I found a thoughtful letter and a card from him, addressed to "My dear friend, Robert," and I knew I must respond. I thanked him for his friendship and his interest in me as an American and commended him for his desire to learn English. And then I asked him for a favor. One of my regrets while in Damascus had been my inability to contact Ismat, the Syrian businessman with whom I had spent the final night in Turkey. Ismat had given me a telephone number where he could be reached or where I could leave a message, but when I dialed the number, the receptionist at the other end of the line did not know him. I had tried several times, unsuccessfully, to locate his home or his place of work. Now I saw in this young man's letter an opportunity to respond to a double kindness and to reestablish contact with Ismat. When Mohammad's letter arrived, I learned that he, too, had been unable to locate Ismat. To this day I ponder the identity of this man who came to my rescue at a moment of need, only to disappear from my life forever.

After my visit to the National Museum, I spent the rest of the day exploring the historic old city of Damascus. One cannot enter the city without being reminded of Damascus's fame as a mercantile center. In fact, the name "damask" bears witness to the city's reputation for textiles and crafts. Covered bazaars line the narrow entryways into the city, giving the place a touch of authenticity that I had found missing in the bazaars of Istanbul. Mosques, minarets, donkeys, and Bedouin added Oriental flavor to the ancient city. Weavers and artisans in mother-of-pearl, brass, leather, jewelry, antiques, carpet, and weapons made shopping an interesting experience. Buyers, however, especially American tourists, must be particularly careful, for merchants are quite skilled at making a sale, deftly exposing a vulnerable tourist's weakness. The secret to successful buying requires bargaining in a cold and detached manner. It seems that everyone in Syria wants dollars, so tourists must avoid the black market. Secret agents seem to be everywhere, and fines and jail sentences will be imposed upon any who are caught transacting dollars illegally.

As an American, I provided an attractive target for merchants and their assistants, who offered me hot tea and an opportunity to sample their merchandise. Refusal to enter a store was universally taken as an affront to the proprietor's integrity. After several such encounters in the bazaar, and annoyed by the relentless pressure and predictable conversations, I made my way to the city's less commercial attractions by looking straight ahead and ignoring the endless entreaties.

As I emerged from the city's commercial bowels, I headed for the Umayyad Mosque, Damascus' most famous site. This "crown jewel" of the Umayyad Empire, with its minarets, mosaics, and other architectural wonders, speaks of a time when Damascus was the capital of the Arab world (661–750). I was interested in the mosque because it is said to contain the head of John the Baptist. John, the famous forerunner and immediate relative of Jesus, was beheaded by Herod Antipas for his blistering personal attack against Herod for his marriage to his brother's wife Herodias (Mark 6:17). He is revered as prophet by Muslims and Christians alike.

The environs of the mosque also contain the mausoleum of Saladin, considered the greatest Muslim warrior of all time. In 1187, Saladin captured Jerusalem from the Crusaders, after defeating their armies decisively on the strangely shaped ridge near the Sea of Galilee known as the Horns of Hattin. This defeat brought an end to the Latin Kingdom of Jerusalem (1099–1187) and ensured that Islamic worship would continue on the Temple Mount without interruption to the present day. Whereas Muslims regard Saladin as a saintly figure, Christians also admire and respect him for his honesty, fairness, and bravery. After reading his biography, I too became an admirer, convinced that Saladin was head and shoulders above the other heroes of his day and quite possibly one of the greatest humans ever to have lived.

A few blocks south of the mosque is perhaps Damascus's most famous street, a road known in antiquity as "the Street Called Straight." According to the Book of Acts, it was on this street that an early Christian named Judas lived, and it was here that St. Paul recovered his sight at the hands of Ananias (9:10–18) following his conversion. Today, Straight Street (also known as the Via Recta) consists of the streets of Bab Sharqi and the Suq Medhat Pasha, a covered market. Bab Sharqi Street, filled with small shops, leads to the old Christian quarter of Bab Touma (St. Thomas' Gate). At the end of Bab Sharqi Street one reaches the House of Ananias, an underground chapel that was the cellar of Ananias's house.

It was dark by the time I neared the House of Ananias. As I walked by, a young man standing at the door of a shop engaged me in a conversation. He told me that he was a Lebanese Christian, temporarily exiled from his war-torn country and endangered home. He was working for a business owned by a Christian family, he said, and many of the homes and shops in this district belonged to Christians. He invited me into the shop for an unpressured look at his wares, offering to follow it with a private tour of Ananias' Chapel, to which he had access even though it was already closed for the night. That was an offer I couldn't refuse.

The shop's merchandise and furnishings were impressive. The young salesman had told the truth, for as I was seated at a beautiful inlaid table, surrounded by linens, finely embroidered tablecloths, and exquisite silver tea sets and trays, I felt no pressure whatsoever to buy. The items easily sold themselves. Had I come to Damascus to purchase Middle Eastern decor for my home, I need have visited only this one shop. The temptation to purchase exotic luxury items, unavailable at such bargain prices anywhere in the West, was hard to resist.

At the conclusion of the tea ceremony, the young Lebanese escorted me down the street and through a courtyard to a lady who handed him a large key. At the end of the yard we came to some steps that led to the locked underground chapel. The room, said to be the oldest place of Christian worship, is believed to mark the spot where St. Paul was taken for safekeeping when certain Jews in the city sought to apprehend him as a traitor. A legend states that an underground tunnel connected this spot with the city walls, which explains how the new Christian convert eluded his would-be captors and escaped from the city by being lowered in a basket under cover of darkness to freedom beyond the city walls. A vivid painting of Paul's dramatic escape hangs in the small chapel of Saint Ananias.

Later that night, after I returned to my hotel room, I was greeted by several of the hotel's guests who were anxious to meet an American.

One man was going to Beirut, Lebanon on business the following day. He invited me to join him for the ninety-minute ride, and though I found the offer quite tempting, my passport clearly indicated that the nation was unsafe and off-limits to Americans. The country was locked in so desperate a civil war that the beautiful city of Beirut had become a wasteland, its beauty scarred by daily shellings and guerilla warfare. The presence of PLO refugee camps, Israeli troops, and Syrian forces scattered about the country added to the high level of violence and insecurity. Various Americans and other Westerners stationed in Beirut had recently been taken hostage by Muslim extremists, so Americans living in Lebanon had been urged to leave the country and no American tourists were allowed in.

Despite its allure, Beirut was not the main reason I wanted to visit Lebanon. For me, the primary attraction was Baalbek, approximately fifty miles northeast of Beirut and less than ten miles from the Syrian border. There, near the northern end of the Bekaa Valley, stands the temple complex of Baalbek, one of the most impressive monuments from the Roman period and the most important tourist attraction in Lebanon. Situated atop a high point in the Bekaa valley, the ruins are one of the most extraordinary and enigmatic holy places of ancient times. Biblical scholar and tour guide LaMar Berrett describes the massive site as follows: "The visitor is not immediately aware that the columns he sees are among the tallest ever erected, the stones the largest ever used, and the whole group of edifices the biggest of its kind ever built."[5]

Baalbek is known to be one of the oldest cities in the world, its history dating back around five thousand years. The Phoenicians settled in Baalbek as early as 2000 BCE and built their first temple dedicated to the sky god Baal, from which the city got its name. During Roman times, the sanctuary was a pilgrimage site similar to Delphi. Trajan's biographer records that the emperor consulted the oracle there.

The Golden Age of Roman building at Baalbek (called Heliopolis by the Romans) began in 15 BCE when the emperor Augustus began construction of the great Temple of Jupiter. This temple, the single largest religious edifice erected by the Romans, was completed soon after 60 CE. Though it is not known why the Romans built this huge pagan complex in this rather remote part of the empire, it is certain that the

---

5. Lamar C. Berrett, *Discovering the World of the Bible* (Nashville: Thomas Nelson, 1979), 471.

project required funding from the entire Roman realm. During the next three centuries, as emperors succeeded one another in the imperial capital of Rome, Baalbek/Heliopolis would be filled with the most massive religious buildings ever constructed in the far-reaching Roman Empire. These monuments functioned as places of worship until Christianity was declared the official religion of the Roman Empire in 313 CE, at which time the Byzantine Christian emperors desecrated thousands of pagan sanctuaries.

In the 1700s, European explorers began to visit the ruins, and in 1898 the German emperor William II organized the first restoration of the ancient temples. Today Baalbek is famous for its annual summer festival, the Baalbek International Festival, touted as the oldest and most prestigious cultural event in the Middle East.

The following morning I awoke early, as was my custom while traveling in the Middle East. I found it almost impossible to sleep later than 6:00 a.m. while staying in any city in this part of the world, on account of the customary early rising by the street vendors. For those who need an additional reminder, the call to prayer that emanates regularly from Muslim minarets, beginning at dawn, provides a fail-safe "wake-up call."

Prior to my departure for Jordan, I crossed the Barada River to inspect some of the city's more modern neighborhoods. I walked along broad boulevards and found shopping areas and office complexes still closed, adhering more closely to western business hours. Behind a cluster of buildings I came to a small park, where along one side of a building I saw a huge painted portrait. The smiling, benevolent-looking figure was the nation's ruthless dictator, General Hafez al-Assad. Dictators around the world often used the walls of prominent buildings as galleries to portray themselves in flattering poses and heroic proportions, and I was reminded of the contrasting privilege and responsibility that come with living in a democratic society, where ordinary citizens are counted on to make extraordinary contributions.

Returning to my hotel, I picked up my luggage and headed to the bus station for a journey to Amman, so near—a mere 115-mile journey—and yet another Middle-Eastern border-crossing away.

15

Wilderness Wanderings: Jordan and the Sinai

TRAVEL ENTRY #46: FROM DAMASCUS TO AMMAN

CROSSING THE BORDER BETWEEN Syria and Jordan was the single-most vexing experience of my journey. For three and a half hours my fellow travelers and I stood in the rain at the border waiting for our bus to clear customs. Our unlocked luggage, awaiting inspection, sat in the rain as well. For some reason, the customs officials were paying particular attention to our bus. Like scavengers, they unscrewed panels, pounded metal parts, and literally stripped the vehicle clean. I had never before witnessed the disassembly of a means of public transportation, so I watched the process with keen interest. If the Syrian officials at the Turkish border seemed observant, their Jordanian counterparts made them look like amateurs. Lengthy delays were customary at border crossings, but scrutiny of this sort certainly was not. Rumors began to circulate as to the cause of the unusual delay. Surely something suspicious, like a bomb threat, had provoked it. Though I never learned the cause, when I arrived in Amman, I was asked by representatives of the bus company to sign an official complaint. As an American traveling through a part of the world where bizarre incidents are often the norm, I felt I should remain uninvolved, so I declined the request.

Earlier, as I rode the bus toward the Jordanian border, I met two travelers, one an Arab poet from Jerusalem who had lived in Amman for twenty-two years and the other an Arab Christian named Mazen, who also lived in Amman. Mazen entertained me with stories about desert Bedouin, the tent-dwelling nomads commonly found in the regions bordering the Arabian Desert. His characterization of Bedouin as honest, reliable, generous people who cared for the needy and protected strangers reminded me of the Turkish tobacco farmer and his family, who had exhibited precisely those virtues when I was in need of shelter several nights earlier. There seems to be a bit of Bedouin spirit in every Arab soul, for such qualities characterize Middle Easterners as a whole.

When I arrived in Amman, the capital of Jordan, it was 10:00 p.m. The exhausting 125-mile journey—including delays—had taken over twelve hours. I probably could have made better time traveling by bicycle. Something seemed strange, almost eerie, as I walked the few blocks from the bus station to my hotel; I felt I was walking through a ghost town. The bus station was deserted, as were the streets and sidewalks. How unlike the Middle East! Even at the hotel everything was extremely quiet. The only person I saw was the hotel clerk, who explained, in broken English, that I had arrived on a national holiday. Today was King Hussein's birthday, a mandatory though somewhat awkward celebration, for Jordan had only recently become a kingdom. The festival was bereft of pageantry and tradition in a country where nearly two thirds of the population was Palestinian and where allegiance was more sociological than political.

TRAVEL ENTRY #47: CONVERSING WITH PALESTINIANS IN AMMAN

At al-Monzer Hotel in Amman, I had a chance encounter with two Palestinian refugees, Mustafa and his son Muhammad. Mustafa had worked as a turbine mechanic in Israel but had lost his job eighteen months earlier at the start of the Intifada, a series of uprisings in the occupied territories that included demonstrations, strikes, and rock-throwing attacks on Israeli soldiers. Mustafa had lost his property, then his job, and he and his family of ten were now living in the Gaza Beach Camp for refugees. He had come to Jordan with Muhammad in hopes of finding a way for his eldest son to study in Germany. The family's options were severely limited. They couldn't go back to Israel, and immigration to the United States was prohibitively expensive and simply out of the question. Even a visit to neighboring Egypt was restricted to a limited number of days, with severe penalties for noncompliance; an extension of even a single day meant imprisonment, and the current Jordanian policy prohibited Palestinian immigration.

Mustafa and I met during two evenings to speak about the prospects for peace in the Middle East. My position was that the history, aspirations, and fate of the Jews and the Palestinian Arabs were intimately intertwined. Each group wants recognition, acceptance, independence, sovereignty, and territorial identity. Both seek worldwide approval and support from external allies and from one of the world's superpowers; and each side fears total destruction or complete denial by the other. Yet neither officially recognizes the other's existence.

The Jewish position seems clear: since 135 CE, when the Roman emperor Hadrian completed the suppression of the Jewish revolt in Palestine, the pain of the Diaspora, compounded by intense racial persecution, was an ever-present motivation for Jews to return to their biblical home and to create a state in Israel as a refuge. Many Jews feel that Israel is the fulfillment of biblical prophecy and the culmination of a long-standing dream to establish life under a government of their own choice.

Current Palestinians suffer from similar circumstances of homelessness, and their desire for self-determination and a national homeland also arouses strong worldwide support. The Palestinians, like the Jews, claim to be driven by religious conviction based on the promises of God, and they consider Palestine their homeland since earliest biblical times. While maintaining a legal and moral claim on their homeland, those who remain in the West Bank and Gaza have been forced to choose between exile and living under Israeli occupation. They are obsessed with the dream of a government of their own choosing—an option that seems increasingly elusive. Of the ten million people currently living between Jordan and the Mediterranean Sea, 49 percent are Palestinian. One million of those are citizens of Israel. The other four million are stateless residents of the West Bank and Gaza, who live under Palestinian jurisdiction, subject to conditions imposed by Israel.

Mustafa's suffering prevented him from agreeing with my assessment. He saw no parallel between the history and circumstances of Jews and Palestinians. For him, the starting point in any discussion required acknowledgement that Palestinians in Israel had been deprived of basic human rights. They could not vote, assemble peacefully, choose their own leaders, travel without restrictions, or own property without fear of its being confiscated. As a people, they were branded by Israeli officials as terrorist, and even minor demonstrations brought the most severe punishment from the military authorities. He claimed that Palestinians were arrested and held without trial for extended periods of time, that some of his people were tortured in attempts to force confessions, that their own lawyers were not permitted to defend them in the Israeli courts, and that appeals were costly and fruitless.

Palestinians, he said, were convinced that some of the Israeli political leaders were trying through subtle harassment to force another exodus of Arabs from the occupied territories. As an example, he mentioned that oranges and other perishable farm products grown by Palestinian Arabs were not permitted to be sold in Israel if they competed with Israeli produce. In such cases, the produce had to be given away, dumped, or exported to Jordan. He claimed that the oranges and vegetables of activist families were often held up at the Allenby Bridge, the border crossing with Jordan, until they spoiled. And in some areas of Israel, the Palestinian farmers were not permitted to replace the fruit trees that died in their orchards.

The litany of grievances continued. Palestinian schools and universities were frequently closed down, educators were arrested, bookstores padlocked, library books censored, and children were left on the street or at home for extended periods of time, without hope of employment. Any serious altercation between these idle and angry young people and the military might result in the sending of bulldozers into the community to destroy homes. He claimed that Israeli settlers were as guilty as any Arabs in initiating violence but were seldom if ever arrested or punished.

Mustafa's primary concern, shared by Palestinians but also by many Americans and by a majority of external observers, is the extensive building of Jewish settlements in the West Bank. Since 1977, when the Likud party gained control of the government, the effort to take Arab lands has become one of Israel's top priorities. Mustafa remained hopeful for a lasting solution to the problems of the region, even though the immediate future seemed bleak.

Israelis and Palestinians have taken starkly different approaches to redress their grievances. Without ever abandoning their ambitious goal of a uniquely Jewish nation—with boundaries similar to those in the time of King David and surrounded by peaceful neighbors—the Jews have been willing to progress in incremental steps, even compromising temporarily when necessary. The Palestinians, on the other hand, have habitually refused to compromise and have remained committed to the position of "all or nothing." This uncompromising stance has led to world sympathy but limited gains, whereas the Israelis have made significant progress.

Recent events, including the victory of the radical Islamic movement Hamas in the 2006 Palestinian elections, are threatening to dramatically reshape Palestinian relations with Israel and the rest of the world. Hamas, which emerged during the first Palestinian Intifada (in 1987) as an offshoot of Egypt's Muslim Brotherhood, favors the creation of a Palestinian nation on land that now includes Israel rather than the two-state solution long prescribed by the United Nations.

There seem to be three basic views to relations between the Jews and the Palestinians:

1. a hopeful position for Palestine—parity and statehood for Palestinians will lessen the Arab-Israeli hostility and lead to Arab acceptance of the State of Israel;

2. a hopeful position for Israel—the unequivocal acceptance of Israel's existence by a major portion of the Arab world will result in a solution for the Palestinians;

3. a pessimistic position—no permanent peace can come to the Middle East so long as a Jewish state exists in the heartland of the Arab world. From the Israeli perspective, the flip side of this skeptical attitude views granting self-determination to the Palestinians as the first step toward the destruction of Israel.

Our conversation ended on a hopeful note when Mustafa extended an invitation for me to visit him at his home in Gaza a week later, when I would be in Israel. I took down his address and directions to his home, fully intending to visit him if at all possible. One of the objectives of my sabbatical journey was to conduct frank discussions on Arab-Israeli issues with individuals on both sides of the fence, and this dialogue was a great start. I hoped to be able to interview Israeli Jews shortly, when I reached Israel.

TRAVEL ENTRY #48: AMMAN AND ITS ENVIRONS

I originally planned to enter Israel via the Allenby Bridge, a temporary bridge across the Jordan River built in 1968 that connects the nation of Jordan with the West Bank city of Jericho. Since the border was only twenty-five miles from Amman, I could travel there easily by bus or taxi.

During the 1970s, this bridge was the scene of a large and uninterrupted flow of people going back and forth between the two countries. The situation changed dramatically in the 1980s, when waiting lines at both sides of the border extended for hundreds of yards and only a trickle of people were allowed through. I knew from a previous trip to the Middle East that anyone interested in visiting Jordan and Israel should do so in that order, for if one's passport was stamped first in Israel, it would not be honored subsequently in Jordan.

When I inquired about crossing the Allenby Bridge (known in Jordan as the King Hussein Bridge), I learned that I could not do so without special documentation from the Department of the Interior, accompanied by a photograph, customs stamps, and a return ticket to Jordan. Today was Wednesday, and I was told that the earliest I could enter Israel would be Sunday and possibly not until Monday. Friday is the Jordanian Sabbath, Saturday is the Jewish Sabbath, and on Sunday only a select number of people are allowed to cross. This information made my decision a simple one: I would instead enter Israel from Egypt, via the Sinai. After completing my visit to Amman and its environs I would proceed to Petra, the remote rock-hewn site located 170 miles south of Amman, and then continue to Aqaba, my transit point to the Sinai.

EXPLANATORY ENTRY #31: A BRIEF HISTORY OF AMMAN

The city of Amman was settled as far back as 3500 BCE. Built originally on seven hills (like Rome and Istanbul), Amman has expanded considerably in recent times to encompass nineteen hills. Its early heyday was around 1200 BCE, when it was the capital of the Ammonites, of Old Testament fame. Greeks and Romans later erected their own cities, and during Greco-Roman times (third century BCE) the city became known as Philadelphia. Under the influence of Roman culture, Philadelphia was reconstructed in typically grand Roman style with colonnaded streets, baths, and an amphitheater. As a member of the Decapolis, a group of ten cities on the eastern frontier of the Roman Empire in Syria and Judea (renamed Palestine in 135 CE), Philadelphia continued to prosper due to its location on the King's Highway, the main commercial route between Arabia and Damascus. The city flourished after the Arab conquest in the seventh century, but declined gradually in importance after that. When Abdullah moved the seat of his newly formed government to Amman in

1921, it was a village of less than two thousand inhabitants. Since then, Amman has grown rapidly into a modern, sprawling metropolis of over two million people. The city's antiquities include the Roman Theater, cut in part out of the solid rock of the Citadel Hill. Many ancient sites were pillaged over time, and stones were removed for use as building materials during later periods, but the theater at Amman remained intact. Today it seats six thousand people and is still used for special occasions.

As on other occasions in my travels, I had a difficult decision to make after my visit to Citadel Hill. Having a half day before I left for Petra, I could visit only one of two important sites: the ruins of Jerash (ancient Gerasa), the best preserved example of a provincial Roman city and one of the most spectacular ruins in the entire Middle East, or the famous Mount Nebo, with its unparalleled view of the biblical Promised Land. Since I had already visited Pompeii and viewed the spectacular Roman ruins of Ephesus, I decided to forego a visit to Jerash and instead take the King's Highway south to the ancient city of Madaba, twenty miles from Amman, to view its celebrated ancient mosaics. Close to Madaba, directly east of the northern end of the Dead Sea, stands Mount Nebo, said to be the place where Moses first viewed the Promised Land and where he died.[1]

I had no trouble getting to Madaba by bus, where I took a taxi to Saint George's Greek Orthodox Church to view the town's most important and famous attraction: a mosaic map of Egypt and Palestine, with a detailed map of Jerusalem that depicts how the city looked in the sixth century CE. The viewing arrangement had been made on the bus by a young Christian boy, who led me to the taxi driver, also a Christian. Most visitors to Madaba come in tour buses and therefore bypass natives, but it is obvious that local Christians are proud of their heritage and eager to display their artistic and historical knowledge of the mosaics.

The town of Madaba stands on a tell, a vast mound in the middle of a battle-scarred plain. The site reached its prominence during the Byzantine era (fifth and sixth centuries CE), and most of the mosaics date from this period. Madaba was destroyed by Persians in 614, then occupied by Arabs until an earthquake in 747 (the same earthquake that destroyed Jerash) caused the site to be abandoned until the nineteenth century, when two thousand Christians from the town of Kerak, sixty miles to the south, settled here. In rebuilding the city the settlers uncov-

---

1. See Numbers 27:12–14; Deuteronomy 32:49; and Deuteronomy 34:5–6.

ered the priceless mosaics that have made Madaba famous. Many homes and churches were built over the Byzantine church mosaic floors.

Saint George's Greek Orthodox Church was built over the map mosaic in 1896, on the site of an earlier basilica. The beautiful map in the mosaic floor is the only one in the world that shows Jerusalem during the early sixth century. The original map, stretching forty-five feet by fifteen feet, included over two million tiles. The map portrayed the area from Egypt to Syria, though only a few fringe pieces remain to complement the central portion of Jerusalem and the Dead Sea. Of the principal buildings depicted in this map of Jerusalem, the most interesting is the Church of the Holy Sepulcher. The walls and gates of the city are very clear. Saint Catherine's Monastery at Mount Sinai and other monasteries are also depicted on the map.

The taxi driver waited while I viewed the mosaics, and then drove me six miles to Mount Nebo (which means "height"), the highest point of a ridge called Pisgah ("point"). Even though the skies were hazy at this time of the year, caused by the Dead Sea's heavy evaporation, the panoramic view of the craggy terrain and of the Dead Sea and Jericho in the distance was as I imagined from biblical references. On a clear day, I am told, one can see Jerusalem.

TRAVEL ENTRY #49: WILD, WONDERFUL PETRA

The following morning I boarded an express bus bound for the fabled site of Petra. Visitors arriving at Petra are surprised at the scope of the site, for this isn't one big monument but a collection of dozens of huge carvings and canyons set against a backdrop of technicolored sandstone cliffs. The site is entered by the Bab-es-Siq, the 1,200-meter-long gorge formed by tectonic forces aeons ago. The passage is only eight feet wide in places, amid red cliffs that tower to heights of three hundred feet. This narrow entrance, frequently entered on horseback, is a magnificent introduction to the wonders of Petra itself. Parts of the Roman paved road through Petra remain, as do large sections of the water channels the Nabatean Arabs cut into the cliff walls to pipe water into their city.

As they traverse the Siq, visitors catch tantalizing glimpses of Petra's premier attraction: el-Khazneh—the Treasury. Made famous by *Indiana Jones and the Last Crusade*, the third film in the Indiana Jones series, it is one of the largest and most complete monuments at Petra. Cut completely from the cliff face, it stands 100 feet wide and 141 feet high, its colonnaded façade indicative of Nabatean imaginative skill when carving the rose-colored sandstone. The structure, with its three interior chambers, was carved in the first century BCE as a tomb for a Nabatean king, making the designation "the Treasury" a misnomer. The name, more recent, is due to local Bedouin stories that once the city was abandoned—due to an earthquake and the fall of the Roman Empire—pirates used the site to hide treasure.

Beyond this point the valley widens, allowing some of the hundreds of tombs and cave dwellings that comprise the site to come into view. Many of the stone carvings are huge, with elaborate façades carved directly from the rock face. Two thousand years of wind and water erosion have taken their toll, though the exquisiteness of workmanship coupled with the multi-colored beauty of the rock is still obvious. A four-thousand-seat theater, first constructed by the Nabateans around the time of Christ but later refurbished by the Romans, is another standout.

About halfway between the Treasury and the theater a steep path leads to the High Place of Sacrifice (el-Mabdah in Arabic), providing a stunning view of the city ruins below. The arduous ascent is the ideal way to appreciate Petra's natural beauty and the extensive Nabatean use of the site's many valleys and mountaintops. This particular "high place," believed to have come from the biblical-era Edomites who inhabited the land before the Nabateans, is considered the best preserved high place from the ancient biblical period. A forty-minute climb up a series of stairs, ramps, walkways, and paths brought me to the summit of Jabal Mabdah. Several processional ways once led up to the High Place of Sacrifice, which comprised two adjacent altars used for the sacrifice of animals. An open central court contained a small raised platform, shallow benches around three sides, and a nearby pool with water channels and drains. The view of the valley far below, with its Nabatean and Roman monuments, included a triple-entrance arched gate and a colonnaded street. This area, the center of the city in Roman times, featured a variety of buildings on both sides of the road.

My descent via the Wadi Farasa route followed the main Nabatean processional way past additional monuments and cultic installations. The path passed the ruins of an ancient Roman military settlement. An assignment to this remote outpost must have been both strange and compelling for the legions sent to defend this portion of the Roman province of Arabia. It is believed that as many as seven thousand people lived in Petra during its Roman heyday.

My self-guided tour of Petra ended with a visit to the rock-cut royal tombs at the east end of the central valley. The Palace Tomb, one of Petra's largest buildings, is believed to be a copy of a Roman palace. Three stories high, it boasts Petra's largest façade. The nearby Urn Tomb contains a Greek inscription indicating that the building was used briefly as a Christian church in 447 CE. At this spot I saw several Bedouin and other enterprising individuals selling jewelry. I was attracted by the authentic Jordanian artwork and purchased two bracelets, hand-crafted by Bedouin, one onyx and the other turquoise. I knew I could purchase items such as these in the gift shops of Amman, but was happy to skip the urban middlemen and to create a memorable experience of this enchanting place and its local residents.

As I looked into the timeless features of the Bedouin around me, I wondered about their ancestry. Who were the original Nabateans, and what could one learn of those remarkable stone-carving masters forgotten for hundreds of years? The Nabateans were a nomadic Arab people from the region of Nabatea in the northwest Arabian Desert who ranged between northern Arabia and southern Syria. In the sixth century BCE, when Babylon depopulated the kingdom of Judah, the Edomites took their place. The Nabateans in turn filtered into Edom. They eventually came to control the major trade route between Mecca and Damascus, as well as the Spice Route between Mecca and Gaza. For four hundred years they thrived in the valley.

At first, using this desolate impregnable spot as a hideout, they plundered caravans going between Arabia, Syria, and Egypt. Eventually they stopped plundering and began exacting a high toll for safe passage. During the third and second centuries BCE they became settled villagers and by 100 BCE were ruled by a monarch, King Aretas II. The first great monuments in Petra appeared around this time. Under Aretas III (86–62 BCE), the Nabateans extended their kingdom as far north as Damascus. At their peak around the time of Christ, the Nabateans were trading not only with Palestine, Egypt, and Syria but also with Greece, Rome, and even China. The Romans conquered Petra shortly thereafter, annexing the Nabatean territories in 106 CE. In 363 an earthquake destroyed buildings and damaged the vital water management system, forcing many inhabitants to leave. The Byzantines established an outpost here, and then later so did the Crusaders, in whose hands it remained until 1189. The ruins of Petra were an object of curiosity in the Middle Ages and were largely abandoned after that. Petra was lost to the world until 1812, when Johann Burkhardt, posing as a Muslim, gazed with wonder into the valley.

TRAVEL ENTRY #50: AQABA TO MOUNT SINAI

There is much to explore at Petra, and two days are a minimum for those who really want to absorb the fascinating setting. My travel clock was ticking, however, so that evening I boarded a minibus and traveled fifty miles to Aqaba, Jordan's port city on the Gulf of Aqaba. The site was made famous by the twenty-eight-year-old British officer T. E. Lawrence (better known as Lawrence of Arabia), who in 1916 marched across eight hundred miles of desert with a scratch force of Arabs and managed the surrender of the Turkish garrison guarding the Ottoman port.

The northern tip of the Gulf of Aqaba had a strategic value, then as now, for it forms the boundary of four countries: Egypt, Israel, Jordan, and thirteen miles south of Aqaba, Saudi Arabia. A few miles west of Aqaba, across the gulf, lies Eilat, Israel's southernmost city and that country's sole access to the Red Sea. Israel occupied the Sinai from 1967 until 1979, but returned it to Egypt as part of the historic peace treaty based on the Camp David Accords. During their occupation, the Israelis developed the Sinai economically, building a network of paved roads and developing attractive beach resorts along the western and southern shores of the Gulf of Aqaba.

Unlike most cities in the Middle East, Aqaba is a clean and modern city, and I decided to spend the evening walking near the waterfront, on a circular drive that took me past the presidential palaces. As I neared the palace complex, I encountered a detachment of four Jordanian guards eating their evening meal along the vacant roadway. At first they regarded me with distrust, but their suspicion lessened as we communicated through sign language and verbal snippets in Arabic, French, and English. I learned that President Hussein, who had come to Aqaba several days earlier to celebrate his birthday, was still there. Abiding by Middle Eastern hospitality, the security guards invited me to join them for dinner and I gladly accepted.

After dinner, walking as far west as the road allowed, I looked across the bay toward the Israeli city of Eilat, knowing that though only a few miles separated Aqaba from Eilat, ideologically they were as far apart as two planets. I thought of Muhammad and Mustafa, the father and son I had met in Amman, and of the untold millions of young people in the Middle East who long for freedom and are willing to take great risks and undergo additional hardship in search of a better way of life. My heart was filled with compassion for the Palestinians who feel trapped and are desperate to disengage from the unending cycle of violence, hatred, and distrust. I contemplated the next step in my journey, visiting Israel and the occupied Palestinian territories, wondering what insights and experiences I would gain there that might enable me to think more hopefully about the future of this powder keg region.

The forty-mile ferry ride from Aqaba to Nuweiba, the port of entry to Mount Sinai (called Jebel Musa by the Arabs) was less than memorable. In addition to the usual hassles and border delays, spending four and a half hours on a crowded ferry was not my idea of fun. There is a fast ferry nowadays—a hydrofoil—which, though quite expensive, takes only about ninety minutes. But one still has to buy tickets and go through customs, and that can take hours. I'm not sure the hydrofoil option was available in 1989, but I was unaware of it. At the ferry landing I located a dilapidated taxi heading to Dahab, an attractive beach resort halfway between Nuweiba and Sharm el-Sheikh, a luxury resort near the southern tip of the Sinai Peninsula. The crowded taxi forced me to endure yet another forty miles of discomfort.

With its colorful coral reefs and deep dive sites, the Gulf of Aqaba has become a Mecca for divers and sun bathers. While Sharm el-Sheikh serves as the tourist center for the Sinai, Dahab has developed into a tourist spot as well, due to its reasonable prices and newly constructed beach promenade. My impression of Dahab was of a Tahiti-like fairyland with lots of palm trees, cozy restaurants, and tourist huts near the beach. During the summer months the place is quite crowded, attracting globetrotters from across the world to its lively atmosphere. Dahab is also famous for its deep dive sites, known by such fanciful names as The Blue Hole, The Canyon, and The Lighthouse. Due to strong winds and spectacular coral reefs, the town caters to a young crowd interested in windsurfing, diving, and other water sports.

That night I met a young Scandinavian traveler who had spent a year as a high school exchange student in Washington, Pennsylvania, the small college town in the United States where I teach. I knew his host family and we marveled at the coincidence of meeting in this remote location. The next morning, without time even to soak in the beach atmosphere, I joined a group of four for a taxi ride to St. Catherine's, the ancient monastery that lies at the base of the mountain where tradition says that Moses received the Ten Commandments. As we drove inland, the Egyptian desert yielded some spectacular scenery. The taxi climbed the hills of the Sinai for two hours until it reached the monastery at 5,012 feet above sea level.

EXPLANATORY ENTRY #32: ST. CATHERINE'S MONASTERY

A place of refuge since it was founded in the middle of the fourth century CE, St. Catherine's lies in a desert valley overlooking the small settlement of al Milqa, in the shadow of boulder-strewn hills. Christians initially came here to pray near the Burning Bush—where God spoke to Moses—at a small chapel dedicated to St. Catherine, an early Christian martyr.

There is no current archaeological evidence to support the view that the 7,500-foot granite peak called Jebel Musa is the actual Mt. Sinai (also called Mt. Horeb) of the Old Testament, so scholars have proposed alternative locations. The association of Jebel Musa with the biblical Mt. Sinai seems to have first developed in the third century CE, when hermits living in caves on the mountain began to identify their mountain with the ancient holy peak.

The assumed identification of Jebel Musa with the Mosaic site was a powerful attraction to hermits and pilgrims of the early Christian era. The most famous of these was the Empress Helena, mother of Constantine, who visited many of the holy sites in Palestine and who confirmed her belief in the authenticity of this site by constructing the first church in the area. Called the Chapel of the Burning Bush, the sanctuary was constructed where grew a rare specimen of *rubus sanctus*, a species of wild raspberry that the monks believe is the original Burning Bush. This species, which grows in the mountainous areas of Central Asia, is rare in the desert, there being only five other known specimens in the entire Sinai Peninsula.

A monastic community soon developed around the chapel and, to protect both the monks and the chapel from attacks by roving Bedouin, the Byzantine emperor Justinian I built a magnificent basilica and a fortress around the chapel. The great walled monastery found today was the product of later centuries. The basilica was called the Church of the Transfiguration, in memory of the transfiguration of Jesus in the presence of Moses, Elijah, and several disciples on Mt. Tabor in Israel (Mark 9:2–8).

After Helena, the next famous pilgrim to Jebel Musa and the monastery was the prophet Muhammad. Being well treated by the Orthodox Christian monks, Muhammad gave his personal pledge of protection, which became incumbent on all Muslims. This promise ensured the monastery's safety and continued existence. During the Middle Ages, many pilgrims came annually, despite the arduous eight-day journey from Cairo by camel and on foot. Following the Reformation, Christian pilgrimage drastically declined and until the 1950s, no more than eighty to one hundred pilgrims made the journey each year. At that time, the Egyptian government, finding huge oil reserves in the Sinai, paved roads leading to oil fields and mines along the western Sinai coast and also built a dirt road to the monastery at the base of mountain. The Israeli occupation of the Sinai in 1967, followed by its return to Egypt in 1980 and the completion of a paved road, further increased the number of visitors to Jebel Musa. Bus service to and from Cairo and Eilat became available on a daily basis so that today it is not uncommon for a hundred or more pilgrims and tourists to visit the ancient sacred site in a single day.

Access is currently limited to only a select few areas of the monastery, including the Church of the Transfiguration and the Chapel of the Burning Bush. Visitors are prohibited from viewing the invaluable collection of icons and manuscripts kept elsewhere. The library, one of the oldest in the world and second only to the Vatican in possession of priceless books, contains thousands of works, including valuable Greek and Arabic manuscripts. The famous Codex Sinaiticus, the oldest complete edition of the Bible in existence, was discovered here in 1844 by the German scholar Constantine Tischendorf, who was touring the Middle East in search of old manuscripts. He visited four times in the next fifteen years until finally, in 1859, he persuaded the monks to allow him to borrow the entire manuscript. It was never returned. The manuscript remained in Russia until 1933, when Stalin, desperate for money, sold the manuscript to the United Kingdom for £100,000. Today the manuscript is on display in the British Museum.

My visit to the monastery began with the Church of the Transfiguration, built in the shape of a basilica, where a collection of icons is on display. In the apse of the church is a magnificent mosaic depicting the transfiguration of Jesus. Most visitors are not permitted in this section of the church, but when I presented my scholarly and religious credentials, I was permitted to enter the holy site. It was an honor to view this treasure, one of the earliest and most beautiful mosaics of the Eastern Church, preserved in such pristine condition. Behind the altar is the Chapel of the Burning Bush, built over the original site of the burning bush. In a clear break with tradition, the holy altar of the chapel does not stand upon the remains of the martyrs, which is the rule, but above the roots of the burning bush. Pilgrims enter this holiest place of the monastery without shoes, in remembrance of the commandment of God to Moses: "put off your shoes from your feet, for the place on which you are standing is holy ground" (Exodus 3:5).

TRAVEL ENTRY #51: CLIMBING MT. SINAI WITH ROB

Later that afternoon I met a forty-six-year-old Dutchman named Rob. Tall, slim, and about my age, he could have passed for my twin. We immediately bonded and developed a strong friendship as we traveled together for the next three days. Rob, who had signed up for a room in the village next to the monastery, agreed to join me in a two-hour climb to the top of the mountain later that night in time to witness the Sunday morning sunrise.

I awoke at 3:00 a.m. and by 3:15 Rob joined me as we silently made our way along the moonlit path. The Sinai was so bright that night that we hardly needed the flashlights we had been given. The starlit sky was spectacular. The distant stars seemed so close I felt I could reach out and touch them. God also felt near. I understood why ancient inhabitants of the Sinai and even Bedouin today worshipped the moon god, Sin (from which the Sinai gets its name). The moon is a compelling force in the desert, so forceful that it elicits wonder and praise. But it was Moses who was able to go beyond the sun and the moon, powerful forces in that awesome landscape, to the personal God, Yahweh, behind those forces and communicate directly and intimately with that God. His faith and experience carved a path for the Israelites but also established a roadmap for future followers.

At the peak of Jebel Musa we relived biblical history. A small chapel stands there, dedicated to the Holy Trinity. Constructed on the ruins of a sixteenth-century church, the chapel is believed to enclose the rock from which God made the tablets of the Law. In the western wall of the chapel is a cleft in the rock where Moses is said to have hidden himself as God's glory passed by (Exodus 33:22). Seven hundred and fifty steps below the summit is the plateau known as Elijah's Basin, where Elijah spent forty days communing with God in a cave (1 Kings 19:9–18). Nearby is a rock on which Aaron, the brother of Moses, and seventy elders stood while Moses went alone to receive the tablets of the Law (Exodus 24:14). Beneath the summit stands the plain where the Israelites are said to have camped while Moses ascended the mountain and where the Israelites erected the first tabernacle.

Archaeology has confirmed the impression given by written sources of a sacred topography mapped by monks and pilgrims onto the terrain around the monastery. A number of small monasteries, chapels, and hermits' cells, as well as a dense network of paths were constructed around the Sinai before the Arab conquest in the seventh century CE. More significantly for pilgrimage, a series of prayer niches were built along the path that led from the monastery to the peak of Mt. Sinai. These marked significant spots where pilgrims might glimpse a view of the distant peak. All such marks on the local landscape provided a succession of mini-goals for pilgrims on their way to the summit. The importance of Jebel Musa, above and beyond its association with Mt. Sinai, is that it allows pilgrims to relive the story of faith—and make the narrative their own. According to a Middle Eastern expression, the best way to keep a trail alive is to walk on it, because every time you walk on it, you create it again.

Jebel Musa stands 7,363 feet above sea level, about 2,350 feet above St. Catherine's. There are two ways up the mountain. The easier, less direct way carved by the Egyptian authorities in the nineteenth century, takes longer but can be traversed on foot or on horseback. The other approach entails climbing 3,750 steps, built with rocks by pious monks. This short but difficult ascent, which begins at the south side of the monastery, is the route we took.

As Rob and I began our climb, the silence was broken by the arrival of tourist buses at the base of the alternate route. The thought of sharing the mountaintop with a crowd of tourists, transported effortlessly to the mount by modern conveyance, was initially disconcerting. The previous day, at the base of the mountain, I had prayed for a special experience. I suppose I anticipated some private, mystical encounter with the divine on the summit, and feared that others might detract from my personal epiphany. My prayer was answered, but not as I had imagined. I had prayed for some*thing* special, and God had given me some*one* special, Rob.

We arrived at the summit around 5:15 a.m. and were surprised to find several others already there. They had spent the night on the mountaintop, having climbed with backpacks and sleeping bags the day before. Perhaps they considered us to be intruders, much like I considered the tourists behind us. A few minutes later, as we watched the sun rise in hushed expectation, a group of pilgrims arrived and began to sing a traditional hymn of praise that was probably sung in churches around the globe that Sunday morning:

> Holy, holy, holy, Lord God Almighty;
> Early in the morning our song shall rise to Thee.

TRAVEL ENTRY #52: ROB'S STORY

The story of Rob's spiritual journey is worth telling. He had grown up in a secular home in Holland. At some point in his midlife he acquired a deep desire to visit a monastery and so signed up for a five-day retreat. When he returned from that experience, others could see he was different. He acquired a passion for people in need and he became extremely generous with his time and his possessions, as though they were no longer his. Rob's monastery stay became his "Damascus road" experience (see Acts 9: 1–31).

This day, on the way down the mountain, Rob embodied the lesson he had learned at the Dutch monastery, for whenever Bedouin appeared, selling food, crafts, or drinks, he bartered in reverse—paying more than was asked. Over the next three days, whenever he was approached by a child or some poor person selling food, some item of clothing, or even jewelry, he regularly purchased the item, paying whatever price was asked, even if several times its value.

"To them it's a lot of money," he said, "but to me it's very little. They need the money; I don't." He found it a joy to share of his abundance, even to allow the less fortunate to take advantage of him. He knew what

Paul also knew, that "God loves a cheerful giver." (2 Corinthians 9:7). "Live simply, trust God in all things, and give lavishly to the poor. This is my motto," he explained. "These are the rules now for my life." At first his act seemed foolish to me—blessedly foolish. But for Rob it was the right way to live, for it is what he felt God had called him to be.

Rob related a vision he once received. In that vision he saw himself with Jesus and the disciples, and he felt compelled to kiss Judas. That experience filled him with love for all in need. His experience is reminiscent of St. Francis of Assisi, whose life was transformed when he encountered a leper.

In every age, individuals come to an awareness that they must live by an underlying principle that animates the universe, the cosmic code of caring for the neighbor who is in need. Dorothy Day, the twentieth-century saint who founded the Catholic Worker movement and spent her life in service to the hungry and homeless, once wrote:

> It is no use saying that we are born two thousand years too late to give room to Christ. Nor will those who live at the end of the world have been born too late. Christ is always with us, always asking for room in our hearts.
>
> But now it is with the voice of our contemporaries that He speaks, with the eyes of store clerks, factory workers, and children that He gazes; with the hands of office workers, slum dwellers, and suburban housewives that He gives. It is with the feet of soldiers and tramps that He walks, and with the heart of anyone in need that He longs for shelter. And giving shelter or food to anyone who asks for it, or needs it, is giving it to Christ . . .
>
> If we hadn't got Christ's own words for it, it would seem lunacy to believe that if I offer a bed and food and hospitality to some man or woman or child . . . my guest is Christ.[2]

When Dorothy Day offered hospitality to others, it was not done for the sake of humanity or even because people in need remind us of Christ, but, as she put it, "because they *are* Christ."

The early followers of Jesus heard that message and knew, like Dorothy Day, Francis of Assisi, Rob, and countless others who have been transformed by the resurrected Christ, that after his resurrection Christ is incarnated in the person of anyone who needs our help.

---

2. Taken from Dorothy Day's essay "Room for Christ" in *By Little and By Little: The Selected Writings of Dorothy Day*, edited by Robert Ellsberg and Tamar Hennessey (New York: Alfred A. Knopf, 1983).

The Sinai, called "a great and terrible wilderness" in the Bible (Deuteronomy 8:15), has been a place of testing and hence a place of growth and cleansing. The desert, and desert-like circumstances in our lives, can also be a place of revelation. Moses, Elijah, Jesus, Muhammad—all came to the desert. They were drawn to the desert because the desert draws people toward God. There is a power in the desert, and a difference of scale. Its vastness of space and sense of timelessness remind humans of their weakness and frailty. Dwellers in the desert and other wilderness places learn to rely less on logic and more on intuition and trust. But it takes a long time to acquire trust; it took the rebellious Israelites forty years of wandering to learn to trust. For Bedouin and other desert-dwellers, however, it becomes a way of life.

In the words of Thomas Cahill: "Each of us has in our life at least one moment of insight, one Mount Sinai—an uncanny, other-worldly, time-stopping experience that somehow succeeds in breaking through the grimy, boisterous present, the insight that, if we let it, will carry us through our life."[3] My experience with Rob reminded me that religion is not real if it remains theoretical. True religion is wonderfully practical: "Religion that is pure and undefiled before God, the Father, is this: to care for orphans and widows in their distress..." (James 1:27). Rob embodied that powerful insight. His conversion resulted in "real religion."

---

3. Thomas Cahill, *The Gifts of the Jews* (New York: Doubleday, 1998), 169.

16

Northern Israel, Galilee, and the West Bank

TRAVEL ENTRY #53: EILAT TO KEFAR MONASH

ROB AGREED TO ACCOMPANY me to Israel. Although he had just come from Israel, and therefore had already seen many of its sites, as I had on an earlier trip, we decided to visit the area along the Mediterranean coast before his return to Holland a few days later.

I had a bit of a scare at the Eilat border crossing. When the security officials ran my backpack through the scanner a fourth time, then a fifth, and still were not satisfied, I knew something was wrong. A glance at the monitor helped me to recognize the cause of their concern, for they were investigating an image of a dagger. It was actually a butter knife, which I had stored in a small side pocket to use for cutting cheese and spreading peanut butter on bread. I retrieved the menacing utensil and after one final trip through the scanner the border guards seemed satisfied and let me pass. In the aftermath of 9/11 such an object might have categorized me as a terrorist, but in 1989 it was simply a cause for concern.

The following morning, after a restful night in a clean, modern hostel in Eilat, Rob and I boarded a bus to Tel Aviv, Israel's former capital and its current commercial and cultural center. The highway ran parallel to the Jordanian border—sometimes no more than a stone's throw away—for at least one hundred miles. Fifteen miles from Eilat I noticed a small road on the left to Timnah, the site of a copper mine dating to ancient times, to the time of King Solomon and possibly even centuries earlier.

We neared Beersheba, once a frontier town on the northern edge of the Sinai desert but now a bustling Israeli city. Every Thursday is market day in Beersheba, when hundreds of Bedouin, both locals and deep-desert nomads, gather to sell their wares. I had originally intended to witness this remarkable event, but because it was Monday, I pressed on. The highway to Tel Aviv continued through a narrow strip of Israeli land. On one side lay the occupied Palestinian territories of the West Bank and on the other side, the Gaza Strip. At one point the distance between them was a mere fifteen miles. I longed to visit Gaza and rendezvous with Mustafa, but the arrangements would be so difficult that I was not sure it would be safe for an American. I didn't want to expose Rob or myself to the risks.

The bus eventually reached Tel Aviv, the first city in modern times to be built, populated, and administered entirely by Jews. Founded in 1909, the city's seafront, skyscrapers, exclusive hotels, nightlife, golden beaches, and attractive setting render it the "Middle Eastern Miami Beach." The city's size and busy lifestyle made it unattractive after our visit to the Sinai, so Rob and I continued to Netanya, twenty-one miles to the north, a lovely resort city known for its relaxed lifestyle and lovely beaches.

There was another reason why I had come to Netanya. Having spoken with Palestinians during my stay in Jordan, I informed Rob of my desire to interview Israeli Jews as well, hoping to get a balanced perspective on the current Arab-Israeli hostility. Rob had an interesting suggestion.

TRAVEL ENTRY #54: A CONVERSATION WITH CHEJE

He knew Cheje Perey, a Dutch lady who lived in Kefar Monash, a small residential community near Netanya. She had arrived forty-five years earlier, when the community functioned as an experimental kibbutz. Her village was close to the West Bank, a mere five miles from Tulkarm, a hot-bed of terrorist activity and a stronghold of the terrorist group Islamic Jihad, which dispatched numerous suicide bombers on deadly missions into Israel. I felt that Cheje's experience, memory, and perspective would be invaluable for my research. When we spoke by telephone from Netanya, she agreed to see us that evening, so we went to Kefar Monash, a village named for a well-known Jewish Australian general who fought with the Allies during World War I. As we gathered in her living room, sipping tea and eating pastries, she spoke from her heart as an Israeli living perilously close to the West Bank.

"Every day I fear for my life," she began. "We live in this country surrounded by hostile enemies and we have been forced to occupy strategic areas such as the Golan Heights, which we cannot give back."

She was referring to the time when Syrians shelled vulnerable Israeli settlements in Galilee from the Golan, settlements similar to hers. It was clear to her that Palestinian terrorists were recruited by Arab states and sheltered in communities close to the Israeli border, where they could be dispatched on frequent raids against defenseless Israeli settlers. The Syrians, she felt, were actively recruiting supporters who would help them drive the Israelis into the sea. The strength of Israel was being tested every day and Israel's resolve could never relax.[1]

"We have paid a heavy toll for our vigilance," Cheje continued. "One of every three families in Israel has lost a family member in combat."

When the topic of Jerusalem came up, she insisted that that city had to remain under Jewish sovereignty: "We can never give back even an inch of our holy city!" Her experience led to a pessimistic view regarding peace in the region. "The Arab countries cannot agree among themselves on policy toward Israel. Furthermore," she concluded, "one can't trust the Arabs."

I came away from our meeting with sympathy for Cheje and her predicament. Safety and security are no doubt central to every person's dignity, wellbeing, and survival, but I knew that Cheje's "Maginot mentality" and deep distrust of the Arabs in general would never lead to peace in the region. Stability in the Middle East—or anywhere else, for that matter—requires a political, economic, and social agenda that guarantees the human rights of every man, women, and child in the region, whether Jewish, Muslim, Christian, or Druze. Such a strategy, I believe, can only come from moderates, who must be afforded every opportunity—and given the resources they need—to rise to positions of prominence in each of those communities.

---

1. Since 1989, Netanya has been the focus of several suicide attacks. The most notorious occurred on March 27, 2002, in which thirty Israelis were killed and 140 were injured when a suicide bomber detonated an explosive device in Netanya's Park Hotel. Over the course of the next several days, multiple suicide bombers targeted additional locations in Israel, including Jerusalem, Tel Aviv, and Haifa. The attack in Netanya occurred during Passover, on the night when the traditional Jewish Seder was being celebrated. Many of the victims were elderly Holocaust survivors gathered to celebrate the festival. The suicide bombers that entered Netanya during this period were known to enter Israel from or near Tulkarm. Tulkarm is only a five-minute drive from Netanya, and the inhabitants of communities such as Kefar Monash, lying along the route, feel particularly vulnerable. Cheje's fears were realistic.

EXPLANATORY ENTRY #33: THE STORY OF FATHER ELIAS CHACOUR

Shortly before my first trip to Israel in 1985, I heard about Elias Chacour, a religious leader who lived in Israel. He was a Palestinian Arab, a priest of the Melkite Greek Catholic Church in the tiny Galilean village of Ibillin. His autobiography, *Blood Brothers*, had just been published, and I believed Father Chacour held a workable solution for the reconciliation of Palestinians and Jews.

Father Chacour was born to an Arab Christian family in 1939, in the village of Biram in Upper Galilee, then a part of Palestine under British Mandate rule. At the age of eight he was evicted, along with his entire village, by the Israeli authorities and he became a refugee in his native country. Because he chose to remain in his homeland, he was granted citizenship when Israel was created in 1948.

In 1965, after seminary studies in Paris, he returned to Israel. In his writings, he recalls two experiences from that time. The first was the moment he stood at the customs line in the port of Haifa, fresh from his studies in Europe.[2] From his place in line he could see his family waiting in a nearby room. When it was his turn to present his passport, he was ushered to an interrogation room where, after a half hour of questioning, he was told to strip.

"Why are you asking me to do this?" he asked.

"You are Palestinian," was the reply.

Elias refused to strip and promptly sat down and began reading a book. After eight nerve-wracking hours, he was finally allowed to enter his home country. His experiment with nonviolent resistance ended successfully.

The second experience took place a few days later, when he decided to visit the village of Biram and stood dumb-struck at its desolation.[3] Surrounded by stone houses, all standing ghost-like in ruins, he passed the shell of his parish church en route to his home on the far side of the village. When he made it to his home, he stepped through the ruined orchard into the house. The roof and attic had been blown up, in addition to one entire wall. In the yard, he found his special fig tree, grafted by his father. Firmly rooted and still green with life, it reminded him of

---

2. Elias Chacour, *Blood Brothers* (Old Tappan, New Jersey: Chosen Books, 1984), 132–33.

3. Ibid., 135–46.

the words his father had spoken when his brother Rudah had brought a gun home to protect his family from the Israeli soldiers who were approaching.

"The Jews and Palestinians are blood brothers," he had said. "We must never forget that."

Elias went back to his car and headed for the Mount of Beatitudes, where Jesus is said to have delivered the famous Sermon on the Mount. Elias was drawn afresh by those ancient words, for as they came into his mind, he suddenly heard them as for the first time: Blessed are the poor in spirit; blessed are those who mourn; blessed are the meek; blessed are those who hunger and thirst for righteousness; blessed are the peacemakers.

He heard them no longer as platitudes, or even as exhortations; they had become prophecies, for each was followed by a promise: the poor in spirit would experience the coming Kingdom; those who experienced suffering would receive comfort; the weak—not simply the weak but those who relied fully upon God's power—would inherit the earth.

The next beatitude, which promised satisfaction to those thirsting for justice and righteousness, stunned him. He realized that this was the pattern Jesus had established throughout his ministry. Whether it was the woman taken in adultery, the blind or crippled persons he had healed on the Sabbath, or the Samaritan outcast, one of the first things Jesus did when he reconciled people to God was to restore human dignity. Suddenly Chacour knew that the first step required for reconciling Jew and Palestinian was the restoration of human dignity. Here, he knew, was the attractive third option between the polarities of violent confrontation and naïve passivity.

Another beatitude—another promise—ran through his head and this one, he said, rattled his thought process like thunderclap after lightening: peacemakers are the children of God. If he, Elias Chacour, was to be a true servant of God and of others, his primary calling was to be a peacemaker. In that moment he was certain he had finally found his path, his identity. A few years later he was sent by his church to study the Torah and the Talmud at the Hebrew University in Jerusalem, where he became the first Arab to gain a higher degree from that institution. In 1965, Father Chacour received his first parish assignment, in the village of Ibillin. What was originally a one-month assignment became a lifetime commitment.

Noticing the lack of educational opportunities for Palestinian youth beyond the eighth grade, Father Chacour created a school for all local children. Beginning with eighty students, in 2001 it had an enrollment of four thousand. He also established a number of additional institutions, including community centers, public libraries, and a summer camp that now accommodates over five thousand children from different religions and denominations in the region of Galilee. In 1995, he founded a technological college and the Center for Religious Pluralism at Mar Elias College.

An advocate of non-violence and someone who not only preaches but embodies the Sermon on the Mount, Father Chacour has received many international peace awards and three times has been nominated for the Nobel Peace Prize. In 2001, he was proclaimed Man of the Year in Israel and five years later was appointed Archbishop of Galilee. Father Chacour provides each of us with a liberating perspective. Like Rob, who was changed by a vision and like St. Francis of Assisi, who met a leper one day and in embracing him saw the face of Jesus, Father Chacour has taught Christians to see Jews and Palestinians as blood brothers.

TRAVEL ENTRY #55: HAIFA AND AKKO

After our visit with Cheje, Rob and I traveled by bus to Haifa, Israel's chief port and the country's third largest city. Haifa was to be my point of transit to the old walled city of Akko (Acre), further up the coast. While in Haifa, I intended to visit the Baha'i Shrine, world center of the Baha'i faith. Rob had heard that Haifa was set in a beautiful location, comparable to that of San Francisco, so he was happy to tag along. He also wished to visit the Carmelite monastery, situated on the ridge of Mt. Carmel, near the traditional site where the prophet Elijah is said to have performed a miraculous sacrifice while confronting the pagan prophets of Baal (1 Kings 18:17–46). Rob wanted this site to be his final memory of Israel, for the next day he would return to Tel Aviv for his flight to Holland.

The one-hour bus ride along the coast from Netanya to Haifa took us through the heart of the Plain of Sharon. We passed prosperous villages, each well-tended and flourishing. Since biblical times, this region had been covered with malarial swamps and shifting sand dunes. When the Israelis declared statehood they began planting eucalyptus trees by the millions, using the extensive sponge-like root systems of those trees to soak up the brackish water. Soon orange groves were planted and in a short time the disease-stricken area blossomed into one of the most fertile regions in the country.

Fifteen miles north of Netanya we drove by the ruins of Caesarea, once the Roman capital of Judea and Palestine. Built in the year 22 BCE by King Herod the Great, Caesarea was named in honor of Emperor Augustus Caesar. Herod, who was very ambitious, wanted a fine harbor to integrate his region more fully with the economy of the empire. Since there was no adequate natural harbor south of Mount Carmel, he constructed an artificial port by sinking enormous stones, twenty to thirty tons each, into the sea until he created a first class harbor. He also created a seawall with an imposing promenade, and after that an economic and political center, complete with an amphitheater, a hippodrome, a magnificent forum, and a theater with a spectacular view of the sea. Due to a lack of fresh water at Caesarea, Herod commissioned the construction of a high-level aqueduct to transport water from springs eight miles away on the southern slopes of Mount Carmel. It was in Caesarea, this remote setting approximately seventy miles from Jerusalem, that the apostle Paul was held prisoner for two years (Acts 23:22—26:32) while awaiting the trial that eventually sentenced him to Rome in chains.

After the site was destroyed in 1291, Caesarea gradually became covered by sand and was largely forgotten until the twentieth century, when a pilot flying over the site spotted the ruins and contacted the Israeli Department of Antiquities. Excavations began in 1956. The large amphitheater has been reconstructed and portions of the impressive aqueduct still remain.

TRAVEL ENTRY #56: THE BAHA'I CENTER IN HAIFA

The next morning, as we climbed the steep streets of Haifa, located on the northern slope of Mount Carmel, we paused to enjoy the wonderful view of the bay and harbor. Across the bay, less than ten miles away, was Akko, the 4,000-year-old Canaanite and Phoenician port city, whose fortress had withstood Napoleon's famous siege in 1799. Before us stood the Baha'i Shrine and Gardens, one of Haifa's most impressive attractions.

The Baha'i faith began in Persia in 1844, when a Muslim named Mirsa Ali Muhammad declared that he was the "Bab," the Gateway to God. He was shot to death in 1850, at the age of thirty-one, but was succeeded by Mirsa Hussein Ali (1817–1892), who took the name Baha'u'llah. He fled to Turkey, where he proclaimed himself Imam (a quasi-messianic designation) in 1868. He was exiled and held captive in Acre (Akko) for twenty-four years, until his death in 1892. During his incarceration he wrote his doctrines, which became the basis of the Baha'i teachings. His disciples brought the body of the Bab secretly to Palestine from Persia and in 1909 buried him in Haifa. The shrine of the Bab, with its monumental dome, dominates the Haifa cityscape. Nearby, in beautifully tended gardens, stands the classical archive building of the Baha'i religious community, whose faith has spread across the world.

Because I had come to Haifa to learn more about the Baha'i faith, I attached myself to one of the guides at the shrine and began a lengthy conversation on Baha'i teachings and symbolism. Baha'is believe that religious truth is progressive, not final. God, the Father of all humans, educates the human race through a series of prophets who have appeared in succession throughout history to guide humans. I was told that all prophets, including Moses, Zoroaster, Buddha, Christ, Muhammad, and more recently Baha'u'llah, preached the same message. The Baha'i faith emphasizes the unity of God, the unity of the prophetic message, the oneness of all religions, and the oneness of the human race. Everything at the Baha'i Center is deliberate and symbolic of its understanding of truth. The holy numbers—nine and nineteen (the nine-pointed star, the nineteen terraces)—the gardens, the orange trees, the human race, all are interrelated; death, rebirth, and reincarnation are part of a common process, underscoring the reality that all things are in a state of flux toward progression. Only God is unchanging and therefore perfect; all else, whether society, religion, or revelation, is progressive.

I found myself agreeing with some of the points made by my Baha'i tutor, particularly the condemnation of prejudice and the service role of religion in establishing and perpetuating peace at every level of life. Rob seemed infatuated by the more mystical teachings of the religion, which supported his understanding of the universe as the body of God and therefore sacred.

Later that day, following our visit to the slope of Carmel, associated with events in the ministry of the prophet Elijah, Rob and I parted. I learned a great deal from this new friendship, and the lifestyle he modeled during our time together continues to instruct me.

TRAVEL ENTRY #57: AN EDUCATED JEWISH PERSPECTIVE ON THE NEW TESTAMENT

At lunch I met a Jewish lady whose daughter was in a PhD program at Ohio State University. When I told her that I was a professor of Religious Studies as well as an ordained Christian minister, she asked if she could speak candidly about the Christian scriptures. This was precisely the sort of conversation I desired but rarely experienced during my journey. The usual response when people learned the nature of my profession or my faith was a change of topic or silence. But I hadn't come to Israel for either of those options. Here, in the only true democracy in the Middle East, I expected honesty. And that's what I got.

"Do you know that the gospels are full of errors and are considered ludicrous by Jews?" she began.

"What do you mean?" I countered. "Could you give me some examples?"

That's all the encouragement she needed. She told me that the idea of Jesus healing on the Sabbath, which according to the New Testament was offensive to Jews, would never have been viewed as problematic by them. Jewish doctors, she said, are required to provide healing for the sick whenever they need help. Jews in Jesus' day would certainly not have encouraged or even allowed needless suffering, not on the Sabbath or on any other holy day. Another far-fetched concept to her was the passage about Jesus visiting Jews who tended swine near the Sea of Galilee. No Jewish person would go near pigs, she declared, much less raise them.

Then she turned to the Christian teaching about the Virgin Birth of Jesus. That, she announced, was sheer nonsense. "Don't Christians know that this idea came from the mistranslation of the Hebrew prophets? And don't they realize that the original passage [Isaiah 7:14] had nothing to do with the birth of a messiah or the distant future but referred to the birth of a royal child of the sixth century BCE?"

She took a deep breath and paused for effect. Then she moved on to her next point, the inconsistent portrayal of Pontius Pilate in the gospels. In her estimation, historians were unanimous in their agreement on one consistent trait in Pilate's character—his brutality. Pilate was a terrible despot. He would not have cared to save Jesus, as the gospels suggest. After all, he had killed hundreds of Jews, including on the eve of Passover. The idea that he might release someone to please the Jews was simply incredible.

She also saw serious flaws in the crucifixion narrative and in the accounts of the resurrection of Jesus. She indicated that another person named Jesus had been crucified six months before the biblical Jesus and perhaps caused confusion. And even if it had been Jesus of Nazareth on the cross, the account states that he only hung on the cross a few hours. He had probably swooned before he was taken from the cross, and later revived. In her opinion, it was more likely that Jesus had left Jerusalem to stay with Essenes, and then upon his return his followers believed he had been resurrected.

Her final argument was quite astute. When Paul said there were many eyewitnesses to the resurrection, he wrote this in a letter to people who lived in faraway Corinth, who could not have checked on the story's veracity. As far as she was concerned, the New Testament was simply not believable. It was edited and changed repeatedly by early Christians and eventually was written for an audience in Asia Minor and Europe. Christianity, she was sure, never had a large following in Palestine or among the Jews of the time. The reasons were obvious.

I was impressed at her knowledge, but even more amazed by the power of her conviction. She really believed that Christians were either ignorant, misinformed, or profoundly naïve. Since the purpose of my trip was to listen, learn, and absorb, I did not feel compelled to debate every point she had made. That path is not always appropriate. I was conscious that American Christians can be arrogant or downright ugly when dealing with people of other cultures and faiths. And so I said very little.

I smiled and congratulated her on her chutzpah. I indicated that all interreligious debate is challenging and that each point she had raised had, for me, a convincing rejoinder. I told her that it was quite likely that the Gadarenes, who tended swine, were not Jewish, and that the Virgin Birth was not simply based upon an ancient mistranslation of the Septuagint version of Isaiah 7. Doctrines like the Virgin Birth do not stand alone but are explained by more profound beliefs, such as the doctrine of the incarnation. The belief that Jesus is the incarnation of God's love on earth is central to Christianity. That affirmation underlies doctrines such as the Virgin Birth and the resurrection. I pointed out that all doctrinal formulations are matters of faith. When religion becomes propositional—a scheme based on facts that can be proven or disproven—such approaches to religion come close to the fundamentalisms that plague us all. Religion is a matter of trust and allegiance, and ultimately it is love that wins the heart, I explained, not law, or ritual, or fear of divine retribution.

That idea led to a discussion of hermeneutics—the study of biblical interpretation. Throughout history, Jews, Christians, and Muslims have developed hermeneutical approaches that configure with evolving beliefs: geographically, historically, rationally, culturally, and scientifically. This is a phenomenon, as the Baha'i guide argued so persuasively earlier that day, which is undeniably true for every religion. Though religious people often seem content in the perception that their faith is built upon fact, over time many come to realize that no intellectual foundation rests upon indisputable evidence. To a certain extent, all things—whether institutions, philosophies, science, rationality, even the nature of faith—evolve. Christianity, as we know it in the West, has undergone numerous permutations before it got to us. Early Christianity had to be translated into a Hellenistic culture, then a Roman culture, then a barbarian (northern European) culture, before it was brought to the New World, where it evolved even further.

Generally speaking, the faith practiced by most Christians in North America is far different from the faith of the earliest Christians in Galilee and Judea. If Christians in the West wish to experience original Christianity, they should attend Pentecostal services or travel to Africa, where many believers adhere to forms of Christianity far closer to first- or second-century Christianity than those practiced in the West. Faith—true religion—is *sui generis*; it is unique to each person. Like a gift, it must be accepted and enjoyed, not proven or disproven.

EXPLANATORY ENTRY #34: ACRE/AKKO AND CRUSADER HISTORY

Anyone interested in Crusader history will want to visit the ruins of the many remarkable desert castles and citadels built in the eastern Mediterranean by those intrepid medieval Christian warriors. At some point they must also visit Akko. The city of Acre (pronounced Akko in Hebrew and Akka in Arabic), ten miles north of Haifa and twelve miles south of Lebanon, is centuries apart from Haifa, its modern cousin across the bay. Renowned as the most impregnable port in the East, Akko remains a city of bastions and battlements. For those in search of history, Acre does not disappoint.

Acre dates back to the Canaanite era. Because of its strategic location, commanding the approach from land and sea to the fertile Jezreel Valley, the city underwent attacks by all of the region's power brokers. Egypt conquered it, as did Assyria. Queen Cleopatra of Egypt held it for a time. Here Herod the Great entertained Caesar. The city rose to prominence as a seaport and commercial trade center (for there was as yet no other city or settlement in the region; Haifa would not be settled until much later) and reached its zenith during the period of the Crusades. The First Crusade was launched in 1099 and five years later, after the conquest of Jerusalem, King Baldwin I succeeded in conquering Acre. Merchants from Venice, Pisa, and Amalfi developed the city's commercial center, making Acre the key port in the eastern Mediterranean as well as the primary crossroad in the flow of traffic between Europe and the Holy Land.

Military power and governmental rule, however, lay in the hands of orders of knights, who had taken vows to protect both pilgrims and the kingdom of the Crusaders. Various orders established centers in the city, but the largest and most important was the Order of the Knights of St. John, also known as the Hospitalers on account of their hospitals and their care of the sick. The Knights of St. John occupied the center of Acre, where they erected the enormous military and governmental citadel that has been excavated and may be seen by the public.

In 1187, when Saladin defeated the Crusaders in the famous battle of the Horns of Hattin (approximately twenty-five miles to the east, near the Sea of Galilee), most Crusader cities, including Acre, fell into Saracen hands. Three years later the knights of the Third Crusade, led by Philip Augustus of France and Richard the Lionheart, arrived. Though they failed to retake Jerusalem, they were successful in recapturing Acre. In 1192, the stronghold became the capital of the Crusaders' Kingdom in the Holy Land. In 1291, Acre fell to the Muslim sultan al-Khalil. Acre's conquerors destroyed everything, and what they could not destroy they covered with earth and rock. For centuries, Acre remained a forgotten village. During the eighteenth century it underwent a period of reconstruction under the Turks.

Today, buried beneath the 200-year-old Turkish settlement, is the partially excavated Crusader center, its peculiar rooms connected by a network of tunnels. One of these halls, named the "Crypt" because of its location at the lowest level of the fortress, is an impressive hall that once served as a great dining room and guest hall. It is quite likely that Marco Polo was among the guests received in this reception room, for he is known to have visited Acre on his historic voyage to China. During the nineteenth century, Akko was gradually overtaken by neighboring Haifa. When the British captured Palestine in the World War I, Haifa, with its larger harbor, became the administrative center of the district and Akko's importance dwindled.

TRAVEL ENTRY #58: FROM AKKO TO ROSH PINNA

That evening I boarded a bus to Rosh Pinna, in Upper Galilee, near Israel's eastern border with the Golan Heights. My goal in Upper Galilee was to view the ruins of Hazor, the largest Palestinian city built during the entire biblical period.

The forty-mile trip crossed the narrowest section of the country, parallel to the border with Lebanon just a few miles to the north. A few miles from Rosh Pinna the bus skirted the town of Safed, Israel's highest settlement, from which one can see all of western Galilee. Together with Jerusalem, Hebron, and Tiberius, Safed is considered a holy city by Jews, a place where Sephardic Jews went when they were persecuted in Spain. Here Jewish intellectuals launched the complex mystical interpretation of their faith called Cabala. I arrived at Rosh Pinna after nightfall and spent the night in a youth hostel. Rosh Pinna, established in 1882 on barren rocky land about seven miles north of the Sea of Galilee, was the first modern Jewish settlement in Galilee. Its name, meaning "cornerstone," was chosen from Psalm 118:22: "The stone that the builders rejected has become the chief cornerstone."

The next morning I hitched a ride on a school bus taking children for an outing to the archaeological site of Hazor. The bus left very early, but public transportation was infrequent in this remote area, and I welcomed the ride.

EXPLANATORY ENTRY #35:
THE ARCHAEOLOGICAL RUINS OF HAZOR

Hazor was strategically located on the Via Maris, the sea route that connected Egypt with Syria. Destroyed many times, as the *tel* of Hazor indicates, Hazor is composed of twenty-one layers of cities superimposed one on top of another over a period of thousands of years.[4] It is the largest and most important archaeological mound in northern Israel.

Hazor is mentioned in ancient documents from Egypt, Palestine, and Assyria, where it is cited along with Babylon and other cities of similar size. The documents indicate that it was a major center of commerce in the Fertile Crescent. During the Middle Bronze period (1950–1550 BCE), the walled city of Hazor was surrounded by a moat and consisted of 180 acres. The site is huge, particularly when compared with the fortified city of Jerusalem, which was only thirteen acres in size during the time of King David. With a population of forty thousand people, Hazor was the largest city in Canaan.

The archaeological site is divided into two separate areas: the Upper City (the *tel*), covering thirty acres, was elevated and heavily fortified, with a citadel at its highest summit; and the Lower City, fortified with huge ramparts made of packed earth. The Lower City was settled during the eighteenth century BCE, probably by a wave of immigrants later known by the Greek name of Hyksos. These bands, which entered the Near East around 1900 BCE, began moving southward, erecting fortifications that would become the power base for invasions of Egypt. The Hyksos finally gained control of Egypt around 1720 BCE, at which time they replaced the native dynasty with their own and established their capital in the Delta region of the Nile.

It was perhaps during this time that Joseph, one of the twelve sons of Jacob, rose to power in Egypt. The Hyksos would have welcomed foreigners such as Joseph, for they regularly appointed naturalized Semitic officials to high administrative positions. When a native dynasty reconquered Egypt around 1570 BCE, it destroyed the Hyksos capital, enslaving those Semites who remained in the Delta region of Egypt.

Although the *tel* was identified as Hazor in 1928, it wasn't until the 1950s that Professor Yigael Yadin and a team of archaeologists from the Hebrew University in Jerusalem first excavated the site. During the summer of 1969, further excavations at Hazor produced the "prize discovery," an underground water system from the Israelite period—the largest one of its size. It dates back to the time of the Israelite king Ahab (869–850 BCE) and measures eighty-two feet long, thirteen feet high, and thirteen

---

4. Whereas "tell" is an Arabic word meaning "an artificial mound formed by the accumulated remains of an ancient settlement," in Israel—and in the Hebrew language—the archaeological term is commonly abbreviated as "tel."

feet wide. It ends in a pool thirty-three feet deep, which extends below the water table, assuring water to the inhabitants even when the spring outside the *tel* was inaccessible to the residents during a siege.

TRAVEL ENTRY #59: TABOR, THE MOUNT OF TRANSFIGURATION

From Hazor, the road to Jerusalem passes through the eastern region of the Galilee and then runs parallel to the Sea of Galilee before crossing the mountainous backbone of the West Bank (ancient Samaria). This is the land of the Bible, and like the Bible it bears witness to spiritual attainment and bloody conflict.

My first stop was the Arab village of Daburinya, at the foot of Mount Tabor, close to Nazareth, where Jesus grew up. I left my backpack in the care of a shop owner near the base of the mount and began the physical ascent to the summit 1,477 feet above the base. Mount Tabor, a defining feature in the valley, is a cone-shaped, symmetrical mountain. The road up the steep slope zigzagged back and forth toward the summit, reminiscent of the climb to Alp d'Huez, the fabled stage of the Tour de France, with its twenty-one switchbacks. As I hiked I pondered the mountain's rich history, wondering whether Jesus as a boy might have climbed here with his family or friends, for Mount Tabor was only six miles from Nazareth.

On account of its distinctive setting, Tabor has regularly attracted worshippers and mystics. In antiquity, mountains and high places were often venues for worship, and Tabor was preeminent in that regard. In the second millennium BCE there was here a Canaanite shrine to Baal, as on Mount Carmel and Mount Hermon. In the period of the Judges (twelfth century BCE), the Israelite prophetess Deborah and her general Barak gathered their forces on the mountain in spiritual preparation for war against Sisera, the general of Hazor (Judges 4:12–16). Verse fourteen suggests that the forces had gathered on the mountaintop to worship Yahweh. As early as the sixth century CE, three churches were built on the summit of Tabor, in memory of the three tabernacles that Peter proposed at the time of the Transfiguration. Today two monasteries, one Franciscan and the other Greek Orthodox, share the spot.

The significance of the mountain in the history of Christianity begins in the fourth century, at which time the transfiguration of Jesus was connected with this locality. In Matthew 17:1–3 we read that Jesus went up into a high mountain with his disciples, Peter, James, and John: "and he was transfigured before them, and his face shone like the sun, and his clothes became dazzling white. Suddenly there appeared to them Moses and Elijah, talking with him."

Together with his resurrection, the transfiguration became one of the central themes in the theology and iconography of Christianity, particularly of the Eastern Church. The appearance of the transfigured Christ also exerted a decisive effect on the development of mysticism in Eastern Orthodox monasticism. The influence of the transfiguration may be discerned even to the present day in the current of mysticism found in the monasteries at Mount Athos in Greece, the oldest surviving monastic community in the world. There, on an isolated, sea-battered peninsula in northeastern Greece, lies a unique monastic republic which, though part of Greece, is governed by its own local administration. On the sacred mountain of Athos the monks hope to attain, through asceticism, the "uncreated light" of Tabor and thus to experience mystic union with the divine.

The main attraction of Mount Tabor for modern visitors is not the religious tradition or the rich mystical lore that surrounds the sacred site but simply the magnificent view of the Jezreel Valley, Israel's largest and most fertile valley. To the north stretch the green mountains of Galilee, with the Sea of Galilee and the unmistakable Horns of Hattin. Further north, dominating the distant landscape, sits the snowy cap of majestic Hermon (9,230 feet above sea level). To the east lie the Jordan Rift Valley and the Transjordanian Mountains; to the west, the mountains around Nazareth, and beyond, near the Mediterranean, the Carmel Ridge. To the south are the mountains of Samaria, including at its base Mount Gilboa, with the imposing mound of ancient Bet Shean, one of the most interesting sites in Israel. The view from Tabor's summit provides a unique orientation to Israel's terrain, which in turn serves as a lens into the historical and cultural peculiarities of this ancient land.

TRAVEL ENTRY #60: FROM TABOR TO JERUSALEM

As I was leaving Tabor, a tourist offered me a ride to the shop near the base of the mountain, where I had left my backpack. He then drove me to Nazareth, where I spent the night in a hospice run by Catholic nuns.

The following morning I boarded a bus filled with Israelis heading to Jerusalem via the West Bank. At the border, a squad of Israeli soldiers came on board, brandishing their weapons. I became alarmed at their presence, fearing a problem ahead. But when they took assigned seats at the front and the rear of the bus, I realized they were there for our protection. Israelis were not welcomed in the West Bank, and we were going through the city of Nablus, a hub of Palestinian nationalism and a thorn in Israel's side since New Testament times, when it was the Samaritan heartland. Nablus was now a major city under Palestinian authority. With its population of one hundred thousand, it is one of the largest Palestinian cities in the Middle East and a center of nationalism.

Nablus, known as Shechem in biblical times, lies thirty-seven miles north of Jerusalem. A much older site than Jerusalem and because it is mentioned regularly in the Bible, it holds religious significance to the three major Abrahamic faiths. It is situated in a strategic position between two ancient commercial routes, one connecting the Israeli coast to the Jordan Valley and the other linking Galilee with Jerusalem and the Negev. Because of its central location, in a valley between Mount Gerizim and Mount Ebal, King Jeroboam, the first king of the Northern Kingdom (Israel), designated Shechem to be his capital. The Shechem Pass was the strategic gateway to the heart of Canaan.

According to the book of Genesis, Abraham built an altar on this spot (12:6–7), considered by the faithful as the first place the patriarch stopped when he and his party entered Canaan. The Bible states that on this occasion God confirmed the covenant he had made originally with Abraham regarding the possession of the land of Canaan. At a later date, Joshua, the conqueror of the Promised Land, assembled the Israelites in Shechem and encouraged them to reaffirm their adherence to the Torah (Joshua 8:30–34).

Earlier, before the conquest of the land, Moses had indicated that the tribes should gather at this spot to re-enact the covenant, half the tribes standing upon Mount Gerizim to represent the blessings promised for faithfulness to the Torah, and the other half on Mount Ebal to represent the curses promised for unfaithfulness (see Deuteronomy 11:26–32; 27:11–13). These texts underscore the centrality of Shechem for the Hebrew covenant and why this site became the first center of the Israelite tribal confederacy.

Nablus is presently the home of a small community of Samaritans, who live in their own quarter on the western side of the city. In New Testament times there was animosity between Jews and Samaritans, for the former worshipped God in the temple at Jerusalem, whereas the Samaritans maintained that the true worship of God was on Mount Gerizim, which they recognized as the place where Adam offered sacrifices and therefore was the sole divine center on earth. In this context it is interesting to note the discussion that Jesus had with the Samaritan woman at the Well of Jacob, located nearby (see John 4:20–23).

Shechem is considered one of the world's authentic sacred sites. Under different circumstances, I would have spent several days there, absorbing the controversial social and spiritual setting, but there were no bus stops for Israelis on this route and the bus continued cautiously, wandering in serpentine fashion past small Arab villages. A half hour later, midway between Shechem and Jerusalem, we passed the road to Shiloh, the religious center of Israel prior to the conquest of Jerusalem by King David. Eventually the bus entered the outskirts of Jerusalem and came to a stop at the Arab bus station on Nablus Road, near the Muslim Quarter. I entered the holy city of Jerusalem through the famous Damascus Gate.

17

Jerusalem in Legend and History

JERUSALEM IS THE MOST venerated site on earth. Its role in history is out of all proportion to its size, its economic importance, or even its political significance. Its status as a "holy" city is evidenced by the abundance of shrines and places sacred to the three monotheistic religions. Consequently, the city is visited annually by pilgrims and tourists from across the world.

To its inhabitants, whether Jewish, Muslim, or Christian, whether ancient or modern, Jerusalem's status has never seemed surprising. Sought after by prophet and pilgrim, king and caliph, mystic and warrior alike, Jerusalem is regarded as the halfway house between heaven and earth. The very names associated with Jerusalem—Calvary, Ophel, Haram al-Sharif, Via Dolorosa, the Western Wall, al-Quds, Zion—call out like friends from distant childhood.

Yet Jerusalem is more than legend, for four thousand years of history are inscribed in its stones and walls. Throughout this span, Jerusalem has witnessed thirty-six wars. Seventeen times it has been reduced to ashes; it has risen eighteen times. No city's rulers have come from such a variety of cultures and places, including from ancient Assyria, Babylon, Egypt, Persia, Greece, and Rome to modern Ottoman and Anglo. Yet despite its many conquerors and all the sacred esteem, Jerusalem has remained exceedingly provincial and in the backwaters of world importance until recent times. It has known only two periods of true greatness—one ancient and the other modern—and these have been separated by two thousand years.

Civilizations arise because of geographic and geological considerations, foremost among them a significant river or body of fresh water. Yet ancient Jerusalem had neither of these. Its location, lack of natural wealth, difficulty for agriculture, and dearth of sufficient water, inform us that it should not be numbered among those cities considered truly great. Yet Jerusalem alone has achieved immortality as the focal point of the spiritual energies of Judaism, Christianity, and Islam. What it lacked was made up for by an idea. The ancient Hebrews became a nation on an idea, and that idea made them unique. Jerusalem, in the words of the author and novelist, Leon Uris, became "the magnificent crown of that idea ... Of all the cities founded by the ancients, Jerusalem alone retains her ancient glory and her special relationship to God. It is here that reality, miracle, and illusion all tumble around together, where a lovely touch of madness remains unconquered by man's folly."[1]

The mosaic map in Madaba, discovered in present-day Jordan in 1884 but made during the reign of the Byzantine emperor Justinian (527–565), reflects the sacred geography of the Christian world that had developed since the time of Constantine, two centuries earlier. On the map, Palestine is depicted as the Holy Land with Jerusalem, bearing the legend "The Holy City of Jerusalem," at the center and clearly the center of the world. The map was probably placed there as a guide for Christian pilgrims in their travels.

EXPLANATORY ENTRY #36: JERUSALEM IN LEGEND AND HISTORY

Jewish Lore

According to ancient Jewish legend, Jerusalem lies at the very center of the inhabited world and is the place where God created Adam. Built on the summit of the sacred mountain of Zion, the temple in Jerusalem linked heaven and earth, for it symbolized the reality that sustains the life of the cosmos. When Solomon erected the temple in the eleventh century BCE, Jews acknowledged the inner sanctuary to be the actual dwelling of God on earth.

Despite religious and political opposition, David was responsible for securing the site on which the temple was later built. The story of the purchase of the threshing-floor of Araunah, the Jebusite, explains how this site came to be acquired. The narrative of 2 Samuel 24:15–25 provides a divine authorization for the erection of David's altar in Jerusalem. The Chronicler (1 Chronicles 22:1 and 2 Chronicles 3:1) makes clear that

---

1. Leon and Jill Uris, *Jerusalem, Song of Songs* (New York: Bantam, 1985), 4.

this became the site of Solomon's Temple. Scholars believe that before David's time the site had been set aside by the Jebusites (the Canaanite inhabitants of Jerusalem prior to David's capture of the site) as sacred. Threshing-floors, as flat open spaces, were quite suitable for religious assemblies, especially during harvest time. The presence of a great rock, revered to this day in the Muslim shrine (the Dome of the Rock) over the site, would undoubtedly have had some profound religious significance for the Jebusites. Most probably it functioned as a primitive rock-altar, continuing to be used as such by the Israelites, for after David erected his altar there it was eventually incorporated into the inner sanctuary of Solomon's Temple. It later came to be regarded in Jewish lore as the foundation stone of the world. Thus, as the very first part of the world to be created, it was considered the navel or center of the earth and therefore comparable to the Greek *omphalos*.

The furnishings of the temple were full of cosmic symbolism, as was in effect true for the temple as a whole. The very conception of such a building was founded on the belief that a correspondence existed between the earthly and the heavenly worlds. Yahweh's house in Jerusalem was intended to be a copy, or symbol, of the cosmic abode. In this way Israel's worship emphasized the power of Yahweh over the natural order.

Various features of the temple furnishings have been thought to illustrate such a symbolism. The great bronze sea (altar of cleansing) was symbolic of the vast primeval ocean, the four groups of oxen that supported it being tokens of the four seasons of the year. The decoration of the temple with palm trees and cherubim, as well as the ornamental pomegranates on the masonry, all suggest the fertility of the earth, or more precisely, the paradise garden where Yahweh dwelt. The free standing pillars, set up at the front of the sanctuary and oriented eastward, were viewed as sacred pillars, possibly as symbols of the cosmic pillars that formed a gateway for the sun to pass through every morning. Such features were designed to stress the divine power over the created order and to establish the temple as a source of blessing for the land and people of Israel. We need not suppose that every Israelite worshipper was conscious of this underlying mythological explanation of the sanctuary, but it seems certain that those who worshipped there believed that the temple was a supernatural source of power and that from the temple the divine blessing and life flowed out to Israel and the world.

The temple also represented the Garden of Eden. Karen Armstrong argues that the creation account found in the second chapter of Genesis illustrates what the divine meant for the Israelite worshippers in Solomon's Temple:

> Eden was a place where there had been easy access to the heavenly world. Indeed, Eden was itself an experience of the sacred . . . In the Temple there were two large candlesticks; in Eden there were two trees, which, with their power to regenerate themselves each year, were common symbols of the divine. Eden was an experience of that primal wholeness which human beings all over the world sought in their holy places. God and humanity were not divided but could live in the same place; the man and woman did not know that they were different from each other; there was no distinction between good and evil. Adam and Eve, therefore, existed on a plane that transcends all opposites and all divisions: it is a unity that is beyond our experience and is quite inconceivable to us in our fragmented existence, except in rare moments of ecstasy or insight. It was a mythical description of that harmony which people in all cultures have felt to have been meant for humanity. Adam and Even lost it when they "fell" and were ejected from the divine presence and barred from Eden. Yet when the worshippers entered Solomon's Temple, its imagery and furnishings helped them to make an imaginary return to the Garden of Yahweh and to recover—if only momentarily—a sense of the paradise they had lost. It healed in them that sense of separation which, we have seen, lies at the root of the religious quest. The liturgy and architecture all aided this spiritual journey to that unity which is inseparable from the reality that we call "God" or the "sacred."[2]

According to Genesis 2:10–14, Eden was the source of the world's fertility. In its midst was a river that divided into four streams once it left the garden and fructified the rest of the earth; one of these streams was called Gihon, the spring at the base of Jerusalem that played a part in the Jerusalem festivals (see Psalm 46:5, which attests to the mythological belief in a fertilizing river that flowed through Zion to bless the land). "The idea of this river is vitally related to the belief in the presence of God, for just as in paradise a life-giving river was thought to flow, so Jerusalem was looked upon as a paradise on earth, a place where God's presence was to be found."[3] The full meaning of Jerusalem as the place where God's pres-

---

2. Armstrong, *Jerusalem*, 51–52.
3. R. E. Clements, *God and Temple* (Philadelphia: Fortress, 1965), 72.

ence is known and revealed becomes explicit in Isaiah's prophecy in Isaiah 2:2–4, where it is to become the spiritual center of the universe.

Jerusalem in Muslim Lore

The Islamic perspective on Jerusalem is similar to the Jewish, though the explanation is more complex. The starting point for Islam—the great ideal—is *tawhid*, "making one." Individual Muslims are enjoined to order their lives so as to make God their chief priority; when they achieve this personal integration, they will experience the unity which is God. The whole of human society also must achieve this unity and bring all its activities under the aegis of the sacred. Muslims are thus called to engage in a ceaseless struggle (*jihad*) to restore all things, both in the human and the natural world, to the primal perfection envisioned by God. Over the years, Jerusalem has played a centralizing role in helping Muslims visualize and achieve this ideal.

Like ancient Jews, the earliest Muslims also considered Jerusalem—particularly the Temple Mount—as the center of the earth. When Muhammad taught his initial converts to prostrate themselves in prayer before Allah as an outward sign of their interior submission, he told them to face Jerusalem, the spiritual center of the Jews and Christians who worshipped the one God. This *qiblah* (direction of prayer) marked their new orientation away from their tribe toward the primordial faith of humanity. It also expressed Muhammad's sense of solidarity and continuity with those who followed the revelation of previous prophets, including Adam, Noah, Abraham, Isaac, Ishmael, Job, Moses, David, Solomon, and Jesus. This vision of the essential unity of the religious quest of humanity would profoundly affect Muslim policy in Jerusalem. Later, when it became clear that the Jews in Arabia would not accept the newer revelation, Muhammad made the congregation turn and pray facing Mecca instead. This change of *qiblah* indicated that Muslims would not bow to one of the established religions but only to God.

Muslims continued to consider Jerusalem as a holy city, indeed as the third holiest site in the Islamic world after Mecca and Medina. Jerusalem had been a symbol that had helped them to form a distinct Islamic identity, to leave behind the pagan traditions of their ancestors and seek a new religious family. Jerusalem had been crucial in this process and would always occupy a special place in the Islamic spiritual landscape.

Muslims claim that the Prophet Muhammad also visited Jerusalem, conveyed there miraculously by the angel Gabriel. Around the year 620, prior to the *hijrah* (the migration to Yathrib/Medina), Muhammad flew through the night to Jerusalem on a winged horse named Buraq and came to rest on the Temple Mount. There Gabriel and Muhammad climbed through the seven heavens up a ladder that extended from the Temple Mount to the divine throne. Muhammad's ascent to the highest heaven was the ultimate act of Islam, a return to *tawhid*, the unity from which all being derives.

Muhammad's vision of the essential unity of the religious quest of humanity would profoundly affect Muslim policy in Jerusalem. Karen Armstrong points out that "Muslims had a rather different sacred geography from their predecessors. Because everything came from God, all things were good, so there was no essential dichotomy between the 'sacred' and the 'profane' as in Judaism. The aim of the *ummah* [Muslim community] was to achieve such integration and balance between divine and human, interior and exterior worlds, that such a distinction would become irrelevant. There was no intrinsic 'evil'; no 'demonic' realm, standing over against the 'good.' Even Satan would be forgiven on the Last Day. Everything was holy and had to be made to realize its sacred potential. All space, therefore, was sacred and no one location was holier than another."[4]

EXPLANATORY ENTRY #37: ISLAMIC EXPANSION UNDER THE EARLY CALIPHS

When Muhammad died in 632, he had united almost the whole of Arabia under his leadership. His successor, Abu Bakr, was forced to crush a rebellion by tribes who broke from the *ummah*. The tribes maintained that they had pledged their loyalty to a leader, not an ideology, and at the Prophet's death they considered themselves released from further obligation. So the new caliph sent his best generals to bring the defectors back into the fold. In 633, Muslim armies began a series of campaigns in Persia, Syria, and Iraq. By the time of Abu Bakr's death in 634, Islam was in full control of Arabia; one army had driven the Persians from Bahrain and another had entered Palestine and conquered Gaza.

---

4. Armstrong, *Jerusalem*, 221.

The Caliph Umar and al-Aqsa Mosque

After Abu Bakr's death, the caliph Umar (Omar), one of the most austere and passionate followers of Muhammad, continued the military campaigns in both Persia and Byzantium. The Arab armies continued their advance into Palestine and Syria. In 635, they entered Damascus after a six-month siege. The Muslims seized Jerusalem in 637, in the most peaceful and bloodless conquest the city had yet seen in its long and tragic history. Once the Christians had surrendered, there was no killing, no destruction of property, and no expulsions or forced conversions.

After visiting the Christian holy places, Umar saw the need for a place where the Muslims could worship without annexing Christian property. When he declared a desire to see the site of Solomon's Temple, he was taken to the Temple Mount, which, ever since the Persian occupation (614–629), had been used as the city dump. When the Muslims gazed at the vast and desolate expanse, they were horrified. As part of their mandate to sacralize the world, they felt a duty to reconsecrate a place that had been so desecrated. After consulting with the Jews on the best place for prayer, Umar went to an abandoned Christian church building at the southern end of the platform, where Emperor Justinian had built a basilica and where the present Mosque of al-Aqsa stands. After cleansing the spot, he began to pray and read from the Qur'an.

The Caliph Abd al-Malik and the Dome of the Rock

Toward the end of the seventh century, a distinctive new culture began to take shape, one that blended the cultural sophistication of Rome and Persia with the teachings of the Prophet. The caliph Abd al-Malik (685–705), a particularly able ruler, began the process of replacing the old Byzantine and Persian systems with a new Arab administration built on the theocratic ideal.

Once he had established a measure of peace and security, Abd al-Malik turned his attention to Jerusalem, to which he was devoted. He repaired the city walls and gates, which had been damaged in the recent disturbances, but his greatest contribution to the city was the Dome of the Rock, which he commissioned in 688. In Jerusalem, Christians had magnificent churches, monuments such as the Church of the Anastasis (the Church of the Holy Sepulcher), the shrine on Calvary associated with the death and burial of Jesus; the impressive New Church of Saint

Mary Theotokos (known as the Nea Church), built on the southern slope of the Western Hill by the Byzantine emperor Justinian to commemorate the doctrine of Mary as "God-bearer"; the Basilica of Holy Sion, built around the Upper Room, where the Holy Spirit had descended on the apostles on the birthday of the Church; and the extraordinary Church of the Ascension on the Mount of Olives, which, when illuminated at night, was one of the great sights of Jerusalem.

To make sure that the new Muslim building was equally brilliant, Abd al-Malik employed craftsmen and architects from Byzantium, some of whom may have been Christian. The caliph chose to build his dome around the rock that was believed to mark the site of the Holy of Holies in the Temple. Because it had long yielded access to heaven, both Jews and Muslims came to regard the rock as the foundation of the temple, the center of the world, the entrance to the Garden of Eden, and the source of fertility. Later Muslims would believe that Muhammad had ascended to heaven from this rock after his Night Journey and that he had prayed in the small cave beneath. But in 688 this event had not yet been definitely linked with Jerusalem. From a very early date, however, the Muslims felt that a visit to their new shrine took them back to the primal harmony of paradise.

The Dome of the Rock is unique in the Islamic world. It is not a mosque and has no large space for prayer. Instead it is a shrine, a reliquary. The monument, rising majestically from the most ancient holy place in Jerusalem, was a dramatic assertion that Islam had arrived and was here to stay. The Dome of the Rock, the first major piece of Muslim architecture, served as a spiritual map for Muslims. It became the archetype of all future Muslim shrines, for it replicated the basic symbolism of Mecca and the kinship that Muslims felt between the two sites. In the Meccan mosque, the square of the Kaaba led to the circle of the *tawaf*, reflecting the journey from earth to eternity. There was a similar pattern in the Jerusalem shrine. The square of the rock and its cave symbolized the earth, the origin and starting point of the quest. It is surrounded by an octagonal structure, which, in Muslim thought, is the first step away from the fixity of the square. It thus marks the beginning of the ascent toward wholeness, perfection, and eternity, replicated by the perfect circle of the dome. The dome itself, which would become such a feature of Muslim architecture, is a powerful symbol of the soaring ascent to heaven. But it also reflects the perfect balance of *tawhid*, its exterior matching its internal dimension. It illustrates the way the divine and the human, the inner and the outer worlds, fit and complement one another as two halves of a single whole.

By the end of the seventh century, both Mecca and Jerusalem were seen as the Garden of Eden, the center of the earth, and were associated with Adam and with Abraham and the sacrifice of his son. Jews had always imagined their temple as the source of the world's fertility, and now Muslims proclaimed, "All sweet water originates from beneath the Rock." The Last Judgment would take place in Jerusalem, God would defeat the forces of evil there, and the dead would rise on the Last Day and congregate in the Holy City. Therefore to die in Jerusalem was a special blessing. It was said that Muhammad's friends had wanted to bring his body to be buried in Jerusalem, the resting-place of the prophets and the place of resurrection. On the Last Day the Kaaba itself (Mecca's holiest shrine), they believed, would be brought to Jerusalem—a frequent recurring myth that shows how deeply fused the two were in the Muslim imagination.[5]

EXPLANATORY ENTRY #38:
THE OLD CITY OF JERUSALEM

The Old City of Jerusalem sits on a plateau that overlooks the Kidron Valley to the east and the Hinnom Valley to the south. It is divided into a narrow eastern hill—the site of the Temple Mount and of the ancient Jebusite city conquered by David, known in the later biblical period as Zion—and the Western Hill, which overlooks the temple and which contains the suburban area known in the later biblical period as the Upper Town. The northwestern side, connected to a range of hills, rises even higher. The Old City, which encompasses these three areas, is surrounded by a circular wall erected from 1537 to 1541 by the Ottoman ruler Sultan Suleiman the Magnificent. These walls, still standing, are two and one-half miles long and average forty feet in height. They completely encircle the city and include thirty-four towers and seven gates (an eighth gate was added later).

The impressive medieval walls of the Old City cradle four quadrants—Jewish, Armenian, Christian, and Muslim. Like most Oriental cities, Jerusalem had long been divided into quarters, inhabitants tend-

---

5. Ibid., 236–42.

ing to settle in various districts according to their religion and ethnic origin. Prior to the Crusades (twelfth and thirteenth centuries), Armenians lived together with Muslims from North Africa, as did Muslims from Iran, Afghanistan, and India. As late as the fifteenth century, there were neighborhoods in the south of the city where Jews and Muslims lived side by side. The same held true for the northeastern quadrant, where Christians and Muslims lived together. After the expulsion of the Crusaders, the divide became increasingly more evident. Under Mamluk rule and certainly by the time of the Ottoman Sultan Suleiman the Magnificent, the four quadrants were laid out roughly as we know them today.[6]

TRAVEL ENTRY #61: TRAVERSING HEZEKIAH'S TUNNEL

In 1985, during my first visit to Jerusalem, I entered the city from the east by way of the Jericho Road, traveling in air-conditioned comfort aboard a modern tour bus, with all the details of my itinerary predetermined. Now, four years later, I needed no guide to lead me, no itinerary to follow, and I had no schedule to keep but my own. The thrill of the first visit still lingered, but now I was more focused. This time I would savor each experience, enjoy every success, and appreciate every setback—and no matter what happened, I would have no regrets.

After locating a hostel in the Old City, near the Jaffa Gate, I headed toward Hezekiah's Tunnel, the 1,777-foot rock-cut water tunnel that can be explored by anyone who isn't claustrophobic or afraid of the dark and who doesn't mind getting wet. I walked to the Temple Mount and continued along the present city walls to the eastern slope of the Hill of Ophel, the site of the old Jebusite city captured by King David (see 2 Samuel 5:6–10) and known henceforth as the City of David. In the Kidron Valley, near the eastern base of the hill on which the ancient city had been built, is the famous Gihon Spring, early Jerusalem's water supply. The Hebrew name Gihon (meaning "to gush forth"), reflects the flow of the spring, which is intermittent, its frequency varying with the seasons of the year and annual precipitation.

As the city's only freshwater source, the Gihon Spring probably determined the original location of Jerusalem. Its waters were later diverted into Jerusalem's ancient water supply. Three water systems have tapped the Gihon Spring at various times in history, the oldest of these known

---

6. For a map of Old Jerusalem and its environs, see Appendix O.

as Warren's Shaft, after its modern discoverer, Captain Charles Warren. That system consists of a forty-foot-deep vertical shaft, part of an ancient sinkhole, and at the base a series of tunnels that gave the inhabitants of the city protected access to the water of the spring, which lay outside the city wall.[7] Because the Gihon Spring lies in the Kidron Valley, near the base of the Ophel Hill, the Jebusites (and the Israelites later) could not include it within their city wall without exposing the wall's defenders to possible assault from attackers positioned on the adjacent Mount of Olives, the slope across the Kidron Valley.

The next water system to be built was known as the Siloam channel, dated to Solomon's time. As an aqueduct that irrigated nearby fields through openings in the channel wall, its position along the southern length of the Kidron Valley, outside the city wall on the eastern slope of the Ophel, indicates that it was used during a peaceful period.

The third water system is Hezekiah's Tunnel, the latest and most impressive of the water systems built into the City of David. As long as water had to be hauled through Warren's Shaft one bucket at a time or across the exposed Siloam channel, Jerusalem was vulnerable. King Hezekiah (715–687 BCE) therefore overcame this problem with a remarkable engineering feat, initiated prior to 701 BCE, when Jerusalem and the Kingdom of Judah were besieged by the Assyrian forces under Sennacherib. Hezekiah ordered a tunnel dug through bedrock to divert water from the Gihon Spring to the Siloam Pool, on the other side of the city. Hezekiah's idea succeeded (see 2 Kings 20:20; 2 Chronicles 32:30); the tunnel was completed in time to withstand the siege and Sennacherib failed to capture Jerusalem. To this day water flows from the spring to the pool.

The Siloam Inscription, found in 1880 by accident near the Siloam end of the tunnel, tells us how the tunnel was made. It describes how two groups of workers, equipped with wedges, hammers, and picks, started boring at opposite ends simultaneously and eventually met deep underground. The text says one group heard the sound of the other, so

---

7. Warren's Shaft has attracted much scholarly attention and public interest over the years and the debate concerning its function in ancient times—or when it came into use—continues. Recent excavations by Ronny Reich and Eli Shukron suggest that this natural shaft, located beneath the ancient city, may never have been used to draw water, for there appear to be no rope marks at the top to indicate that it had been used for that purpose. Nevertheless, it is possible that a platform was constructed at the top of the shaft, which would have enabled buckets to be used successfully for water retrieval. For an expanded discussion of Warren's Shaft, see pages 252–54.

they knew which way to go. To compensate for the lack of air vents, the workers kept the ceiling high—as high as eighteen feet near the Siloam end but as low as five feet in the northern part, where the tunnel passes through some of the harder rock strata.

The first person in modern times to go through Hezekiah's Tunnel was Edward Robinson, the famous American explorer whose travels mark the beginning of modern archaeology in Palestine. Robinson, who crawled through the tunnel with his friend Eli Smith, made the first accurate survey of it in 1838.

At first he attempted to go through from the Siloam end, where the ceiling was high. But after eight hundred feet he made a mark with the smoke of his candle and turned back, for the ceiling had become so low that he could not advance without crawling on all fours. Three days later, more appropriately dressed, he and Smith tried again, this time starting from Gihon. In several places they found they could advance only by lying down and dragging themselves along on their elbows. At length they arrived at their previous mark and successfully proceeded to the other side, measuring the length of the passage at 1,750 feet.

I arrived at the entrance to the tunnel late in the day and found it devoid of tourists. Purchasing a candle from the tunnel's lone attendant, I struck a match and stepped into the Gihon Spring, rolling the pant legs of my lightweight khakis as far up as possible, conscious that at some point the water might reach my waist. The gate closed behind me and I proceeded cautiously into the darkness of the tunnel.

Crossing the spring, I moved slowly along the serpentine path. The floor of the tunnel was rough-hewn at this point and I inched along its slick bottom. The water deepened, and soon I was waist-deep. My heart was pounding, no doubt from a combination of fear and excitement. I realized that if a mishap were to occur, no one would find me or come to my rescue until the following day. Suddenly, without warning, a gush of air came at me from a gap to my right. The candle flickered alarmingly and I was on the verge of utter darkness. Using my free hand to cup the horizontal flame, I moved deeper into the tunnel, past the hazard. The gush of air, I learned later, came from the opening of Warren's Shaft.

I proceeded deeper into the preternatural passage, guarding my source of light as if my life depended on it. Each step propelled me closer to my goal, but possibly also toward another gust that surely might extinguish my light. I questioned why I had entered the tunnel so brazenly and so ill-prepared. I had trusted the Arab attendant, but he was young and uneducated. Doubts flooded my mind: perhaps he was merely a surrogate who didn't think to warn me about the dangers ahead or to provide me with adequate equipment for my exploit; maybe he was anti-American. I had no certain answers, but it was simply too late to turn back. I had come in search of adventure, and I was certainly getting my money's worth.

Coming eventually to a long straight section of the tunnel, my confidence returned and I began to move more quickly. After about twenty minutes, the passage began to twist and turn. Detecting a change in the height of the ceiling at this point, I knew I had reached the spot where the workers on the Gihon side must have heard the sounds of the team from the south coming through the rock. Apparently, the southern team began at a higher point on the hill, for after meeting the team from the spring they lowered the floor so the water from Gihon would flow to the Pool of Siloam. Despite the meager lighting, I noticed a series of wrong turns and dead ends, each corrected quickly by the tunnelers. An abrupt difference in the height of the ceiling confirmed that I stood at the original point of meeting. The tunnel straightened again and soon the ceiling began to rise.

The tunnel bent to the left and before long a sliver of twilight appeared ahead. Night was falling and there was very little daylight left. Then, as if confirming my worst premonition, I saw a gate at the point where the tunnel flowed into the pool, but the gate was closed. If it was locked, I would be stuck in a soggy dungeon for the next ten to twelve hours. My heart pounded as I contemplated my fate.

Although the gate opened when I pushed it, my jubilation was short-lived, for when I looked across the pool to the stairway leading to the exit, another gate appeared at the top of the stairs. And this one was locked. Fortunately, there was just enough room at the top of the gate for my slim body to pass through. Warmth returned as I unrolled my wet pant legs and stepped into the streets of Jerusalem. As the lightweight khaki dried quickly in the warm evening air, I reveled in my accomplishment.

18

Jerusalem: Jewish Center of the Labyrinth

TRAVEL ENTRY #62: WEST JERUSALEM

ON FRIDAY MORNING, THE start of Jerusalem's three-day weekend, I needed to plan my activities carefully. In this ecumenical setting, Friday functions as Islam's Holy Day (not necessarily the entire day, but Muslim males are enjoined to attend mosque during the noontime prayer service), Friday sundown until Saturday sundown is the Jewish Sabbath, and Sunday is the Christian Sabbath.

Knowing that many Jewish sites would be closed on Saturday and that buses might not be running that day, I decided to spend Friday in Jerusalem's New City, commonly known as West Jerusalem. My list included the Holocaust Memorial (Yad Vashem) and the Israel Museum, with its archaeological display and the Shrine of the Book, home to a collection of Dead Sea Scrolls found in caves near the ruins of Qumran in 1947. But the first order of business was a trip to the Hadassah Medical Center in the district of Ein Kerem.

The hospital, the largest medical center in the Middle East and the most modern in Jerusalem, stands on a hilltop several miles from downtown Jerusalem. Despite its medical fame, the facility is renowned for its stained-glass windows, designed by Marc Chagall, one of the most illustrious painters of the twentieth century. Having seen an exhibit of Chagall's paintings in Philadelphia, I was fascinated by the unusual coloration, folk symbols, and floating figures of animals, fish, and flowers.

At the Jaffa Gate I boarded Bus No. 19 and headed for the medical center. Thirty minutes later I stood in the hospital's Abbell Synagogue, gazing at the remarkable windows. The light emanating from the twelve stained glass windows bathed the synagogue in a special glow. Every pane of the exquisite windows represents a microcosm of Chagall's world—real and imaginary—of his love for his people, his deep sense of identification with Jewish history, and his early life in Russia. The Bible was his primary inspiration, particularly Genesis 49, where Jacob blesses his twelve sons, and Deuteronomy 33, where Moses blesses the twelve tribes. The dominant colors used in each window were inspired by those texts as well as by the description of the breastplate of the high priest in Exodus 28:15, colored gold, blue, purple, and scarlet and embedded with twelve gems including emeralds, turquoise, sapphire, blue jacinth, agate, beryl, lapis lazuli, and jasper. Each window features a specific color and contains a quotation from the individual blessings. Even the most casual visitor is overwhelmed by the vivid imagery.

I left the synagogue inspired, departing with a sense of indebtedness for the profound ways in which the Jewish heritage had impacted my own life as well as the self-understanding of the Western world. I thought of Abram, who in the second millennium BCE first heard a mysterious voice calling him to go forth into the unknown and to shape a new destiny. He trusted that voice and became a new person. Abraham would become the father of the monotheistic tradition and the patriarch of a great nation, a nation with a unique role among the nations.

In *The Gifts of the Jews*, Thomas Cahill argues that the Jews gave the world a whole new vocabulary for an inner landscape of ideas and feelings that had never been known before: "Because of their unique belief—monotheism—the Jews were able to give us the Great Whole, a unified universe that makes sense and that, because of its evident superiority as a worldview, completely overwhelms the warring and contradictory phenomena of polytheism. They gave us the conscience of the West, the belief that this God who is One is not the God of outward show but the 'still, small voice' of conscience, the God of compassion, the God 'who will be there,' the God who cares about each of his creatures, especially the human beings he created 'in his own image,' and [who] insists we do the same."[1]

For Cahill, the Jews gave us not only the Outside—our historical perspective—but they also gave us the Inside—our inner life; they made history real to human consciousness for the first time. Ancient Israelites gave us belief in the Promise and hope for the future—that it would be truly new and full of surprise. Biblical writers did not envision the

---

1. Cahill, *The Gifts of the Jews*, 239–40.

movement of history to be cyclical, as other societies had imagined. As a result, each moment, like each destiny, can now be viewed as unique and unrepeatable. "[History] is a process—it is going somewhere, though no one can say where. And because its end is not yet, it is full of hope—and I am free to imagine that it will not be just process but progress." Cahill is right. We can hardly get up in the morning or cross the street without being Jewish. We dream Jewish dreams and hope Jewish hopes. Most of our best words—*new, adventure, surprise; unique, individual, person, vocation; time, history, future; freedom, progress, spirit; faith, hope, justice*— are the gifts of the Jews.[2]

EXPLANATORY ENTRY #39: YAD VASHEM

The Holocaust Memorial presented a stark contrast to the luminous Chagall windows. Whereas the synagogue was radiant and uplifting, Yad Vashem was the opposite. The memorial was dimly lit and designed for reflection; darkness pervaded the exhibits, and one had the feeling of passing through the "valley of the shadow of death." In this haunting place of memory, one feels a deep need for silence, spiritually, physically, and psychologically; silence in which to remember; silence in which to try to make some sense of the memories; silence because there are no words strong enough to deplore the terrible tragedy of the Holocaust.

Built on the top of the Hill of Remembrance, Yad Vashem Holocaust Memorial opened to the public in 1957. On the grounds are a building dedicated to the memory of the Holocaust victims, a museum with a permanent exhibition, and the world's foremost center for Holocaust research and documentation. The library contains the largest and most complete collection of Holocaust literature in the world. Stored in the archives are more than fifty-eight million pages of original documents, including thousands of personal testimonies—written, dictated, or videotaped—by Holocaust survivors. Gentiles who rescued Jews are honored in the tree-lined Avenue of the Righteous of the Nations, which leads to the museum.

At the end of the museum is the Hall of Names, a partial list with over three million names of Holocaust victims. The Hall of Remembrance is a solemn structure that allows visitors to pay their respects to the martyred dead. On the floor are names of the six death camps and some of the

2. Ibid., 240–41.

concentration camps and killing sites throughout Europe. In front of the memorial flame lies a crypt containing ashes of victims. The Children's Memorial is hollowed out from an underground cavern, where memorial candles, a customary Jewish tradition for remembering the dead, are reflected in a dark and somber space.

I had come to Yad Vashem to pay homage to the millions of Jewish people who, stripped of everything, particularly their human dignity, were murdered in the Holocaust. I pondered the experience of Holocaust survivor Elie Wiesel, who in his heart-wrenching autobiographical account recalls his first night in the extermination camp at Birkenau, the reception center for Auschwitz. Only fifteen years old at the time, he had just been separated from his little sister and his mother, who were headed to the ovens:

> Never shall I forget that night, the first night in camp, which has turned my life into one long night, seven times cursed and seven times sealed. Never shall I forget that smoke. Never shall I forget the little faces of the children, whose bodies I saw turned into wreaths of smoke beneath a silent blue sky. Never shall I forget those flames which consumed my Faith forever. Never shall I forget that nocturnal silence which deprived me, for all eternity, of the desire to live. Never shall I forget those moments which murdered my God and my soul and turned my dreams to dust. Never shall I forget these things, even if I am condemned to live as long as God Himself. Never.[3]

The late Jewish scholar Emil Fackenheim indicated that there can be no explanation for Auschwitz or the Holocaust. He maintained that no redeeming voice can ever be heard from the extermination camps because Auschwitz is "a unique descent into hell ... It is an unprecedented celebration of evil. It is evil for evil's sake." To respond with despair or to merely forget, Fackenheim argued, would be further victories to Hitler, and thus impossible. In an essay titled "Jewish Faith and the Holocaust," he affirmed that while no *redeeming* Voice can ever be heard from Auschwitz, there is a *commanding* Voice. Though no purpose, religious or non-religious, can ever emerge from Auschwitz, there is an appropriate response. That response can be summarized in four declarations:

---

3. Elie Wiesel, *Night* (New York: Bantam Books, 1982), 32.

1. There can be no second Auschwitz, no second Bergen-Belsen, no second Buchenwald—anywhere in the world, for anyone in the world.

2. The Jewish people must survive, as a people. In order to survive, they are commanded to remember the victims, lest their memory perish.

3. Jewish people are forbidden to despair of humanity and their world. They cannot escape into either cynicism or otherworldliness, lest they cooperate in delivering the world to the forces of Auschwitz.

4. Jews are forbidden to despair of the God of Israel, lest Judaism perish.[4]

Fackenheim, called the philosopher of the Holocaust, very nearly became one of its victims. Born in Germany and ordained a rabbi in Berlin in 1939, he fled to Canada in 1940, where he had a long, illustrious scholarly career. He formulated the "614th commandment" (adding one to the 613 found in the Torah): there must be no slackening of Jewish faith because that would be to grant Hitler a posthumous victory.

Jews and Christians share a patrimony that demands an effort to overcome evil with good. Christians and Jews must remember, collectively and cooperatively, the lessons of suffering and persecution—of crusades, inquisitions, and pogroms—not with any desire for vengeance or as an incentive to hatred, but to overcome evil. Christians must join hands with Jews and also with Muslims and with people of all religions, races, and creeds and remember. "For us, to remember," said Pope John Paul II on March 23, 2000 during a brief ceremony held in the Hall of Remembrance at Yad Vashem, "is to pray for peace and justice, and to commit ourselves to their cause. Only a world at peace, with justice for all, can avoid repeating the mistakes and terrible crimes of the past."

EXPLANATORY ENTRY #40: THE ISRAEL MUSEUM

The Israel Museum is one of the great museums of the world and an absolute "must see" on any visit to Jerusalem. It is located in a lovely area

---

4. Emil L. Fackenheim, "Jewish Faith and the Holocaust," in *The Ways of Religion*, ed. by Roger Eastman (New York: Harper & Row, 1975), 332–44; see particularly page 337. Reprinted from Emil L. Fackenheim, *The Quest for Past and Future: Essays in Jewish Theology* (Bloomington, IN: Indiana University Press, 1968).

of West Jerusalem, in a cluster of buildings and parks that also includes the Hebrew University and the government quarter, where the Knesset, the Israeli parliament, is situated.

Across the street, southwest of the Knesset, are the pavilions of the Israel Museum, the beautiful and spacious complex that houses Israel's treasures. The museum, which opened in 1965, contains the Shrine of the Book, the Archaeological Museum, and two art museums. The Israel Museum, the largest and most important cultural institution in the country, includes five hundred thousand works of art, archaeological and anthropological exhibits, and ethnographic displays. It also houses unique finds, such as the Dead Sea Scrolls—the oldest Biblical manuscripts in the world—relics from the time of Bar Kokhba (second century CE), and the largest collection of Judaica in the world.

The Archaeological and Antiquities Museum houses exhibits covering all the periods, from the Early Stone Age (about 500,000 BCE) through the Canaanite, Biblical, Roman, Byzantine, Arab, and Crusader periods to the Ottoman period.[5] One of the new displays at the museum is the Model of Jerusalem in the Late Second Temple Period. The model recreates Jerusalem in 66 CE, the fateful year when the Great Revolt by the Jews against the Romans erupted, resulting in the destruction of the city and the temple. The ancient city was then at its largest, more than twice the size of the Old City today. The model thus reflects ancient Jerusalem at its peak. Produced under the direction of Prof. Michael Avi-Yonah of the Hebrew University of Jerusalem, the model took four years to complete.

Visitors interested in the archaeology of Israel are urged to visit the Rockefeller Archaeological Museum, situated in a magnificent white limestone building in East Jerusalem. This excellent museum, built with a grant from John D. Rockefeller, stands just north of the city wall near Herod's Gate. The museum, opened in 1938 before the founding of the State of Israel, was run independently for most of its history but it is now associated with the Israel Museum. The collection is based on finds unearthed during the early years of archaeological activity in the country (1890–1948), when key sites, among them Jerusalem, Megiddo, Ashkelon, Lachish, Samaria, and Jericho, were excavated. The wealth of finds includes some of the most important artifacts uncovered in this land to date.

5. For a chronology of events in Israel and the rest of the Holy Land, consult Appendix E.

Jerusalem: Jewish Center of the Labyrinth 249

The crowning moment of my visit to the Israel Museum was a stop at the Shrine of the Book, an onion-top-shaped building designed to resemble the jar covers in which the Dead Sea Scrolls were discovered. The building, opened in 1965, is considered a milestone of modern architecture. The corridor leading to the main hall resembles a cave, recalling the mysterious surroundings in which the ancient manuscripts were discovered.

The center of the round building displays scrolls containing the oldest extant text of the Old Testament, sections of the book of Isaiah written about 100 BCE. Other texts are displayed on the outside walls. The cases on the lower floor contain finds from Masada, dating from the period when the uprising by the Jewish Zealots was put down by the Roman siege in 73 CE; they were found during excavations in 1964 and 1965.

The Dead Sea Scrolls are considered by many to be the greatest archaeological find of the twentieth century. These ancient manuscripts were discovered between 1947 and 1956 in eleven caves near Khirbet Qumran, on the northwestern shores of the Dead Sea. They are approximately two thousand years old, dating from the third century BCE to the first century CE. In general, they were written on parchment, with the exception of a few written on papyrus. The vast majority of the scrolls survived as fragments, with only a handful found intact. Nevertheless, scholars have managed to reconstruct from these fragments approximately 850 different manuscripts of various lengths.

On the basis of the scrolls and excavations at the site, most scholars have concluded that Khirbet Qumran and its environs were inhabited by a sect of Jewish Essenes. This sect existed side by side with Pharisees, Sadducees, early Christians, Samaritans, and Zealots, who together comprised the Jewish society of the land of Israel in the Late Hellenistic-Roman period—from the rise of the Maccabees through the destruction of the Second Temple (167 BCE–70 CE). The sectarians, who had divorced themselves from the main body of the Jewish people, espoused fervent messianic beliefs. Having left Jerusalem following a harsh dispute with the Jerusalem priesthood regarding theological and ritual matters, it became their goal to return to the city in order to restore the "desolate" Temple (as they perceived it).

The question of when the sectarians first began to settle in Qumran is still the subject of much debate. It is believed that an unknown personality referred to in the scrolls as the Teacher of Righteousness established the community in the second half of the second century BCE. As for its end, the general consensus is that the community met its fate in 68 CE, when the Roman army destroyed the settlement on its way to suppress the revolt that had broken out in Jerusalem.

The discovery of the Dead Sea Scrolls represents a turning point in the study of the history of the Jewish people in ancient times, for never before has a literary treasure of such magnitude come to light. Thanks to these remarkable finds, our knowledge of Jewish society in the land of Israel during the Hellenistic and Roman periods as well as the origins of rabbinical Judaism and early Christianity has been greatly enriched.

TRAVEL ENTRY #63: SATURDAY MORNING IN THE WEST BANK

Early Saturday morning I walked through the Damascus Gate to the Arab Bus Station. On Saturdays (the Jewish Sabbath), Israeli buses do not run, but in the Old City region there are Arab Palestinian bus lines that serve nearby Arab villages. I wanted to visit two places: Emmaus, the village where the risen Christ appeared to two disciples (Luke 24:13–35), and the Old Testament site of Gibeon, where a famous gladiatorial contest occurred to resolve a dispute between the armies of Ishbosheth (son of King Saul), under Abner, and of David, under Joab, by having twelve men from each side fight (2 Samuel 2:12–28). The plan failed because the twenty-four men killed each other at the pool.

Today two places vie for consideration as the biblical Emmaus: el Qubeiba, a village about twelve miles northwest of Jerusalem, and Amwas, several miles further west. Each is located in the West Bank, but I visited only one—el Qubeiba. As soon as I reached the outskirts of Jerusalem, I entered the Judean hill country, where geography, history, and religion are closely interwoven. It was clear that this was the land of the Bible: on the left was the Mountain of Joy, thought to be the site of Samuel's tomb, and on a hill to the right, excavations confirmed the site of Gibeah, where Saul, the first king of Israel, lived and reigned. Two miles farther a road forks off to the village of er-Ram (Ramah), the home of the prophet Samuel.

On its way to el Qubeiba, the small minibus passed stony fields, mostly bordered by low stone walls, and vineyards with old towers, such as Jesus mentioned in Matthew 21:33. With its clusters of trees, el Qubeiba resembles an oasis among the barren hills, its high altitude providing a panoramic view of the hill country to the western coastal plain. Upon entering the village, I passed a convent and shortly afterwards arrived at the entrance to the Franciscan church. Inside the church, in the left nave, are the foundations of an ancient house.

From Jerusalem to el Qubeiba is approximately seven miles as the crow flies. This distance would correspond to the sixty stadia in Luke's account of the two disciples' walk to Emmaus. Excavations have disclosed that the place was inhabited in pre-Christian times. When the Crusaders attempted to identify Emmaus, el Qubeiba was ascribed greater importance than was Amwas, its distance from Jerusalem being more in keeping with Luke's report. And from the thirteenth century onwards the pilgrim way led from Akko (Acre) to Jerusalem via el Qubeiba.

In the twelfth century Crusaders built a monastery, a church, and a castle at el-Qubeiba. During the following centuries the church was destroyed, like most others. In 1861, the Franciscans received the land as a gift and in 1900 erected the present church over the remains of the medieval one. When the Crusader church was discovered, the ruins of a house were also found in the left nave. Today this is regarded as the house of Cleopas, which Jesus is said to have entered with the two disciples, and it has been preserved as a memorial of the breaking of bread in Emmaus (Luke 24:28–30). Behind the church are the extensive ruins of a wide Roman road, dating from Jesus' day, as well as the ruins of houses belonging to an ancient settlement. These remains indicate that this village must have been an important trading center in New Testament times.

After my visit to el-Qubeiba and a futile wait for public transportation, I decided to walk to Gibeon, approximately two miles away. It was still morning and the hike seemed attractive on this beautiful fall day. When I arrived at the site of the celebrated pool a couple of Arab youngsters were hanging out, proud to show me the famous site but unable to communicate their knowledge effectively. The water system, cut entirely from solid rock, includes a great cistern, thirty-seven feet in diameter and eighty-two-feet deep with a circular staircase of seventy-nine steps cut out of the rock. Actually the pool was never used to hold water but was part of a waterworks that assured the citizens of water even during times of siege. To reach the water required a descent to the base of the cistern and then a walk through a tunnel 167 feet long that descended ninety-three additional steps. At the bottom was the cistern room filled with water from the main spring outside the city wall. The armed contest between Saul and David's men probably took place around this cistern.

TRAVEL ENTRY #64: SATURDAY AFTERNOON IN OLD JERUSALEM

After a productive morning in the West Bank, I returned to Jerusalem to explore the Old City's Jewish Quarter. Later that day I had an appointment with Marian Lewin-Epstein, who had lived in Washington, Pennsylvania until 1948, when she moved to the newly founded State of Israel. In Washington, her many friends encouraged me to contact her during my sabbatical visit. She and her husband, Dr. Jack Lewin-Epstein, lived about a mile southwest of the Old City. Jack was the former dean of the dental school at Hadassah, where Marian volunteered as a tour guide. I looked forward to my visit with this educated Jewish couple.

My first stop was "Warren's Shaft," a vertical rock-cut shaft located just south of the Temple Mount, outside today's Old City. The shaft connected biblical Jerusalem (the City of David) to the spring of Gihon and Hezekiah's Tunnel, which I had traversed recently. For some reason this part of Jerusalem—the original heart of the ancient city—attracts me like no other. Perhaps the magnetism comes from knowing that the area's escarpments, wall, and rock-hewn water systems were viewed by David, Solomon, Hezekiah, Isaiah, Jeremiah, Ezra, Jesus, Paul, and so many other biblical figures.

For one who has taught a biblical course every semester over a thirty-year career, it is natural to identify with the lives of the men and women of Jerusalem who climbed steep paths to draw water from the Gihon Spring; who hewed Hezekiah's tunnel to protect its spring from Assyrian invasion; who listened to Jeremiah plead and exhort and who gazed from their walls at the Babylonian army that laid siege to the city; who worked with Nehemiah to rebuild the city walls; who listened to Ezra proclaim the words of Torah by the Water Gate; who followed Jesus to the Pool of Siloam and witnessed his holistic healing and teaching ministry.

The City of David is located on a low, narrow spur (the Hill of Ophel) south of the Old City. A settlement existed here in the Bronze and Iron Ages, of which remains of fortifications and buildings have been found. The ancient city was built on a hill of hard limestone, in which underground water created karstic caves. "Karst" is a geological term that describes an irregular region of sinks, caverns, and channels caused by groundwater as it seeps and flows through underground rock formations. The Gihon Spring, the only source of water of the city, emerges in the Kidron Valley, at the eastern base of the City of David. It made the founding of the City of David possible and sustained its existence for thousands of years.

Warren's Shaft consists of a steeply sloping tunnel which then flattens and winds under ancient Israelite and Canaanite city walls toward a narrow forty-foot shaft. The entrance to Warren's Shaft is located midway down the eastern slope of the City of David, within the ancient city's walls. At its easternmost end is a narrow, irregularly shaped vertical shaft some six feet wide and forty feet deep. That shaft drops to a cavity in the bedrock attached to the Gihon Spring. By going down the tunnel to the shaft and lowering a bucket on a rope, ancient inhabitants of Jerusalem could bring up water from the bottom of the shaft. Thus, in time of siege it was possible to draw water safely from the spring without venturing outside the walls. The vertical shaft at the end of the system was considered to be impenetrable from the outside.

The debate over the shaft's date raised an intriguing question. In 2 Samuel 5:8, when King David attacked Jebusite Jerusalem to conquer it, he declared: "Whoever would strike down the Jebusites, let him get up the *tsinnor*," a word commonly translated as "water shaft." Did Warren's Shaft provide the route by which David's forces penetrated the city?

The meaning of *tsinnor* is problematic—the New English Bible translates *tsinnor* as "grappling hooks," suggesting that the word refers to grappling hooks that were used to scale city walls—and a parallel description of the city's conquest by David (1 Chronicles 11:6) fails to mention the term. Some scholars who accept the reference to *tsinnor* as "water shaft" argue that David conquered the city not by getting *up* the water shaft, but by getting *into* the water system, that is, by discovering and capturing the Jebusite water source. Once this was done, the Israelites were in a position to deny the city water. According to this theory, surrender was preceded by thirst, and not by a surprise attack up some potentially impassable vertical shaft.

Until recently, the tunnel leading to Warren's Shaft was a dead end; visitors peered down the shaft at its end, listened to the water from the spring whispering below, and then climbed up and out the way they climbed down and in. But recent study opens up an entirely new understanding of the shaft system. A newly excavated passageway at the tunnel's end, ten feet up the wall and accessible by steps, opens to a whole new set of excavations. It seems that the wide tunnel leading to Warren's Shaft, hewn during the Middle Bronze Age (eighteenth to seventeenth century BCE), didn't aim for that shaft at all, but instead around and above it, into the hole recently opened up, then emerging from the hillside above a large storage pool. The passage was carved through soft limestone which ran above harder dolomite. Current research indicates that Jerusalem's Canaanite residents would have traveled through the tunnel system under the city wall and out the hillside, where they would have stepped onto wooden platforms above the pool. From these platforms people dropped buckets and filled them with water.

EXPLANATORY ENTRY #41: THE CARDO

As I strolled through the Jewish Quarter to my appointment with Marian, I came across a sign pointing to the ruins of the "Cardo," and I stopped to explore the site. In ancient Roman city planning, a cardo was a north-south-oriented street in cities, military camps, and colonies. Sometimes called the Cardo Maximus, the street served as the center of economic life. Derived from the same root as cardinal, the cardo was the axis of the city; it was lined with shops, merchants, and vendors. Most Roman cities also had a Decumanus Maximus, an east-west street that served as a secondary main street. A forum was normally located at the intersection of the Decumanus and the Cardo. The Cardo in the Old City of Jerusalem provides an example of this Roman layout.

After the Jewish rebellion of 70 CE, when the Jews were crushed by Roman troops, Jerusalem was left in ruins. In the ensuing years, Jerusalem, the center of the Jewish world, became little more than a base for the Roman army. Some Jews remained on the hill to the south of the Roman camp, which Josephus, the first-century CE Jewish soldier and author had mistakenly called Mount Zion. By the time of his writing, people had forgotten that the original City of David had been on the Ophel hill; they assumed that David had lived in the Upper City in the better part of town, where their own kings and aristocrats resided. Today this hill is still called Mount Zion, but to distinguish it from the original, it is now commonly spelled "Mount Sion."

After the destruction of Jerusalem in 70 CE, the Jewish Christians returned from the region of the Decapolis, where they had fled for refuge, and settled alongside the Jews on Mount Sion. They met in one of the houses that had survived destruction, later identified with the "Upper Room" where Jesus had celebrated the Last Supper and where the disciples had seen the risen Christ and received the Holy Spirit. Jews and Jewish Christians mingled in that part of the city called Sion, and it seems that a substantial number of Jews converted to Christianity here during this period.

After a brief examination of the reconstructed Cardo, I exited the Old City through the Zion Gate at the extreme south end of Old Jerusalem and proceeded south along Mount Sion. Since the fourth century, as is evidenced by churches built at that time, this hill has been revered as the place where Jesus celebrated the Last Supper with his disciples and where, according to tradition, the apostles met after the Ascension of Jesus (Acts 1:13–14). This area, part of the Upper Town in the first century, was once within the city wall, and is sacred to the Jews because they believe David is buried here.

On the eastern slope of Mount Sion is the traditional site of the palace of Caiaphas, the high priest at the time of Jesus' arrest and crucifixion. Jesus was brought here after his arrest in Gethsemane. The cell dungeon where Jesus stayed is still visible, as is the courtyard where Peter denied the Lord three times. Farther south, the remains of buildings dating from the time of Herod have been discovered. One of these buildings contains a room that is now used as a synagogue. An adjoining room contains the Tomb of David, one of the most sacred of all sites to the Jews, second only to the Western Wall. The tomb, made of stone, is covered with embroidered cloths and topped with silver Torah crowns and Torah rolls.

On leaving David's Tomb, I came to the steps leading to the Cenacle, the Upper Room of the Last Supper. In addition to being revered as the place where Jesus established the Eucharist, the Upper Room is believed by some to have been the place where 120 disciples were gathered when the Holy Spirit came upon them on the day of Pentecost (Acts 1:1–42), the birthday of the Church. The large hall, with two Gothic columns supporting a vaulted ceiling, was renovated by the Franciscans, after Pope Clement IV transferred the care of this site to them in 1342. In the sixteenth century, Sultan Suleiman drove out the Franciscans, allowing the Muslims to use the Upper Room as a mosque. A large square stone opposite the Muslim *mihrab* (the prayer recess) is thought to be the place where Jesus sat at the Last Supper.

TRAVEL ENTRY #65:
A CONVERSATION WITH MARION LEWIN-EPSTEIN

After making my way past some of the city's most revered sites, I finally arrived at the home of the Lewin-Epsteins, a lovely modern apartment southwest of Old Jerusalem. Marion was expecting me and we sat down for afternoon tea and animated conversation as we spoke of my trip and shared memories of her hometown of Washington, Pennsylvania. We discussed educational opportunities for American students in Israel, a topic I was pursuing at the time, and then the conversation turned to current affairs and Arab-Israeli relations. Marion indicated that until recently, many Jews and Arabs in Jerusalem had been friends, but that had changed dramatically since the start of the Intifada.

After the Six-Day War of 1967, when Israel achieved a stunning victory over three Arab armies, the nation more than tripled its territory. But more importantly, Israeli forces moved into ancient Jerusalem and took control of the entire Old City, including the Western Wall, thereby fulfilling the age-old quest of the Jews to return to their holy city. The war changed mental maps in the Middle East as much as it did the political landscape, altering hopes and fears.

For Israelis, 1967 was a time of euphoria. For the next twenty years, Israel prided itself on running an "enlightened" occupation, and the Palestinians largely acquiesced to Israeli rule. Israel tapped into a deep pool of cheap labor, employing 40 percent of the Palestinian work force by the mid-1980s and selling its goods to a captive market. Palestinians earned more as construction workers, waiters, and gardeners in Israel than they would at home. Roads were open, and travel was uninhibited. Israelis had their cars fixed in Gaza and spent weekends sampling hummus and pomela in the desert oasis of Jericho. Many Palestinians picked up Hebrew, went on day trips to Tel Aviv's beaches, and even listened to Israeli pop songs. But Israel also cracked down on any display of Palestinian nationalism.

For Palestinians, the negative impact of 1967 took time to develop. Gradually, the vocabulary of the Palestinian struggle changed. At first it was anger and searing loss. Their sense of identity—and their rage—was sharpened by the spread of Jewish settlements in the occupied territories.[6] By 1987, thousands of youths grew impatient waiting for Arafat

---

6. As of July 2009, over three hundred thousand Israelis lived in West Bank settle-

and his colleagues to turn the tables on the occupiers and launched their own uprising against the Israelis. The resentment at occupation boiled over in December. The spark for the Intifada, as it became known, was a Gaza traffic accident in which an Israeli driver killed several Palestinian laborers. The first Intifada lasted six years and did not end until Israel and the Palestine Liberation Organization agreed to recognize each other's existence.

There were interim peace deals in the 1990s, aimed at a "two state solution." But Yasser Arafat, an Egyptian-educated former civil engineer whose Fatah organization carried out raids inside the conquered territories, refused to give up his demand that Palestinian refugees be allowed to return to villages in Israel. Israel's response was to continue building settlements on Palestinian territory. Granting Palestinian refugees the right of return to their former land was viewed as an existential threat, for Israelis know that the return of Palestinians to what is now Israel would soon render Jews a minority in their own state.

The latest Palestinian uprising, resulting in the deaths of over forty-three hundred Palestinians and eleven hundred Israelis, cemented Israel's determination to cut itself off from the Palestinians. Prime Minister Ariel Sharon removed all Israelis from Gaza in 2005 and began building a separation wall in the West Bank. Younger Palestinians, meanwhile, feel let down by Fatah and the old secularists and are turning to radical Islam as an alternative. During the first Intifada, youngsters threw stones at Israeli tanks and ran away, whereas youngsters of the new generation seek to annihilate themselves as well as their Israeli enemy.

Palestinian children today are tougher and more aggressive than the preceding generation; they have fewer opportunities, and therefore are less hopeful. Raja Shehadeh, a Palestinian writer and lawyer in Ramallah, quotes a saying: "When you lose a nation, you resort to religion." And that is what is happening to young Palestinians: they're turning to Islam for perspective and for answers.

My conversation with Marion, less than two years into the original Intifada, indicated that a sea-change was occurring in the Arab-Israeli neighborhoods. Both groups were fearful and pessimistic; each was demonizing the other, and neither group seemed to hold out hope for a

---

ments, over twenty thousand lived in settlements in the Golan Heights, and an additional one hundred and ninety-two thousand settled in East Jerusalem, annexed by Israel.

lasting solution. As I listened, I realized that at another level Jews and Palestinians are fatally alike: they both suffer from a powerful and justifiable sense of victimization—the Jews over the Holocaust, the Palestinians over the loss of land and many of their rights—and this blinds each to the others' tragedy.

Palestinians have never felt as hopeless as they feel today. And they are turning their weapons on each other in a power struggle between Fatah and Hamas. Hundreds of Palestinians died in bloody street battles in Gaza during 2006 and 2007, more than one-third of the total killed by Israel in the same period. Radicals have gained strength, especially in Gaza. The Palestinian Authority, a product of interim peace accords between Israel and Fatah, appears close to collapse. Palestinians with ties to the West are leaving; they don't expect the occupation to end.

Still, the Palestinian population inside the territories is rising, due to a high birth rate. There will soon be more Muslims than Jews in the lands comprising historic Palestine. Demography, more than politics or religion, will most likely be what drives Israeli policy. If Israel hopes to remain both Jewish and democratic, it will need to make a deal. As Jonathan Kuttab, a Palestinian human rights lawyer has argued persuasively, any permanent and lasting peace must lead to a two-state solution. On the Israeli side, such a solution must include: (a) withdrawal to 1967 borders [any changes to these boundaries must be by agreement on a swap basis]; (b) dismantling of its West Bank settlements; (c) making possible some form of shared status for a united Jerusalem, the capital of both parties; (d) and offering a viable solution to the refugee problem. For its part, the West Bank and Gaza would have to be demilitarized to remove any security threat to Israel. Furthermore, all Arab neighbors must pledge to honor Israel's legal borders and its right to live in peace under these conditions. The solution may be obvious, but it cannot be implemented without political will on both sides.[7]

By the time I left Marion Lewin-Epstein's home, Shabbat, the Jewish day of rest, was over. The mood seemed festive as people strolled about, talking excitedly or simply window shopping. The sidewalks in Jewish neighborhoods began to fill with people and the roads with cars as families emerged from their Sabbath rest. Though secular Jews sometimes

---

7. Jimmy Carter deals with these and other concerns in his recent work, *Palestine: Peace Not Apartheid* (New York: Simon & Schuster, 2006), including his dismay at the segregation wall built by Israel through the Palestinian West Bank.

drive cars on the Sabbath in Israel, many avoid doing so in Jerusalem. Conservative Jews and Reform Jews may drive on the Sabbath, but only for specific purposes such as going to synagogue or visiting family and friends. While not strictly following the biblical prohibitions, they purportedly observe the spirit of the Sabbath day. Orthodox Jews, however, do not drive on the Sabbath, for starting a car involves lighting a fire, and kindling fire is one of the thirty-nine types of work that the Torah prohibits on the Sabbath.

TRAVEL ENTRY #66: MEA SHEARIM

Jerusalem is a city of neighborhoods, secular and religious groups generally living apart in their own sharply defined areas. The contrast between these neighborhoods can be as dramatic as the contrast between Israelis and Palestinians. One neighborhood I wished to visit was Mea Shearim, Jerusalem's ultra-Orthodox quarter, and Saturday evening seemed like the perfect time to do so.

Mea Shearim, an Old World enclave in the midst of a city aspiring to modernity, represents a living museum, its residents having preserved the traditional ways of life that existed for centuries among ultra-Orthodox Jews in the ghettos of Northern and Eastern Europe. In many ways Mea Shearim's residents live in a medieval world, every aspect of daily life following its solemn rules and rituals. They live and dress in the same somber style as did their European ancestors.

The quarter has one of Jerusalem's highest population densities, making life there intense, public, and ceremonious. Houses tend to be small, shabby, and airless, with privacy almost nonexistent—about a third of the people living more than three to a room. The sexes are strictly segregated, with customers in line at a shop standing in separate queues designated for males and females. Many men in Mea Shearim engage full time in study and worship, while their wives raise large families—typically seven or eight children, since birth control is forbidden. Although they depend on charity for support, ultra-Orthodox communities are close knit, and have a well-developed welfare and mutual aid system.

The residents of Mea Shearim are not a cohesive religious group. They are splintered into rabbinical sects and Hasidic movements. Discord, strife, and conflict mark their relations with each other. Each sect dresses a bit differently. Typically, though, men and boys wear heavy, black frock coats and fur-trimmed hats, regardless of the season. Women wear long-sleeved, modest clothing; in some groups, they wear thick black stockings all year long, even in summer. Because married women must cover their hair, they wear a variety of head coverings, from wigs to headscarves. Some extreme Orthodox sects require married women to cut their hair short and wear scarves. The men have beards and some grow long side curls, called *peyos*.

The daily language for many ultra-Orthodox Jews is Yiddish, a German-Jewish dialect. They refuse to speak Hebrew, Israel's official language, which they view as a sacred tongue, to be used only in prayer and learning and not to be debased through daily, irreverent use. The more moderate sects, however, will speak Hebrew. Most Mea Shearim inhabitants see Jewish sovereignty in the Holy Land as a sin since the Messiah and the End of Days have not yet arrived. They see the State of Israel as premature and in violation of Holy Scripture. The more radical sects do not even recognize the State of Israel. They refuse to pay taxes, serve in the armed forces or accept aid from the government. Some go so far as to believe the Holocaust was God's retribution for Zionist efforts to create a Jewish state.

When I entered the Jerusalem Gate onto Ein Yaaqov Street, I passed a large multi-lingual sign that warned against immodest dress while in the quarter. The sign also made it clear that men had to wear hats. Knowing that ultra-Orthodox Jews are intolerant of those not sharing their beliefs and that "modesty patrols" walk the streets, I made sure to conform to the rules as much as possible. I had worn slacks and a shirt, for I knew that shorts or any scanty clothing is considered insulting. Since I had not brought a hat with me, I improvised and placed a handkerchief over my head, hoping that the residents would respect my sincerity. I also did not carry a radio or a camera, for I knew such items caused offense. My tour was brief, for the inhabitants were mostly indoors. Had I come earlier in the day, I would no doubt have seen a great deal of activity, for people are constantly in the street on Shabbat, coming to or from *schul* (a Yiddish word that emphasizes the synagogue's role as a place of study).

Mea Shearim has at least fifty synagogues and as many Torah schools and *yeshivas*. Most are simple and unadorned facilities. Some are just a single street-side room with benches as the only furniture. Others may be in houses or attics. Only a few resemble a typical classroom. Strict, authoritarian education is the primary tool for instilling values in their young, and children spend most of their time in school, where the curriculum is devoted almost exclusively to religious studies.

19

Jerusalem: Christian Center of the Labyrinth

TRAVEL ENTRY #67: SUNDAY MORNING IN JERUSALEM

SUNDAY WAS MY FINAL day in Jerusalem. I had purchased a bus ticket to Cairo and would be leaving Israel on the morrow. Most of the places I expected to visit before my departure—the Western Wall, the Temple Mount, the Via Dolorosa, and the Church of the Holy Sepulcher—I had seen during a previous trip. This time I wanted to add one more site to the list, the Ophel Archaeological Garden at the foot of the Temple Mount, south of the Western Wall. I also hoped to spend some time in the Old City's labyrinthine alleys and bazaars.

Because time wends slowly in the Middle East, Jerusalem's exotic bazaars still exist. The crowds, the energy, the cramped space all survive amid shadowy passageways and arcades as ancient as bartering itself and as permanent as the search for a good bargain. These can be found in the Arab market—the *souk*—that occupies a jumbled maze of narrow alleys in the Old City. About a million tourists visit the Old City each year, adding the *souk*'s bustle in their quest for everything from olivewood carvings and sheepskin rugs to headdresses and spices. The quality of merchandise has declined since the Six-Day War of 1967, when Israel captured the Old City, but shoppers can still sift out genuine Bedouin apparel, saddle bags and rugs, Persian carpets, and valuable antiques from the mass of trinkets. In doing so, they must rise to the challenge of Middle Eastern haggling, hold on to their wallets and purses, and steel their wits.

Since my hostel was on the western side of the city, near the Jaffa Gate, I followed David Street into the *souk*. David Street contains more than one hundred stalls jammed together in a claustrophobic space. As I made my way through the maze of bazaars, I reached an alley that led to additional bazaars and eventually to the Damascus Gate. I continued straight ahead, following the Street of Chains to the Western Wall and the Temple Mount. Serious shopping would have to wait until my return trip later in the day.

The current Jewish Quarter, which has been rebuilt and today looks almost brand new, was the center of Jewish life in Jerusalem for eight hundred years. It is located on the remains of the Upper City from the Herodian period (37 BCE–70 CE). The oldest synagogues are below street level because at the time they were built, Jews and Christians were prohibited from building anything higher than the Muslim structures. The Great Synagogue, as the Hurva was known, dates back to Rabbi Yehuda Hanassi, who came from Poland in 1701 with five hundred disciples. After the Rabbi died it fell into decay (hence the name *hurva*, "ruin"). The synagogue was rebuilt in 1856, but was damaged in the War of 1948 and then destroyed after the Jordanians took control of the Old City. The beloved Hurva was reconstructed once again and rededicated in 2010. Nearby is the Ramban Synagogue, built on ancient ruins in 1267 CE. Named for Rabbi Moshe ben-Nahman Ramban (Nachmanides), who had come from Spain, it is the most ancient synagogue in the Old City. Ramban helped rejuvenate the Jewish community in Jerusalem in the thirteenth century, after it had been wiped out by the Crusaders.

A large plaza at the northern end of the Jewish Quarter offers access to the Western Wall, the largest of the sites venerated by the Jews. In 1967, after Jewish forces captured the Old City, the densely built site was cleared and made into a huge open square. The location near the wall is divided by a fence with a small area for women on the right and a larger area for men on the left. When Rome destroyed the Second Temple in 70 CE, only one outer wall remained standing. The Romans probably would have destroyed that wall also, but it may have seemed unnecessary, it being not even part of the Temple itself, just an outer wall surrounding the Temple Mount.[1] The size of some of the stones (known as ashlars) may also have made their removal practically impossible. The largest ashlar is forty-five feet long, fifteen feet deep, fifteen feet high, and weighs more than one million pounds.

---

1. For a site plan of the Herodian Temple Mount in Jerusalem, including walls, gates, and buildings, see Appendix P.

For the Jews, this remnant of what was the most sacred building in the Jewish world quickly became the holiest spot in Jewish life. Throughout the centuries, Jews from throughout the world traveled to Palestine, and immediately headed for the Western Wall (the Kotel) to thank God, for it was the only accessible part of the Temple. The prayers offered at the Kotel were so heartfelt that non-Jews began calling the site the Wailing Wall. Praying at the sixty-five-foot-high wall is a unique experience, one that makes believers feel as close as it is possible to get to the Almighty. Over the years, worshippers have inserted into joints of the wall scraps of paper representing messages and prayers they hope will be answered.

Around the corner from the Western Wall, below the southeastern corner of the Temple Mount, is the Ophel Archeological Garden. The excavations reveal twenty-five hundred years of Jerusalem's history in twenty-five layers of ruins dating back to the time of King Solomon in the tenth century BCE. The archaeological excavations feature a number of remains from the First Temple period, including administrative buildings that served Jerusalem from the tenth to the eighth century BCE.

The most notable of the remains excavated on the Ophel come from the late Second Temple period (from the time of Herod until the destruction of the temple in 70 CE). Wide streets were paved at the foot of the Temple Mount to afford hundreds of thousands of pilgrims easy access to the temple. A section of one such street, with shops along both sides, can be seen in the northern part of the excavation site. Other finds from this period include Jewish ritual baths, a grand Herodian staircase that connected the City of David on the Ophel Hill with the southern entrance to the Temple Mount (known as the Hulda Gates), and sections of a massive overpass known as Robinson's Arch. Excavation indicated that the monumental structure was a stairway that led up from the main street in the valley and then turned right to the entrance to the Royal Portico at the Temple Mount's southern summit. The overpass enabled the multitude of visitors—Jews and Gentiles alike—to ascend to the Royal Portico without mingling with the pilgrims entering the temple compound through the Hulda Gates following their immersion in a ritual bath.

Another impressive discovery from the Second Temple period is the ancient staircase on the southern end of the Temple Mount, leading to the Western (Double) Hulda Gate, through which worshippers entered the Second Temple compound. Extending along the base of the southern section of the wall, these stairs were originally 210 feet wide. The thirty steps, laid alternately as steps and landings, were conducive to a slow, reverent ascent. Today we can see only half their length; the remainder lies under a Crusader structure, built against the southern wall of the Temple Mount in order to protect the western gate during the Crusader period. At that time, the southern wall of the Mount served as the city wall, and the center of government was located on the Temple platform. Today much of the western gateway (Double Gate), built about two hundred feet west of the Eastern Hulda Gate, including the internal passageway, remains intact under the al-Aqsa Mosque, but it is only accessible with permission.

The Temple Mount

After completing my condensed sojourn through three thousand years of history, I left the Ophel Archaeological Garden and entered the Temple Mount, the most famous and contested religious site in the world. Nowhere else do holy places of the three monotheistic world religions lie so close together as on the Temple Mount, Israel's old Temple Square. This place is the holiest site for Judaism, for in this location stood the Temple of Solomon (completed 950 BCE and destroyed 587 BCE by the Babylonians).

Known to Muslims as Haram al-Sharif (the Noble Sanctuary), the Temple Mount is dominated by two major Muslim religious shrines, the Dome of the Rock (built c. 690) and the al-Aqsa Mosque (built c. 710, this sanctuary is named after the Quranic reference to Jerusalem as the "Remote Place," for it was the most distant sanctuary visited by Muhammad).

The spot is important for Christians for it is mentioned many times in the New Testament. It was in the Temple that Jesus was presented as a baby; it was here that the twelve-year-old boy disputed with the scribes and later came to pray as an adult; Jesus chased money changers and other merchants from the courtyard of the Temple, turning over their tables and accusing them of desecrating a sacred place with secular ways; also, Jesus predicted the destruction of the Second Temple, which occurred in 70 CE.

Today both Israel and the Palestinian Authority claim sovereignty over the Temple Mount, which remains a key issue in the Arab-Israeli conflict. A Muslim Waqf (administrative council) has managed the Haram al-Sharif continuously since the twelfth century, when the Muslims reconquered the Kingdom of Jerusalem from the Crusaders. Since taking control of the area in the Six-Day War, the Israeli government has permitted the Waqf to retain internal administration of the site. Under this arrangement, Jews and Christians are permitted to visit the site. As a security measure to prevent Intifada-related riots from destroying the site, the Israeli government has agreed to enforce a ban on non-Muslim prayer on the site. Non-Muslims who are observed praying on the site are subject to expulsion by the police.

The Temple Mount is a large flat-topped construction built over a natural hill. The history of this place begins with Abraham, who was ordered by God to sacrifice his son Isaac on Mount Moriah, which the Talmud indicates was the place where the Temple was later built. God intervened to prevent the human sacrifice when a ram appeared in Isaac's place. The account of the sacrifice is central not only to Judaism but also to Christianity and Islam. Christians view Isaac as a prefigurement of Christ. Isaac, like Jesus, was his father's only son. He carried the wood for the offering, much as Jesus carried the cross. According to Genesis 22, the journey from Beersheba to Mount Moriah (the distance from Beersheba to Jerusalem is fifty-three miles) took three days, the time that Jesus was in the tomb. Christians argue that Jesus, the only-begotten Son of the Father, was the perfect sacrifice, the complete substitute for humanity. The tradition of the sacrifice is also important for Muslims, for according to the Qur'an "the son of Abraham" was taken to Moriah as a sacrifice. Most Muslims accept the biblical account, but believe it was Ishmael, and not Isaac, who was the subject of the story.

Solomon's Temple (the First Temple) stood for almost four hundred years until it was destroyed by Nebuchadnezzar in 587 BCE. On their return from exile in Babylon the Israelites removed the rubble and built the Second Temple, which was completed in 516 BCE. By comparison with Solomon's Temple, the Second Temple was modest. Around 19 BCE, to win popularity with the Jews and an eternal name for himself, King Herod embarked on building a temple complex far grander than what existed. Despite his reputation as a tyrant, Herod was an extraordinarily skilled administrator and a visionary builder.

Herod began his work on the Temple by enlarging the area by three times, to a size equal to twenty-five football fields, surrounding it with huge walls. The project took some eighty years and required eighteen thousand workmen. The Temple complex that Jesus knew was in fact the largest manmade platform in the ancient world, being about one mile in circumference and nearly forty acres in size. The floor of the plaza, which could hold up to a quarter of a million people, was effectively a roof covering a network of chambers and over two dozen cisterns.

The huge walls are still visible on the southern and eastern side and on the southern half of the western side. Fifteen feet thick, they rose to a height of 120 feet above the plaza. In the southeast corner they reach a height of 213 feet above the Kidron Valley. They were made from hand-carved stone blocks, each weighing on average nine thousand pounds—about the weight of a full grown elephant. The largest of these are forty feet long and weigh over forty tons. Perhaps even more impressive than the size of the ashlars is the artistic work that went into each layer of stone, for craftsmanship, not mortar, held the walls together.

On the Temple platform itself, the supporting walls were surmounted on three sides by colonnaded porches in the Greek style. Covering the entire southern end of the platform, the covered Royal Portico, similar to the basilica in a Roman forum, gave people shelter from the rain and shade in the summer. This grand hall, the largest structure on the Temple Mount, was divided into a central nave and side aisles by four rows of forty columns each. At the eastern end of the nave, an apse provided the setting for meetings of the Sanhedrin—the supreme Jewish legislative, religious, and judicial body. This Royal Stoa was six hundred feet long and soared to one hundred feet at its highest point. The awe-inspiring sight, covered in gleaming white marble, towered above the southern supportive wall. The Temple Mount was a brilliant spectacle.

One of the great architectural ironies of history is that five years after its completion, the Temple Mount was destroyed by the Romans while they suppressed a Jewish revolt. That was the end of the Jewish Temple and the end of the sacrificial rites. Rabbis replaced priests, synagogues became places of prayer, and only the Western Wall (Wailing Wall) stayed on as the reminder of the Temple. But long after it had been destroyed, the rabbis would claim: "Whoever has not seen the Temple of Herod has never seen a beautiful building in his life."[2]

In antiquity, a number of gates enabled pilgrims and others to enter the Temple Mount. Once on the platform, visitors found an intricate

---

2. B. Batria 3B. Cited in Armstrong, *Jerusalem*, 132.

arrangement of courts, each one more holy than the last, leading to the sacred Temple. First pilgrims entered the Court of the Gentiles, where traders and money-changers worked and the only section where non-Jews were allowed. Notices warned foreigners not to proceed further, on pain of death. Beyond the barrier was the Court of the Women, a screened-off area with a raised gallery that enabled the women to watch the sacrifices in the temple courtyard. Next came the Court of Israel, reserved for male Jews, and finally the Court of the Priests, which contained the great altar of sacrifice.

This gradual approach to the inner sanctum "reminded pilgrims and worshippers that they were making an *aliyah* (ascent) to a wholly different order of being. They had to prepare themselves by undergoing various rites of purification, which heightened this sense by putting them at some distance from their normal lives. They were about to enter the separate sphere of their holy God, and for the duration of their visit they had to be in the same state of ritual purity as the priests . . . The whole of reality was somehow condensed into this segregated space."[3]

By the first century CE, the symbolism of the Temple appears to have changed; it was now experienced as a microcosm of the entire universe. Josephus, who once served in the Temple as a priest, explained its cosmic imagery. The Court of the Gentiles was associated with Yam, the sea of primal chaos, which stood over and against the ordered world of the sacred. The Hekhal (the Temple's central section), represented the whole of the created world; its curtain symbolized the four elements and the entirety of the heavens; the lamps on the great candlestick (menorah) stood for the seven planets, and the twelve loaves of shewbread recalled the signs of the zodiac and the twelve months of the year. The incense altar with its thirteen spices signified that all things come from God and for God (*Jewish War* 5:211–17). The layout and design of the Temple Mount thus presented a perspective that the world leads inexorably to God. Just as the high priest walked through the Hekhal to the ultimate reality, symbolized by the Temple's inner sanctum, so pilgrims journeyed through life on earth to the divine, which lay beyond and gave meaning to the whole.

Many of the ancient entryways into the Temple Mount have been sealed and are no longer functional. Today non-Muslim visitors enter from the Western Wall plaza via a ramp through the Mughrabi Gate (the

3. Armstrong, ibid., 132–33.

Gate of the Moors), where they find themselves in the spacious Muslim area. Gardens take up the eastern and most of the northern side of the platform; the far north of the platform houses an Islamic school. In the center of the courtyard, on a raised platform, stands the Dome of the Rock.

Dominating most of the width of the Temple Mount on the south side is the grey-domed al-Aqsa Mosque and its neighboring buildings, the Museum for Islamic Art and the White Mosque for women. The present mosque rests on very ancient substructures and has been restored several times. The Stables of Solomon, a subterranean chamber located in the southeastern corner of the Mount, is said to have been used for the horses of King Solomon's chariots and mounted warriors. While this legend is almost certainly not accurate, it is known that the Crusaders used this structure as stables.

Going north from al-Aqsa one passes the large Purification Fountain, where Muslims wash their feet and remove their shoes before entering al-Aqsa and the Dome of the Rock. Beyond the fountain one climbs a broad flight of steps to the upper platform. Like the steps on the other sides of the platform, these are spanned by beautiful pointed arches. The stairs at the northwest corner are believed by some archaeologists to be part of a much wider monumental staircase, mostly hidden or destroyed, and dating from the Second Temple era.

The Dome of the Rock is one of the most important monuments of Islam. On the outside one's gaze is first drawn to the brilliant blue, green, yellow, and white Persian tiles with which the Ottoman Sultan Suleiman (1520–1566) decorated the exterior of the building. The impressive effect of the Dome of the Rock results from a combination of sumptuous furnishings, well-designed proportions, and the elegance of the gilded aluminum dome. The diameter of the inner rotunda and the height of the dome are almost identical; the overall height (177 feet) is slightly more than the overall diameter (171 feet). This beautiful octagonal-shaped edifice is not a mosque, but was built to safeguard the holy Moriah rock, which, according to some old maps and traditions, is the center of the earth. In addition to the traditions that associate this rock with Abraham's sacrifice and with Muhammad's Night Journey, another tradition, recorded in the Talmud, indicates that the world was created from this foundation stone. The rock in question is the bedrock at the peak of the hill, about forty by fifty-two feet, which rises seven feet above the level of the Temple area. The rock is the summit of Mount Moriah.

According to Jewish tradition, the rock formed the base of the Jewish altar of burnt offering. Archaeologist Leen Ritmeyer has provided extensive support for the Jewish tradition, arguing not only that the ancient Jewish Temple stood on the area now occupied by the Dome of the Rock but that a rectangular depression measuring four feet four inches by two feet seven inches on the north side of the rock marked the center of the Holy of Holies in the Temple, the exact spot where the Ark of the Covenant was once situated.[4] A hole in the rock is said to have been used to drain the blood into a natural cave below.

I was fascinated by the beauty and the tradition associated with the Temple Mount, but since I had visited the area previously, this time I hoped to explore areas of the Mount not ordinarily seen by tour groups. But I soon discovered that the area is patrolled by plain clothed guards who watch one's every move and seem to know even what one is thinking, for whenever I approached restricted areas, they appeared without notice, issuing shouts and warnings. I headed toward the Golden Gate, on the Eastern Wall, whose entrance Jews and Muslims associate with the site of the Last Judgment. To counter the Jewish belief that the Messiah would enter the city through this gate, the Arabs walled up the entrance and also laid out a cemetery outside, in front of the gate. The site is apparently off limits, for as soon as I approached the area a guard materialized, yelling and waving me away. Fearing an incident, I decided to leave the premises on my own terms.

EXPLANATORY ENTRY #42:
WALKING THE LABYRINTH IN JERUSALEM

We are living at a time when people want more than abstraction; they want to know directly, to see for themselves, to touch something tangible. And so they go to Jerusalem. The city of Jerusalem, sacred to one-third of the world's population, draws people to itself like a magnet. For those twenty-six thousand who live in the Old City, packed into an area less than one mile square, the city is a haven, like the fulfillment of a prophecy. The most important thing about those who come to Jerusalem is

---

4. Leen Ritmeyer, "The Ark of the Covenant: Where It Stood in Solomon's Temple," in *Secrets of Jerusalem's Temple Mount*, by Leen and Kathleen Ritmeyer (Washington, DC: Biblical Archaeology Society, 1998), 99–110.

their variety. They come from all walks of life, and from every corner of the globe; they come because they believe in something and are bound by their fierce devotion to the city's timeless quality.

The Old City, a focal point of faith over three thousand years, has been an oasis of calm for Jews, Christians, and Muslims alike in the midst of one of the world's most troubled regions. Each quarter of the city clings close to its central shrine: Jews to the Western Wall, Muslims to the Temple Mount, Armenians to the Cathedral of St. James, and other Christians to the Church of the Holy Sepulcher. Some of the world's greatest dramas have been enacted within the city walls. For Christians, what happened here—the death and resurrection of Jesus—changed the world.

The Via Dolorosa

The Via Dolorosa, the "Street of Sorrows" or Way of the Cross, is the traditional pathway Jesus took from Pilate's judgment hall to Calvary. The tradition of following the Via Dolorosa dates to the Byzantine period. During Holy Week, thousands of pilgrims come from all over the world to walk in the footsteps of Christ. Each Friday at 3:00 p.m., a ceremony led by Franciscan priests is conducted along the Via Dolorosa, beginning at Station 1, and prayers are made at each of fourteen Stations of the Cross, as originally determined by the Crusaders. Nine stations are based on the gospel accounts and five are based on tradition. Protestants have seven, and Catholics have fourteen stations. The first seven stations wind through the Muslim Quarter; the last five are inside the Church of the Holy Sepulcher.[5]

According to the gospels, Jesus was brought to the residence of Pilate for his trial. Tradition says this was located at the Antonia Fortress, a garrison for soldiers stationed in Jerusalem. Investigators have shown it had four massive towers, with walls over fifty feet high; unfortunately, almost nothing remains of the fortress. A place known as the Lithostrotos, a pavement in the courtyard where Jesus was sentenced to death by Pilate and crowned with thorns, remains, but archaeology states that the type of pavement found here was laid in the second century CE by the emperor Hadrian as part of a marketplace.

---

5. For a listing of the fourteen Stations of the Cross (Roman Catholic Version) see Appendix K.

For centuries pilgrims have followed the narrow pathway of the Via Dolorosa. As many as forty Stations of the Cross have been marked out. Yet there is little to prove that this is the correct route. Pilgrims should keep in mind that the Stations of the Cross are not so much historical sites as points marking stages in the procession. In addition, centuries of rubble have raised the street level far above what it was in Jesus' time and the roadway has been altered by later buildings. For many, greater importance should be placed on the spiritual over the physical journey that Jesus took on that first Good Friday.

The Church of the Holy Sepulcher

The Church of the Holy Sepulcher, known as the Church of the Anastasis (Resurrection) to Eastern Orthodox Christians, is situated in the Christian Quarter, on the highest part of the Old City. The site encompasses a hill called Golgotha, where Jesus was crucified, and the tomb (sepulcher) where he was buried. The name Golgotha is derived from a Hebrew word meaning the "place of a skull," where tradition says Adam's skull was buried. The name was later translated into the word "Calvary," Latin for "skull." The Church of the Holy Sepulcher has been an important pilgrimage destination since the fourth century, and for a majority of Christians it remains the most sacred site on earth.

Unlike many historical sacred sites, which often turn out to be based more on pious tradition than historical fact, most historians and archaeologists agree that the Church of the Holy Sepulcher is probably located over the actual tomb of Christ. Some dispute this, for the site became a church only three hundred years later, and today it stands within the city walls. The Bible states that the crucifixion occurred outside the city walls, since according to Jewish law, events such as crucifixions could not occur within a city, and no one could be buried within the precincts of the Holy City of Jerusalem. However, evidence shows that during the Second Temple period, when Jesus was crucified, the hill of Golgotha lay outside the city walls, thus making it possible to put his body to rest there.

The question of whether Christ's tomb really was on the spot indicated in the Church of the Holy Sepulcher continues to be asked. In 1867 a peasant who wished to cultivate some land just beyond the city walls near the Damascus Gate accidentally discovered a burial cave that came to be known as the Garden Tomb. In 1883, General Charles Gordon, famous for his Egyptian campaigns and world renowned as a man of deep spirituality, arrived in Jerusalem. His identification of the site as the hill of Golgotha led many Protestants to accept this peaceful garden setting beyond the city walls as authentic. By that time, Protestants had begun to question the authenticity of the traditional site of the tomb within the Church of the Holy Sepulcher, which in those days was dark and dismal. It was crowded with priest, monks, and pilgrims, mainly from Eastern countries, who often disputed with one another over rights to light candles and to hold ceremonies in various parts of the church. The Protestant newcomers did not feel at home here and could not imagine that this site could be the authentic burial place of Jesus. In this frame of mind, they welcomed alternative suggestions, particularly since Protestants were devoid of any proprietary share in the Church of the Holy Sepulcher, which was divided among the Greek Orthodox, Roman Catholic, Armenian, and Coptic Churches.

We now know that the area north of the Damascus Gate was an extensive cemetery that dates back to the eighth and seventh centuries BCE, long before the time of Jesus. We also know more about tombs from the Second Temple period, when Jesus lived, and not a single tomb from Second Temple times has been found in this area.

The evidence for equating Golgotha with the present Church of the Holy Sepulcher is actually quite impressive. In *The Holy Land: An Oxford Archaeological Guide*, Jerome Murphy-O'Connor lists numerous supportive arguments, including that (1) the Christian community of Jerusalem held worship services at the site until 66 CE (according to church historian Eusebius); (2) even when the area was brought within the city walls in 41–43 CE, it was not built over by the local inhabitants; (3) the Roman Emperor Hadrian built a Temple of Venus over the site in 135 CE, which could be an indication that the place was regarded as holy by Christians, causing Hadrian to claim it for traditional Roman religion; (4) the local tradition of the community would have been scrutinized carefully when Constantine set out to build his church in 326 CE, because the chosen site was inconvenient and expensive. Substantial buildings had to be torn down, most notably the temple built over the site by Hadrian. Just to the south was a spot that would have been otherwise perfect—the open space of Hadrian's forum; (5) the eyewitness historian Eusebius claimed that in the course of the excavations, the original tomb was discovered.

These arguments lead to the following conclusion: although we cannot be certain that the Church of the Holy Sepulcher is the site of Jesus' burial, there is no other site that can lay nearly as weighty a claim, and therefore we really have no reason to reject the authenticity of the site.

The site remained buried beneath the pagan temple until the fourth century, when Emperor Constantine the Great converted to Christianity. Showing an interest in the holy places associated with his new faith, he commissioned four churches to be built throughout the Holy Land. Each of these, including the Church of the Annunciation in Nazareth; the Church of the Nativity in Bethlehem, where Christ was born; and the Eleona Basilica, erected on the Mount of Olives to commemorate the place where, according to Christian tradition Jesus taught his disciples the Lord's Prayer, was associated with salvation history (that is, with places of revelation and the redemption of humanity). The most important of these, the Church of the Holy Sepulcher, was begun in 326 CE.

To understand the context for this building activity, historically and theologically, we must go back in time. Constantine had become emperor in the West after his victory at the Milvian Bridge. In 323 he defeated Licinius, emperor of the eastern provinces, and became sole ruler of the Roman world. Constantine had attributed his dramatic rise from obscurity to the God of the Christians, and though he had little understanding of its theology and delayed his baptism until he was on his deathbed, he continued to be loyal to the church. He also saw in Christianity the potential to serve a cohesive role in his far-flung empire.

Because Constantine was unable to visit Palestine, he sent instead his Christian mother, the dowager empress Helena, who arrived in Jerusalem during the excavations for the tomb. She may even have been present when the tomb was discovered. Shortly after her arrival in Jerusalem, discovery of various religious relics began in and around the city, the most significant of these being several crosses of execution found in a subterranean Roman cistern. The empress identified two of these as belonging to the two thieves crucified with Jesus and the other as the True Cross, one of Christianity's most important relics. The discovery of these relics in Jerusalem at a time when Christianity had just become the official religion of the Eastern Empire had important repercussions for the city's development. Jerusalem was transformed from a relatively insignificant, provincial city in the Roman Empire to the focus of pilgrimage and adoration by a major religion other than Judaism. This also marked the beginning in the city of inter-religious rivalry, which would be joined three centuries later by the advent of Islam. The basilica of Constantine, known as the Martyrium or the Church of the Anastasis, was formally dedicated in 335, with an oration by Constantine's biographer, Eusebius, bishop of Caesarea. The Martyrium was to be a "witness" to the resurrection and a memorial to Christ.

Constantine had achieved his purpose. In building his Martyrium, he had demonstrated the centrality of the new faith to his empire. Previously, Aelia Capitolina (as Jerusalem was known by Romans since 135 CE) had been off the spiritual map of most Christians, but Constantine had taken possession of the center point of Roman Aelia and transformed it into a Christian holy place, a New Jerusalem. As a gesture that immediately captivated the Christian imagination, Christians soon started to evolve their own mythology about the place, locating the city at the heart of their spiritual sensibility. Recalling the old tradition that Adam had been buried there, they also came to believe that Abraham had bound Isaac for sacrifice there. This new Christian holy place was inspiring the same kind of belief and legend as had the old Jewish Temple. It had become a symbolic "center," where divinity touched humanity in a unique way. The Martyrium represented "a new start for humanity, a fulfillment of the religion of Abraham and a new era in Christian history."[6]

The Crusaders began a massive reconstruction of the Church of the Holy Sepulcher, which was to be completed in 1149, in time for the fiftieth anniversary of their conquest of the city. Golgotha, which up till then had been outside in the open, was incorporated into the main body of the church as a raised side chapel, and tombs for the conqueror of Jerusalem, Godfrey of Bouillon, and Baldwin I, the first king of the Crusade kingdom, were installed in a grotto under the rock of Golgotha. The Constantinian courtyard was covered with a Romanesque church, connected to the rotunda by a great arched opening.

The new church was a triumph: the Crusaders had brought all the scattered shrines on the site—the tomb of Christ, the rock of Golgotha, and the crypt where Helena was said to have found the True Cross—into one large Romanesque building. Mosaics and colored marble adorned the walls in a way both brilliant and elegant, a splendor that is hard to imagine today in the present gloomy building. To this day the Church of the Holy Sepulcher, though somewhat altered, has retained its two

6. Armstong, *Jerusalem*, 181–83.

sacred focal points and its two related buildings, as can be seen from outside by the two domes of the building.

Ownership of the Church of the Holy Sepulcher today is shared by six religious communities. The three primary custodians of the church, first appointed when Crusaders held Jerusalem, are the Greek Orthodox, the Armenian Apostolic, and the Roman Catholic churches. In the nineteenth century, the Coptic Orthodox, the Ethiopian Orthodox, and the Syrian Orthodox acquired lesser responsibilities, which include shrines and other structures within and around the building. An agreement regulates times and places of worship for each group.

The chaotic history of the Church of the Holy Sepulcher is evident in what visitors see today. Byzantine, medieval, Crusader, and modern elements mix in a clash of styles, and each governing Christian community has decorated its shrines in its own distinctive way. In many ways, the church is not what one would imagine for the holiest site in all Christendom, and it can easily disappoint. But at the same time, its noble history and immense religious importance is such that a visit can also be very meaningful. My experience was clearly in the latter category.

TRAVEL ENTRY #68: THE CENTER OF THE LABYRINTH

When I arrived at the Church of the Holy Sepulcher, I expected that a quick tour would suffice, since I had visited the site with a tour group several years earlier. That familiarity led me to underestimate its impact.

To get the layout of the church, it is a good idea to visit the nave first.[7] Known as the Catholicon, this Greek Orthodox cathedral features a large iconostasis (a screen decorated with icons) flanked by the thrones of the patriarchs of Jerusalem and Antioch. Above is a colorful cupola, decorated with an image of Christ and other icons. A stairway on the right inside the entrance leads to Golgotha (Calvary), the place where Jesus was crucified. On the rock are two chapels, rich in mosaics. The first is the Catholic (Franciscan) Chapel of the Nailing of the Cross, which is Station 11 on the Via Dolorosa. On the vault and on a Medici altar from Florence is featured a twelfth-century mosaic of Jesus being nailed to the cross. To the left of the altar is a statue of Mary, which is Station 13 (Jesus' body removed from the cross and given to Mary). Turning left past the Stabat Mater Altar, which according to tradition is

---

7. For a site plan of the Church of the Holy Sepulcher, see Appendix Q.

where Mary stood while her son was being crucified, one comes to the Greek Orthodox Crucifixion Chapel. Under its altar is the hole in the rock that held the cross.

The north side of the church, on the opposite side of the Catholicon, is the Latin (Roman Catholic) part. Here one finds both the private Franciscan chapel that serves their adjoining monastery and a large square Chapel of St. Mary Magdalene. This part of the church contains columns from various periods, including a few ornate Corinthian columns from the original fourth-century building. These are known as the Archway of the Virgin because it is said that the risen Christ appeared to his mother on this spot. At the east end of the north aisle is the chapel of the Prison of Christ, which according to an early tradition housed Jesus and the two thieves before the crucifixion. The chapel probably originated as a liturgical station where the passion and death of Christ were commemorated.

Nearby is a stairway that descends to the large Chapel of St. Helena, owned by the Armenians and known to them as the Chapel of St. Gregory. Tiny crosses scratched by medieval pilgrims mark the passageway to the place where Helena found what she believed to be the true cross. Painted on the bedrock is a ship with the inscription: "O Lord, we have arrived." When the Crusader church was built, pilgrims traveled to this spot in the belief that it had been the site of the crucifixion.

Returning to the entrance and walking west, I arrived at the focal point of the church. Known as the Rotunda or Anastasis, this round area preserves the location and shape of Constantine's fourth-century Church of the Resurrection built on the site of Christ's tomb. Surmounted by a large dome, completed in the 1960s, the Rotunda diameter is about 67 feet and its height is 112 feet. Underneath the large dome is the Holy Sepulcher and inside are two small chapels. The shrine, referred to as the Edicule and supported by scaffolding due to earthquakes, is not terribly attractive. The current structure was built after the severe fire of 1808.

When I approached the Angel's Chapel in the Edicule, a Greek Orthodox monk motioned for me to enter. As I did, he showed me a stone, set in marble, said to be the one that the angel rolled away from the door of the sepulcher at the resurrection. Next, he beckoned me to enter through a low door into the tiny Chapel of the Holy Sepulcher, where I saw the marble slab marking the place where Jesus was buried. This is Station 14 of the Via Dolorosa and the holiest site in Christendom. Here a marble slab covers the place where the body of Christ was laid and from which he rose from the dead. A vase with candles marks the spot where his head rested. The slab, installed here in the 1555 reconstruction, was intentionally cracked to deter Ottoman looters.

The monk allowed me a moment of privacy. This sacred place represented the destination of my sabbatical journey, but in some way also the center of my spiritual labyrinth. Having come to this point, physically, spiritually, and geographically, I felt I had reached a milestone. I emerged from this place of encounter feeling like a newborn child, full of promise. The priest handed me a small icon as a memento, a cross with a two-dimensional figure of Jesus painted upon it. Noting my gratitude, he handed me prayer beads to remind me that this place was a symbol of the Center, which is Christ, but also the commencement of a new phase in my outward journey toward the circumference, which is God.

Icons, prayer beads, crucifixes—all are unfamiliar to Protestants, but I keep these treasures as symbols of my experience in that small chapel and as reminders of my intention to affirm the unity of Christians (Romans 12:5) by valuing the symbols, traditions, and ways of Christians different from myself.

Christians have traditionally considered the Edicule—or the Catholicon, the nave next to the Rotunda—as the center of the earth. Since the tenth century the spot has been marked by an *omphalos*, a stone chalice. Many modern Christians disagree with this assessment for they view the center of the Christian labyrinth not as a building, or even a place, but as the person of Christ, who rose from the grave in an act that defies knowledge and convention. "Why do you look for the living among the dead?" the women were told when they came to the tomb after the crucifixion. "He is not here, but has risen" (Luke 24:5). For Protestants, the central symbol of the Christian faith is an empty tomb.

EXPLANATORY ENTRY #43:
THE MIRACLE OF THE BLUE FLAME

Each year, on Holy Saturday, the eve of Easter as celebrated by Orthodox Christians, a remarkable ceremony known as the miracle of the Holy Fire takes place at the Church of the Holy Sepulcher, when the Greek Orthodox patriarch of Jerusalem symbolizes the resurrection by lighting the "holy fire" in the Chapel of the Angel, which has been sealed since Good Friday. The event takes place every single year, on the same time, in the same manner, and on the same spot. No other miracle is known to occur so regularly and for such an extensive period of time; one can read about it in sources as old as the eighth century CE.

In order to be as close to the tomb as possible, pilgrims camp around the tomb-chapel, waiting from Holy Friday afternoon in anticipation of the wonder on Holy Saturday. The miracle happens at 2:00 p.m., but already around 11:00 a.m. the church is a boiling pot of excitement. At that point the Orthodox Arab Christians sing traditional songs with loud voices accompanied by the sound of drums. At 1:00 p.m. the songs fade out and there is silence, a tense silence electrified by the anticipation of the great manifestation of the power of God that all are about to witness. At that point a delegation of local authorities elbows through the crowds. Even though these officials are not Christian, they are an integral part of the ceremonies. During times of Turkish occupation they were Muslim Turks; today they are Israelis. For centuries these officials have been a part of the ceremony, their function representing the Romans in the time of Jesus. The Gospels speak of Romans that went to seal the tomb of Jesus, so that his disciples would not steal his body and claim he had risen. In the same way the Israeli authorities on Easter Saturday come and seal the tomb with wax. Before they seal the door it is customary that they enter the tomb to check for any hidden source of fire, which could produce the miracle through fraud. Just as the Romans were to guarantee that there was no manipulation after the death of Jesus, likewise the local Israeli authorities are to guarantee that there is no fraud.

When the tomb has been checked and sealed, the congregants chant the *Kyrie eleison* ("Lord have mercy"). At 1:45 p.m. the patriarch enters the scene. In the wake of a large procession he encircles the tomb three times, whereupon he is stripped of his royal liturgical vestments, carrying only his white alb, a sign of humility before the power of God, which he is about to witness. The oil lamps had been blown out the preceding night, and now all remains of artificial light are extinguished, so that the church is enveloped in darkness. Holding two large unlit candles, the patriarch enters the Chapel of the Holy Sepulcher, first into the small room in front of the tomb and from there the tomb itself.

Diodorus, the patriarch of Jerusalem since 1982, was once asked what happened when he entered the sepulcher. He replied:

Jerusalem: Christian Center of the Labyrinth 279

I find my way through the darkness towards the inner chamber in which I fall on my knees. Here I say certain prayers that have been handed down to us through the centuries and, having said them, I wait. Sometimes I may wait a few minutes, but normally the miracle happens immediately after I have said the prayers. From the core of the very stone on which Jesus lay an indefinable light pours forth. It usually has a blue tint, but the color may change and take many different hues. It cannot be described in human terms. The light rises out of the stone as mist may rise out of a lake—it almost looks as if the stone is covered by a moist cloud, but it is light. This light each year behaves differently. Sometimes it covers just the stone, while other times it gives light to the whole sepulcher, so that people who stand outside the tomb and look into it will see it filled with light. The light does not burn—I have never had my beard burnt in all the years I have been patriarch in Jerusalem and have received the Holy Fire. The light is of a different consistency than normal fire that burns in an oil lamp. At a certain point the light rises and forms a column in which the fire is of a different nature, so that I am able to light my candles from it. When I thus have received the flame on my candles, I go out and give the fire first to the Armenian patriarch and then to the Coptic. Hereafter I give the flame to all people present in the church.

While the patriarch is inside the chapel, the crowd is in darkness and the atmosphere is very tense. When he emerges with the two candles lit and shining brightly in the darkness, a roar resounds through the church.

The miracle is not confined to what actually happens inside the little tomb, where the patriarch prays, for the blue light is reported to appear and be active outside the tomb as well. Every year many believers claim that this miraculous light ignites candles, which they hold in their hands, of its own initiative. All in the church wait with candles in the hope that they may ignite spontaneously. Often closed oil lamps do light spontaneously, according to a number of signed testimonies. Persons who experience the miracle for themselves usually leave Jerusalem changed, and for those who attend the ceremony, there is always a "before and after" the miracle of the Holy Fire in Jerusalem.

As with any other miracle, there are people who believe it is fraud and nothing but a masterpiece of Orthodox propaganda. They believe the patriarch has a lighter inside the tomb. These critics, however, must confront a number of problems. Matches and other means of ignition are recent inventions. Only a few hundred years ago lighting a fire was an undertaking that lasted much longer than the few minutes during which the patriarch is inside the tomb. One might believe he had an oil lamp burning inside, from which he kindled the candles, but the local authorities attest to having checked the tomb and to finding no light inside. The strongest arguments against a fraud, however, are not the testimonies of the patriarchs but of the thousands of independent testimonies by pilgrims whose candles were lit spontaneously in front of their eyes without any possible explanation.

Miracles, of course, cannot be proved. Faith is required for a miracle to bear fruit in the life of a person and without this act of faith there is no miracle in the strict sense. Each of us, like the patriarch of Jerusalem, must come to that center. We must enter the silence, kneel in humility and expectation, and encounter the fire for ourselves. When we do, we must leave that center and embark on the outward journey, conveying the fire to those in need of it. As Richard Mouw explains, "It is in pursuing the well-being of others that we realize our own well-being."[8]

TRAVEL ENTRY #69: TRIALS AT THE CENTER: REMINDERS OF THE "REAL" WORLD

My day ended with a walk through the heart of the Arab *souq*, where the colors, aromas, and wild mixture of peoples created a kaleidoscope back in time. The crowded walkway was filled with the scents and sounds of people buying and selling. Some of the stalls and displays jutted out into the narrow space, making the going slow and tedious. Knowing that pickpockets were everywhere, I took proper precautions. I had left most of my valuables, including my fanny pack, in storage back in the hostel, as all I carried was my passport and a wallet, safely stored in one of my front pockets.

At one point, as I mingled with the crowds, I felt a tug on my pants but when I checked my pocket my passport was still there. A man ahead of me turned his head and gave me a glance, making me suspicious, so I reached into my pocket once again and this time discovered that my wallet had been stolen—from my front pocket! Fortunately, I had taken very little cash with me, but my wallet did contain some traveler's checks

---

8. *Uncommon Decency* (Downers Grove, IL: InterVarsity, 1992), 11.

and a bus ticket. I marveled at the skill of the pickpocket, who had taken an item from my front pocket without my knowing it and then had the nerve to look back for my reaction.

At first it seemed ironic that something negative, something so much a part of the "real" world like having my wallet stolen, could happen at the height of my pilgrimage. I recalled that "illumination"—the middle stage in the "hero's adventure"—included trials, in addition to fulfillment. In retrospect, the experience in the bazaar, which came immediately after my visit to the Holy Sepulcher, seemed essential for the next stage of my journey. I needed to place my trust in someone higher—the risen Lord—and not upon tangible things such as expertise, skill, or even possessions. These would always let me down.

Like the rainbow after a storm, the day ended on a positive note, for when I returned to the hostel, two Christian Arab boys were waiting in the lobby. They had seen my wallet lying in an alley and found the hotel receipt that indicated where I was staying. The money was gone, but I appreciated their intention. Their visit might have been part of the scam, but that's not how I saw it. My bus ticket was there, heartening me for the journey ahead.

PART THREE

Return

As the Israelites discovered when they left Mt. Sinai and as all pilgrims learn, one cannot remain forever at the center—whether it be a mountain, an oasis, or a religious retreat. When the cloud moves by day or the pillar of fire by night, people of faith—sojourners—must move out. And as they do, they discover that the Center goes with them, energizing them, empowering them, and directing them on the inward/ outward journey of life.

After seven days in Israel, it was time to move on, to Egypt and beyond. My time in Israel had been well spent. I had visited remarkable places, met amazing people, and carried in my heart and mind priceless insights and memories to last a lifetime. There was more to see, but I simply couldn't view it all. Bethlehem, Masada, Jericho, Qumran, and Capernaum, these I had visited earlier. Eight days remained before my return flight to the U.S., barely enough time to travel to Cairo, visit the Egyptian Museum, view the great pyramids at Giza, and witness the wonders of Luxor (ancient Thebes), which for hundreds of years served as the religious and political center of Egypt.

20

Entering Egypt

TRAVEL ENTRY #70: JOURNEY TO CAIRO

BUSES RUN REGULARLY FROM Jerusalem to Cairo by way of the Egyptian border at Rafah, at the southwestern end of the Gaza Strip. This border area, under United Nations control, was managed by the Israelis until it was evacuated in 2005 as part of Israel's unilateral disengagement plan.

The bus to Rafah left Jerusalem at 7:00 a.m. and proceeded west through the early morning traffic toward Tel Aviv. After fifteen miles we turned south and headed along the Valley of Elah, where the ancient Israelites fought against the Philistines and where David slew Goliath with a smooth stone from a nearby brook. We followed the Mediterranean coastline past the cities of Ashdod and Ashkelon and skirted the Gaza Strip. Slowing down for several checkpoints along this volatile region, we finally arrived at the border. Eventually, after a two-hour delay, we commenced the interminable ride across the northern tier of the Sinai Peninsula.

This vital land bridge—a triangular tongue of land 175 miles wide and 250 miles in length—has long served as the sole connecting link between Africa and Eurasia. In ancient times numerous out-of-Africa migrations passed through this region, including migrations shared by hominids and humans during interglacial periods.

Since the establishment of the modern nation of Israel, the Sinai has witnessed numerous wars, including the War of 1956, when Israel, France, and Great Britain attempted to take the Sinai and the Suez Canal from Egypt. Although international political pressure forced the invaders to withdraw, Israel succeeded in winning guarantees of a largely demilitarized Sinai. In 1967, during the Six-Day War, the Israeli air and land forces were successful beyond all expectations. Israel's forces moved west through the Gaza Strip and the Sinai desert to the Suez Canal. The Israeli viewpoint was that the occupied lands should be kept and traded for a secure peace with the Arabs. In 1973, during the Yom Kippur War, Israeli forces crossed the Suez Canal and advanced to within sixty miles of Cairo before the war's conclusion.

Following the Israel-Egypt Peace Treaty of 1979, Israel agreed to withdraw from the Sinai Peninsula, in exchange for peace and normalized relations with its neighbor. In 1979, the leaders signed a peace treaty on the White House lawn. Israeli President Menachim Begin and Egyptian President Anwar Sadat both received the Nobel Peace Prize for their work. The two nations have enjoyed peaceful relations to this day. Final Israeli withdrawal from the Sinai occurred in 1982. In addition to relinquishing control over the strategic region, Israel also gave up the Alma oil field, valued over $100 billion, which Israelis discovered and developed. The Israelis would have had energy independence for the foreseeable future had they held on to it.

The bus arrived in the coastal town of el Arish, about twenty-five miles west of Rafah, around lunchtime, where we stopped to stretch our legs, eat, and enjoy the scenery. With a population around one hundred thousand, el Arish is the center of social and cultural activity in North Sinai. The town is known for its beautiful beaches and palm trees bordering the seacoast and it is fast becoming a resort town, with five-star hotels. A welcome relief to the Sinai's lunar landscape, it is located near the mouth of the Wadi el Arish, a stream that drains most of the central and northern Sinai during the rainy season but dwindles to a dry bed in the summer. In biblical times, the stream marked the traditional southwestern boundary of Canaan (Numbers 34:5) and of the tribe of Judah (Joshua 15:4).

As we continued along the coastal road toward Cairo, six hours by bus, we occasionally passed Bedouin encampments and were reminded of the simple yet deeply gratifying customs preserved by these nomadic and semi-nomadic indigenous peoples. When we reached the Suez Canal, we felt rejuvenated, as when one comes to an oasis. On the other side of the canal, less than one thousand feet away, lay the continent of Africa, viewed by anthropologists as the original homeland of humanity.

The Suez Canal is one hundred miles long and runs between Port Said on the Mediterranean Sea and Suez on the Red Sea. Considered the deepest artificial canal in the world, the canal allows transportation between Europe and Asia without circumnavigation of Africa. About 7.5 percent of world sea trade, including the majority of Europe's oil, is carried via the canal today. The canal has no locks because the terrain is relatively flat.

At el Qantara we crossed the canal by ferry. As the ferry departed, local youngsters jumped into the canal. Their efforts were designed to impress the passengers in hopes that they might toss coins in the water. A refreshing swim in the water seemed to beat the alternatives: going to school or getting a job.

EXPLANATORY ENTRY #44: CAIRO (AL-QAHIRA)

Cairo straddles the Nile River 140 miles upstream from the port city of Alexandria, immediately south of the point where the river leaves its desert-bound valley and breaks into two branches of the low-lying delta region. Officially known as al-Qahira, Cairo is huge. With its sixteen million inhabitants, it is the seventh most populous metropolitan area in the world and the most populous metropolis in Africa.

Old Cairo (al-Fustat) was founded in 648 CE near other Egyptian cities and villages, including Heliopolis, Giza, and the old Egyptian capital, Memphis.[1] The Muslim founders built Fustat as a military garrison for Arab troops because Memphis, the capital of Egypt when they came into power, had an alien religion and was therefore objectionable to the Muslims. Al-Qahira (Cairo) was officially founded in 969 CE as an imperial capital and it absorbed Fustat.

During its history, various dynasties added suburbs to the city and constructed important structures that became famous throughout the Islamic world, including al-Azhar Mosque, which was expanded in 988 to include a school of religion. Al-Azhar became the world's oldest university and an unrivaled institution for Islamic theological studies. When Saladin established his rule in 1171, Cairo remained an important center of the Muslim world and continued its reputation as one of the greatest centers of culture and learning in the world. Slave soldiers (Mamluks) eventually seized Egypt and ruled from their capital at Cairo from 1250 to 1517, when they were defeated by the Ottomans.

In 1798 Napoleon's army landed in Alexandria and advanced to Cairo, where it captured Cairo with little resistance. During the three-

---

1. For a chronology of Egypt's history, consult Appendix F.

year occupation (1798–1801), Egypt came out of its long dark age. A major advance occurred when Champollion, the father of Egyptology, deciphered the ancient Egyptian writings on the famous Rosetta Stone. The French built schools and colleges and wrote the *Description de l'Egypte*, the most comprehensive reference on the country's geography and culture. Following Napoleon's brief occupation, an Ottoman officer named Muhammad Ali (1769–1849) made Cairo the capital of an independent empire that lasted from 1801 to 1882. Under Muhammad Ali's rule, Cairo prospered both economically and culturally. Not only was the infrastructure of the city rebuilt, but a new city center was also planned according to European standards. It was constructed by French city planners and engineers over a large swampy flood plain.

Ismail Pasha, known as Ismail the Magnificent (1830–1895), ruled Egypt from 1863 until he was removed at the behest of the British in 1879. This grandson of Muhammad Ali modernized Egypt, but also put the country heavily in debt. He greatly expanded Cairo, building an entire new city on its western edge modeled on Paris. His desire to reconstruct Cairo according to the European standard of cities is evident from a statement he made in 1879: "My country is no longer in Africa; we are now part of Europe. It is therefore natural for us to abandon our former ways and to adopt a new system adapted to our social conditions."

Ismail launched vast schemes of internal reform on the scale of his grandfather, including a vast railroad-building project that saw Egypt rise from having virtually no railways to the most railways per habitable kilometer of any nation in the world. Ismail dreamt of expanding his realm over the whole Nile and over the whole African coast of the Red Sea. Ismail was also deeply committed to the building of the Suez Canal. He agreed to, and oversaw, the Egyptian portion of its construction. When the canal finally opened, Ismail held a festival of unprecedented scope, inviting dignitaries from around the world.

These developments left Egypt deeply in debt to the European powers, and they used this position to wring concessions out of Ismail. At length the inevitable financial crisis came. Unable to raise loans for an insurmountable national debt, in 1875 he sold his Suez Canal shares to the British government for £4,000,000, and this was immediately followed by foreign intervention. Cairo came under British control until Egypt attained independence in 1922.

Tahrir Square is the center of Cairo. This modern district contains most of the city's travel agencies and tourist offices, as well as many inexpensive hotels. Many of Cairo's foreign embassies and banks are in Garden City, south of Tahrir, once a model of urban planning but now almost as crowded as the rest of Cairo. These western areas of Cairo, built on the model of Paris, are marked by wide boulevards, public gardens, and open spaces.

South of Garden City, on the right bank of the Nile, is Old Cairo, the oldest part of Cairo. Of the world's major religions, three are represented by some of their most ancient relics in this section. Old Cairo includes remnants of an old Roman fortress; the first Arab settlement (al-Fustat); the Coptic Quarter, with its many fine churches; and the Ben Ezra Synagogue, which is Egypt's oldest and dates to the ninth century. The Coptic Museum, built in 1908 and located within the Roman fortress in Old Cairo, houses the largest collection of Christian Coptic treasures in the world.

The Copts are one of the oldest Christian communities in the Middle East. They are native Egyptian Christians, descendants of ancient Egyptians who remained faithful to Christianity when most of the Egyptians converted to Islam. Although integrated in the larger Egyptian nation, the Copts have survived as a distinct religious community and today comprise around 10 percent of the native population. They pride themselves on the apostolicity of the Egyptian Church, whose founder was the first in an unbroken chain of patriarchs. The number of Copts within Egypt is slowly declining due to higher emigration rates caused by harassment and discrimination at the hands of Islamic extremist groups.

A walk through Cairo's medieval Islamic district, two miles east of Tahrir, reveals some of the finest ninth- to seventeenth-century Islamic architecture anywhere in the world. Having grown up haphazardly over the centuries, this eastern sector is filled with small lanes and crowded tenements. While western Cairo is dominated by the government buildings and modern architecture, the eastern half is filled with hundreds of mosques and other Muslim landmarks. It also includes the Khan al-Khalili, one of the largest and most famous bazaars in the world.

TRAVEL ENTRY #71: WELCOME TO CAIRO

When I arrived at Tahrir Square, the transportation hub of Cairo, I met a young college graduate from Wisconsin named John. He had reserved a double room at the Anglo-Swiss Hotel and was looking for a roommate. The hotel was located near the Egyptian Museum and was a short walking distance from the square. Many of Cairo's inexpensive hotels are hidden on the upper floors of downtown office buildings, and I was pleased to learn that the higher the floor, the quieter the room. The Anglo-Swiss was on the seventh floor, and I was not disappointed. Doubles went for LE 14 (Egyptian pounds), which added up to $3 per person, breakfast included. The cost, the location, and the ambiance made this an ideal base during my stay in Egypt.

The following morning I headed east to Cairo's Islamic district. My goal was to visit al-Azhar (the venerable Islamic theological institution) and to purchase an attractive folio-size copy of the Qur'an. I had studied Arabic with a personal tutor for the past two years and I was anxious to try out my new linguistic skills. I wandered into the Khan el-Khalili, its patchwork of alleys and shop-fronts running endlessly along this part of the city. Naguib Mahfouz, the Egyptian novelist who won the 1988 Nobel Prize for literature, set his novel *Midaq Alley* in Khan el-Khalili. There is a lot to see here, but just finding one's way around is the greatest challenge.

The *souq* (bazaar), noted for selling good-quality clothing, spices, souvenirs, traditional jewelry, and perfumes at reasonable prices, is for many the most entertaining part of Cairo. At one point a teenager materialized at my side and we struck up a conversation, he in halting English and I in even more basic Arabic, for the Arabic I had learned was designed to give me a reading ability of the Qur'an and not a conversational facility. When the youngster learned that I intended to purchase a copy of the Qur'an, he tugged at my arm and indicated that he would take me to a shop where I could purchase the scripture for the same price as a native Muslim, rather than the inflated price charged to a foreigner. I emerged from the bookshop with a leather-bound folio version, its frontispiece and first chapter richly decorated in color. The price was about the cost of a used paperback in the United States.

With the copy of the Qur'an in plain view at my side, my young guide then escorted me to al-Azhar, where I expected to be received warmly. But as we entered through the gate I heard a shout and we were instantly surrounded by a group of Muslims—I couldn't tell whether they were students or self-appointed guards. Their angry remarks and intimidating looks let me know that I was trespassing. When my newfound companion intervened on my behalf, one of the sentries pointed to the Qur'an in my bag and asked me to open it. I could see this was a test of some sort, for he indicated that I should start reading. His facial features softened after a while but I guess my Arabic skills were less than convincing, for with a motion of his hand he dismissed me and I had no recourse but to leave. Later I learned that there is a specific gate where visitors can enter, for a fee, but the rude reception and my inability to communicate effectively left me frustrated and disappointed.

EXPLANATORY ENTRY #45: CAIRO'S QUANDARY

I've been to many of the world's great cities and witnessed severe urban degradation, but Cairo's social and environmental problems may be unparalleled. The first thing I noticed was the traffic: I had seen crazy traffic before, but Cairo's traffic had to be the craziest. Traffic merges without discernible pattern to create the most abysmal snarls imaginable. In Cairo, stop-and-go traffic is simply the norm. But that is not the worst problem. There seem to be no rules of the road, at least none that are discernable. Red lights do not necessarily mean "stop" or even "slow down," and assuming that a green "walk" light means that it is safe for pedestrians to cross the street could be deadly. Cars flood through red lights with impunity, horns blaring to warn those who might consider getting in the way. Whoever has his nose in front apparently has the right of way.

To the outsider, the behavior of motorists and pedestrians in Egypt's capital defies common sense. The underlying system, however, follows its own logic. After some observation, I arrived at certain rudimentary conclusions: in Cairo, pedestrians are an obstruction to be eliminated; red lights are a nuisance to be ignored; and the horn is indispensable. The dilemma is compounded by the fact that Cairo, the largest city in Africa, is growing by thirty-five hundred newcomers every day.

Cairo is also facing a housing problem. The lack of satisfactory and affordable housing has forced many poor Egyptians to live in cemeteries called "City of the Dead." Within these cemeteries live entire communities of Egypt's urban poor, forming an illegal but tolerated, separate society. More than five million Egyptians live in these cemeteries.

Cairo's rapid population growth has contributed to many environmental problems. The air pollution in Cairo is a matter of serious concern. Air quality measurements in Cairo record dangerous levels of lead, carbon dioxide, sulfur dioxide, and suspended particulate matter concentrations due to decades of unregulated car emissions, urban industrial operations, and trash burning. Cairo also has many unregistered lead and copper smelters that heavily pollute the city. The results are a permanent haze over the city, with particulate matter in the air reaching over three times normal levels. It is estimated that up to twenty-five thousand people a year in Cairo die due to air pollution-related diseases. It is further estimated that the high lead content of the air can retard a child's IQ on average by four points.

EXPLANATORY ENTRY #46: BRIEF OVERVIEW OF EGYPTIAN HISTORY

The Nile is Egypt. This has been true since the introduction of agriculture at least six thousand years ago. Of Egypt's population of about eighty million, 95 percent live on the banks of the Nile, the longest river in the world (4,145 miles). From the first cataract at Aswan to the Mediterranean Sea, the mighty river meanders through the Egyptian countryside, bringing water to an otherwise parched land. Until the completion of the Aswan High Dam in 1971, the annual flooding of the Nile dictated the rhythm of Egyptian life, inundating its delta and river valley with a twenty-five- to fifty-foot wall of water and silt. The river, now regulated by elaborate irrigation systems, remains the lifeblood of a country that still depends on agriculture.

Deserts flank the Nile Valley. On one side of the road are lush groves of date palms, fig, banana, and mango trees, and fields of sugar cane, corn, and squash. On the other side, a few feet away, desolate sand dunes stretch as far as the eye can see. Lower Egypt (so named because of the northward flow of the Nile) includes the Delta and the Cairo region, while Upper Egypt is the whole of the Nile Valley to the south.

The world's first "united nation" was formed when Upper and Lower Egypt became one in 3100 BCE and formed the first of thirty dynasties of pharaohs. For two thousand years Egypt enjoyed a magnificent civilization.[2] A united government, a 365-day year, a system of writing for keeping records, a firm belief in life after death, medical science, the science of astronomy, material wealth, sea trade, and knowledge of art and architecture were a part of the Egyptian genius that was to inspire the Greek, Roman, and western civilizations that followed.

---

2. For additional information, consult Appendix F.

During the Eighteenth Dynasty (c. 1550-1295), under the rule of Thutmose III (1479-1425), Egypt expanded its borders to the Euphrates River and reached the zenith of its power. But after Pharaoh Amenhotep IV (1353-1336) changed his name to Akhenaton (also spelled Akhenaten and Ikhnaton) and instigated a religious revolution in Egypt—introducing a kind of monotheism based on worship of the sun god, Aton—Egypt was never the same. Following the reign of Ramses III (1186-1155), the last of the great pharaohs, the grandeur ended. Wave after wave of invaders overran the country: Assyrians, Persians, and finally in 332 BCE the successors of Alexander the Great, who kindled a final blaze of cultured glory. The library of Alexandria became the universal center of learning and all eyes turned toward Egypt. In the year 30 BCE, however, the glory ended when Cleopatra and Antony committed suicide. With their deaths, Egypt became a Roman province and lost its independent power in the ancient world.

EXPLANATORY ENTRY #47: THE EGYPTIAN MUSEUM

Like most people, I always considered the land of the Nile a dream destination. Talk of Egypt fills the mind with fantastic images of grand civilizations and ancient times. The Nile River Valley, settled since the dawn of prehistoric times, yields abundant evidence of its rich culture. And what better way to explore those antiquities than at the Museum of Egyptian Antiquities, known commonly as the Egyptian Museum.

The museum, set on the banks of the Nile, on the north side of Tahrir Square, houses the world's most complete collection of Egyptian antiquities. Built in 1900, the museum has one hundred and thirty-six thousand items on display, with hundreds of thousands more in its basement storerooms. Many of these are reserved exclusively for purposes of research. The writers of the *Lonely Planet* guidebook reckon that if visitors spend one minute on each item, it would take nine months to see them all. To be sure, the museum can be daunting in the sheer numbers of its antiquities on display, but there is an order to its layout and it is a goldmine—figuratively and literally—for anyone wanting to study Egyptian antiquities.

The museum's ground floor follows the history of ancient Egypt. If visitors turn directly to the left after entering and make the complete tour of the rectangle, while at the same time inspecting the side rooms of the main galleries, they will follow in chronological order the history of

Egypt. In so doing, they will encounter row upon row of mummies and shapely decorated coffins, statues and figurines, hieroglyphic tablets, jewelry, papyrus scrolls, war chariots, funerary furnishings—absolutely everything one can associate with ancient Egypt.

I approached a staff worker and asked to see the Stele of Merneptah, one of the most important Jewish antiquities in the museum. On my own, I would never have located it in the museum's vast collection. The black granite stone is eight feet high, four feet wide, and two feet thick. Called the "Israel Stone," it contains the earliest mention of "Israel" outside the Bible (the stele is dated to 1209/08 BCE). In line 27 of the text, the word "Israel" appears in hieroglyphics. The inscription tells of the defeat of various peoples, including the Hittites, the Philistines, and, in line 27, of "Israel."

In the center of the north gallery, Room 3 is devoted to the Pharaoh Amenhotep IV (Akhnaton), who for a brief period—the so-called Amarna Age (c. 1350–1330)—decreed that only one god, Aton, could be worshiped publicly in Egypt. The new pharaoh espoused a god devoid of human characteristics. In the Egyptian language, *aton* was a noun meaning "disk of the sun." In the mind of the young Amenhotep IV, however, the Aton was no mere disk: he was the sublime living sun disk—there was none other than he. Aton became represented by the hieroglyphic symbol of a disk radiating rays that terminated in hands, which held the *ankh*, or symbol of life. Thus, the deity that Egyptians were now under obligation to worship had neither statuary nor legend nor human appearance to lend him credibility.

Unlike his predecessors, Amenhotep IV was less interested in pursuing an aggressive foreign policy than in effecting a religious revolution in Egypt. To dramatize the break with the powerful bureaucrats and the established priesthood of the high god Amon (Amen-Re), the sun god, in the sixth year of his reign he abruptly moved the capital two hundred and fifty miles north to the desert frontier near the modern Tell el-Amarna. Once there he radically changed the state religion, demoting Amon and elevating the marginal god Aton, who represented the sun at midday, to sole god. To prove his devotion, he changed his name to Akhnaton (meaning "The Splendor of Aton"). According to the official doctrine during this period, the king of Egypt was not the son of an earthly father but bodily the godly son of Aton and a human mother.

In effect, Akhnaton became the world's first monotheist. He closed all the temples of Egypt, erased the name Amon from all monuments, changed the plural "gods" to god, and called his new capital Akhetaton ("Horizon of Aton"). Akhnaton was an impractical idealist, however, whose attempt to reform Egypt resulted in failure. He had no sons, and his successor, the famous king Tutankhamon, died while still a teenager.

Recently a new understanding has emerged of this royal city. The capital was built not merely to house the Egyptian government, but also to represent the cosmos. Although the short-lived city was only inhabited on the east side of the river, boundary markers were found on both sides of the river, indicating the margins of the symbolic universe. The city was chosen for its peculiar landscape setting, which aligned with the movement of the sun. East of the city were cliffs, with an opening that coincided with the center of the city. The break in the cliffs served as a gateway for the sun's path across the city on its daily east-west journey.

Every day the king and the residents of this isolated city—mostly bureaucrats—enacted a cosmic ceremony, mimicking the pattern of the sun. The ritual began in the morning, when the king entered his electrum chariot from his royal residence at the north end of the city. He proceeded southward to the official quarter, the center of the city, following a special route aligned with the north-south axis. The official quarter contained the offices of the government, the main Aton temple, and a large palace, the setting for the ceremonial public activities of the king. In the evening, the pattern was reversed. On both occasions, in the morning and in the evening, people would line the streets along the designated path, honoring the divine king's presence and power. The symbolism was obvious: the sun controls the celestial axis (east to west) and the king controls the terrestrial axis (north to south). Each day the two primary actors—father (solar disk) and son (king)—met at noon, symbolizing cosmic stability, wellbeing, and peace.

Ahknaton's reform—essentially the first monotheistic faith in history—was soon rescinded by subsequent pharaohs, including Tutankhamon, and was erased from public memory. Akhetaton, the revolutionary capital city, was abandoned and fell prey to the sands of time. In 1887 an Egyptian peasant woman digging in the ruins came upon some clay tablets, and Akhnaton's royal archives were unearthed. The archives, consisting of some four hundred tablets inscribed in Akkadian cuneiform (known as the "Amarna letters") contain correspondence between vassal princes in Canaan and the Egyptian king. The letters point to a time of political change and disorder in Canaan and have been the subject of much scholarly debate. The disturbance seems to have been occasioned, at least in part, by the relaxation of Egyptian rule coupled with raids by bands of brigands called 'Apiru.

Some years ago it was fashionable to date the Exodus to this period and to equate the 'Apiru (also known as Habiru) with the invading Hebrews. This theory has since been called into question or abandoned by nearly every biblical scholar, as new evidence has come to light which points to a later date for the Exodus: the thirteenth century, perhaps early in the reign of Ramses II (1279–1213).

Not all of Akhnaton's influences ended in failure. Into the visual arts, for example, he breathed a new and vibrant life. Early in his reign, the pharaoh assembled his royal sculptors and made it clear that pharaohs would no longer be depicted in stiff, expressionless poses. As the unique son of the Aton, Akhnaton insisted that he be portrayed in all of his individuality. The resulting sculptures were both unique and peculiar, for Akhnaton was grotesque in appearance. He had slanted eyes, pulpy lips, and a knobby chin; other features—a huge gourd-shaped head supported by a long and slender neck, a potbelly reminiscent of a woman in early pregnancy, gigantic thighs and matchstick shins—were strangely effeminate, and it was speculated he suffered a glandular disorder that resulted in bodily deformation.

The sculptors took him at his word—and then some, possibly exaggerating his physical grotesqueness. But a new naturalism swept through Egyptian art, evident from statuary to reliefs to painting. For the first time, Egyptians were allowed to view their pharaoh in the intimate surroundings of home and family. Similarly, in long, curved lines, humans and animals came alive; the elderly showed their age, married couples were portrayed with warmth, children looked like children instead of stunted adults, and birds seemed to fly rather than appearing lifeless and frozen as they had in earlier eras. The art thus promoted by Akhnaton would far outlive both the heretical pharaoh himself and the god that he championed.

One of the finds at the deserted city includes the bust of Nefertiti, Akhnaton's beautiful wife. The famous bust of Queen Nefertiti shows her in a royal headdress with a brightly painted face under a crown. Her bust, now in Berlin's Altes Museum, is one of the most copied works of ancient Egypt. It was attributed to the sculptor Thutmose, thought to have been the official court sculptor of Akhnaton, and was found in his workshop by a German archaeological expedition digging in the ruins of Amarna during its 1912 excavations.

The upper floor of the Egyptian Museum contains the museum's most spectacular displays. Here one finds countless coffins, amulets, *ushabtis* (figurines or servant statues placed in the graves of the deceased), chariots, and household items. Here, too, is the Royal Mummy Room, housing eleven pharaohs from the New Kingdom, Egypt's golden age (c. 1570–1070 BCE). The collection includes the mummy of Ramses the Great (Ramses II), often considered as "the Pharaoh of the Exodus," the ruler when Moses and the Israelite slaves were released from bondage.

The highlight of the collection is the display containing the fabulous tomb artifacts of the Pharaoh Tutankhamon, whose nearly intact tomb Howard Carter found in the Valley of the Kings in November 1922. In the "Great Gallery," on the upper floor, the treasures from Tutankhamon's tomb occupy almost two sides of the museum. Chariots, gloves, jewelry, the famous mask—many of the antiquities from his tomb are on display. Tutankhamon's tomb contained four gilded shrines nested one inside the other. The innermost of these covered a stone sarcophagus, which remains in the tomb. Inside the stone sarcophagus were three coffins— the innermost being made of 242 pounds of solid gold. Two of the three coffins are on display in the same room, along with stunning jewelry. Tutankhamon's mummy was enclosed within the third coffin. The head and shoulders of the young monarch were covered with a gold funerary mask, actually a portrait-effigy of the king. The mask, also of solid gold, weighs twenty-four pounds.

The religion of the ancient Egyptians was dominated by their funerary cult, but far from being obsessed with death itself, they saw it as a brief interruption. The idea of an eternal and actual death was incomprehensible to them. Human life, assuming certain precautions were taken, would last forever. Because life on earth was relatively short, they built their houses of mud. But they built their tombs of stone, since life after death was eternal.

21

Egypt's Monuments of Civilization

TRAVEL ENTRY #72: AN UNFORGETTABLE RIDE

AFTER MY VISIT TO the Egyptian Museum, it was time to see Egypt's monuments in their original setting. The pyramids of Giza, only seven and a half miles southwest of Tahrir Square and easily accessible by bus, taxi or minibus, beckoned. I hailed a "service taxi"—a minivan, actually—and sat on the bench seat behind the driver. A few passengers were in the back seat and a lady on the window seat next to me. We headed out into the busy afternoon traffic. Before long the van was packed, with two men squeezed between me and the door. Just when it seemed that the vehicle was about to burst from its load, the driver stopped to pick up one additional passenger—a lady with shopping bags. She crouched down in the landing next to the double doors and the van merged with the flow of traffic.

We approached one of Cairo's notorious traffic circles, where caution is thrown to the wind. As we careened into the first turn, surrounded by traffic, the door latch broke loose and the doors swung open. Before anyone could react, the lady with the bags let out a cry and fell from the vehicle onto the pavement, her valuables scattered across several lanes of the highway.

Cairo's drivers, apparently, are forever prepared for the unexpected, and our driver was no exception. He came to an abrupt halt and miraculously, so did the vehicles behind us. The rest of the traffic either swerved away from us or saw what was happening and came to a stop as well, forming a protective wall around the fallen passenger. Given the traffic conditions, I marvel that a chain reaction of collisions did not occur and that the lady was not run over. The men closest to the door got out to help the lady, who was then placed in the front seat, next to the driver. Her arm and leg were badly skinned and she had a nasty bruise on her forehead. The driver tried to take the woman to the hospital but she refused and insisted that she be dropped off at a stop near her home. Stubbornness—or modesty—prevented her from seeking proper health care. There are a great many people limping around Cairo, and I suspect that many have been injured in similar accidents.

EXPLANATORY ENTRY #48: THE PYRAMIDS OF GIZA

After my harrowing experience, I arrived at the Giza plateau and gazed in amazement at the Great Pyramid of Khufu (known in Greek as Cheops). A few hundred yards southwest of the Great Pyramid lies the slightly smaller pyramid of Khafre (Greek, Chephren), one of Khufu's successors who is commonly considered the builder of the Great Sphinx, and a few hundred yards further southwest is the smaller pyramid of Menkaure (Greek, Mycerinus), Khafre's son and successor. The three pyramids are offset from each other at a 45-degree angle, so that without obstruction each faces the four cardinal points of the compass.

The Great Pyramid, the first to be built in Giza, dominates the plateau. Originally 481 feet high (due to erosion and the theft of its capstone its current height is 455 feet) and 755 feet long on each side, it covers thirteen acres (eight football fields) at its base. The structure's current rough-hewn appearance is due to the absence of original polished casing stones, some of which weighed more than fifteen tons. For over fifty centuries, this edifice has challenged the imaginations of all who have visited it.

The largest and oldest of the Seven Wonders of the Ancient World, the pyramid has remained one of the most mysterious structures of the world. Completed in 2560 BCE,[1] it is in every respect a remarkable feat. But what was its purpose? Was it a tomb for a pharaoh, designed to satisfy a ruler's yearning for immortality, or was it something far more? Some believe it holds lost secrets to mankind's past. Additional questions remain, tantalizing scholars and dreamers for centuries. If the pyramid was merely a tomb, why—along with its companion pyramids of Khafre and Menkaure—was it laid out with such mathematical precision, align-

---

1. This is the generally accepted date; if the complex was built during the reign of Khufu, the date would have to be adjusted backward.

ing exactly with the world's compass points? Buildings today can't be built with such precision without astronomical instruments. And why was there no evidence of ancient burials found within the pyramid?

The building of the Great Pyramid, the largest stone structure ever built, remains a remarkable feat. Herodotus, the Greek historian in the fifth century BCE, estimated that construction may have required one hundred thousand workers for twenty years. The pyramid was constructed of cut and dressed blocks of limestone, basalt, or granite, its core made primarily of low quality limestone blocks taken from a quarry south of Khufu's Great Pyramid. These blocks weighed from two to four tons on average, with the heaviest used at the base of the pyramid. An estimated 2.4 million blocks were used in the construction. High quality limestone from the hills of Tura, about nine miles away on the other side of the Nile, was used for the outer casing. Granite quarried nearly five hundred miles away in Aswan with blocks weighing as much as sixty to eighty tons was used for the King's Chamber and relieving chambers.

The Great Pyramid of Giza is the main part of a complex setting of buildings that includes a number of smaller satellite edifices, known as "queens" pyramids, mortuary temples, causeways, small tombs surrounding the pyramid for nobles, and most noticeably the Great Sphinx. There are three known chambers inside the Great Pyramid, the lowest cut into the bedrock upon which the pyramid was built. This chamber, the largest of the three, remains unfinished. The middle chamber, known as the "Queen's Chamber," is the smallest; two narrow shafts extend from the chamber toward the outer surface of the pyramid. The purpose of the chamber remains uncertain.

At the end of the lengthy series of entrance ways leading into the pyramid interior is the structure's main chamber, the "King's Chamber." This chamber, the highest of the three and placed almost exactly at the center of the pyramid, was originally 17.25 x 34.5 x 20 feet, comprising a double 10 x 10 cubit square, and a height equal to half the double square's diagonal. This is consistent with then-available geometric methods for determining the Golden Ratio phi, which can be derived from other dimensions of the pyramid.

The King's Chamber is a dimly lit room with the broken base of a sarcophagus at one end. The sarcophagus was hollowed out of a single piece of Red Aswan granite and has been found to be too large to fit through the passageway leading to the King's Chamber. Whether the sarcophagus was ever intended to house a body is unknown, but it is too short to accommodate a medium height individual without the bending of the knees (a technique not practiced in Egyptian burial) and no lid was ever found. Although there is little to see in the chamber, the experience of being inside something so old is amazing. Here, deep within the heart of the Great Pyramid, many discern an aura of sacredness.

The King's Chamber contains two "air shafts" that ascend out of the pyramid and point directly to the star Thuban and the star Alnitak, in the Orion constellation. The Queen's Chamber has two air shafts which also align to stars as well. These air shafts were supposedly used for ventilation, but given the fact that all four were found to be closed off at both ends and only discovered by accident, Egyptologists conclude that they were designed for ceremonial purposes, thereby allowing the pharaoh's spirit to rise up and out into the stars.

Five boat pits surround Khufu's Pyramid on the south and the east. Two of these are believed to have been used by the pharaoh during his lifetime. One boat, which now serves as a museum, has no nails but was held together with ropes and pegs. These boats may have been intended for the pharaoh's use in the afterlife or to accompany the Sun-God on his journey.

For safety's sake—and also to protect the monuments—Egyptian law prevents visitors from climbing the pyramids. Each night, however, a number of tourists bribe the guards and climb them anyway; consequently, each year a number die.

In a depression south of Khafre's pyramid sits the Great Sphinx, an enormous statue of a creature with a human head and a lion's body. It is 240 feet long and 65 feet tall—seven stories high and nearly a football field in length, the largest surviving sculpture from the ancient world. It is also the earliest colossal sculpture erected by the Egyptians, so old that for much of history the Egyptian pharaohs worshipped it as a god.

The name "sphinx" was first given by the Greeks to a fabulous creature that had the head of a woman, the body of a lion, and the wings of a bird. The Great Sphinx of Egypt, however, has the body of a lion and the head of a king wearing his headdress. Because it resides within part of the funerary complex credited to Khafre, it is generally accepted that the Sphinx was built by Pharaoh Khafre (c. 2558–2532) during the Old Kingdom, the age of the great pyramid builders. There is speculation that the monument may be older than this, however, for an inscription within the Great Pyramid, dating from 600 BCE, records that Pharaoh Khufu—Khafre's grandfather—carried out repairs on the Sphinx's tail and headdress. Some believe that the Sphinx may have been built by Khufu; others, dating it as far back as 3100 BCE, before the unification of Upper and Lower Egypt, think that the Old Kingdom temples were simply built around it. If so, the Sphinx would predate the earliest phase of Stonehenge, and be among the most ancient monuments from antiquity that have survived intact into modern times.

The original purpose of the Sphinx is unknown. It may have been built to symbolically guard over the Giza plateau, where it faces the rising sun, and it may have been a portrait of Pharaoh Khafre, the royal headdress that it wears being particular to pharaohs. It was the focus of solar worship in the Old Kingdom because its animal form, the lion, has long been a symbol associated with the sun in ancient Near Eastern civilizations.

The area occupied by the Sphinx was once a quarry. The Sphinx was likely carved out of the bedrock with stone hammers and copper chisels, and as it was being sculpted, a large defect was found in the rock near its hindquarters. Its builders consequently extended the body with large blocks of high-quality Tura limestone—the same stone that encases the pyramids—to cover up the fault, and as a result, the Sphinx's head is far too small for its 240-foot-long body. After the Giza necropolis was abandoned, the Sphinx was buried up to its shoulders in sand. Because the figure was built of soft sandstone, it would have disappeared long ago had it not been buried.

The statue is crumbling today because of wind, humidity, and the smog from Cairo. Attempts to restore the image have not been very successful, often causing more harm than good. Visitors interested in learning more about the Sphinx and its storied setting can attend the Sound and Light Show. The commentary might not impress listeners, but the dazzling light show and awe-inspiring backdrop of the Sphinx and pyramids surely will. Three times a night in three different languages, the Sphinx plays the role of storyteller, narrating the history of ancient Egypt.

TRAVEL ENTRY #73: AN UNFORGETTABLE BUY

On one of my trips to the pyramids, I stopped at nearby shops in hopes of finding some item that would serve as a lasting reminder of my sabbatical trip. There, in the shadow of the Great Pyramid, I finally found what I was looking for.

During a previous visit to Cairo, I had visited the Papyrus Institute, where my wife and I witnessed a demonstration showing how a sheet of papyrus is made from the stem of the papyrus reed that grows in the marshes along the Nile. We were intrigued by the ancient process: the outer rind is first stripped off, and the sticky fibrous inner pith is cut lengthwise into thin strips about fifteen inches long. The strips are then placed side by side on a hard surface with their edges slightly overlapping, and then another layer of strips is laid on top at a right angle. The strips are then soaked in water to increase adhesion. While still moist, the two layers are mashed into a single sheet, which is then dried under pressure. After drying, the sheet of papyrus is polished with a round stone or similar object. At the end of the demonstration, Susan and I purchased several replicas of ancient Egyptian art made on authentic papyrus sheets by students at the institute.

This time, as I strolled through one of the shops, inundated by the enormous quantity of items available for purchase, my eyes were drawn to a large painting placed over one of the doorways. The painting, illuminated by various lights, depicted a scene of a pharaoh and his wife on a papyrus skiff, hunting along the Nile. It was the largest and most stunning papyrus painting I had ever seen, its gold and silver leaf paint shining brilliantly in its museum setting. I wondered whether I could afford the painting, but using bargaining skills honed over time, including the technique of leaving and returning days later (successful bargaining requires patience coupled with an air of detachment), I was able to reduce the price to about one-fifth the original. It was still expensive, but definitively affordable.

Once I reached a price I could live with, I had to address a further issue: could I get it home? The shopkeeper answered that question with a brief demonstration. He brought out a ladder and removed the 32 x 48-inch papyrus from its temporary mounting. Rolling the picture like a scroll, he inserted it into a long tube, and handed it to me. That clinched the deal and I emerged from the store the proud owner of an authentic Egyptian work of art. Rather than entrusting it to the vagaries of overseas shipping or to the mercies of a potentially unscrupulous shopkeeper, I took it to my hotel for safekeeping and registered it with the owner until my departure for the United States several days later. I carried the painting on the flight home and today it hangs over a mantel in my college office, the object of scrutiny and admiration by generations of students.

EXPLANATORY ENTRY #49: THEBES, THE ANCIENT CAPITAL OF EGYPT

The city of Luxor, 416 miles south of Cairo, is also known by its classical Greek name, Thebes. It is located on a wide and straight stretch of the river that was chosen by the pharaohs of the Eleventh Dynasty (c. 2125–1782) as their capital of Upper Egypt. The city was the capital of Egypt again during most of the Eighteenth Dynasty (c. 1550–1295), though the administration probably remained located at Memphis for much of this time. With the Nineteenth Dynasty (1295–1190) the seat of government moved permanently to the Delta. The archaeological remains of Thebes offer a striking testimony to Egyptian civilization at its height and are a magnet for thousands of tourists each day of the year.

Whereas the modern town of Luxor, with its population of roughly three hundred and eighty thousand, is unimpressive, ancient Thebes was a mighty and prosperous city of a million inhabitants. In *The Iliad* Homer described Thebes as the richest and mightiest city in the world. It reached its glory about 1500 BCE, when names such as Tutankhamon, Hatshepsut, Amenhotep III, and Akhnaton would have been household names in Thebes. After 1000 BCE, however, Thebes was in decline. In 661 BCE the city was sacked of what riches remained by Ashurbanipal, king of Assyria. But its temples, built to last through eternity, still remain.

For hundreds of years temples, statues, obelisks, columns, and sphinxes made this area the central place of worship for the Egyptians and a religious center of the god Amon (also spelled Amun or Amen), the first universal god in Egypt.

The Egyptian pantheon, with its multitude of gods portrayed as animals, often bewilders foreigners. "What monsters are revered by demented Egypt?" asked the Roman satirist Juvenal. "One part worships the crocodile. Another goes in awe of the ibis, which feeds on serpents. Elsewhere, there shines the golden effigy of the long-tailed monkey." To the earliest Egyptians, however, there was nothing demented about their worship. The power of the gods was plainly visible in the natural world—in the Nile itself, a miraculous wellspring of life amid the desert wastes, and in all of the river's inhabitants: the beasts that grazed on its floodplain, the creatures that swam in its waters or slithered along its banks, the birds that rose from its shallows to circle the sky above. It was entirely fitting that immortal gods should reveal themselves in these creatures—that Horus should appear as a falcon, Khnum as a ram, Thoth as an ibis, Hathor as a cow, and Sobek as a crocodile. What the Egyptians worshipped was not the animal itself but the divine spirit that animated it, a pliant force that could take many forms.

As civilization developed, the deities were imagined in more human terms, but because of ancient prior practices of revering animals, the Egyptians fused three ideas: nature, animal, and human. An example of this type of fusion is the goddess Hathor, who might appear as a human or a cow. When she was given a human body, she still retained the element of a cow with horns upon her head. The god Thoth had the head of an ibis, Horus the head of a falcon, and Anubis the head of a jackal.

The Egyptians saw gods in the heavens as well. The rising sun was the god Re embarking on a boat that would carry him to the western horizon. There he would transfer to a nighttime vessel and sail through the afterworld until he reached the dawn once more. Even the Egyptian story of the creation was based on an event they witnessed in the world around them. During severe floods, the huge earthen mounds known as tortoise backs might be swallowed up by the Nile, forcing those who lived there to take refuge at the fringe of the desert. Those humps were the first islands that emerged as the flood receded. To the Egyptians, such mounds represented Creation, when the primeval mound of the universe rose from the waters of Chaos.

The myth varied in its detail from place to place, and even the identity of the Creator was open to argument. At various times, the priests of Memphis, Heliopolis, Hermopolis, and Thebes each claimed their city as the site of the creation, and each ascribed the feat to its local god. But the rivalries made little difference. Each village and community usually had its local deities, and temples were built for them. Sometimes a universal god, such as Amon, became incarnate in the pharaoh, whose name included that of the god.

TRAVEL ENTRY #74: DAY ONE IN UPPER EGYPT

I arrived in Luxor after an exhausting overnight train ride. I had taken the slower train in order to mingle with locals and not with tourists, but also because the cheap second-class ticket was hard to pass up. I definitely got my money's worth! The seats were so crowded and uncomfortable that stretches of sleep were short lived. On account of terrorist attacks, the Egyptian government now puts restrictions on trains foreigners may take between Cairo, Luxor, and Aswan, allegedly so that the government can assure tourists' safety. Tourists are generally allowed to take most daytime or overnight air-conditioned express trains but not second- or third-class ordinary trains.

After finding an inexpensive hotel near the train station and stashing the few belongings I had not left locked up in Cairo, I headed toward the Luxor temple ruins. Having only three days to explore Upper Egypt, I decided to spend the first day viewing the archaeological remains on the East Bank of the Nile.

The ancient city of Thebes consisted of three areas known today as Luxor, Karnak, and the West Bank.[2] The ruins of the temple complexes at Karnak and Luxor are located on the East Bank of the Nile, within the modern city. The interior of Luxor Temple is a blend of architectural styles from the New Kingdom through the Roman era, but it holds together beautifully, particularly at night, when a sound-and-light show draws crowds to Luxor. The even more sumptuous Karnak Temple, two miles north of the Luxor temple, is the greatest monument to Thebes's ancient glory. Its huge hypostyle hall, an assembly of 134 colossal columns, is large enough to accommodate Paris's Notre Dame Cathedral (James Bond fans will remember an irate Jaws chasing Agent 007 through the temple in the 1977 film, *The Spy Who Loved Me*).

Immediately opposite Luxor, across the Nile, lie the monuments, temples, and tombs of the West Bank necropolis, a vast area stretched across three square miles of desert. The most famous site on the West Bank is the Valley of the Kings, about five miles from the Nile, where the tombs are richly decorated with painted carvings. A number of imposing mortuary temples rest on the West Bank, the finest of which is Deir el-Bahri, erected by Queen Hatshepsut. The Ramesseum, memorial temple of Ramses II, houses fragments of the enormous colossus that inspired Shelley's poem *Ozymandias*. Ruins of administrative buildings and the mortuary temple of Ramses III, the richest pharaoh of all, constitute Medinet Habu. Also on the West Bank are some three hundred Tombs of the Nobles, with nine burial chambers of particular interest. The Valley of the Queens houses several outstanding tombs for wives and sons of the most powerful pharaohs.

---

2. For a map of this region, see Appendix R.

TRAVEL ENTRY #75: DAY TWO IN UPPER EGYPT—THE WEST BANK (WEST THEBES)

That night, after attending the melodramatic Sound and Light show at Karnak, I joined a group of likeminded travelers who had gathered at the hotel to discuss the possibility of hiring a local tour guide to take them across the Nile to visit the tombs and mortuary temples of the vast West Thebes necropolis. One member of the group had met a guide who promised to purchase admission tickets and provide transportation on the West Bank. I agreed to participate. The next morning, eight of us met early, knowing that the necropolis should be seen first thing in the day, before the onslaught of tour groups. We met up with the guide and crossed the Nile on the local ferry. Two taxis awaited us on the other side and we proceeded to visit several temples and tombs, led by our knowledgeable guide.

The West Bank (West Thebes) contains a valley in which over sixty royal tombs have been found. There, for a period of nearly five hundred years, tombs were constructed for the kings and powerful nobles of Egypt's New Kingdom; only sixteen of the known sixty-four tombs can now be visited by the unprofessional tourist.

Most of the tombs follow a similar plan: three corridors in a line leading to the burial chamber. Designed to resemble the underworld, the long inclined rock-cut corridors descended through one or more antechambers to the burial chamber itself. Some have rooms along the second and third corridors, used to store furniture, jewelry, and other items that were buried with the pharaoh to ensure that his continued existence in the afterlife would be pleasant and successful. Also present in the tombs were ritual magical items and equipment that may have been used by the kings in their lifetime, some having been specially constructed for the burial.

Some of the tombs are quite plain but many are highly colorful and would have been stunning to see stuffed with glistening treasures. The walls are usually painted with scenes of pharaohs, gods, stars, and hieroglyphs. The texts and images, generally with a religious theme, are taken from ancient Egyptian funerary texts (commonly known as *The Book of the Dead*), a collection of religious spells and incantations intended to help the spirit of the deceased to be preserved in the afterlife.

Ramses II (1279–1213) ruled for sixty-seven years during the thirteenth century BCE, the height of ancient Egypt's power and glory.

Several factors, including his extraordinarily long reign, the wealth available in the state coffers, and the pharaoh's personal vanity, meant that Ramses, of all the ancient rulers, left what is perhaps the most indelible archaeological mark on the country. Most splendid of these, in accordance with New Kingdom royal burial practices, would have been his memorial temple, the Ramesseum: a place of worship dedicated to the pharaoh—god on earth—where his memory would have been kept alive after his passing from this world. Surviving records indicate that work on the project began shortly after the start of his reign and continued for twenty years.

On the extreme south end of the West Bank necropolis lies the complex of Medinet Habu. There are four different constructions here, including the mortuary temples of Ramses III (1186–1155) and of Thutmose III (1479–1425). Mortuary temples were built for the purpose of performing ceremonies in memory of a king or queen. The mortuary temple of Ramses III, which resembles closely the nearby Ramesseum, is one of the best preserved and most impressive monuments in the West Bank. Aside from its intrinsic size and architectural and artistic importance, the temple is probably best known as the source of inscribed reliefs depicting the advent and defeat of the Sea Peoples during the reign of Ramses III.

Because the funerary temple of Queen Hatshepsut (1479–1458/7), located at the base of majestic cliffs, is one of the biggest draw cards in Egypt, tourists generally flock to the location. The focal point of the Deir el-Bahri complex is a colonnaded structure known as the Djeser-Djeseru (meaning "the Holy of Holies"). The structure was designed and implemented by Senmut, royal steward and architect of Hatshepsut (and commonly believed to be her consort), to serve for her posthumous worship and to honor the glory of Amon and the other gods.[3]

---

3. Hatshepsut's temple was dedicated to the god Amon, but it also contained chapels for Anubis and Hathor. As god of the heavens and god of the cemetery, Anubis supervised the passage of the soul to the judgment hall in the West. There the hearts of the dead were weighed against the feather of truth. Anubis, called the son of Osiris, presided over the tombs and is portrayed as a jackal-headed god. Hathor, the goddess of love, joy, and sky, is portrayed as a woman wearing a headdress with horns and a red disc between the horns. She is sometimes represented as a cow. At Deir el-Bahri she is portrayed nursing Pharaoh Amenhotep II. She was regarded by the Greeks as Aphrodite.

Hatshepsut was one of the most famous of all women rulers in Egypt. With the exception of women in the Bible, she is the first great woman recorded in history. Because of the Egyptian desire to concentrate royal blood, Hatshepsut had married her brother Thutmose II (1493–1479), and at his death, she became regent. Thutmose III was then only ten to twelve years old. To reinforce her regency and to become "king," Hatshepsut appropriated male titles and attributes, including the symbolic beard of authority. Twice before in Egypt's history a queen had usurped the kingship, but it was a new departure for a female to pose and dress as a man.

Her nephew (as well as stepson and husband), Thutmose III, wanted the kingdom, but because he could not get it from his aunt (as well as stepmother and wife), he became jealous and angry. In 1458, when the great queen died after a lengthy rule, Thutmose III became king. His first act after Hatshepsut's death was to destroy the statues in her temple and to erase her name and image wherever they appeared. When he died in 1425, he left a great empire, which lasted for three hundred years. Ironically, the temple of Hatshepsut has endured for over three thousand years.

TRAVEL ENTRY #76: CYCLING IN AFRICA

The following day, my last in Upper Egypt, I fulfilled a cyclist's dream. Having cycled across the North American continent and more recently in Europe and Asia, I felt that my journey would not be complete without biking in Africa. So I rented a bicycle and spent the morning cycling along the historic Nile. Later that day I crossed the Nile, touring the West Bank by bike. Pedal power, accompanied by blue skies and light winds, enabled me to revisit the sites I had seen all too quickly or not at all the day before. I was particularly captivated by the stunning temple complex of Queen Hatshepsut, which I had seen from a distance earlier, and the mortuary temple of Ramses III, the richest pharaoh ever. The latter was a highlight, for it contained the best carvings and reliefs I would see in Egypt.

That afternoon I went shopping for family and friends as well as for myself. My trip was coming to an end, and I no longer needed to be limited by the size of my backpack or what my shoulders could bear. There were many souvenir shops in Karnak where numerous hawkers competed for my attention. The souvenirs they offered were clearly unique to Egypt: basalt scarabs, painted stone tablets inscribed with hieroglyphs, gold and silver cartouches, statues, papyrus scrolls, silver jewelry, alabaster and onyx vessels, and other curios.

An experience came to mind from the previous day, when a young man at one of the West Bank monuments had singled me out. Approaching with an air of secrecy, he took from his coat pocket an object, which he unwrapped briefly. Allowing me a glance, he then motioned for me to follow him to a more secluded place, where we could negotiate a price. As I walked a few paces from the group, the tour guide indicated they would wait for me. I'm sure he had witnessed this scenario repeatedly and might possibly have been party to the scam. When the con man noted my interest, he quoted a high price, but still a fraction of the value of such an object on the black market. I smiled, indicating that we understood one another, and then proceeded to bargain. I may have paid a couple of dollars for the item, well worth it to me but no doubt a disappointment for the seller.

What he showed me looked like a piece of funerary pottery, with lovely painted figures and a text from the *Book of the Dead*. The fragment was made to look like an object of great antiquity, with blackened strips of cloth attached to the back as if it had been taken from a mummy. It was illegal to sell antiquities in this fashion but I enjoyed the charade, knowing that the object was a clever imitation.

TRAVEL ENTRY #77: LEAVING EGYPT

After three days in Luxor, it was time to leave this amazing place, once the greatest city of the world. Although nothing physical lasts forever, the ancient Egyptians were right about one thing. While their temples—and other monuments—may no longer link heaven and earth, they still connect the past and the present.

I headed for Cairo on the overnight train, this time in first class. Though it was not a sleeper, I had the railroad car practically to myself. At one point, to alleviate the boredom and to stretch my legs, I wandered through the second-class compartments. There I met an American woman, who begged me to stay. Several young Egyptian men had been harassing her and she felt desperate. We acted as if we were friends, traveling together, and that seemed to work, for there were no more incidents of that sort during the rest of the trip.

After a few days in Cairo, it was time to head for the airport. Since my flight was scheduled to leave before daybreak, I ordered a cab the night before. That would save an extra hotel stay and ensure that no last-minute surprise would keep me from my departure time. I also had some concerns about my airline ticket. The original ticket had been stolen in Geneva, and because it was still valid, there was always a chance somebody might try to use it. In this case two of us would be vying for the same seat, and since my replacement ticket was not the original issue, I might be out of luck. Fortunately, the seat was empty when I boarded the plane.

When I arrived at the airport, something unexpected happened—something that had not previously occurred on my trip: I became violently sick. Even though I had traveled through many unsanitary places on my journey, I had not once been ill. I figured that I must have let down my guard toward the end. As I examined the possible causes, I narrowed them down to the fresh sugar cane drink I had purchased in Giza a day earlier (the cup had been rinsed in a bucket of standing water) or possibly to the *kushari* I had eaten in a cheap restaurant earlier that day. *Kushari*, a dish made of macaroni, rice, lentils, and tomato sauce, is served with an accompanying sauce that, like salad dressing, needs to be shaken.

I had been alone at the table when a street urchin joined me. I had already partaken of the sauce before his arrival, but when the boy joined me, he took the bottle and shook it while holding the open top with his filthy hand. When I saw his black thumb, which had probably not been washed for weeks, I felt nauseous and immediately left the restaurant. No doubt this youngster repeated the practice every day at that restaurant, and my digestive system was unprepared for the result.

The symptoms of nausea, it turned out, were not simply caused by revulsion. I felt sick during the entire flight home, with vomiting and diarrhea. The culprit was probably giardiasis, a disease that plagues many a traveler in the developing countries of the world. The symptoms may have been further exacerbated by the flight. A lady on the airplane noticed my distress and gave me a small bottle of sherry that she had purchased on the flight.

"Drink this," she said. "It always helps me when I get sick."

I drank it to be polite. But I only felt worse.

Epilogue

Living in the Center

Huston Smith, in his masterful introductory study, *The World's Religions*, writes that we are living at a time when world cultures are not simply meeting but colliding, "hurled with the force of atoms... The change that this new situation requires of us all—we who have been suddenly catapulted from town and country onto a world stage—is staggering." He tells of Diogenes, an exceptional individual who stated some twenty-five hundred years ago: "I am not an Athenian or a Greek but a citizen of the world." Today, Smith argues, we must all struggle to make these words our own. "We have come to the point in history when anyone who is only Japanese or American, only Oriental or Occidental, is only half human. The other half that beats with the pulse of all humanity has yet to be born."[1]

On December 5, after a late departure from Cairo and a missed connection in New York City, I landed at the Pittsburgh airport after midnight, and Susan was there to welcome me home.

In some respects everything was the same as when I had departed fifty-seven days earlier: the airport, the car, the neighborhood, my home, all was as I had left it. And yet in other ways everything had changed, for I had been to the Center—various centers, it seems—and I had returned a citizen of the world. The closing chapter charts out the responsibilities that come with global citizenship.

---

1. Huston Smith, *The World's Religions*, 7.

22

Becoming a Third-phase Person

GLOBAL CRISIS

It is no secret that our world is in a state of crisis. The prognosis is bleak and the conditions may be irreversible. The tip of the iceberg, evident to almost everyone nowadays, is the environmental fate of our entire planet. During the second half of the twentieth century we learned that deterioration in the quality of the air we breathe, the water we drink, and the soil in which we grow our crops seriously threatens our continued life and well-being on this earth.

In addition to environmental degradation and anticipated ecological factors such as unpredictable weather patterns, increasing number and severity of storms, and sea-level rise, we can add pandemics and the outbreak of new diseases, species extinction, malnutrition and widespread famine, terrorism, violence and crime, the breakdown of the family, increased addictive behavior, unemployment, corporate scandals, an increasing income gap between rich and poor, religious fanaticism and sectarian wars, and the list goes on and on.

The current crisis involves many factors: ecological, political, economic, sociological, and ethical. At its core, however, the problem is spiritual. The crisis of spirit, dubbed "the impoverishment of soul" by Matthew Fox, one of today's leading spiritual teachers, is particularly evident in our Western civilization today. It is characterized by imbalance, or more accurately, by dissociation between the spiritual and physical realms of life.

The current generation outpaces all others in history in terms of wealth, health, education, and convenience—yet it doesn't seem to be happier or more content than preceding generations. Perhaps, in our passion for acquiring things, we have actually lost something profound—

something so valuable that we would never knowingly sell it or trade it away. Some may refer to values, standards, or patriotism, but what it comes down to is the loss of the sacred.

Rather than being rooted in a spiritual worldview and in principles espoused by the traditions of the world's great religions, particularly in their mystical approaches to reality, modern humans see the world through the lenses of crass materialism, scientism, and positivism. In his thoughtful volume, *Man and Nature: the Spiritual Crisis in Modern Man* (1997), Islamic scholar Seyyed Nasr takes the reader through history and explores the causes of the desacralization of nature in the West and the resultant ecological crisis we face today. He demonstrates how the West, by divorcing science from spirit, has wrecked havoc on our planet. He also argues that the Christian faith helped accelerate this process when it removed elements of its metaphysical doctrines that kept nature as a part of the divine.

Whether the current crisis is curable is debatable, but it will clearly require massive cultural reorientation. More importantly, it will require a transformation of the human spirit and a commitment of will. Only a relationship of genuine harmony with nature and a love of nature's God can transform humans from consumers to caretakers.

When historians look back at the start of the twenty-first century, it is hoped that they might remember it most for two commitments: as a time when the peoples of the world made a profound commitment to one another and made an equal commitment to nature.

One of the goals of my sabbatical trip was to visit museums and sites associated with the archeology and religion of the Middle East. Often, as I walked through the vast sites and examined the artifacts from the archaeological eras of ancient history, I also pondered more recent eras of the West, known successively as the Dark Ages, the Renaissance, the Enlightenment, Romanticism, and Naturalism. What had caused such drastic shifts in the pendulum of civilization? Did classical brilliance have to be followed by regression, as occurred in Europe? Did Arab civilization, so advanced during the Middle Ages, need to collapse so mightily in the face of colonialism and the Industrial Revolution, when the West gained its technological supremacy? Though technology, warfare, plagues, and climate were factors, somehow the answers seemed far more complex and elusive than during the dawn of civilization.

I pondered the future, wondering whether the world's Eastern, Middle Eastern, African, and Western peoples would ever live as equals, sharing technological, cultural, and spiritual treasures with one another in a new golden age of peace and prosperity. There have been numerous attempts over time to envision utopias, their composition, and the conditions that might enhance their arrival. My thoughts wandered to the approaching millennium. Would environmental degradation and spiritual disregard lead to future Dark Ages, perhaps even to the end of civilization as we know it, or could humanity finally get it right?

Despite the grave problems in our world today, many of them centered in the eastern Mediterranean world, I now understand why people fall in love with this region and why some devote their lives to solving the intractable problems that plague it. Because it is the birthplace of Western civilization and the source of its three guiding religions, to dismiss it or to let it descend into anarchy would be a rejection of our roots, and ultimately, failure for humankind.

GLOBAL CITIZENSHIP:
A PROFOUND COMMITMENT TO NATURE

The central defining characteristic of spirituality is an individual's sense of connection to a much greater whole. At its heart, spirituality involves an emotional experience of awe and reverence. As such, it's something that is highly desired, fervently sought, endlessly disagreed upon, and thoroughly fascinating.

The world we live in today is the world we know through scientific observation, a much different world from the classical world where Western civilization first emerged. At that time, there was greater continuity between religion, culture, and nature. Today, however, we are experiencing a discontinuity unequaled in its order of magnitude. That is why there is suspicion and misrepresentation among the religions of the present time and why we are experiencing new fundamentalisms: Islamic, Jewish, Christian, Buddhist, Hindu, and Shinto.

Fundamentalism is a defensive tactic. It is one reason why few of the religions of the world are dealing with the ecology issue on a widespread scale. They simply do not feel equipped to deal with this new challenge. By not accepting a responsibility for the fate of the earth, there is a failure of religious responsibility to the divine, as well as to the human. We seem not to realize that as the outer world becomes damaged, our sense of the divine is degraded correspondingly.

Why did our ancestors have such a wonderful idea of God? Because they lived in an awesome world. They wondered at the magnificence of whatever it was that brought the world into being. This led to a sense of adoration. This adoration, this gratitude, we call religion. But now, as the outer world is diminished, our inner world is drying up.

Religion involves the sense of God, of the human, of creation, and of revelation. All of these aspects belong together, and they cannot be treated separately. We would have no sense of the divine without creation. Speculatively, we could talk about God as being prior to or outside creation or independent of creation, but in actual fact there is no such being as God without creation.

Pagans are seen as idolatrous because they worship the forces of nature and depict the divine in natural images and forms. But the divine always appears in some embodiment; no one ever worshiped matter as matter. Whatever is worshiped is seen as a mode of divine presence. Prior to the advent of monotheism, the divine was experienced by peoples generally as an all-pervasive presence of mysterious power in the universe. Biblical people drew together this all-pervasive presence in a transcendent, divine, personal creator related by covenant to a special people. People in the West, who inherited this outlook, gained a great deal, including a historical perspective, a sense of personal identity, and a sense of community. But they gradually lost the outer world, and when the outer world is lost, much of the inner world is lost as well.

Christianity allows for both the immanence and transcendence of God. The two polarities, however, must be maintained in tension. Excessive emphasis on the immanence of God can limit the divine to the range of purely natural phenomena. Excessive emphasis on the transcendence of God, however, can lead to apathy toward nature or even to misuse of its resources, thereby contributing to the destruction of the planet.

Of course, we have to recognize that immanence—this divine presence in creation—is understood differently in our present historical context than by our primal ancestors. Primal peoples related to nature immediately and intuitively; they simply observed and admired the natural world about them. Time was eternal—it moved in ever-renewing, seasonal cycles of change—and the universe existed as it always was and always would be. Humans could not really interfere with that or change it.

In the biblical world, however, a new sense of history came into being, an awareness that the universe emerged into being at a definite moment. Modern science, though it perceives the universe through a different set of intellectual lenses, with the aid of microscopic and telescopic instruments, reinforces the biblical perspective. Gradually, the Western world has come to understand that the universe is not simply a given, and that it did indeed have a beginning in time. And time, we have discovered, is irreversible. Our modern scientific view of the universe thus coincides with the biblical realm rather than with the non-biblical world.

There is something very important about the origin of the universe as we now know it. The beginning of the universe, we now understand, involved articulated energy constellations bound together in an inseparable unity. The various parts of the universe, while outwardly differentiated, were once inwardly bonded together in a comprehensive intimacy of each particle with every other particle.

Ecotheologian Thomas Berry indicates that at the beginning of the universe there were two forces: an expansive force, which resulted in a diversification process, and an attractive or gravitational force, which pulled things together in profound intimacy. While this attraction that everything has for everything else is vital, nobody knows its nature. Isaac Newton (1642–1727), who noted the laws of gravitation, said he did not know what gravitation was, and to this day no one can tell us what gravitation is. But we do know that these antithetical forces, the attractive force and the explosive force, together constitute what is called the curvature of the universe. According to Berry, "Everything that exists comes into existence within this context, the curvature of space. If this rate of emergence had been a trillionth of a fraction faster or a trillionth of a fraction slower, the universe would have either exploded or collapsed . . . If the attraction overcame the expansion, it would collapse. But if the expansion overcame the attraction, then it would explode."[1] Gravitation, built into this process, binds everything together so closely that nothing can ever be separated from anything else. Alienation, therefore, of one human from another or of humans from nature, is only a perception, for it is a cosmological impossibility.

---

1. *Befriending the Earth*, edited by Stephen Dunn and Anne Lonergan (Mystic, CT: Twenty-Third Publications, 1991).

As Berry points out, the other thing that is so important to this process is the relationship of origin: everything in the universe is derived from the same source. Science indicates that, and so does theology. If that is so, then everything in the universe is cousin to everything else. There is literally one family in the universe, one bonding. Community is not something we humans invented. And if the planet is a single community of existence, then all living beings are interconnected and all things are vital. In a universe where everything is related by origin, nothing is unimportant, nothing is marginal.

The current crisis of humanity is, in essence, a crisis of a lack of relationship. Humans are out of touch with themselves—with one another, with nature, with their past, with their future—but also with the Creator, the God of the universe. As this crisis grows, so does the yearning for relatedness. And that is the good news. Crisis precedes transformation and actually fuels or serves as a catalyst for transformation.

In the journey of life upon which we have all embarked, the most important task is to cultivate a sense of trust. Nothing will serve us better than a profound and ever deepening trust in the Creator, the sovereign power that keeps the vast panorama of universal existence moving along. Yes, the world is in poor shape, and many of its problems grow worse with each passing day. We must do what we can, but we must not fall into despair. If we focus on the big picture, we will realize that the universe is in a continual state of change. And we must remember that our planet is only a small part of the whole, that our crises are but fleeting instants in the eternity of time. There is perfection to the order and flow of this grand universe that is not absent from our tiny earth or our present time.

RECAPTURING THE SACRAMENTAL SENSE OF REALITY

John F. Haught, professor of theology at Georgetown University, argues that when it is wholesome, religion maintains four components: sacramental, mystical, silent, and active. Each of these dimensions suggests a distinct "way" of being religious, he argues, "but religion is most healthy and alive when it blends all four ways harmoniously. And it begins to dissolve into something other than 'religion' whenever any of the four aspects is isolated from contact with its three partners. In the actual world of religious life, such sundering of one aspect from the others is not unusual. But when this splintering occurs, religion rapidly decays into magic, escapism or obsession with esoteric teachings, or into cynicism, iconoclasm or vacuous activism."[2] When, on the other hand, religion concretely preserves the four components in a balanced way, it will function in an ecologically supportive way.

What fascinates me most about these aspects is the sacramental dimension. Religion is sacramental in the sense that it can speak of unspeakable mystery only through the use of symbols, or what theology calls sacraments. A sacrament, in its broadest sense, includes any object, person or event through which religious consciousness is awakened to the presence of sacred mystery. Historically, most of religion's sacraments have been closely related to nature. For example, the luminosity of sunshine, dawn, and dusk; the experience of wind or breath; the purifying power of clean water; the fertility of soil and life—all of these natural phenomena, and many more, have been used by religions to symbolize the way in which ultimate mystery affects us.

Since nature provides many of the fundamental sacraments of human religion, it is easy to see how the conservation of nature is indispensable for the survival of religion. If we lose the environment, we lose God as well. And it is equally true that when religion loses touch with its sacramental origins, it begins to grow indifferent to the natural world. A sacramental vision, Haught reminds us, makes nature, at least in a fragmentary way, transparent to divinity. In this sense it concedes to nature an inherent value without allowing it to become a substitute for God. According to this Christian perspective, nature is worth saving not because it is sacred, but because it is sacramental.

Of course, religion can exaggerate its sacramental side. It does so when it loses its association with mysticism, its essential polarity, as well as silence and action, another set of opposites that exists in a sort of tension with sacramentalism. When mysticism is lost, the sacrament becomes an end in itself, losing its symbolic value. But mysticism alone, if it diminishes the value of nature by looking exclusively beyond the natural order, can decay into sheer escapism. Occasionally it has even gone to the extreme of hating the earth and everything natural. Mysticism and sacramentalism are necessary, as are silence and action, but they need to be delicately balanced. Mysticism dissociated from a vigorous sacramentalism promotes the doctrine of "cosmic homelessness," whereas

---

2. *The Promise of Nature* (Mahwah, NJ: Paulist, 1993), 73–75.

sacramentalism without the mystical aspect of religion collapses into idolatry or pure naturalism (the view that nature is all there is).

In his book *The Luminous Dusk*,[3] Professor Dale Allison explores the loss of wonder in Western society and its negative impact on our relationship to the cosmos. Arguing that early Christians favored the desert to the city, finding it natural to practice Christianity in solitude and silence, he laments that modern people forsook the wilderness and filled the cities. And the closer humans came to themselves, the more uncertain and cynical they became.

He mentions a poll of scientists taken some years ago, whose object was to gauge their belief in God. Although few acknowledged a belief in God, of those that did, there was a significantly higher percentage of cosmologists than biologists, and a significantly higher percentage of biologists than psychologists. The results led Allison to conclude that "the closer one's profession took one toward human beings, the less belief [in God] there was."[4]

THREE PHASES OF THOUGHT ABOUT THE SCOPE AND NATURE OF THE FAITH JOURNEY

People who agree with the preceding assessment have been characterized as being in the "third phase" of their faith journey.[5] Third-phase people are uncomfortable with relegating their religion to a private sphere of personal belief and corporate worship. They may not have been taught in church, synagogue, or mosque to think of valued daily activities as "spiritualities," but they would like to think of them this way. Such an understanding of spirituality, what the letter of James calls "pure religion" (2:20 KJV) cannot remain apathetic. A commitment to justice issues in society—saying "no" to the tragic injustices of our times—is a way of saying "yes" to life in its fullness. This form of spirituality encourages us to say "yes" to the healing powers of nature itself and thereby to live lives of deep-seated respect for the environment and all of life.[6]

---

3. Dale C. Allison, Jr., *The Luminous Dusk: Finding God in the Deep, Still Places* (Grand Rapids, MI: Eerdmans, 2006).

4. Ibid., 13.

5. The expression is taken from Dorothee Soelle and Shirley A. Cloyes *To Work and to Love: A Theology of Creation* (Philadelphia: Fortress, 1984).

6. Jay B. McDaniel, *Earth, Sky, Gods & Mortals* (Mystic, CT: Twenty-Third Publications, 1990), 1–4.

The "first phase" way of thinking is said to occur during childhood, when parents traditionally socialize children to the religious norms and practices of their ancestors. For many, this religious way, characterized as one's "isolated childhood village," is rich and meaningful. It offers "security amid uncertainty, hope amid despair, [and] trust amid doubt."[7] In this stage there is little or no encounter with religious pluralism or with the tests of reason and experience. There is as yet no internalized global consciousness or recognition that many of the urgent problems we face today are caused in part by the practices and attitudes of organized religions.

The "second phase" is a critical phase, or possibly even an apathetic reaction to the first phase. In this phase, some abandon prayer and stop attending formal worship altogether, living as post-religious inhabitants of the secular city. For many "second phasers," critical reason becomes the object of their faith and secular humanism becomes their creed.

Just as some people stay in the first phase all their lives, so some remain in the second phase. Indeed, many in the West have been reared in a second-phase way of thinking: the truths of science, not those of religion, are their guide. For them, the second phase is not a transition to something further, but the very norm for an authentic life.

Nevertheless, some move on to a third phase. They do so for different reasons, but almost always as a result of feeling that the second phase lacks "a depth dimension, a sense of mystery, an awareness of the Holy, and a sense of connectedness with all that is. From a third-phase perspective, the second phase fails to recognize that, after all, humans are part of a larger cosmic, and even divine, story. Without a feeling for this larger story, humanism itself becomes arrogant, wrongly proffering a philosophy that humans are the measure of all things."[8] Those who enter the third phase retain an appreciation of critical reason, but have moved beyond secular humanism in search of sacred ground. They have become third-phase believers. This does not mean that they stop praying or stop attending church, for the religious life is best nourished by fellowship and community. But third-phase believers understand their lives as open-ended journeys in which they seek, not an end to ambiguity and uncertainty, but rather breadth, depth, and meaning. They realize that life is a pilgrimage, and that the entire earth can become hallowed ground and therefore the locus of encounter with the living God.

7. Ibid., 4.
8. Ibid., 5.

OBJECTIVE TIME AND EXISTENTIAL TIME: HISTORICAL AND HISTORIC

As we learned in chapter 3, the ancient Greeks had two words for time, *chronos* and *kairos*. While the former refers to chronological or sequential time, the latter signifies "a time in between," a moment of undetermined length understood as a "right or opportune moment." While *chronos* is quantitative, *kairos* has a qualitative nature. In the New Testament, *kairos* means "the appointed time in the purpose of God," the time when God acts (e.g. Mark 1:15, "the *kairos* is fulfilled," referring to an hourglass, when it is filled with the "sand of time").

In the German language, two terms are used to distinguish between temporal events: *Historie* and *Geschichte*. They provide a helpful distinction not only in the study of history but also in considering the accounts and events recorded in the Bible. *Historie* stresses objective facts that can be recognized by all observers, whereas *Geschichte* concerns the subjective meaning to an individual. Although the English language does not have exact equivalents, scholars have found two sets of words for the adjective derivatives of these two German words, namely objective-historical (or simply "historical") for *historisch*, and existential-historical (or "historic") for *geschichtlich*. *Historie* refers to an event that can be proved by general historical science, whereas *Geschichte* refers to events that also take place in time and space but may or may not be provable.

The Bible includes both types of events, but it does not always distinguish between them. Though it is clear that biblical authors consider the latter to be of greater significance, because they convey both lasting and transformative power, it is up to the reader to distinguish what is historic/kairotic from what is historical/chronological. From a religious or spiritual perspective, the fascinating thing about common times, places, persons, and events is that they may serve as "thin places," that is, as vehicles of sacred opportunity and intention, and when that happens, historical "events" become historic whenever chronological time becomes kairotic.

RIDING THE TIDES

One of the great stories of human ingenuity comes from World War II, when the Italian forces were driven out of Eritrea, a country along the Red Sea. In an effort to make a major harbor unusable to the Allies, the

Italians filled great barges with concrete, and then sank them across the entrance to the harbor. When the Allies took control of the region, they inherited a massive problem: finding a way to remove those barges in order to make use of the harbor.

The solution was ingenious. They sealed great empty gas tanks, the kind used by oil refineries to store fuel, and they floated them in the sea above the sunken barges. When the tide went out, they chained the floating tanks to the barges. When the tides came in, the tanks exerted their tremendous buoyancy to tug the barges free from the bay's sucking sand. Think of the power in that sequence of events. The barges were chained to the tanks, and the tanks were dependent upon the tides. The tides were pulled by the gravitational attraction of the moon, and the moon was moving in accord with the entire universe.

"There is a tide in the affairs of men, which, taken at the flood, leads on to fortune; omitted, all the voyage of their life is bound in shallows and in miseries."[9] Shakespeare is saying that the tides not only have great power, but that they cannot be stopped or retrieved. Their lifting strength comes for a few hours and then is gone. And if we miss the flood, then we will be left "in shallows and in miseries." So there are moments in our lives when the tide is up, when opportunities for growth must be harnessed. If ideas are not cultivated as they surface, they may be gone forever. And so it is with the Spirit of God, who is described as a wind that blows where it will. There are times when the hot breath of the Spirit is all around us, when God's presence is palpable. At such times, great opportunities lie close at hand.

Examine the opportunities before you now—opportunities to believe, to repent, to obey, to bind up the brokenhearted, to serve. They might never rise again. Ride the tide while it is yours.

---

9. William Shakespeare, *Julius Caesar*, Act 4, scene 3, 218–24.

Appendix A

ARCHAEOLOGICAL TIMELINE OF THE MEDITERRANEAN WORLD

The material in Appendix A covers diverse cultural and archaeological information, so a timeline is provided below for use as a reference. The timeline, however, cannot be applied indiscriminately to all geographical areas, and readers must not assume that the dating of archaeological periods is the same for cultures around the world.

The Bronze Age, for example, marked a significant development in human culture. Generally, this era succeeded the Chalcolithic (Copper Stone) Age. But the use of bronze came into existence at different times around the world. For instance, bronze technology was known in Thailand as early as 4500 BCE whereas in the Americas, bronze was introduced after 1000 CE. Asia Minor was among the first regions to gain bronze-producing technology, beginning as early as 3000 BCE. Because Asia Minor experienced a long-lasting Bronze Age, its inhabitants succeeded in producing sophisticated tools and weapons. Some civilizations in the world never produced bronze, so the term Bronze Age does not apply to them.

The Iron Age is the last principal period used for classifying prehistoric societies. Its date and context vary depending on the country or geographical region. Classically, the Iron Age is taken to begin in the twelfth century BCE in the ancient Near East, ancient Persia, ancient India, and ancient Greece. In other regions of Europe, it started much later. The following information holds true for much of the Middle East (the dates are approximate and vary widely, even across the region).

The Paleolithic Age (500,000–15,000 BCE)

The Paleolithic Age (Old Stone Age) refers to the long period of prehistory during which human artifacts first appeared. During the Lower Paleolithic period (500,000–70,000 BCE), tools were fashioned and used for hunting and protection; where available, caves and rock shelters were used as dwellings. The temperate climate of the Lower Paleolithic was replaced in the Middle period (70,000–35,000 BCE) by a drier, harsher climate with heavy snowfalls. The ensuing glacial period brought about a change in life-styles and technological abilities, evident by innovations in the shapes of stone tools. During the Middle Paleolithic, burial customs of the Neanderthal provide the first evidence of ritual practices. In the Upper Paleolithic Age (35,000–15,000 BCE), when the weather again turned cold and dry, *Homo sapiens*, the ancestor of modern man, replaced Neanderthal Man. Stone-cutting reached its technical peak during this period, together with such important developments as multicolored paintings made on cave walls and the production of ornaments.

The Mesolithic Age (15,000–9000 BCE)

The Mesolithic Age was a transitional period, from the Old Stone Age to the New Stone Age. It was roughly coterminous with the later stages of the Ice Age in Europe, when the glaciers began retreating. As climatic changes occurred, animals and humans were forced to adapt. Animals became smaller in size and faster than before, so humans developed smaller stone tools made from obsidian and flint and lighter weapons. Hunting and the collecting of plants continued to be the main supply of food, but humans began storing food for later consumption. Domestication of animals began during this period, including that of the dog.

The Neolithic Age (9000–5500 BCE)

Following the relatively static Mesolithic period, the Neolithic Age, considered the beginning of civilization, was the scene of major developments and changes caused by human beings, notably the emergence of towns. Because this period saw major changes in human evolution, it is referred to as the Neolithic Revolution. Two important events caused this change: the cultivation of plants and the domestication of wild animals. Once humans settled down, history became compressed and progress was swift. Whereas the Paleolithic period had lasted one-half million years, the Neolithic lasted forty-five hundred years, the Chalcolithic twenty-five hundred years, the Bronze two thousand years, and the Iron Age a mere five hundred years.

In order to protect their crops, humans left their caves and rock shelters and lived closer to their fields. This led to the creation of a great variety of polished stone implements and to the development of new social forms based upon a settled agriculture and the accumulation of wealth. The emergence of village life brought with it major religious advances as well as significant developments in the art, architecture, farming, fire baked pottery and ceramics, advanced tools, and weapons.

It was during the Neolithic period that communities and villages emerged across the Middle East. These communities were characterized to a large degree by self-sufficiency, providing their own food and making tools, weapons, utensils, and clothes out of local materials. A central feature of the period was the manufacture of hand-made pottery. Adequate security led to the development of customs and laws, which became the basis of society.

The Chalcolithic Age (5500–3000 BCE)

During the Chalcolithic Age, the most striking development was the use of copper. Previously, the only material that humans had used to make weapons was natural stone, but in this period they learned to process and shape copper for stronger weapons and also for ornamental use. Metallurgy developed first in Anatolia, which possessed rich deposits of copper. Copper was also mined in Cyprus, the Negev desert in Israel, and around the Persian Gulf. The number of towns, typically built near rivers or lakes or in rich valleys, increased considerably during this period. The discovery of copper led to the development of trade between local and remote towns, with a network of trading centers where they exchanged commodities. The need for record-keeping resulted in the development of writing.

The Early Bronze Age (3000–2000 BCE)

By the start of the Early Bronze Age, inhabitants of the Middle East learned how to make bronze, a mixture of copper and tin. From this alloy, together with copper, gold, silver, and electron (an alloy of gold and silver), they made all of their weapons, ornaments, and utensils. During this period metallurgy becomes as prominent as agriculture. Facilitated by the growth of trade, the Early Bronze Age was characterized by the rise of urbanization and the proliferation of city states.

The Middle Bronze Age (2000–1550 BCE)

The Middle East reached a high level of civilization in the Middle Bronze Age, at which time this region became a world leader in art, urban planning, sculpture, and pottery. Many of the towns were fortified for defense purposes, indicating that there was a big struggle for power between local states and tribes. The significant increase in production and surplus of metal products made possible the export of such items to other communities and kingdoms in the area. This activity of trade, exchange, and profit made the Middle Bronze Age one of the first international periods in history. Movements of people impacted the political pattern of the Near East during this period, including the Amorites, Hittites, Hurrians, Hyksos, and possibly the Israelites.

The Late Bronze Age (1550–1200 BCE)

The Late Bronze Age was characterized by competing powerful kingdoms and their vassal states, including New Kingdom Egypt, Assyria, Babylonia, the Hittites, and Mitanni. Extensive contacts took place between these states and the Aegean civilization, and the copper trade played an important role. This period ended in widespread collapse, which affected much of the eastern Mediterranean and Middle East; Hattusa, the Hittite capital, was violently destroyed then, along with Troy, Miletus, Tarsus, Alaca Huyuk, Alisar, Carchemish, Ugarit, and other cities that had been part of the Hittite Empire.

The Bible contains a record of the transition from the Bronze to the Iron Age (1 Samuel 13:20–22). In the war between Israelites and Philistines, featured in the books of 1 and 2 Samuel, the ability of the Israelites to master iron technology was of great strategic importance. However, despite the new developments in metalworking, the transition to the Iron Age about 1200 BCE should be understood primarily for the political change it brought to the Near East. Out of the destructions of the Bronze Age emerged classical Greek culture and biblical Israel. When one considers the contributions these two cultures have made to Western civilization, it becomes clear that the change from the Bronze to the Iron Age in the eastern Mediterranean represents one of the most momentous revolutions in human history.

The Iron Age (1200–550 BCE)

The Iron Age in the Ancient Near East is believed to have begun with the discovery of iron smelting and smithing techniques in Late Bronze Age Anatolia (c. 1300 BCE). By 1500 BCE, Anatolia's use of iron produced weaponry superior to bronze. The use of such weapons by the Hittites was a major factor in the rapid rise of the Hittite Empire. Other groups possessing iron at this time includes the Sea Peoples, who introduced iron technology into Asia, as well as the Dorians with respect to Greece. Military technology designed to complement the use of iron came from Assyria, which may well have considered Troy an outpost, for the iron trade between the two places was well established by that time, with the Assyrians jealously guarding their trade secrets of production.

The Iron Age is divided into two subsections, Iron I and Iron II. Iron I (1200–1000 BCE) illustrates both continuity and discontinuity with the previous late Bronze Age. Certain new features appear in the Transjordan and coastal regions of Canaan, indicative of the appearance of the Aramaeans and the Sea Peoples. Iron II (1000–550 BCE) witnessed the rise of the states of Judah and Israel, small states that exercised considerable control over their particular regions due in part to the decline of Assyria and Egypt from about 1200 to 900. Beginning in the eighth century, Assyria reestablished its authority over the eastern Mediterranean area and exercised almost complete control. The northern state of Israel came to an end after a withering siege in 722/721 by King Sargon, and its inhabitants were taken into exile. The southern state of Judah escaped defeat, but its freedom was short-lived, for it was eventually destroyed by the Chaldean (Neo-Babylonian) kings who conquered Jerusalem in 586 and took many of the inhabitants into exile in Babylon.

Historical Periods (550 BCE–present)

The Iron Age is usually said to end in the Mediterranean region with the onset of Hellenism and the Roman Empire, in India with the onset of Buddhism and Jainism, in China with the onset of Confucianism, and in Northern Europe as late as the early Middle Ages.

Appendix B

CHRONOLOGY OF ROMAN HISTORY

753–510 BCE: The Monarchy.
[The dates for early Rome prior to 389 BCE are uncertain.]

510–30 BCE: The Republic

30 BCE–192 CE: The Early Roman Empire

30 BCE–41 CE: The Julian Emperors

30 BCE–14 CE. Augustus became first emperor of Rome.

27–25. The original Pantheon was constructed under the consulship of Marcus Agrippa.

14–37. Tiberius was the ruler during the time of Jesus.

41–68: The Claudian Emperors

54–68. Nero became emperor at the age of sixteen.

64. Rome burned, and Nero accused the Christians.

69–96: The Flavian Emperors

70. Destruction of Jerusalem by Titus after a four-year war.

70–72. The Coliseum was built; it was inaugurated by Titus in AD 80.

79. Mount Vesuvius erupts and buries Pompeii and Herculaneum.

96–180: The Five Good Emperors

98–117. Trajan. He launched massive building campaigns, including roads; he greatly extended the borders of the empire and erected Trajan's Forum in Rome, the largest of the forums.

117–138. Hadrian constructed a line of fortifications from the Rhine to the Danube; in Britain, he constructed a 73-mile-long defensive wall.

192–284: Collapse of the Empire

284–395: The Late Empire

284–305. Diocletian persecution—the last of the emperors who persecuted the Christians.

306–337. Reign of Constantine the Great; from 312–324 he ruled as emperor of the West.

312. Constantine defeated Maxentius at the battle of Milvian Bridge. This became a turning point in the history of Christianity.

313. Edict of Milan—Christianity was given equal rights with other religions.

319. The first basilica of St. Peter's was built by Constantine.

325. Council of Nicaea.

330. The seat of the empire was moved to Byzantium (Constantinople) by Constantine.

364. The Roman Empire was divided, with Rome as the capital of the Western Empire.

379. Theodosius proclaimed Christianity the state religion.

395–476: The Collapse of the Western Roman Empire

395. The Roman Empire was permanently divided into eastern and western halves.

410. Alaric's sack of Rome.

476. Traditional date for the fall of the (Western) Roman Empire. Romulus Augustulus, the last emperor of Rome after a thousand-year era, was deposed.

476–1453: Perpetuation of Rome in the East (Byzantine Empire)

1054. The Great Schism divided medieval Christendom into Western (Latin) and Eastern (Greek) branches, which later became the Roman Catholic Church and the Eastern Orthodox Church.

1201–1204. Fourth Crusade.

1204. Constantinople was sacked on Good Friday by zealous European Crusaders en route to the Holy Lands. Venetian fleets profit greatly as a result.

1063–1073. St. Mark's Basilica was built in Venice.

1173–1372. Tower of Pisa was constructed in three stages.

1300–1600: The Italian Renaissance: Prospect and Retrospect

1436. The *Duomo* was completed in Florence by Brunelleschi.

1445–1510. Sandro Botticelli, Italian painter during the early Renaissance. The *Birth of Venus* and *Primavera* rank among the masterpieces of Florentine art.

1449–1492. Lorenzo de' Medici (The Magnificent); his rule constituted the high point of the Florentine Republic. With his death, the center of the Renaissance shifted from Florence to Rome.

1450–1626. Construction of the current St. Peter's Basilica in Rome.

1452–1498. Savonarola. Dominican priest known for his anti-Renaissance preaching, book burning, and destruction of artwork. He was executed in Florence.

1452–1519. Leonardo da Vinci. One of the greatest painters of all time and perhaps the greatest inventive genius ever to have lived; often described as the prototypical "Renaissance man."

1471–1481. Construction of the Sistine Chapel (commissioned by Pope Sixtus IV).

1475–1564. Michelangelo. Italian Renaissance painter, sculptor, architect, and engineer. Two of his best known works, the *Pietà* and the *David*, were sculpted before he turned thirty. He is equally famous for his important paintings in the Sistine Chapel, including the scenes from Genesis on the ceiling and the *Last Judgment* on the altar wall. He also designed the dome of St. Peter's Basilica.

1503–1513. Julius II's ruled as Pope. A patron of the arts, Julian laid the foundation stone of the new St. Peter's Basilica in 1506; he commissioned Michelangelo to paint the ceiling of the Sistine Chapel and to create sculptures for his tomb, originally intended for St. Peter's Basilica but now found in the church of San Pietro in Vincoli (St. Peter in Chains).

1504. Michelangelo completed his sculpture *David*.

1508–1512. Michelangelo painted the ceiling of the Sistine Chapel.

1513–1521. Leo X (Giovanni de' Medici) was Pope. To raise money for the arts and other projects, he promoted the sale of indulgences on an unprecedented scale. Martin Luther's protest sparks the Protestant Reformation.

1515. Michelangelo completed his sculpture *Moses*.

1535–1541. Michelangelo painted his *Last Judgment* on the altar wall of the Sistine Chapel.

1554. Pope Paul IV decreed that all Jews must be segregated into their own quarters (ghettos).

1564–1642. Galileo Galilei. Italian figure who championed heliocentrism; called the "Father of Modern Science."

1600–Present.

1610. Galileo published *The Starry Messenger*, an account of his telescopic observations in favor of a heliocentric theory of the universe.

1633. Galileo was tried and sentenced by the Holy Office of the Inquisition in Rome.

1656–1667. St. Peter's Square was constructed (designed by Bernini).

1861–1878. Victor Emmanuel II ruled as the first king of unified Italy.

1870. Rome became the capital of Italy.

1929. The Lateran Treaty; the Italian state restored the diplomatic status of the Vatican, which had been lost from 1860–1870, when Italy seized all papal territories. The independent State of the Vatican City was established.

1946. The monarchy was abolished and Italy became a republic.

Appendix C

CHRONOLOGY OF GREEK HISTORY (INCLUDING THE BYZANTINE AND OTTOMAN ERAS)

4000–1200 BC: Bronze Age Greece.
This was the period of the Minoan civilization (2700–1450) in Crete and the Mycenaean civilization on the mainland. The Bronze Age on the mainland was called the Helladic civilization; the late Helladic Age is the Mycenaean Age (1600–1200). This period is the historical setting of the epics of Homer and of much other Greek literature.

3000. Human settlement on the present-day site of Athens begins.

c. 1600–1550. The volcanic eruption on the Aegean island of Thera (Santorini) is believed to have contributed to the collapse of the Minoan civilization.

1200–700 BC: The Dark Ages.

1200. The Dorians invaded Greece and destroyed the Mycenaean civilization. Sparta was settled by Dorians as a military camp.

1200. Troy was captured and destroyed.

1100. Greeks began colonizing the Ionian coast of Asia Minor.

c. 800. First temple to the goddess Artemis was built at Ephesus.

776. The first Olympic Games were held.

750. Homer's epic poems, *The Iliad* and *The Odyssey*, were composed. Poet Hesiod lived.

750–500: Archaic Period.

750–561. Athens became a republic. Greek law developed.

594. Solon (605–527) became archon at Athens. Serfdom was abolished and government by property owners was instituted.

560–546. The Greek city-states along the western coast of Asia Minor came under control of the Lydians and their king, Croesus.

550. King Croesus conquered Ephesus and rebuilt the Temple to Artemis.

546. The Persians (under King Cyrus) conquered the Lydians.

499–479: PERIOD OF THE PERSIAN WARS.

490. Battle of Marethon, quite possibly the single most important battle in Greek history. The Greeks stopped the first Persian invasion under Darius.

480. Battle of Thermopylae. The Spartans sacrificed three hundred warriors so the main force could escape. The Persians were led by Xerxes, son of Darius.

480. Battle of Salamis. Greeks defeated the Persian fleet at the Bay of Salamis.

479. Battle of Plataea. Though the Persians entered Athens and destroyed the Acropolis, the Greek armies defeated the Persians at Plataea, ending the Persian expansion into Europe.

479. Athens set up the Delian League, a confederacy of cities around the Aegean Sea. Sparta formed the rival Peloponnesian League.

479–431: GOLDEN AGE OF ATHENS (THE AGE OF PERICLES).

This was the period of the rise of the Athenian Empire and classical Greece. It was a time of democratic government and the beginning of Western civilization.

479. The *Charioteer*, one of the most celebrated sculptures of the ancient world, was crafted by an unknown artist.

468. Sophocles, Greek playwright, defeated Aeschylus for the Athenian Prize.

461–429. The Age of Pericles. Pericles, Athenian statesman, began a period known as the Athenian Golden Age.

456. The Temple of Zeus at Olympia was completed.

449. Herodotus (c. 484–425) wrote the history of the Persian Wars, the first historical work of Western civilization.

449. The Temple of Hephaestus was built in the Agora in Athens.

447–438. The Parthenon was built.

431–404: Second Peloponnesian War.

Sparta defeated Athens in this war. Socrates (c. 470–399) wrote and taught during this period.

421–407. The Erechtheum was constructed on the Acropolis.

411. Thucydides wrote an account of the Peloponnesian war that ended this year. His *History of the Peloponnesian War* ranks among the world's great literary works.

404. Athens fell to Sparta, thus ending its Golden Age.

404–371: Sparta's Supremacy over Athens.

399. Socrates was tried and condemned to death.

395–387. The Corinthian War, fought between Corinth and Thebes against Sparta, resulted in a weakening of the Peloponnese. This weakness allowed for the subsequent invasions by the Macedonians and the conquests of Alexander the Great.

387. Plato founded his Academy in Athens.

334–197: Hellenistic Age.

359–323. The period of the Macedonian Empire.

343. Aristotle (384–322) became a tutor to Alexander of Macedonia.

338. Philip II of Macedonia defeated Athens and Greece became a part of the Macedonian Empire.

336. Alexander the Great (356–323) succeeded Philip II.

335. Aristotle opened his Lyceum.

334–323. Alexander conquered the Persian Empire. Alexander affected the history of the world by spreading Greek civilization and language. Through his efforts, Greek culture became a world culture.

241–197. Attalos I ruled Pergamum. Under Eumenes and Attalos, Pergamum became a center of arts and science.

197. The Romans first conquered Macedonia and Greece.

197–159. The reign of Eumenes II (called the "Pericles of Pergamum") was the Golden Age of Pergamum.

190. The Altar of Zeus was built on the acropolis at Pergamum.

Appendix C   337

159–138. Attalos II ruled in Pergamum. He was involved in many important public works projects, including building magnificent stoas in Athens and dredging the harbor at Ephesus.

147 BCE–529 CE: ROMAN RULE.

147. Greece became a Roman province and the Hellenistic Age ended.

146. The destruction of Corinth by Lucius Mummius resulted in the city's abandonment for a century.

131. Herod Atticus built a large stadium on the site of the later Panathenian Stadium, built for the first modern Olympics in 1896.

44. Corinth was founded as a Roman colony by order of Julius Caesar.

52 CE. St. Paul visited Greece during his second missionary journey (49–53).

54–57. St. Paul spent three years in Ephesus during his third missionary journey, at which time he wrote important letters to the Corinthians. He wrote his most important epistle, *Romans*, from Corinth c. 58, toward the conclusion of his third journey.

100. Library of Celsus was built in Ephesus.

130–200. Galen, one of the greatest physicians of antiquity, was born in Pergamum and practiced medicine in its asclepion.

324. Constantine defeated Licinius in a battle near Adrianople and became ruler of the entire Roman Empire.

325. The Council of Nicaea was convened by Constantine. The first Christian ecumenical council resulted in the creation of the Nicene Creed and resolved the dispute over the nature of Jesus in relation to God the Father, thereby repudiating Arianism.

330. Constantine (Roman ruler from 306–337) chose Byzantium to be the new capital of his empire. He changed its name to Constantinople and dedicated the city to the Virgin Mary.

359. Constantinople became the capital of the Eastern Roman Empire.

360. The original Hagia Sophia was constructed during the reign of Constantius II (337–361), Constantine's son.

361. Julian the Apostate (Roman ruler from 355–363) became the last person to consult the oracle at Delphi.

364–378. Emperor Valens constructed a vast aqueduct system to provide water for Constantinople.

391. The Christian emperor Theodosius I the Great (emperor from 379–395) made Christianity the official religion of the empire. Theodosius was the last emperor of both the Eastern and the Western Empire.

393. Theodosius abolished paganism in the empire.

429. The Edict of Theodosius II (Eastern Roman emperor from 408 to 450) abolished the Olympian religion and forcibly Christianized the temples on the Acropolis.

451. Council of Chalcedon. The Fourth Ecumenical Council defined further the nature of the Trinity and resulted in the Chalcedonian Creed, which declared Jesus to be "fully human and fully divine."

527–1453. BYZANTINE AGE.

The Byzantine Age was a second golden age that lasted for one thousand years.

527–565. Justinian I was Eastern Roman Emperor during this period. Justinian is considered one of the most important figures in late antiquity.

529. Justinian closed the Academy in Athens, founded by Plato over nine hundred years earlier.

529–534. Corpus Juris Civilis. This code or collection of Roman law remains the basis of civil law in many modern states.

532. The Nika riots in Constantinople. The destruction that took place provided Justinian with the opportunity to erect a number of splendid buildings, notably the domed Hagia Sophia.

532–537. Justinian constructed the Hagia Sophia in Constantinople. For one thousand years it was the largest cathedral in the world.

726–843. The Iconoclastic Controversy. This movement, described by most historians as a watershed in Byzantine history, dominated the history of the Byzantine Church in the eighth and ninth centuries. As the use of icons—sacred images—gained importance in the Byzantine world, a long-standing opposition to images (known as Iconoclasm) resurfaced. The issue led to the Second Council at Nicaea in 787.

787. The Seventh Ecumenical Council met at Nicaea to resolve the issue of iconography. The Council sided with the Iconophiles, who favored the use of icons. This decision emphasized the growing cultural separation of the Eastern and Western bodies of Christendom that led to the Great Schism of 1054.

1054. The Great Schism divided medieval Christendom into Western (Latin) and Eastern (Greek) branches, namely the Roman Catholic Church and the Eastern Orthodox Church.

1201–1204. Fourth Crusade.

1204. Constantinople was sacked on Good Friday by zealous Crusaders en route to the Holy Lands.

1204–1261. The period of Latin rule proved to be the most disastrous in the history of Constantinople. The Crusaders sacked the city of its treasures and the looting went on for years.

1453–1822: OTTOMAN EMPIRE.

1453. Sultan Mehmed II conquered Constantinople and instituted Turkish rule in Greece.

1822–PRESENT: INDEPENDENCE.

1822. Greece declared its independence and defeated Turkey in 1829 (Greek War of Independence).

1873. Heinrich Schliemann discovered "Priam's treasure" in the ruins of Troy.

1876. Schliemann discovered additional treasure at Mycenae, including a gold mask dubbed "the Mask of Agamemnon."

1881–1893. The French cut a canal in the vicinity of Corinth, thereby joining the Adriatic and the Aegean seas while separating the Peloponnesus from the Greek mainland.

1924. Greece proclaimed itself a republic.

1955. Istanbul "pogrom"; most Greeks in Turkey left their homes for Greece.

Appendix D

CHRONOLOGY OF ANATOLIAN HISTORY

Prehistoric Period	**500,000–2,000 BCE**
Paleolithic Age (Old Stone Age)	500,000–15,000 BCE
Mesolithic Age (Middle Stone Age)	15,000–8,000
Neolithic Age (New Stone Age)	8000–5500
Chalcolithic Age (Copper Stone Age)	5500–3000
Early Bronze Age	3000–2000
Hatti Period	2500–2000
Assyrian Trading Colonies	1950–1750
Historic Period	**2000 BCE Onward**
Hittites	2000–700
Early Hittite Period	2000–1750
Old Hittite Kingdom	1750–1500
Middle Hittite Kingdom	1500–1430
Imperial Hittite Kingdom	1430–1180
Neo Hittite City States	1180–700
Phrygian Period	1200–700
Urartian Kingdom	860–580
Lydian Period	700–546
Persian Period	546–333
Hellenistic Period	333–133
Roman Period	133 BCE–395 CE
Byzantine Period	395–1453
Ottoman Period	1300–1923
Modern Turkey	1923–present

Appendix E

CHRONOLOGY OF CANAAN (ISRAEL AND THE REST OF THE HOLY LAND)

[including relevant events from Jewish and Islamic history]

When speaking of chronology, one must differentiate between relative and absolute chronology. Absolute chronology is tied to fixed dates—events which are known to have occurred on a specific date. Relative chronology places events in their chronological order but without a fixed date. Most of the biblical events are dated relatively rather than absolutely. For this reason many chronological charts have differences in specific dates BCE or CE, but generally agree on the relative order of most events.

PALEOLITHIC AGE	400,000–14,000 BCE
MESOLITHIC AGE	14,000–8,000
NEOLITHIC AGE	8000–4250
CHALCOLITHIC AGE	4250–3300
EARLY BRONZE AGE	3300–1950
MIDDLE BRONZE AGE	1950–1550
Patriarchal Period	1850–1700
LATE BRONZE AGE	1550–1200
Egyptian Captivity	1550–1250
IRON AGE I	1200–918
Period of the Judges	1200–1025
United Monarchy	1025–926
IRON AGE II	926–539
Northern Kingdom (Israel)	926–722
Southern Kingdom (Judah)	926–586
Neo-Babylonian Period	605–539
PERSIAN PERIOD	539–332
HELLENISTIC PERIOD	532–63

Early Hellenistic	532–198
Late Hellenistic	198–63
ROMAN PERIOD	**63 BCE–324 CE**
Early Roman	63 BCE–135 CE
Late Roman	135–324
BYZANTINE PERIOD	**324–640**
Early Byzantine	324–491
Late Byzantine	491–640
EARLY ISLAMIC PERIOD	**630–1174**
Pre-Umayyad	630–661
Umayyad	661–750
Abbasid	750–969
Fatimid	969–1171
Seljuk	1071–1174
CRUSADER PERIOD	**1099–1291**
Early Crusader	1099–1187
Late Crusader	1187–1291
LATE ISLAMIC	**1174–1918**
Ayyubid	1174–1263
Early Mamluk	1250–1401
Late Mamluk	1401–1516
Ottoman	1516–1918
MODERN	**1918–PRESENT**

10,000–8000 BC. NATUFIAN CULTURE.

Natufian culture is significant to the study of anthropology and archaeology for it provides evidence:

- of the beginning of agriculture, humanity's first attempts to harness nature. The presence of sickles demonstrates that humans here were making the transition from food collecting to food producing. Two complete limestone mortars and fragments of basalt pestles found at one site provide evidence that humans were learning to cultivate and store grain, an initial step toward urban living;

- of religious thought. Natufian people were obviously aware of the mystery of death and seemed to believe in life after death, for they buried their dead in fetal positions, with limestone "pillows" beneath their heads and useful objects at their feet;
- of domestication of animals. Some Natufian sites reveal evidence that wild goats, pigs, and oxen were penned or tamed.

9000–2000 BC. Pre-Biblical Period.

The oldest known communities on the earth were in the Holy Land. These include Damascus and the West Bank city of Jericho, where an urban center developed around 8300 BC.

6000. A settlement is established at Ugarit, on the coast of Syria. Ugarit is one of the oldest sites in the world.

3100. Mari. This site was the most westerly of the Sumerian states and an important stop on the trade route between the Persian Gulf and the Mediterranean.

2400–2250. Ebla. This site in ancient Syria served as a major commercial center at this time. It was destroyed by the famous Sargon of Akkad and his grandson Aram-Sin (2300–2250).

2000. Baalbek settled by the Phoenicians. Excavations reveal that this site had been inhabited for hundreds of years before its settlement.

2000: Biblical (Hebraic) Period begins.

1900. A wave of immigrants known as the Hyksos entered the Near East at this time. They began moving southward, erecting fortifications as power bases for invasions of Egypt.

1850–1700. Traditional dating of the Patriarchal Period, the age of Abraham, Isaac, and Jacob.

1800–1650. The city of Hazor is greatly enlarged. The city walls enclosed an area of 180 acres, making it the largest enclosed city built during the biblical period.

1720–1570. Hyksos (Semitic foreigners) ruled Egypt.

1700. Mari destroyed by King Hammurabi, the compiler of the famous law code.

c.1650. Joseph in Egypt.

1600. Ebla destroyed by the Hittites.

1350–1330. The Amarna Letters provide a detailed account of this period of Egyptian domination in Canaan during the reign of Pharaoh Ahkenaton.

c. 1250. Moses led Hebrew slaves out of Egypt.

c. 1250–1200. Migration of Hebrews to Canaan.

c. 1200. Sea Peoples (Philistines) from Crete invaded southern Canaan. They occupied much of the region by 1050.

c. 1200. Ugarit was destroyed by the Sea Peoples.

1187. The attempted invasion of Egypt by the Sea Peoples.

c. 1025–1005. Saul ruled as first king in Israel.

c. 1005–965. David ruled over Israel.

c. 965–926. Solomon ruled over Israel.

c. 950. Solomon's Temple built in Jerusalem.

c. 926. Israel was divided into Israel (Northern Kingdom) and Judah (Southern Kingdom)

722. The Assyrians under Sargon II (721–705) captured Samaria and took Israel into captivity, thereby bringing the Northern Kingdom of Israel to an end.

701. Hezekiah's Tunnel, a 1,777-foot rock-cut tunnel under the city of Jerusalem, was built at a time when Jerusalem and the Kingdom of Judah were besieged by Assyrian forces.

605–562: BABYLONIAN PERIOD

586. Nebuchadnezzar destroyed Jerusalem and the Temple of Solomon and ended the Davidic dynasty. He took many of the inhabitants of the Southern Kingdom of Judah into captivity in Babylon.

586–538. Babylonian Exile.

539–332: Persian Period.

539. Babylon captured by Cyrus, king of Persia.

538. Cyrus issued an edict encouraging exiled Jews to return to Jerusalem.

520–515. Second Temple was constructed on the site of Solomon's temple.

c. 500. By this time the Arabian tribe of the Nabateans had established their capital at Sela ("the Rock"), known today by its Greek name, Petra.

333. The Battle of Issus. Alexander the Great defeated the forces of the Persian Darius III in the great battle for supremacy in Asia.

332–63: Hellenistic Period.

336–323. Alexander the Great conquered most of the known world, expanding Greek thought and culture.

333. Alexander the Great founded the city of Jerash.

323. Alexander the Great died. In the power struggle after Alexander's death, the part of his empire that included Israel changed hands at least five times in just over twenty years. Babylonia and Syria were ruled by the Seleucids, and Egypt by the Ptolemies.

305–280. Seleucus Nicator reigned over the Seleucid Empire. He founded Antioch on the Orontes, the most famous of sixteen cities named "Antioch" that he built in honor of his father, Antiochus. Seleucus, a Macedonian officer of Alexander the Great, was successor and ruler over most of Alexander's Asiatic empire. The Seleucid dynasty lasted 247 years, until the spread of the Roman Empire into the region in the first century BCE.

305. Israel came under Ptolemaic (Greek-Egyptian) rule.

c. 250. The Hebrew Torah became the first part of the Jewish Scriptures to be translated into Greek (Septuagint).

198. Israel came under Seleucid (Greek-Syrian) rule.

175–163. Antiochus IV, Epiphanes promoted Greek culture and attempted to Hellenize all Jews.

142–63. The Hasmonean Dynasty. The Maccabean uprising eventually led to a period of Jewish independence and autonomy under the Hasmoneans, to which the Maccabees belonged. During this period the community at Qumran began, from which came the Dead Sea Scrolls.

86–62. Aretas III ruled as Nabatean king at Petra. The theater at Petra was carved from the rock at this time, and the city is assumed to have taken on a Hellenistic aspect.

64. The Roman general Pompey brought the Seleucid Empire to an end and made Antioch the capital of the Roman province of Syria.

63 BCE–324 CE: Roman Period.

63. Pompey, the Roman general, brought the Hasmonean Dynasty to an end with the capitulation of Jerusalem. Pompey made the region part of the Roman Empire.

40–4. Herod the Great ruled as a vassal of Rome. He built the port city of Caesarea and greatly enlarged the temple in Jerusalem.

15. Baalbeck's golden age began when the Roman emperor Augustus constructed the great Temple of Jupiter, the single largest religious edifice ever erected by the Romans.

9 BCE–40 CE. Aretas IV ruled as Nabatean king at Petra. Some of the rock-cut tombs date to this period.

6 BCE–100 CE. New Testament Period.

c. 6 BCE. Jesus was born in Judea.

CE

27–30. Ministry of Jesus of Nazareth.

26–36. Pontius Pilate served as Roman governor of Judea.

30. Crucifixion of Jesus. First Christian community formed in Jerusalem on the Day of Pentecost.

33. St. Paul is converted to Christianity while en route to Damascus to persecute Christians.

46–58. Paul's missionary journeys.

46–48. Paul's First Missionary Journey. Christianity expanded to Asia Minor.

49. Jerusalem Council.

49–53. Paul's Second Missionary Journey. Christianity expanded to Europe.

54–58. Paul's Third Missionary Journey. Paul spent three years in Ephesus during this period. During his third journey he wrote epistles to Corinth and Rome.

54–68. Emperor Nero's reign.

58. Paul's arrest in Jerusalem.

64. Nero blamed the great fire in Rome on Christians; local persecutions follow.

66–70. First Jewish revolt against Rome.

c. 68. Martyrdom of Peter and Paul in Rome.

70. Roman armies under Titus, son of Vespasian, sacked Jerusalem and destroyed the Temple. End of Second Temple period in Judaism. Nearly one hundred thousand Jews were captured and taken to Rome in chains.

73. Fall of the mountain fortress of Masada, the final Jewish resistance against Rome.

c. 90. Jewish Council of Jamnia planned the reconstruction of Judaism and its survival after the destruction of Jerusalem.

96. Emperor Domitian instituted emperor worship. The epistles of John and Revelation are written in response to the ensuing crisis for Christians.

98. Death of John, last of the apostles.

100. End of the Christian Apostolic Period and start of the Patristic Period.

105. The Nabatean kingdom fell to the Romans, and Petra became the capital of the Roman province of Arabia. The native dynasty came to an end, but the city continued to flourish.

132–135. Second Jewish revolt against Rome. Emperor Hadrian rebuilt Jerusalem as a Roman city and called it Aelia Capitolina. He forbade Jews, under penalty of death, from entering the city. He also changed the name of the province from Judea to Syria Palestina "Syria of the Philistines." Henceforth, the region has been called Palestine.

135. The Roman Emperor Hadrian built a Temple of Venus over the traditional site of the hill of Golgotha in an attempt to claim the site for traditional Roman religion. This action provides evidence that the site was regarded as holy by Christians.

249–251. First major persecution of Christians under Emperor Decius.

256. Dura-Europos was conquered and destroyed by native Persians known as the Sassanids. The city is known today for its most celebrated remains, the world's oldest preserved synagogue. The reconstructed synagogue may be seen in the Damascus National Museum.

303. Persecution of Christians began under Emperor Diocletian.

313. Edict of Milan. Emperor Constantine legitimized Christianity with legal sanction.

324–640: BYZANTINE PERIOD.

Christianity spread rapidly after Constantinople (Byzantium) was made the capital of the eastern half of the Roman Empire.

324. Jerusalem passed into Christian hands. The city soon became a pilgrim and tourist center. The Byzantines felt that the Temple Mount should remain in ruins, as tangible evidence that Jesus' prophecy of the Temple's destruction had been fulfilled. The area around the Temple Mount became a residential quarter. The remains of over twenty Byzantine-period dwellings, comprising dozens of rooms, have been uncovered in the Ophel Archaeological Garden.

325. Council of Nicaea.

326. Excavation of the site of the crucifixion of Jesus began under the supervision of Macarius, Bishop of Jerusalem.

335. The basilica of Constantine, known as the Martyrium or the Church of the Anastasis, was formally dedicated, with an oration by Constantine's biographer, Eusebius, bishop of Caesarea.

451. Council of Chalcedon.

527–565. The monastery of St. Catherine's at the base of Mt. Sinai was built by order of Emperor Justinian I during this period.

570. Muhammad was born in Mecca.

c. 600. The mosaics at Madaba (in the modern state of Jordan) date from this period.

610. Muhammad received a divine visitation that resulted in the command, "Recite." The result of those recitations is the Qur'an, the Muslim Scripture.

622. The Hijrah. This event, the Muslim exodus from Mecca to Medina, marks the beginning of the Muslim calendar.

630–1174: Early Islamic Period.

632. The death of Muhammad. Abu Bakr was chosen as caliph.

633–643. Muslim armies conquered vast portions of the Fertile Crescent and the North African coast, including regions under Persian and Byzantine control.

634. The Muslims captured Damascus and made it the capital of the Umayyad dynasty.

637. Jerusalem was captured by Muslim forces and it became Islam's third sacred city, next to Mecca and Medina.

661–750. Damascus was the seat of the Umayyad dynasty and of the caliphate.

680. The death of Husayn, Ali's son, marked the beginning of the Shi'at Ali ("party of Ali") or Shi'a sect.

688–691. The Dome of the Rock on the Temple Mount was built by Abd al-Malik.

709–715. Al-Aqsa Mosque on the Temple Mount was built by Umayyad Caliph al-Walid.

754. Baghdad became the capital of the Abbassid Empire.

1009. Fatimid Caliph Hakim ordered the destruction of the Church of the Holy Sepulcher. In Asia Minor thousands of Christian buildings were destroyed. These atrocities sparked the Crusades.

1017. The Druze religion was founded by an Egyptian chieftain who drew on a combination of messianic, Gnostic, and incarnational beliefs then current in the Ismaili sect of Islam.

1054. The Great Schism. The Latin Roman Church and the Greek Orthodox Church excommunicated each other.

1055. Seljuk Turks took Baghdad; the Abbasids remained as nominal rulers.

1071. Seljuk Turks defeated the Byzantines at the Battle of Manzikert.

1099–1291: Crusader Period.

1098–1099. The First Crusade. Christian Crusaders took Jerusalem in 1099 and formed the Latin Kingdom of Jerusalem. The Crusaders ruled Jerusalem from 1099–1187.

1149. The Crusaders completed a massive reconstruction of the Church of the Holy Sepulcher.

1171. Fatimid power in Egypt ended with the conquests of Saladin.

1187. Saladin gained control of Egypt, Syria, Mesopotamia, and Israel.

1187. The Battle of Hattin. At that historic engagement, Saladin defeated the Christian invaders, leading to the fall of the Crusader Kingdom of Jerusalem immediately thereafter. The Christians briefly controlled Jerusalem in 1229 and 1241.

1187. Acre (Akko) became the capital of the Crusader's Kingdom in the Holy Land.

1189–1192. The Third Crusade—a two-year war against the Crusaders under the English king Richard I "the Lion-Hearted"—resulted in a truce between the Muslims and the Crusaders. The Palestinian coast came under the control of the Christians and the interior under control of the Muslims; Christian pilgrims were allowed to enter Jerusalem, now under Muslim control.

1193. Death of Saladin. By this time most of the Crusader states had returned to Islamic control.

1204. Armies of the Fourth Crusade attacked Constantinople before moving on to the Holy Land.

1174–1918: Late Islamic Period.

1258. Mongols captured Baghdad. The caliph was killed and the Abbasid caliphate ended.

1453. The conquest of Constantinople by Ottoman Turks. Constantine XI, the last Byzantine emperor, led a force of four thousand troops and succeeded in holding off one hundred and sixty thousand advancing Turks for seven weeks. The city of Constantinople, all that remained of the Byzantine Empire, fell on May 29.

1517. The Turkish Ottoman Empire conquered Palestine and held it for four hundred years.

1537–1541. The impressive medieval walls surrounding the Old City of Jerusalem were erected by the Ottoman ruler Sultan Suleiman the Magnificent.

1838. The first accurate survey of Hezekiah's Tunnel was made by Edward Robinson.

1844. The famous Codex Sinaiticus was discovered here by the German scholar Constantine Tischendorf, who was touring the Middle East in search of old manuscripts.

1867. Charles Warren conducted the first major excavations of Jerusalem, thereby ushering in a new age of biblical archaeology. His most significant discovery was a water shaft, now known as Warren's Shaft, and a series of tunnels underneath the Temple Mount.

1874. Five local Jewish figures founded the ultra-Orthodox Jerusalem neighborhood of Mea Shearim. This settlement was one of the first urban communities outside the Old City walls.

1880. The Siloam Inscription, now located in the Istanbul Archaeology Museum, was discovered at the Siloam end of Hezekiah's Tunnel.

1883. General Charles Gordon identified the Garden Tomb and the hill in which the Garden Tomb is located as the place of crucifixion and burial of Jesus, rather than the traditional setting of those events within the Church of the Holy Sepulcher.

1909. The Jewish city of Tel Aviv was founded. It became the first city in modern times to be built, populated, and administered entirely by Jews.

1917. The port city of Aqaba was captured by the Arab armies under Faisal, the son of Hussein, Sharif of Mecca. Faisal, along with the legendary Lawrence of Arabia, was a leader of the Arab Revolt against the Ottoman Turks.

1917. Jerusalem was taken by the Allies in World War I under General Allenby.

1917. The Balfour Declaration. This declaration by the British indicated the need for a Jewish homeland in Palestine.

1918–Present: Modern Period.

1920. Syria and Lebanon came under French mandate rule.

1922. An emirate called Transjordan was created out of the desert regions east of the Jordan River, with Amman as its capital.

1933. Hitler became chancellor of Germany.

1935. The Nuremberg Laws reduced German Jews to second class citizens.

1939–1945. The Holocaust. The term refers to the unprecedented destruction of an estimated six million European Jews—one-third of all Jews then living in the world—conducted in virtually all areas of Nazi-occupied territory in what are now thirty-five separate European countries, and sent to labor camps in some countries or extermination camps in others.

1947–1956. The Dead Sea Scrolls were discovered in eleven caves near Khirbet Qumran, on the northwestern shores of the Dead Sea. The Dead Sea Scrolls are often considered the greatest archaeological find of the twentieth century.

1947. The United Nations adopted a Partition Plan whereby Palestine was to be partitioned between Israel and Jordan.

1948. The State of Israel was established, the British withdrew, and the Jewish-Arab war began.

1956. The Suez Crisis. When Egypt nationalized the Suez Canal, Israel attacked and occupied nearly all of the Sinai Peninsula.

1957. Yad Vashem Holocaust Memorial was opened to the public in Jerusalem.

1964. The Palestinian Liberation Organization (PLO) was organized to represent the Palestinian people.

1967. Six Day War. Israel captured large portions of territory formerly held by Arab nations, including the West Bank, the Golan Heights, the city of Old Jerusalem, and the revered Western (Wailing) Wall.

1973. The Yom Kippur War. The war began with a surprise joint attack of Israel by a coalition of Arab forces led by Egypt and Syria.

1978. The Camp David Accords led to normalized relations between Egypt and Israel, the first time any Arab nation had recognized the Israeli state.

1987–1993. The first Palestinian Intifada, a Palestinian uprising against Israeli rule. Hamas emerged as an offshoot of Egypt's Muslim Brotherhood, favoring the creation of a Palestinian nation on land that now includes Israel rather than the two-state solution long subscribed by the United Nations.

2000. Second Intifada, also known as al-Aqsa Intifada.

2006. The victory of the radical Islamic movement, Hamas in the Palestinian parliament elections threatened to reshape dramatically the Palestinian relations with Israel and the rest of the world.

Appendix F

CHRONOLOGY OF EGYPT'S HISTORY

Scholars disagree on the dates associated with the chronology of ancient Egypt. Since exact dates differ according to research results, all dates in Egyptian chronologies are therefore approximations. A century ago all dynasties were viewed to be sequential, whereas scholars now know that several existed at the same time. Confusion is also caused by co-regencies and other peculiarities.

Though dating events in Egyptian history is still a subject of research, scholars generally divide ancient Egyptian history (prior to the Roman period) into ten different periods (all dates are BCE):

PRE-DYNASTIC PERIOD (PRIOR TO 3100)

EARLY DYNASTIC PERIOD (3100–2686): FIRST AND SECOND DYNASTIES

OLD KINGDOM (2686–2181): THIRD THROUGH SIXTH DYNASTIES

FIRST INTERMEDIATE PERIOD (2181–2025): SEVENTH THROUGH TENTH DYNASTIES

>This was a period of decline. Princes ruled provinces and there were frequent civil wars.

MIDDLE KINGDOM (2125–1782): ELEVENTH AND TWELFTH DYNASTIES

>This was the classical period, in which art and architecture flourished. The capital of Egypt was moved to Thebes (modern Luxor and Karnak).

SECOND INTERMEDIATE PERIOD (1782–1550): THIRTEENTH THROUGH SEVENTEENTH DYNASTIES

>The Hyksos (Asiatic peoples, likely Semitic or Indo-Aryan) invaded Egypt and controlled it from their capital at Avaris in the Nile Delta. They introduced horses and chariots into Egypt.

New Kingdom (1550–1077): Eighteenth through Twentieth Dynasties

After the Hyksos were driven from Egypt, this was the age of Egypt's supreme power, expansion, and wealth. It was a period of temple building at Luxor, Karnak, Abu-Simbel, Abydos, and Memphis. Famous pharaohs reigned during this period, including Hatshepsut, Amenhotep III, Amenhotep IV (Akhnaton), Tutankhamon, and Ramses II. During this period elaborate tombs were hewn in the Valley of the Kings, and the *Book of the Dead* was written on papyrus.

Third Intermediate Period (1077–656): Twenty-first through Twenty-fifth Dynasties (also known as the Libyan Period).

The international prestige of Egypt declined considerably at this time.

Late Dynastic Period (664–343): Twenty-sixth through Thirtieth Dynasties

The Twenty-sixth Dynasty, also known as the Saite Period, lasted from 664 to 525. During this period Egypt was ruled by client kings established by the Assyrians, and Thebes was destroyed (c. 661 by Ashurbanipal, king of Assyria). The Persians ruled in Egypt from 525 to 404 BC (the First Persian Period) and again between 343 and 332 (the Second Persian Period). This period is also known as the Achaemenid Dynasty or the Thirty-first Dynasty. The Twenty-eighth through Thirtieth dynasties represent the last flowering of native Egyptian rulers.

Macedonian/Ptolemaic Period (332–30)

Alexander the Great, who conquered Egypt at age 24, founded and built Alexandria c. 332. After his death, the Ptolemaic dynasty ruled for 300 years. Cleopatra, the last ruler in the line, reigned from 51–30. In 30 BCE Cleopatra and Antony committed suicide. With their deaths, Egypt became a Roman province and lost its independent power in the ancient world.

Roman Period (30 BCE–395 CE)

42. Saint Mark founded the Patriarchate. Within a half century Christianity spread throughout Egypt. In the second century the Christian Scriptures were translated into the local language, today known as the Coptic language (which was the Egyptian language at the time). By the beginning of the third century CE Christians constituted the majority of Egypt's population and the Church of Alexandria was recognized as one of Christendom's four Apostolic Sees, second in honor only to the Church of Rome.

325. The Council of Nicaea. The most prominent figure of the council was Athanasius, the future patriarch of Alexandria, who played a central role in the formulation of the Nicene Creed.

Byzantine Period (395–641)

Arab Conquest (begins 641 CE)

648. Old Cairo (Al-Fustat) was founded near the old Egyptian capital of Memphis.

969. Al-Qahira (Cairo) was officially founded as an imperial capital and absorbed Fustat. That year marked the founding of al-Azhar Mosque, which was expanded in 988 to include a school of religion. Al-Azhar became the world's oldest university and an unrivaled institution for Islamic theological studies.

1171. Saladin established his rule in Egypt.

1250–1517. Slave soldiers (Mamluks) seized Egypt and ruled from Cairo until 1517, when they were defeated by the Ottomans.

1382. Cairo's bazaar (*souq*), Khan el-Khalili, dates to this period.

Modern Period (1517 to present).

Key political dates during this period include:

1517–1798. Egypt was a Turkish province of the Ottoman Empire.

1798–1801. Napoleon conquered Egypt in 1798, but France was forced by the British to withdraw in 1801.

1801–1805. Egypt was under British control.

1805–1952. This was the dynasty of the Albanian Muhammad Ali, and the last dynasty of Egypt.

1863–1879. Ismail Pasha, known as Ismail the Magnificent (1830–1895), ruled Egypt until he was removed at the behest of the British. This grandson of Muhammad Ali modernized Egypt but also put the country heavily in debt. He launched a vast railroad building project and greatly expanded Cairo, building an entire new city on its western edge modeled on Paris.

1882–1936. The British occupied Egypt.

1889. The Suez Canal was opened to navigation.

1953. Egypt became a republic after being ruled by foreign rulers for 2,800 years.

1954–1970. Gamal Abdel Nasser, the president of Egypt, was the moving force behind the creation of the United Arab Republic in 1958.

1967. Nasser's foreign and military policies were central in provoking the Six Day War against Israel.

1970–1981. The era of Anwar el-Sadat, president of Egypt.

1973. Egypt launched the Yom Kippur War with Israel

1978. Sadat and Israel's Prime Minister, Menachem Begin, signed the historic Camp David Accords. Throughout this period, U.S.–Egyptian relations steadily improved, and Egypt became one of America's largest recipients of foreign aid.

October 6, 1981. Sadat was assassinated by Islamic extremists.

1981–present. Hosni Mubarak is president of Egypt. The original election was subsequently confirmed by popular referendum for three additional six-year terms.

Appendix G

MASLOW'S HIERARCHY OF NEEDS

Maslow's hierarchy is often depicted as a pyramid consisting of five levels: the four lower ones associated with physiological needs, while the top level—termed self-actualization—is associated with psychological needs.

Deficiency needs—physical and emotional—have priority. Once these are met, growth needs drive personal development. The higher needs in this hierarchy come into focus only when the lower needs in the pyramid are satisfied. Once an individual has moved upwards to the next level, needs in the lower level are no longer prioritized. If a lower set of needs goes unmet, the individual temporarily re-prioritizes those needs by focusing attention on the unfulfilled needs, but will not permanently regress to the lower level.

Self-actualization

Maslow discovered that healthy individuals are motivated toward what he termed self-actualization, and noted that self-actualizing people had strikingly similar characteristics. The following descriptions have been compiled from the writings of Maslow and others:

1. *Clearer perception of reality.* Self-actualizing people perceive reality more effectively than others and are more comfortable with it. They have an accurate perception of what exists rather than a distortion of perception by their own needs, and they possess an ability to be objective about their own strengths, possibilities, and limitations. They judge experiences, people, and things correctly and efficiently, and have an unusual ability to detect the spurious, the fake, and the dishonest. They are not afraid of the unknown and can tolerate the doubt, uncertainty, and tentativeness accompanying the perception of the new and unfamiliar.

2. *Acceptance of self, others, and nature.* Self-actualizing persons are not ashamed or guilty about their human nature, with its shortcoming, imperfections, frailties, and weaknesses. They can accept their own human shortcomings, without condemnation. Nor are they critical of these aspects of other people. They respect and

esteem themselves and others. Moreover, they are honest, open, and genuine, without pose or façade. They are not, however, self-satisfied, but are concerned about discrepancies between what is and what might or should be in themselves, others, and society.

3. *Spontaneity*. Self-actualizing people are relatively spontaneous in their behavior, and are far more spontaneous than that in their inner life, thoughts, and impulses. Self-actualizing persons are not hampered by convention, but they do not flout it. They are not conformists, but neither are they anti-conformist for the sake of being so. They might act conventionally, but they seldom allow convention to keep them from doing anything they consider important or basic. They are not externally motivated or even goal-directed; rather their motivation is the internal one of growth and development, the actualization of themselves and their potentialities.

4. *Problem-centering*. Self-actualizing people have a problem-solving orientation toward life instead of an orientation centered on self. They are interested in solving problems, often including the problems of others. Solving these problems is often a key focus in their lives. They commonly have a mission in life, some problem outside themselves that enlists much of their energies. In general this mission is unselfish and is involved with the philosophical and the ethical.

5. *Detachment and the need for solitude*. Self-actualizing people enjoy solitude and privacy. It is often possible for them to remain above the battle, unruffled and undisturbed by that which upsets others. They may even appear to be asocial, an appearance possibly related to an abiding sense of security and self-sufficiency.

6. *Autonomy, independent of culture and environment*. Self-actualizing persons are not dependent for their main satisfactions on other people or culture or means-to-ends, or in general, on extrinsic satisfactions. Rather they are dependent for their own development and continued growth upon their own potentialities and latent resources. The meaning of their life is self-deciding, self-governing, and being active, responsible, self-disciplined persons rather than pawns ruled by others.

7. *Continued freshness of appreciation.* Self-actualizing people have a wonderful capacity to appreciate again and again the basic pleasures of life. They experience awe, pleasure, and wonder in their everyday world, such as nature, children, music, and sexual experience. They approach these basic experiences with awe, pleasure, wonder, and even ecstasy.

8. *The mystic experience, the oceanic feeling.* Self-actualizing people commonly have mystic or peak experiences or times of intense emotions in which they transcend self. During a peak experience, they experience feelings of ecstasy, awe, and wonder with feelings of limitless horizons opening up, feelings of unlimited power and at the same time feelings of being more helpless than ever before. The experience ends with the conviction that something extremely important and valuable has happened so that the person is to some extent transformed and strengthened by the experience, which has a carry-over effect into everyday life.

9. *Oneness with humanity.* Self-actualizing people have deep feelings of identification, sympathy, and affection for other people, and an empathy and compassion for human beings in general. These feelings are, in a sense, unconditional in that they exist together with the recognition of the existence in others of negative qualities that may provoke occasional anger, impatience, and disgust.

10. *Deep interpersonal relations.* Self-actualizing people have deeper and more profound inter-personal relationships than most adults, but not necessarily deeper than children have. They are capable of more closeness, greater love, more perfect identification, and more erasing of ego boundaries than other people would consider possible. One consequence is that self-actualized people have especially deep ties with rather few individuals, and their circle of friends is small. They tend to be kind or at least patient to almost everyone, yet they speak realistically and harshly of those whom they feel deserve it—especially the hypocritical, pretentious, pompous, or self-inflated individual.

11. *Democratic character structure.* Self-actualizing people are democratic in the deepest possible sense. They are friendly towards everyone regardless of class, education, political beliefs, race, or gender. They believe it is possible to learn something from every-

one. They are humble in the sense of being aware of how little they know in comparison with what could be known and what is known by others. They are ready and willing to learn from anyone. They respect everyone as a potential contributor to their knowledge, merely because everyone is a human being.

12. *Ethical means towards moral ends.* Self-actualizing persons are highly ethical. They clearly distinguish between means and ends, subordinating means to ends. Their notions of right and wrong and of good and evil are often not conventional.

13. *Philosophical, pleasant sense of humor.* Self-actualizing people have a keen, agreeable sense of humor. They don't laugh at jokes that hurt other people or are aimed at others' inferiority—unless following a convention. They can make fun of others in general—or of themselves—especially when they are foolish or try to be big when they are small. They are inclined towards thoughtful humor that elicits a smile, is intrinsic to the situation, and spontaneous.

14. *Creativity.* Self-actualizing people are highly imaginative and creative. Potentially inherent in everyone, this creativity is a fresh, naïve, and direct way of looking at things, rather similar to the universal creativity of unspoiled children.

Appendix H

JOHN CALVIN'S INFLUENCE ON THE PROTESTANT REFORMATION

Calvin's Geneva

In 1536, when Calvin first arrived in Geneva, he intended to stay a single night. Having broken with the Catholic Church approximately three years earlier, he had been forced to flee from Paris and then later from his home town of Noyon, where he was briefly imprisoned. He found refuge in the Swiss town of Basle, where in 1536 he published the first edition of his great work, *The Institutes of the Christian Religion*. The preface of the first edition, a letter to Francis I of France protesting his persecution of the Protestants, is a masterpiece of apologetic literature. After its publication, Calvin sought haven in Strasbourg, but warfare in the region of Lorraine forced him to travel by way of Geneva.

The Geneva to which Calvin came was a vigorous, liberty-loving city of some ten thousand inhabitants. It held high rank both as a commercial and ecclesiastical center, and its location at the crossroads of the great trade routes gave it strategic importance. The fires of political independence were burning strong from the recent successful attempt to overthrow the power of the bishop and the ruling House of Savoy. Under William Farel's leadership the small independent republic had recently become nominally Protestant. Its churches had been seized for Protestantism and its four monasteries and a nunnery closed. The Council in charge of political affairs had taken drastic measures to regulate private morals and to compel attendance at sermons. Despite these measures, Geneva's leaders were primarily motivated by political rather than religious consideration. In the city, which was a magnet for exiles and expatriates, the political climate was unpredictable. Because these were perilous times, Calvin wished to travel through Geneva incognito.

When Farel discovered that Calvin was in town, he went to meet him. Farel was then in the midst of a vigorous but unorganized attempt to establish the new Genevan Protestant church. The chaos of the situation required the touch of a master organizer, and Farel was quick to detect in Calvin the helper he needed. Calvin was reluctant to give up the prospect of a quiet life of study at Strasbourg, for he was by nature retiring and studious. But Farel pressed him into service with an argument that was almost an imprecation: "I denounce unto you, in the name of Almighty God, that if, under the pretext of prosecuting your studies, you refuse to labor with us in this work of the Lord, the Lord will curse you, as seeking yourself rather than Christ." Upon hearing these words, Calvin gave up his intended journey and thereby enlisted in the service of Geneva.

The city's moral standards at this time were not particularly high. The virtues of an aggressive, self-governing city were accompanied by all the vices characteristic of a wealthy, pleasure-loving, medieval town. Many inhabitants of the city did not wish to convert to Protestantism. Besides Catholic sympathizers there were many "Libertines"—freethinkers and free-livers—who found Protestantism irksome and were not disposed to make any concessions.

In this situation, Farel struggled to clean up the city and establish Protestantism upon a firm basis. He was a preacher of fiery eloquence but lacked organizing skills. Geneva needed a disciplinarian and an executive, and Calvin met the need, working at once along the two lines that were to dominate his future activity, the establishment of purity of doctrine and purity of living.

In Geneva, Calvin established a system of civic and ecclesiastical governance that rejected Papal authority and created a central hub from which Reformation theology could be propagated. Working with unusual dedication throughout his career, he neglected neither the priestly nor the prophetic duties of his office. Theodore Beza, his early biographer, estimates that Calvin preached 286 times a year, while also lecturing 180 times. His growing reputation brought people from far and near to Geneva in search of his advice, and he maintained a voluminous correspondence, of which four thousand letters remain. Any matter arising in one of the Reformed churches, of which there were a great many by this time, was almost certainly brought to his attention for settlement.

As Calvin advanced in years, he suffered great pain and discomfort from ulcers, kidney stones, and pulmonary hemorrhages, and began to show symptoms of tuberculosis. In the midst of such physical handicaps, Calvin kept up his work as long as he could, preaching when he was unable to walk and being carried to the pulpit in a chair. When his infirmities became such that he was confined to his room, he still kept up an extensive correspondence and continued giving advice to many. He felt that he could not lay down his work while God gave him strength. The day after his death he was buried like any humble citizen, in a plain wooden coffin and without ceremony. It was his own wish that his burial be modest, and that no stone should mark his final resting place. He lived, and died, a poor man.

Calvin was only fifty-five when he died. It is easy to speculate what he might have accomplished had he lived, as John Wesley did, for another thirty years of service. Yet it seems clear that his historic work was accomplished. As early as 1556 John Knox called Geneva "the most perfect school of Christ that ever was on earth since the days of the apostles." While such praise from Calvin's disciple and ardent admirer may be discounted, there is little doubt that by the time of Calvin's death, Geneva was morally the most upright city in Europe. The ecclesiastical system instituted by Calvin (known as the Ordonnances) and defended through many battles had become an established fact. The Genevan state had become a theocracy firmly established on the principles of Scripture, as Calvin understood them.

By 1564, Calvin's theological system, known subsequently as Calvinism or Reformed theology, was complete and embodied as well in his *Institutes*, a systematic presentation of Christian doctrine and life, and further developed in his many volumes of Bible commentary. In fact, his theology scarcely changed in content from that in the first publication of the *Institutes* in 1536, when he was only twenty-seven, though subsequent editions demonstrate a growing elaboration of argument and precision of form. During Calvin's lifetime the *Institutes* went through five editions, being successively revised and enlarged until it grew from six to eighty chapters.

Calvin's Academy

In addition to his pastoral duties, Calvin was a professor. All his life—in Paris, Strasbourg, and Geneva—he taught. On returning to Geneva in 1541, following a three-year exile, he began to teach regularly in the Church of St. Mary the Greater (called the Temple of the Auditorium, or Auditoire, ever since). It was there that the congregation met every Friday in an assembly attended by all the pastors. One of the pastors submitted a topic, and Calvin corrected or commented on what was said. In addition, he gave three theology lessons every week.

For a long time Calvin wished to set up a college—a municipal school system for all children—with the academy as the center of instruction for the very best students. Such a school had been founded in the fifteenth century, but no longer suited the requirements of the day. The establishment in 1559 of the academy, with Beza as rector of what soon became a full university, was Calvin's crowning achievement in the building of a Christian state. It provided free instruction for all grades from primary work through college. Though the need of preparing men for the ministry was an important reason for the establishment of the university, Calvin was also motivated by a profound desire to train an educated Protestant laity. Broadly educated himself, he attracted learned scholars to the school and helped elevate its reputation and extend its influence.

The endeavor flourished. Within five years the numbers had risen to over one thousand in the college and three hundred in the academy. The academy, which attracted students from all over Europe, served as a model for other academies around the world and eventually became the University of Geneva. Lest we think that Calvin was simply founding a university, we must keep in mind that he considered the crown of education to be theology, for which all arts and sciences were a preparation. Students were trained, not for degrees or lucrative employment, but to serve God as preachers or as godly civil servants.

When one examines the life of John Calvin, and the many demands upon his life as a cleric, one wonders how he found the time and energy for education, religious or secular. Yet it was such a priority that in his later years he is known to have taught ten hours a day, six days a week. Such an emphasis on education, however, is not really surprising. The humanism of the Renaissance stimulated unprecedented academic ferment and a concern for academic freedom. Earnest debates took place in the universities about the nature of the church and the source and extent of the authority of the papacy, of church councils, and of princes. The invention of the printing press, while making the Bible increasingly available to the general public, allowed quick broadcasting of ideas. Popular discontent at moral corruption in the church, coupled with the spread of nationalistic fervor, led support for a reformation as never before.

The Protestant Reformation, based upon concepts such as the priesthood of all believers, the importance of the individual conscience, and the supremacy of Scripture, made widespread literacy important.

Martin Luther, Calvin's predecessor in the Reformation movement, had borrowed from the humanists the sense of individualism—that persons can be their own priests—a notion that found popular support, due to the rapid rise of an educated urban middle class in northern Europe. Taking the Augustinian notion of salvation by faith alone to new levels, Luther argued that all individuals were personally responsible for their status before God and that mediation through any but Christ alone was unbiblical. Because Luther and other reformers saw these teachings as stemming from the Bible, they encouraged publication of the Bible in the vernacular and promoted universal education.

The Synod of Dort

During the seventeenth century, Calvinism became the predominant religious belief in the Low Countries. This dominance does not imply, however, that unity existed, for from the beginning bitter controversies between strict Calvinists and more permissive Protestants, known as Arminians, split the region. The Calvinists advocated predestination, while the Arminians, named after James Arminius, a professor of theology at the University of Leiden, championed freedom of conscience. Humanism had a longstanding foothold at Leiden and was partially responsible for a climate of tolerance in the Netherlands.

Arminius questioned the teachings of Calvin and his followers on a number of important points. A year after Arminius's death, his followers presented their views on five of these points in a document called The Remonstrance of 1610, and its proponents became known as Remonstrants. In this document and in later more explicit writings, the Arminians rejected the doctrine of predestination, especially that part of it known as reprobation (that humans are totally unable to save themselves). They held rather to a doctrine of partial depravity, which affirmed that, while human nature has been impaired by sin, the will is still free and able to accept or reject the grace of God.

Besides publicly challenging the doctrines of predestination, sin, and grace, as understood by the Calvinists, the Remonstrants indicated they were unsure of other doctrines, including original sin, justification by faith, the atonement, and even the deity of Christ. That some questioned Christ's deity contributed to the seriousness and bitterness of the controversy. After the death of Arminius in 1609 the drift toward Socinianism, a version of Unitarianism, became more pronounced.

As a result of this controversy, a strong sectarianism developed, which threatened to split the church and provinces of the Netherlands. The situation deteriorated until in 1617 it appeared that there might be civil war. That year the States General of the Netherlands decreed that a synod (a church assembly) should be called to settle the questions troubling the nation and to restore peace. Because the synod convened in the town of Dordrecht (thirty miles southwest of Utrecht), it came to be known as the Synod of Dort (Dort was a contemporary colloquial English term for Dordrecht).

The Synod of Dort (1618-1619) was one of the most remarkable and important gatherings of Protestant delegates ever assembled. It consisted of thirty-five pastors and a number of elders from the Dutch churches, five theological professors, eighteen deputies from the States General, and twenty-seven foreign delegates, including theologians from England. The problems facing the synod were complex, the first issue being the control of the church by the state. The Dutch church was by confession Calvinistic, following Calvin's conviction that the church should be independent of the state while cooperating with it. By 1554 he had won that battle in Geneva, but until the Synod of Dort, the Dutch church favored state control over the church. A second problem was the status of the creeds. The Arminian party, while admitting that the church was guided by its confessions, disliked confessional confinement and sought to have the creeds revised. A third problem, for which the synod is best known, concerned doctrine.

When the Synod of Dort met, the Remonstrants expected that they would be recognized as equals and that the synod would be a conference to discuss disputed questions. Instead, the synod summoned the Remonstrants to appear as defendants, and in due time their doctrines were condemned. The decision of the synod on the five main points of doctrine in dispute came to be known as the Canons of Dort, not intended as a comprehensive explanation of Reformed doctrine but only as an exposition of the five points of doctrine in dispute. The five points, commonly referred to as the "Five Points of Calvinism," are remembered by the mnemonic term TULIP: Total Depravity, Unconditional Election, Limited Atonement, Irresistible Grace, and Perseverance of the Saints.

The prestigious Synod of Dort set the course the Dutch church was to follow for centuries. It also influenced the British delegation on issues ranging from predestination and episcopacy to catechizing and Bible translation at a vital period in the emergence of an "Anglican" identity. The gathering served as an example for the Westminster Assembly held in Britain a generation later. Arminian theology later received official toleration by the Dutch government and has since thrived in various forms within Protestantism, including among Methodists, General Baptists, Seventh-day Adventists, Pentecostals, and charismatic Christians.

Appendix I

FLORENCE: CRADLE OF THE ITALIAN RENAISSANCE

The traditional date for the fall of the (Western) Roman Empire is September 4, 476. That event left Europe fractured and subject to rule by a line of German kings who called their domain the Holy Roman Empire. By the twelfth century, a loose collection of republics began taking shape in the Italian peninsula, where together they aimed to recover the glory of ancient Rome. Their efforts would revitalize Europe and provide a blueprint for the modern Western world.

The foundation of the Renaissance was the city. In the twelfth and thirteenth centuries, Italy witnessed the rebirth of the city, born from the system of feudalism. Within these newly liberated cities merchants, rather than the traditional aristocracy, emerged as leaders of this vibrant urban life in Italy. Lucrative possibilities existed in banking, insurance, trade, and most other activities that would come to be associated with a modern economy. This new style of existence was far removed from the life of the itinerant merchants of the early Middle Ages, traveling peddlers who simply toted their goods from fair to fair. Making new demands upon those who practiced it, this style of life required education—an education directed toward secular ends, not toward the service of the Church, to which almost all academic pursuit had been dedicated for a thousand years. But the real driving force behind the growth of secular learning was the demand for trained lawyers created by the sheer complexity of the new society. The study of the law, in turn, revived enthusiasm for Latin and Greek and the authors of classical times. The result was a phenomenon that came to be known as humanism.

In northern Italy, formerly small towns began building on a massive scale, always with an eye on their neighbors and on their own independence. One ambitious city, Siena, was located on an important trade route between France and Rome. North of Siena was Florence, the other dominant city in the region. These cities became rivals in every respect: culturally, politically, and economically. Initially Siena was superior, but in 1347, the bubonic plague arrived in Europe. Known as the Black Death, it became one of the greatest natural disasters the world had ever seen.

By 1553, it had killed an estimated one-third of the European population. In crowded cities such as Siena, the impact was most devastating. Siena lost over 60 percent of its population in a matter of months and the city would never be a major player again. Other Italian cities suffered similar fates: Milan lost almost half its inhabitants and Pisa lost three-quarters. Florence was hard struck as well; having a population of almost one hundred thousand people on the eve of the Black Death, it would take two centuries before its population would reach the fifty thousand mark again. It would take the region over a half century to recover, but the recovery would be unlike anything the world had ever seen.

For those who lived through the disaster, the net economic effects were actually beneficial. The plague destroyed humans but spared land, buildings, and other commercial assets, so that the gold lying in Florentine vaults was shared by far fewer people. In fact, the Black Death created a cash surplus that would help finance the expensive artistic display of the Renaissance. Though the plague returned at regular intervals to terrify the survivors for another three hundred years, Florence emerged in a class by itself. By the fifteenth century, Florence was perhaps the most glittering example of civic success. An effective sewage system drained into the Arno River, and an increasing number of houses possessed the luxury of an inside toilet. Fireplaces were becoming commonplace; torches provided a primitive form of street lighting, and the streets themselves were evenly paved with slabs of stone.

But something more than urban renewal was taking place. In the first thirty years of the century alone, thirty-four statues, all larger than life and executed with consummate skill, had been erected in the new squares and public buildings—all in the vicinity of the thirteenth-century Palazzo della Signoria, the fortress-palace where Florence's rulers took time off from politics to commission works of art. The Medicis of Florence, one of the wealthiest families in Italy, led the way to regaining the glory that was Rome. They would transform Florence into a new Athens.

The Piazza del Duomo

The Renaissance witnessed an explosion of new ideas, from some of the greatest minds of all times. It produced some of the finest works of art, architecture, and engineering the world has ever known. No other period of Western civilization can boast of producing so much genius.

Florence's gleaming new works were signs of political as well as artistic self-confidence. Commissioned in the course of a prolonged struggle with the dukes of Milan, they were a declaration of the city's faith in its own future. Art and architecture, as much as the gold in Florence's thirty-three banking houses, were clear demonstrations of civic power.

The centerpiece of this effort was a square at the heart of the city, the Piazza del Duomo, featuring the Baptistery of St. John and the cathedral itself, crowned with a magnificent dome, the largest of its day. The octagonal Baptistery, the city's oldest extant structure, dates from the eleventh through the thirteenth centuries. The shape symbolizes the "eighth day," associated with the Day of Resurrection and a symbol for eternal life given through baptism, when one passes to a new life with Christ. Until the end of the nineteenth century, all Florentines were baptized in this church.

In 1329, Andrea Pisano was commissioned to design the first set of doors for the Baptistery. The south doors (main doors) were originally installed on the east side, facing the Duomo, but transferred to their present location in 1452. The bronze casting and gilding was done by the Venetian Leonardo d'Avanzano, widely regarded as one of the best bronze smiths in Europe. The project took six years to complete. Consisting of twenty-eight panels, the twenty top panels of the door contain scenes from the life of John the Baptist and the eight lower panels depict virtues: three theological virtues (hope, faith, and charity) and five cardinal virtues (humility, fortitude, temperance, justice, and prudence).

In 1401, a competition was held to replace the bronze scenes of the north doors of the Baptistery. The winner was Lorenzo Ghiberti, a Florentine designer and goldsmith. Executed between 1403 and 1424, the commission necessitated the establishment of a large workshop in which many of the future masters of the Florentine school received their training. Ghiberti, now widely recognized as a celebrity and the top artist in this field, in 1425 gained a commission for the east doors, on which he toiled for twenty-seven years. These had ten panels depicting scenes from the Old Testament, each panel portraying multiple episodes. Ghiberti employed the recently discovered principles of perspective to give depth to his compositions. The doors themselves are still known by the name Michelangelo used in referring to them as fit to be the "Gates of Paradise." Giorgio Vasari described them a century later as "undeniably perfect in every way and must rank as the finest masterpiece ever created." The current gates are actually gilded bronze reproductions, placed there in 1990 after it was determined that the originals were deteriorating, and could be saved only if they were moved indoors. The originals are housed nearby in the Duomo museum, preserved in containers filled with nitrogen. One of the few original copies, made in the 1940s, is installed in San Francisco's Grace Cathedral.

The Florentines spared no expense in decorating the Baptistery's vast interior, cladding its walls in black and white marble inlaid with geometrical patterns. The mosaic marble pavement contains complex geometric patterns as well. Crowned by a magnificent mosaic ceiling, the mosaic cycle above the high altar depicts the Last Judgment with a gigantic Christ and angels of judgment at each side. At Christ's right hand the saved are depicted as leaving their tombs in joy, whereas at Christ's left hand the damned are depicted as receiving their punishment. This latter part is particularly famous: evildoers are burnt by fire, roasted on spits, crushed with stones, bitten by snakes, and gnawed and chewed by hideous beasts, reminding us of later works by the Flemish painter Hieronymus Bosch such as *The Last Judgment* or the panel *Hell*. Dante Alighieri was christened in this building and undoubtedly grew up looking at these mosaics and images of death and resurrection, which surely impacted him deeply.

In 1420, a competition was held to complete the Cathedral of Santa Maria del Fiore, known as the Duomo. Prosperous Florence wanted to surpass in grandeur its Tuscan rivals, Pisa and Siena, with a more magnificent church. The cathedral, however, lacked a dome. Building a dome for so large a structure involved one of the greatest engineering challenges Italy had ever seen, for it required constructing the largest dome in Christendom. The winner of the competition was the Venetian architect Filippo Brunelleschi. He had been a goldsmith when he placed second to Ghiberti in the 1401 competition, but after his failure in gaining that commission he went to Rome, where he spent two decades studying ancient Roman architecture. One structure in particular—the Pantheon—had a lasting influence on him, and he spent years examining every square inch of its dome, which spanned 142 feet. Although Brunelleschi was ridiculed when he proposed to build a dome for the Duomo without the use of flying buttresses or interior scaffolding, in 1436, after sixteen years of construction, he was vindicated, having completed the largest masonry dome in the world. In order to move the heavy material into place, vertically and horizontally at great heights, he invented elaborate wooden machines, including a clutch, a flywheel, and a crane. The final product, an ingenious dome within a dome, still stands, a remarkable tribute to this brilliant architect. The octagonal cupola, all but equaling the span of the Pantheon, measures 138 feet.

The modern mind has not yet come to grips with the setting of its own birth and the nature of its parent. Was the Renaissance a period or a movement, an evolution or a revolution, an economic phenomenon or spontaneous intellectual combustion? Only one thing is certain: Italy was the seedbed of the Renaissance and Florence its finest flower. Florence's artistic and literary movements inaugurated the Renaissance, altering the way the Western world thought and expressed itself.

Appendix J

THE SEVEN WONDERS OF THE ANCIENT WORLD

The ancient world has bequeathed to us seven particular monuments that have risen above the rest: the seven wonders of the ancient world. This list was primarily a Greek record, for all were part of the Greco-Roman world. The first complete list was probably compiled by Philo of Byzantium (c. 250 BC). Three features were paramount in their selection: size (all were large), great artistry, and great feats of engineering. For people who were traveling across the ancient known world, these were must-see places.

The idea of actually creating a list was conceived in the third century BCE, when Greece was ascending and on the warpath. The armies of Alexander the Great had marched across Persia and North Africa to India. As entire cultures fell before him, great buildings and cities sprang forth from a vision that Greece would dominate the world. As a body of monuments arose, the idea emerged to create a list of places that were truly unique. The list would highlight great Greek artistry and compare its greatest man-made achievements with those of areas they had recently conquered. Seven places were chosen, for the number seven represented perfection. Of the seven, five were Greek (or built by Greek artists and craftsmen) and two—the Great Pyramid of Giza (finished in 2560 BCE) and the Hanging Gardens of Babylon (600 BCE)—were much older.

Of the remaining five wonders, three were in Asia Minor—the Temple of Artemis in Ephesus (550 BCE), the Tomb of Mausolus in Halicarnassus (351 BCE), and the Colossus of Rhodes (280 BCE). The sixth wonder, the Great Statue of Zeus in Olympia (435 BCE), was on the Greek mainland, and the seventh wonder, the Lighthouse at Alexandria (280-250 BCE), was on the island of Pharos, at the mouth of the Nile River in Northern Egypt.

Appendix K

THE FOURTEEN STATIONS OF THE CROSS
(ROMAN CATHOLIC VERSION)

1. The place where Pontius Pilate's judgment hall (the Praetorium) once stood and where *Jesus was condemned to death* (Matthew 27:2–31). This is traditionally the site of the Antonia Fortress, which Herod built on the higher ground immediately overlooking the northwestern corner of the Temple Mount. Within the fortress Jesus was condemned, mocked, crowned, and given the cross to bear. The first station is now a boys' school, and the school stands on the ruins of the Antonia.

2. The place where *Jesus received the cross* (Matthew 27:28–32). Located opposite the Praetorium is the Franciscan Church of the Flagellation, standing on the traditional site where Jesus was scourged and a crown of thorns was placed on his head (John 19:1–2). Over the Via Dolorosa stands the Ecce Homo Arch, recalling the Latin words spoken by Pilate when he pointed to Jesus and said "Behold the Man" (John 19:5). A convent is located near the arch, which tradition says is built over the top of the Lithostrotos, the pavement of Pilate's courtyard where Jesus was condemned to death.

3. The place where *Jesus fell for the first time*.

4. The place where *Jesus met his mother*. This is marked by an Armenian Catholic church.

5. The place where *Simon the Cyrene was compelled to bear the cross of Jesus* (Matthew 27:32; Mark 15:21; Luke 23:26).

6. Recalls the tradition of *Saint Veronica wiping Jesus' face*. This is the house of the traditional Saint Veronica, who, after wiping the sweat and blood from Christ's forehead, is said to have found the imprint of Christ's facial features on the cloth.

7. The place where *Jesus fell the second time*. This is the location of the gate through which Jesus was led outside the city walls.

8. The place where *Jesus consoled the women* of Jerusalem (see Luke 23:27–32). The site is marked by the large Greek Orthodox Monastery of Saint Charalambos.

9. The place where *Jesus fell for the third time*. A Coptic Monastery of the Abyssinian Monks, which is built over the Helena Chapel of the church of the Holy Sepulcher, marks the site. The remaining stations may be found within the Church of the Holy Sepulcher:

10. The place where *Jesus was stripped of his garments and received gall to drink* (Matthew 27:34; Mark 15:23–24; Luke 23:34; John 19:23). This site is located behind the Roman Catholic altar.

11. The place where *Jesus was nailed to the cross* (Matthew 27:35; Mark 15:25; Luke 23:33; John 19:18). Golgotha, the rock of Calvary, may be seen under a glass in the Greek Orthodox chapel, which is built next to the Catholic chapel.

12. The place where *Jesus died on the cross* (Matthew 27:50; Mark 15:25, 37; Luke 23:46; John 19:30). This location is visible in the Greek Orthodox chapel, under the altar.

13. The place where *Jesus' body was taken down from the cross and given over to Mary*. The exact site, according to Catholic tradition, is under the Roman Catholic altar.

14. *The tomb of Jesus*, where he was laid and from there resurrected (Matthew 27:57–61; 28:1–10; Mark 15:42–16:8; Luke 23:50–24:8; John 19:38–20:31). The Holy Sepulcher marks the fourteenth station. The tomb is entered through the small Chapel of the Angel; a low door leads to the sepulchral chamber where a marble slab covers the location where Jesus was buried.

Appendix L

SITE PLAN FOR THE ACROPOLIS AT ATHENS AND ENVIRONS

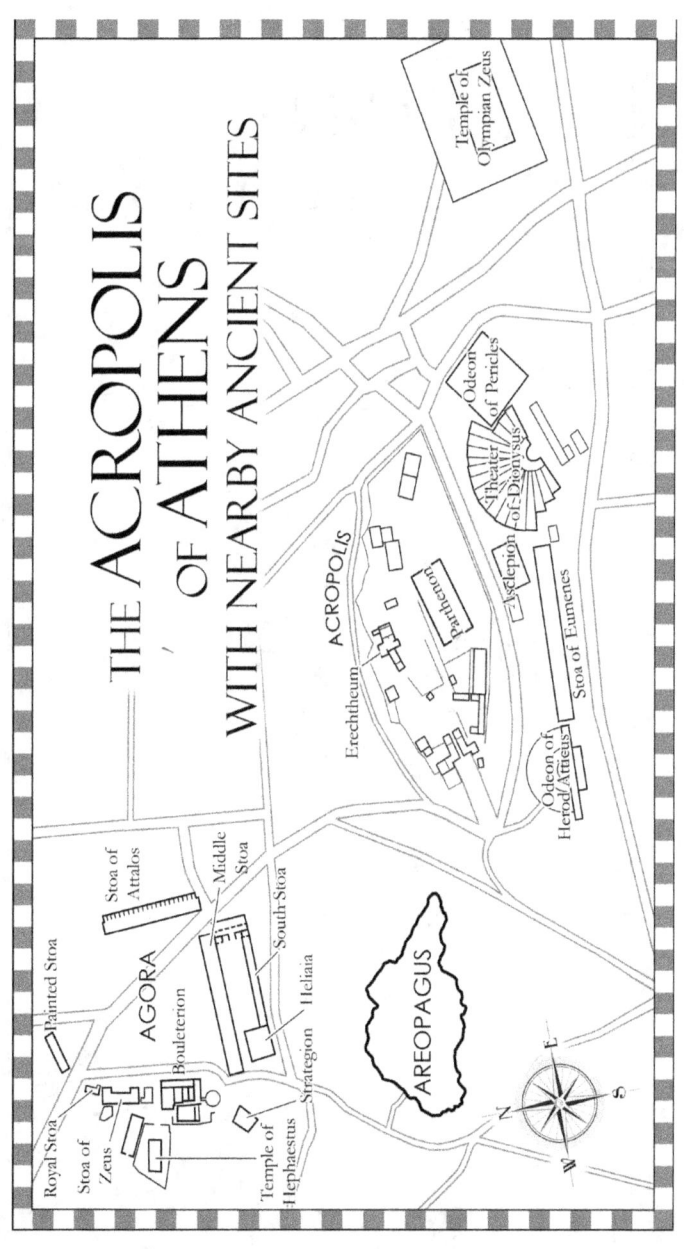

Appendix M

SITE PLAN FOR THE RUINS OF EPHESUS

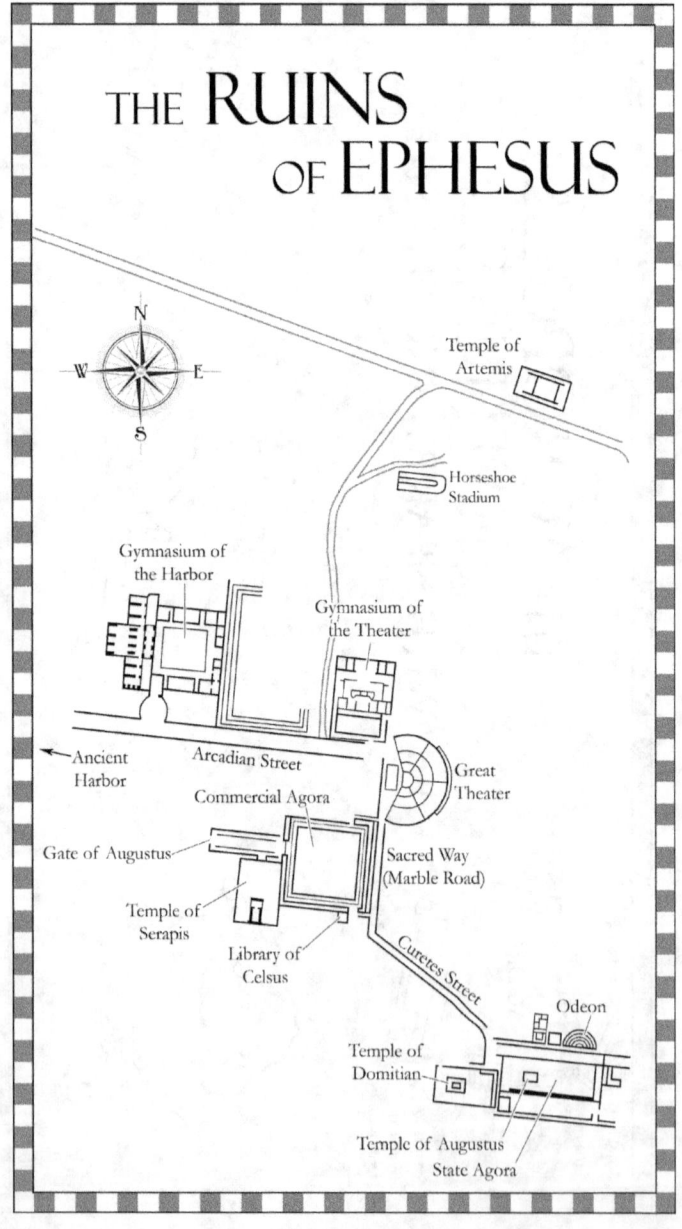

Appendix N

SITE PLAN FOR THE ARCHAEOLOGICAL SITE OF HATTUSA (BOGAZKOY)

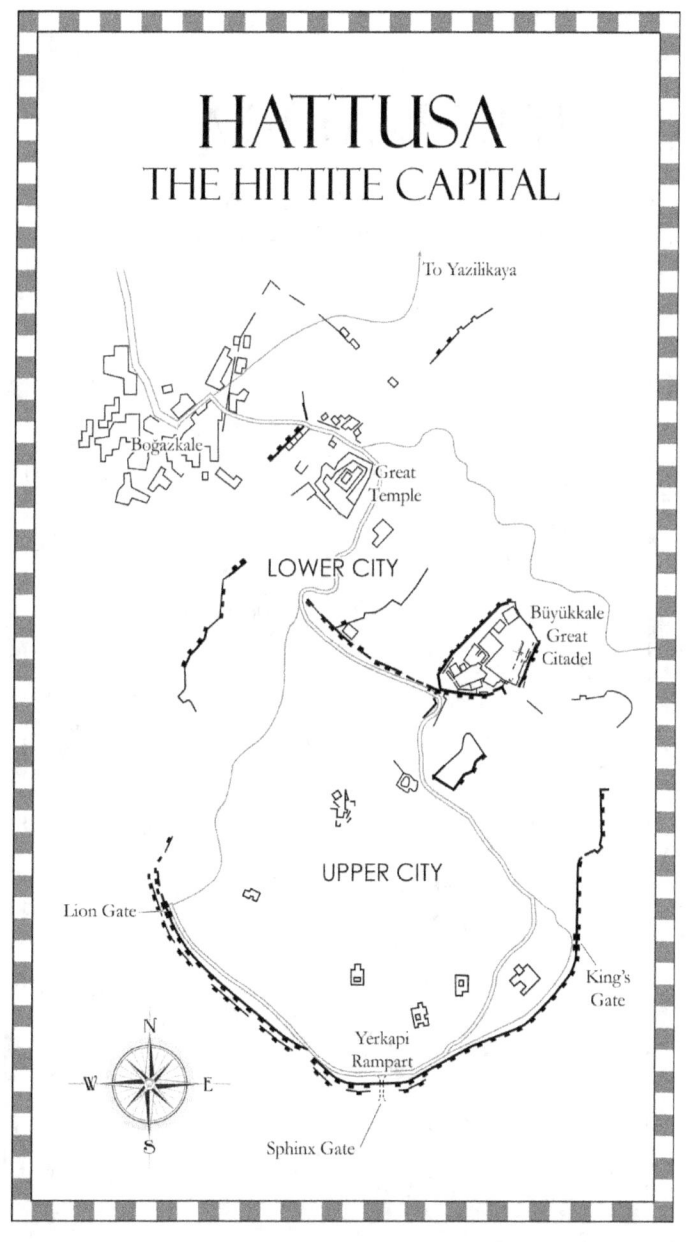

Appendix O

MAP OF OLD JERUSALEM AND ENVIRONS

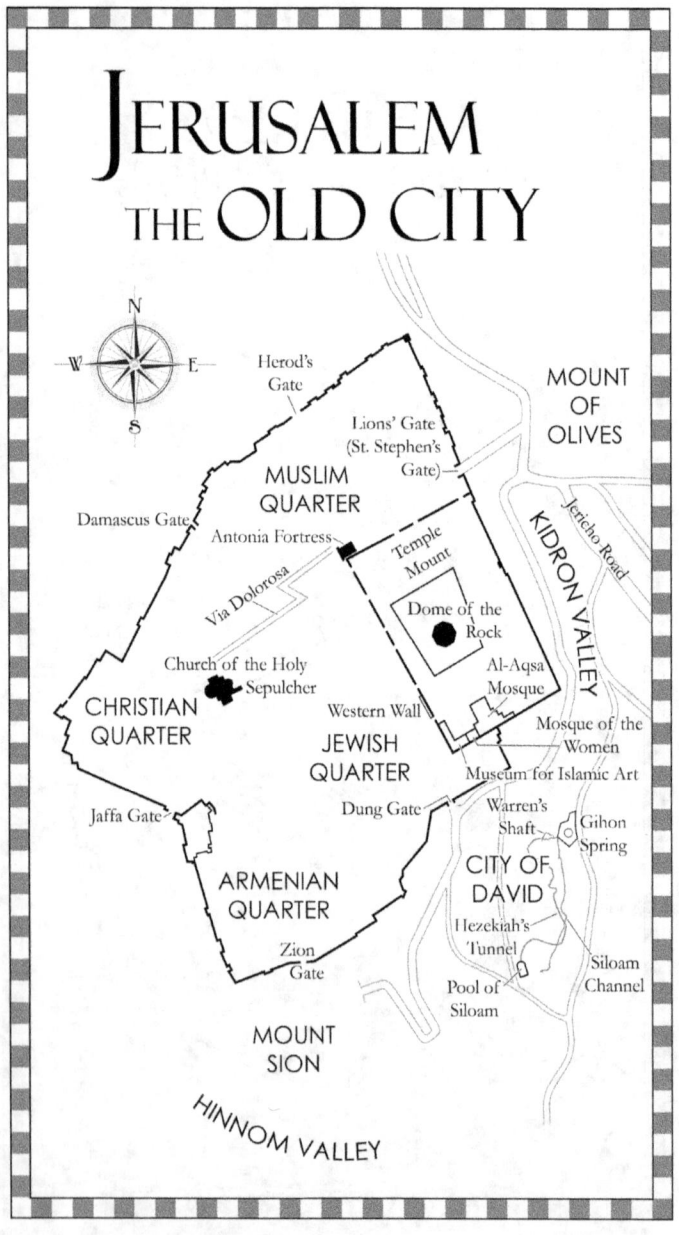

Appendix P

SITE PLAN FOR THE HERODIAN TEMPLE MOUNT IN JERUSALEM

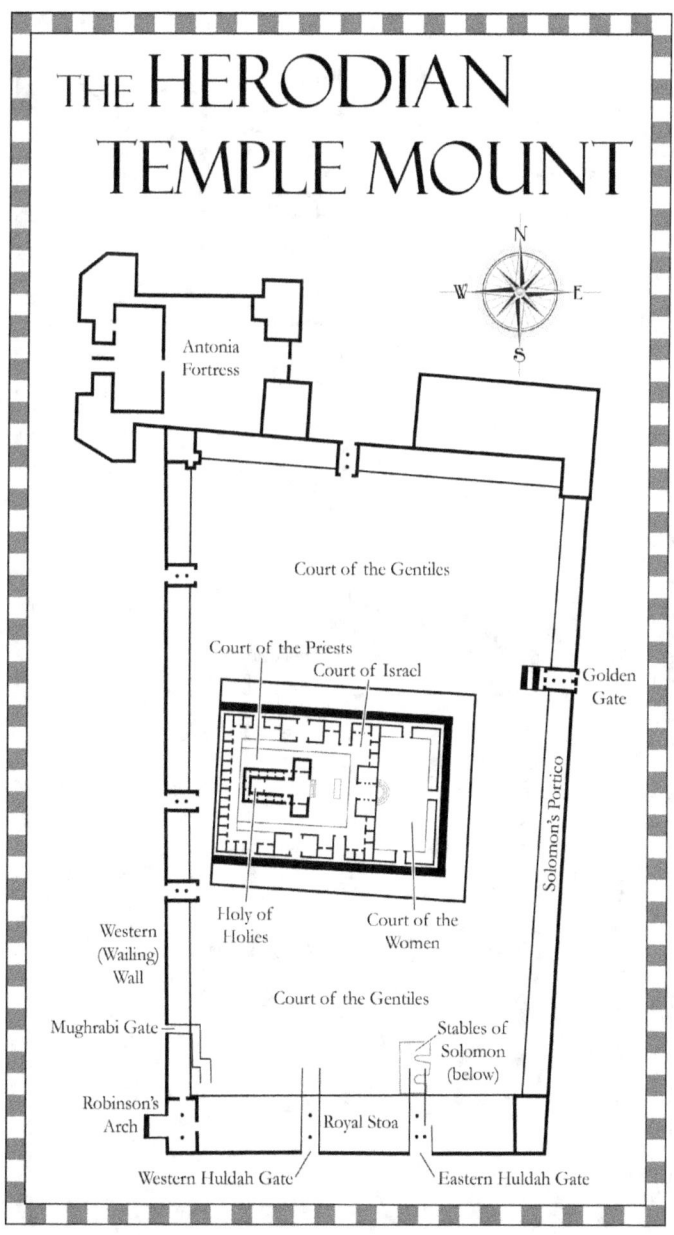

Appendix Q

FLOOR PLAN OF THE CHURCH OF THE HOLY SEPULCHER

Appendix R

MAP OF UPPER EGYPT (LUXOR, KARNAK, AND THE WEST BANK)

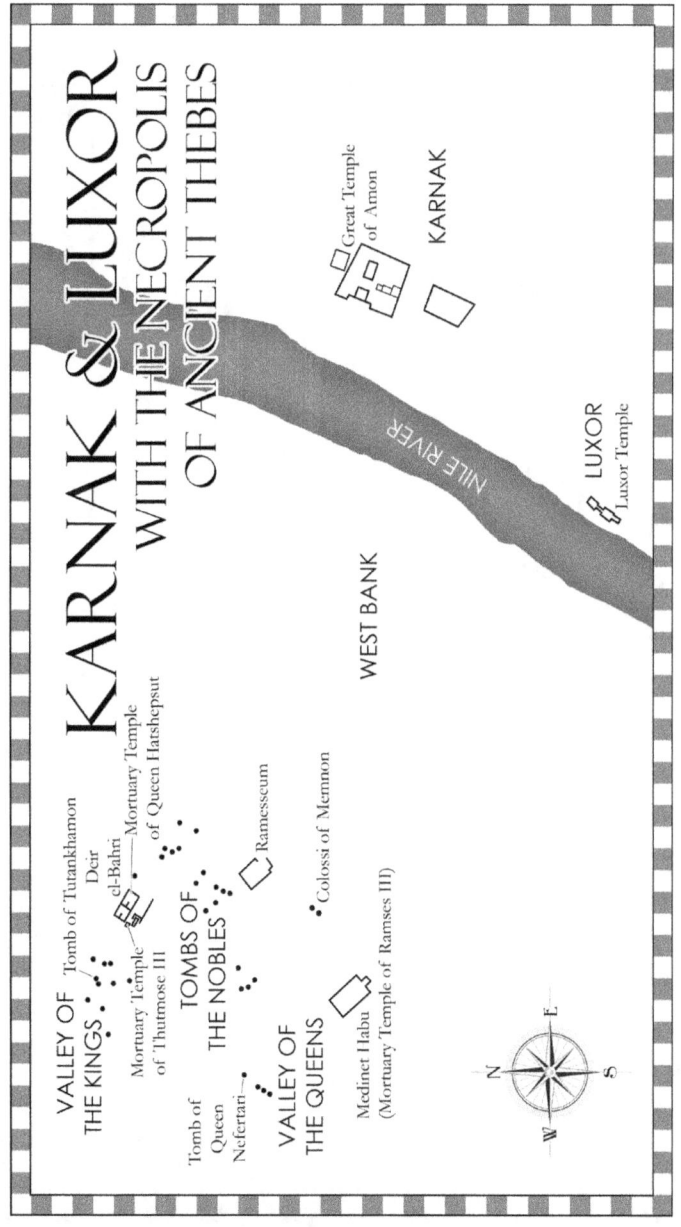

Selected Readings

BOOKS OF GENERAL INTEREST

Archaeological and Geographical Resources

Aharoni, Yohanan. *The Archaeology of the Land of Israel*. Translated by Anson F. Rainey. Philadelphia: Westminster, 1982.

Baly, Denis. *The Geography of the Bible*. 2nd ed. New York: Harper & Row, 1974.

Bean, George E. *Aegean Turkey: An Archaeological Guide*. New York, Frederick A. Praeger,1966.

Murphy-O'Connor, Jerome. *The Holy Land: An Oxford Archaeological Guide* (Oxford Archaeological Guides). 5th ed. Oxford: Oxford University Press, 2008.

Landay, Jerry. *Silent Cities, Sacred Stones*. New York: McCall's, 1971.

The Oxford Companion to Archaeology. Ed. by Brian Fagan. New York: Oxford University Press, 2004.

Whitley, James. *The Archaeology of Ancient Greece*. Cambridge World Archaeology Series. Cambridge: Cambridge University Press, 2001.

Cultural and Mythological Symbolism

Armstrong, Karen. *A Short History of Myth*. New York: Canongate, 2005.

Campbell, Joseph. *The Hero with a Thousand Faces*. Princeton: Princeton University Press, 1972.

———, with Bill Moyers. *The Power of Myth*. Edited by Betty Sue Flowers. New York: Doubleday, 1988.

Eliade, Mircea. *Cosmos and History: The Myth of the Eternal Return*. New York: Harper & Row, 1959.

———. *The Sacred and the Profane: The Nature of Religion*. Translated by Willard R. Trask. New York: Harvest/Harcourt Brace Jovanovich, 1957.

Holm, Jean, with John Bowker, eds. *Sacred Place*. London: Pinter, 1994.

Otto, Rudolph. *The Idea of the Holy*. Translated by John Harvey. Oxford: Oxford University Press, 1923.

Richer, Jean. *Sacred Geography of the Ancient Greeks*. Translated by Christine Rhone. Albany, NY: State University of New York Press, 1994.

Religious and Spiritual Studies

Arberry, R. J. *Religion in the Middle East*. Cambridge; Cambridge University Press, 1969.

Bowker, John. *The Religious Imagination and the Sense of God*. Oxford: Oxford University Press, 1978.

Chitty, D. J. *The Desert: A City*. Crestwood, NY: Saint Vladimir, 1966.

James, William. *The Varieties of Religious Experience*. New York: Macmillan, 1961.
Smith, Huston. *The World's Religions*. New York: HarperSanFrancisco, 1991.

Spiritual Ecology

Allison Jr., Dale C. *The Luminous Dusk: Finding God in the Deep, Still Places*. Grand Rapids, MI: Eerdmans, 2006
Dunn, Stephen, and Anne Lonergan. *Befriending the Earth*. Mystic, CT: Twenty-Third Publications, 1991.
Haught, John F. *The Promise of Nature*. Mahwah, NJ: Paulist, 1993.
McDaniel, Jay B. *Earth, Sky, Gods & Mortals*. Mystic, CT: Twenty-Third Publications, 1990.
Nasr, Seyyed Hossein, *Man and Nature: the Spiritual Crisis in Modern Man*. Chicago: ABC International, 1997 (1968).
Soelle, Dorothee, and Shirley A. Cloyes. *To Work and to Love: A Theology of Creation*. Philadelphia: Fortress, 1984.

Travel Narratives

Dalrymple, William. *From the Holy Mountain: A Journey among the Christians of the Middle East*. New York: Henry Holt and Company, 1998.
Feiler, Bruce. *Walking the Bible: A Journey by Land through the Five Books of Moses*. New York: W. Morrow, 2001.
———. *Where God Was Born: A Journey by Land to the Roots of Religion*. W. Morrow, 2005.

Travel Resources

Berrett, Lamar C. *Discovering the World of the Bible*. Nashville: Thomas Nelson, 1979.
Let's Go: The Budget Guide to Europe. New York: St. Martin. Revised annually.

CULTURAL AND HISTORICAL STUDIES

General Topics and Studies

Grant, Michael, ed. *Greece and Rome: The Birth of Western Civilization*. New York: Bonanza 1986.
Grant, Michael, and Rachel Kitzinger. *Civilization of the Ancient Mediterranean: Greece and Rome*. 3 vols. New York: Scribner, 1988.
Lewis, Bernard. *The Middle East: A Brief History of the Last 2,000 Years*. New York: Scribner, 1995.
TimeFrame (Time-Frame Series). 25 vols. Alexandria, VA: Time-Life, 1987–1990.
Yapp, M. E. *The Making of the Modern Near East*. London: Longman, 1987.

Anatolian Topics and Studies

Bryce, Trevor. *The Kingdom of the Hittites*. Oxford: Oxford University Press 1998.
Ergener, Resit. *Anatolia: Land of Mother Goddess*. Ankara: Hitit Publications, 1988.
Gurney, O. R. *Some Aspects of Hittite Religion*. Oxford: Oxford University Press, 1977.

Hansen, Esther Violet. *The Attalids of Pergamon.* 2nd rev. ed. Ithaca: Cornell University Press, 1971.
Lloyd, Seton. *Early Anatolia.* Baltimore: Penguin, 1958.
———. *Ancient Turkey: A Traveller's History of Anatolia.* Berkeley: University of California Press, 1989.

Arabic and Islamic Topics and Studies

Donner, Fred McGraw. *The Early Islamic Conquests.* Princeton: Princeton University Press, 1981.
Dunlop, D. M. *Arab Civilization to A.D. 1500.* London: Longman, 1971.
Fromkin, David. *A Peace to End All Peace: The Fall of the Ottoman Empire and the Creation of the Modern Middle East.* New York: Avon Books, 1989.
Hayes, John R., ed. *The Genius of Arab Civilization.* Oxford: Phaidon, 1975.
Hitti, Philip K. *History of the Arabs.* New York: St. Martin's, 1964.
Lewis, Bernard. *Islam and the Arab World: Faith, People, Culture.* New York, Knopf, 1976.
Lyons, M. C. and D. E. P. Jackson. *Saladin: The Politics of the Holy War.* Cambridge: Cambridge University Press, 1982.
Peters, F. E. *The Hajj: The Muslim Pilgrimage to Mecca and the Holy Places.* Princeton, NJ: Princeton University Press, 1994.
Schuon, Frithjof. *Understanding Islam.* New York: Penguin, 1972.

Arab-Israeli Studies

Abu-Amr, Ziad. *Islamic Fundamentalism in the West Bank and Gaza: Muslim Brotherhood and Islamic Jihad.* Bloomington: Indiana University Press, 1994.
Burrell, David, and Yehezekel Landau. *Voices from Jerusalem: Jews and Christians Reflect on the Holy Land.* New York: Paulist, 1992.
Carter, Jimmy. *The Blood of Abraham.* Boston: Houghton Mifflin, 1986.
Chacour, Elias. *Blood Brothers.* Old Tappan, NJ: Chosen Books, 1984.
Khalidid, Rashid. *Palestinian Identity: the Construction of Modern National Consciousness.* New York: Columbia University Press, 1997.
Kimmerling, Baruch and Joel S. Migdal. *Palestinians: The Making of a People.* Cambridge: Harvard University Press, 1995.
Lacquer, Walter, and Barry Rubin, eds. *The Israel-Arab Reader: A Documentary History of the Middle East Conflict.* 6th revised and updated ed. New York: Penguin, 2001.
Morris, Benny. *Righteous Victims: A History of the Zionist-Arab Conflict, 1881-1999.* London: John Murray, 1999.
Oz, Amos. *Israel, Palestine and Peace.* London: Vintage, 1994.
Ross, Dennis. *The Missing Peace: The Inside Story of the Fight for Middle East Peace.* New York: Farrar, Straus and Giroux, 2004.
Said, Edward. *The Question of Palestine.* New York: Vintage, 1992.

Byzantine Topics and Studies

Grabar, André. *The Golden Age of Justinian.* Transl. by Stuart Gilbert and James Emmons. New York: Odyssey, 1967.
Grant, Michael. *The Emperor Constantine.* London: Phoenix, 1998.
Kaegi, W. E., Jr. *Byzantium and the Early Islamic Conquests.* Cambridge: Cambridge University Press, 1992.

Lenski, Noel Emmanuel, ed. *The Cambridge Companion to the Age of Constantine.* Cambridge and New York: Cambridge University Press, 2006.
Maas, Michael, ed. *The Cambridge Companion to the Age of Justinian.* Cambridge: Cambridge University Press, 2005.
Mango, Cyril. *The Oxford History of Byzantium.* Oxford: Oxford University Press, 2002.
Norwich, John Julius. *Byzantium: The Apogee.* New York: Knopf, 1992.
———. *Byzantium: The Decline and Fall.* New York: Knopf, 1996.
———. *Byzantium: The Early Centuries.* New York: Knopf, 1989.
Rice, D. T. *Constantinople: From Byzantium to Istanbul.* New York: Stein and Day, 1965.

Canaanite Topics and Studies

Gray, John. *The Canaanites.* New York: Praeger, 1964.

Christian Topics and Studies

Chadwick, Henry. *The Circle and the Ellipse: Rival Concepts of Authority in the Early Church.* Oxford: Clarendon, 1959.
Hussey, J. M. *The Orthodox Church in the Byzantine Empire.* Oxford: Oxford University Press, 1986.
Krautheimer, R. *Three Christian Capitals: Topography and Politics.* Berkeley: University of California Press, 1982.
Pelikan, Jaroslav. *The Emergence of the Catholic Tradition (100-600).* Vol. 1, *The Christian Tradition: A History of the Development of Doctrine.* Chicago: University of Chicago Press, 1971.
———. *The Spirit of Eastern Christendom.* Vol. 2, *The Christian Tradition: A History of the Development of Doctrine.* Chicago: University of Chicago Press, 1974.
Stevenson, J. *The Catacombs.* London: Thames and Hudson, 1978.
Ware, Timothy. *The Orthodox Church.* New York: Penguin Books, 1986.

Crusader Topics and Studies

The Oxford Illustrated History of the Crusades, ed. by Jonathan Riley-Smith. Oxford: Oxford University Press, 1995.
Richard, Jean. *The Latin Kingdom of Jerusalem.* 2 vols. Oxford: North-Holland, 1979.
Riley-Smith, J. S. C., *The Crusades: A Short History.* London: Athlone, 1987.
Runciman, Steven. *A History of the Crusades.* 3 volumes. Cambridge: Cambridge University Press, 1951–54.

Egyptian Topics and Studies

Breasted, James H. *Development of Religion and Thought in Ancient Egypt.* New York: Harper and Brothers, 1959.
Frankfort, Henri. *Ancient Egyptian Religion: An Interpretation.* New York: Harper & Row, 1961.
Gardiner, Sir Alan. *Egypt of the Pharaohs: An Introduction.* New York: Oxford University Press, 1961.
James, T. G. H. *Ancient Egypt: The Land and Its Legacy.* Austin: University of Texas Press, 1988.
———. *An Introduction to Ancient Egypt.* New York: Harper & Row, 1990.

Greek Topics and Studies

Agard, Walter R. *The Greek Mind*. Princeton: D. Van Nostrand, 1957.
Brunschwig, Jacques, and Geoffrey E. R. Lloyd. *Greek Thought: A Guide to Classical Knowledge*. Cambridge: The Belknap Press of Harvard University Press, 2000.
Burkert, Walter. *Greek Religion*. Cambridge: Harvard University Press, 1985.
Cahill, Thomas. *Sailing the Wine-Dark Sea: Why the Greeks Matter*. New York: Doubleday, 2003.
Davies, John Kenyon. *Democracy and Classical Greece*. Cambridge, MA: Harvard University Press, 1993.
Hopper, R. J. *The Early Greeks*. New York: Harper & Row, 1976.
King, Helen. *Greek and Roman Medicine*. London: Bristol Classics Press, 2001.
Parke, Herbert W. *Festivals of the Athenians*. Ithaca: Cornell University Press, 1977.
Parke, Herbert W., and Donald C. W. Wormell. *History of the Delphic Oracle*. 2 vols. Cambridge: Blackwell, 1956 (1939).
Walbank, F. W. *The Hellenistic World*. Cambridge, MA: Harvard University Press, 1981.

Jewish Topics and Studies

Ariel, David. *The Mystic Quest: An Introduction to Jewish Mysticism*. Northvale, NJ: Jason Aronson, 1988.
Cahill, Thomas. *The Gifts of the Jews*. New York: Nan A. Talese, 1998.
Fackenheim, Emil L. *The Quest for Past and Future: Essays in Jewish Theology*. Bloomington, IN: Indiana University Press, 1968
Gilbert, Martin. *The Holocaust: The Jewish Tragedy*. London: Fontana, 1987.
Herzberg, Arthur. *The Zionist Idea*. New York: Jewish Publication Society, 1997 (1959).
Marrus, Michael. *The Holocaust in History*. New York: New American Library, 1989.
Wiesel, Elie. *Night*. New York: Bantam, 1982.

Ottoman Topics and Studies

Shaw, Stamford J. *History of the Ottoman Empire and Modern Turkey*. Cambridge: Cambridge University Press, 1976–77.

Roman Topics and Studies

Barrow, R. H. *The Romans*. Baltimore: Penguin Books, 1962.
Cunliffe, Barry W., Brian Brake, and Leonard von Matt. *Rome and Her Empire*. New York: McGraw Hill, 1978.
Dowden, Ken. *Religion and the Romans*. London: Bristol Classical Press, 1992.
Ferguson, John. *The Religions of the Roman Empire*. Ithaca: Cornell University Press, 1970.
Woolf, Greg. *Cambridge Illustrated History of the Roman World*. Cambridge and New York: Cambridge University Press, 2003.

BOOKS ON PARTICULAR PLACES AND REGIONS BY COUNTRY

Egypt

Baedeker's Egypt (Baedeker's Travel Guides). Baedeker, 2008.
Bernstein, Burton. *Sinai: The Great and Terrible Wilderness*. New York: Viking, 1979.
Edwards, I. E. S., C. J. Gadd, N. G. L. Hammond, and E. Sollberger. *The Pyramids of Egypt*. New York: Penguin, 1985.
Mendelssohn, Kurt. *The Riddle of the Pyramids*. New York: Praeger, 1974.
Nims, Charles F. *Thebes of the Pharaohs*. New York: Stein and Day, 1965.
Portman, Ian. *Luxor: A Guide to the Temples & Tombs of Ancient Thebes*. Cairo: The American University in Cairo Press, 1989.
Romer, John. *The Great Pyramid: Ancient Egypt Revisited*. Cambridge: Cambridge University Press, 2007.
———. *Valley of the Kings*. New York: Morrow, 1981.

Greece

Baedeker's Greece (Baedeker's Travel Guides). Baedeker, 2001.
Finley, M. I. *The Legacy of Greece*. New York: Oxford University Press, 1981.
Hamilton, Edith. *The Greek Way*. New York: Franklin Watts, 1958.

Israel

Armstrong, Karen. *Jerusalem: One City, Three Faiths*. New York: Ballantine, 1997.
Baedeker's Israel (Baedeker's Travel Guides). 3rd ed. Baedeker, 1995.
Coüasnon, Charles. *The Church of the Holy Sepulchre in Jerusalem*. London: OUP/British Academy, 1974.
Parrot, Andre. *The Temple of Jerusalem*. London: SCM Press, 1957.
Peters, F. E. *Jerusalem and Mecca: The Typology of the Holy City in the Near East* New York: New York University Press, 1986.
———. *The Distant Shrine: The Islamic Centuries in Jerusalem*. New York: AMS Press, 1993.
Ritmyer, Leen and Kathleen. *Secrets of Jerusalem's Temple Mount*. Washington, DC: Biblical Archaeology Society, 1998.
Uris, Jill and Leon. *Jerusalem, Song of Song*. New York: Bantam, 1985.

Italy

Baedeker's Italy (Baedeker's Travel Guides). 3rd ed. Baedeker, 1996.
De Franciscis, Alfonso. *The Buried Cities: Pompeii and Herculaneum*. London: Orbis, 1978.
Grant, Michael. *Cities of Vesuvius: Pompeii and Herculaneum*. New York: Macmillan, 1971.
———. *The Roman Forum*. New York: Macmillan, 1970.
———. *The World of Rome*. New York: New York Library, 1961.
Hibbert, Christopher. *Florence: The Biography of a City*. New York: W. W. Norton, 1993.

———. *Venice: the Biography of a City*. New York: W. W. Norton, 1985.
McDowell, Bart. *Inside the Vatican*. Washington, DC: National Geographic Society, 1991.
Norwich, John Julius. *A History of Venice*. New York: Random House, 1989.

Jordan

Taylor, Jane. *Petra*. London: Aurum, 1993.

Syria

Seale, Patrick. *Asad: The Struggle for the Middle East*. London: I. B. Tauris, 1988.
Tibawi, A. L. *A Modern History of Syria Including Lebanon and Palestine*. London: Macmillan, 1969.

Turkey

Baedeker's Turkey (Baedeker's Travel Guides). New York: Random House, 1999.
Bittel, Kurt. *Hattusha: The Capital of the Hittites*. New York: Oxford University Press, 1970.
Kostof, Spiro. *Caves of God: Cappadocia and Its Churches*. Oxford: Oxford University Press, 1972.
Lewis, Bernard. *The Emergence of Modern Turkey*. London: Oxford University Press, 1961.
Mitchell, Stephen. *Anatolia: Land, Men and Gods in Asia Minor*. New York: Oxford University Press, 1993.

BOOKS ON ART AND ARCHITECTURE

Akurgal, Ekrem. *The Art of the Hittites*. New York: Harry N. Abrams, 1962.
Alexander, Robert L. *The Sculptors of Yazilikaya*. Newark: University of Delaware Press, 1986.
Beckwith, John. *Early Christian and Byzantine Art*. New York: Penguin Viking, 1979.
Boardman, John. *The Parthenon and Its Sculptures*. Austin: University of Texas Press, 1985.
Goodenough, E. R. *Jewish Symbols in the Greco-Roman Period: Symbolism in the Dura Europos Synagogue*. New York: Pantheon, 1964.
Goodwin, Godfrey. *A History of Ottoman Architecture*. London: Thames and Hudson, 1971.
Kähler, Heinz. *Hagia Sophia*. Transl. by Ellyn Childs. New York: Praeger, 1967.
King, Ross. *Brunelleschi's Dome: How a Renaissance Genius Reinvented Architecture*. New York: Walker & Company, 2000.
———. *Michelangelo & the Pope's Ceiling*. New York: Walker & Co., 2003.
Krautheimer, R. *Early Christian and Byzantine Architecture*. 4th edition (Pelican History of Art). New Haven, CT: Yale University Press, 1992.
Kuran, Aptullah. *Sinan: The Grand Old Master of Ottoman Architecture*. Istanbul: Ada, 1987.
MacDonald, William L. *The Architecture of the Roman Empire*, 2 vols. New Haven: Yale University Press, 1982, 1986.

———. *The Pantheon: Design, Meaning and Progeny*. Cambridge, MA: Harvard University Press, 2002.

Mainstone, Rowland J. *Hagia Sophia: Architecture, Structure and Liturgy of Justinian's Great Church*. London: Thames & Hudson, 1997 (1988).

Smith, W. Stevenson. *The Art and Architecture of Ancient Egypt*. Second ed., revised by William Kelly Simpson. New York: Penguin Books, 1981.

Sherrard, Philip. *Constantinople: Iconography of a Sacred City*. London: Oxford University Press, 1965.

Wheeler, Mortimer. *Roman Art and Architecture*. New York: Praeger, 1964.

Woodford, Susan. *An Introduction to Greek Art*. London: Gerald Duckworth, 1986.

Scripture Index

OLD TESTAMENT (HEBREW SCRIPTURES)

Genesis

2:10–14	233
12:6–7	228
22:4	265
49	244

Exodus

3:5	207
19–24	151
20:4	186
24:14	208
28:15	244
33:22	208
34:29–30	64

Leviticus

18:24	179

Numbers

22–24	185
27:12–14	199 n. 1
34:5	286

Deuteronomy

11:26–32	228
12:3	100 n. 2
16:21–22	100 n. 2
23:17–18	179
27:11–13	228
32:49	199 n. 1
33:30	244
34:5–6	199 n. 1

Joshua

8:30–34	228
15:4	286

Judges

4:12–16	226

1 Samuel

13:20–22	328

2 Samuel

2:12–28	250
5:6–10	239
5:8	253
24:15–25	231

1 Kings

16:32–33	100 n. 2
18:17–46	217
18:19	100 n. 2
19:9–18	208

2 Kings

5:12	181
20:20	240
21:3	100 n. 2

1 Chronicles

11:6	253
22:1	231

2 Chronicles

3:1	231
32:10	240

Psalms

46:5	233
118:22	224
Isaiah	249
2:2–4	234
7:14	220, 221

NEW TESTAMENT

Matthew

5:3–10	216
6:2	42
17:1–3	226–27
21:33	250
25:40	37
27:2–31	375
27:28–32	375
27:32	375
27:34	376
27:35	376
27:50	376
27:57–61	376
28:1–10	376

Mark

1:15	322
9:2–8	206
15:21	375
15:23–24	376
15:25	376
15:37	376
15:42–16:8	376

Luke

6:20	42
23:26	375
23:27–32	376
23:33	376
23:34	376
23:46	376
23:50–24:8	376
24:5	277
24:13–35	250
24:28–30	251

John

4:20–23	229
6:68	36
17:23–26	37
19:1–2	375
19:5	375
19:18	376
19:23	376
19:30	376
19:38–20:31	376

Acts

1:1–42	255
1:13–14	255
9:1–31	209
9:9	183
9:10–18	190
11:25–26	166
13:1–4	167

13:9	167 n. 2
17:22–31	86
17:28	86
23:22–26	218

Romans

12:5	277

2 Corinthians

9:7	210

James

1:27	211
2:20	320

Revelation

2:13	124

QUR'AN

2.125	9
5.97	10

Subject/Name Index

Aaron, 208
Abbasids, 163
Abd al-Malik, Caliph, 236–37
Abraham, 173, 175, 181, 185, 244; sacrifice of Isaac, 265, 274; at Shechem (Nablus), 228
Abu Bakr, 235–36
Acre. *See* Akko
Acropolis, 85, 87–91, 95, 377; Acropolis Museum, 90
Adam, 8, 61, 229, 231, 233, 271, 274
Aelia Capitolina, 274
Aelius Aristides, 124
Aeneid, 152
Aeschylus, 82
Afghanistan, 149, 163, 164, 239
Agamemnon, 93
Agora (Athens), 85; (Ephesus), 115; (Pergamum), 120, 122
Ahab, King of Israel, 225
Akhenaton, Pharaoh, 293–97, 304
akitu ceremony, 157–58
Akko (Israel), 217, 218, 222–24, 251
Alaca Huyuk (Turkey), 148, 152
Aleppo. *See* Haleb
Alexander VI, Pope, 45, 60
Alexander the Great; Alexander Sarcophagus, 137; and Ankara, 145; battle of Issus, 167; conquests of, 101, 293, 374; death of, 120; and Delphi, 95, 98; legend of birth of, 113
Alexandria (Egypt), 38, 40, 120, 121, 122, 137. 287, 293; lighthouse of, 374
alijah, 267
Allison, Dale, 320
alphabet, 178, 184

Amarna (Egypt), 294–95, 296, 297
Amazons, 89
Amenhotep III, Pharaoh, 304
Amenhotep IV. *See* Akhenaton
Amman (Jordan), 180, 192, 193–94, 197–200
Ammonites, 198
Amon (Egyptian deity), 294, 304, 305, 308
Amphictyonic League, 98
Amsterdam, 17, 19, 25–26
Anastasis, Church, 271, 274. *See also* Holy Sepulcher, Church
Anat (Canaanite deity), 178
Anatolia, 144, 158, 166, 173, 184; cultural timeline, 146–49; definition, 108; Greco-Roman period, 152; Hittite rule, 136, 150, 152; matriarchal civilization, 108–11; Phrygian presence, 151–52; Seljuk Turks, 165–66
Angel, Chapel of the (Jerusalem), 276–80, 376
Ankara (Turkey), 144–46, 158, 159, 166
Anatolian Civilizations Museum, 146–49
Angel's Chapel (Jerusalem). *See* Angel, Chapel of
Annunciation, Church of the (Nazareth), 273
Antakya (Turkey), 104, 166–68
Antioch (Syria). *See* Antakya
Antonia Fortress, 270, 375
Anubis (Egyptian deity), 308 n. 3
Aphrodite (Venus), 100–101, 308 n. 3

Apollo (Olympian deity), 8, 76, 96, 98, 98 n. 1, 107; Temple of (Delphi), 75, 96
Appian Way (Italy), 68, 79
Aqaba (Jordan), 198, 203–4
Aqsa, al-, 236, 268
Arabia, 182, 198, 202, 235
Arabs; Anatolian presence, 167; civilization, 314; conquest of Philadelphia (Amman), 198; and Damascus, 182, 189; Israeli perspective, 213–14; Nabatean, 202; occupation of Madaba, 199; Umayyad dynasty, 183; West Bank (Palestine), 250. *See also* Arab-Israeli conflict
Arab Christian, 215
Arabic (language), 171, 181, 188, 290–91
Arab-Israeli conflict, 179–80, 194–97, 213–14, 215–17, 227–28, 256–58, 264–65, 285–86. *See also* peace in Middle East
Arafat, Yasser, 35, 257
Arameans, 182
archaeology, 377–83; at Acropolis, 87–91; at Akko, 222–24; at Amman, 198–99; at Baalbek, 191–92; at Caesarea, 218; at Cairo, 293–97; cultural timeline (Anatolia), 146–49; at Corinth, 102–3; at Damascus, 182–87; at Delphi, 98–100; at Ephesus, 114–16; at Gibeon, 251–52; at Giza, 299–302; at Hattusa, 153–58; at Hazor, 224–26; at Jerash, 199; at Jerusalem, 238–39, 247–50, 254–55, 262–69; Heinrich Schliemann, 93–94; Istanbul, 136–37; at Jebel Musa (Mt. Sinai), 208; at Pergamum, 120–25; at Petra, 200–203; at Pompeii, 74–77; at el Qubeiba (Emmaus), 251; at Roman Forum and the Palatine, 53–55; at Thebes, 304–5, 306–9; timeline of Mediterranean world, 325–29; at Ugarit, 178–79
architecture; at Acropolis (Athens), 87–91; at Agora (Athens), 85; at Akko, 222–24; at Amarna, 295; at Baalbek, 191–92; at Caesarea, 218; at Cappadocia, 159–60; at Coliseum, 65–66; at Corinth, 100–103; at Damascus, 185–86; at Delphi, 98–99; at Ephesus, 111–16; at Florence (Duomo), 43–44, 370–73; at Geneva (Old Town), 33; at Giza, 299–302; at Hattusa, 153–58; at Istanbul, 128–31, 132–36; at Naples, 73–74; at Pantheon (Rome), 53; at Pergamum, 120–25; at Petra, 200–202; at Piazza Navona (Rome), 62; at Pisa, 47–48; at Pompeii, 74–75; at Roman Forum, 53–55; Romanesque style, 46, 48, 274; at St. Peter's Basilica (Vatican), 56–59; at Temple Mount (Jerusalem), 236–41, 252–55, 264–69, 271–77; at Temple of Olympian Zeus (Athens), 85; at Thebes, 304–5, 306–9; at Venice (St. Mark's Square), 40–42. *See also* Seven Wonders
Areopagus (Athens), 85–86
Arish, el-, 286
Aristotle, 49
Ark of the Covenant, 269
Armenians, 167, 238, 239, 270, 272, 275
Arminians, 366–68
Arminius, James, 366
Armstrong, Karen, 4, 7, 233, 235
art; at Acropolis (Athens), 87–90; at Amarna (Egypt), 296–97; at Athens, 92–94; at Cappadocia, 160–62; catacombs, 67–69; at Delphi, 99–100; Dutch painters, 26; at Ephesus, 109–110; at Florence, 43–47, 370–73; at Geneva, 34–36; at Hattusa, 156–58; at Istanbul, 134–36,

Subject/Name Index

art – continued
140; at Madaba, 199–200; at Pergamum, 122–24; at Pompeii, 74–77; at Roman Forum, 55; in Solomon's Temple (Jerusalem), 232–34; in St. Peter's Basilica (Rome), 57–59; Sistine Chapel, 59–61; Vatican Grottoes, 69–70; at Venice, 40–42. *See also* Michelangelo
Artemis (Greek deity), 109–13; Temple of (Ephesus), 111–14
Artemision. *See* Artemis, Temple of
Ascension, 255
Asclepion (Athens), 90; (Pergamum), 121, 124–25
Asclepius (Greek deity), 55–56, 90; Temple of (Pergamum), 124
Asherah (Canaanite deity), 100, 178
Ashkelon (Israel), 248, 285
Ashurbanipal, King, 304
Asia Minor, 111, 113, 119, 139; definition, 106
Assad, Hafez al-, 180, 192
Assyria, 182; archaeological artifacts, 136; King Sennacherib and Jerusalem, 240, 252; presence in Canaan, 223, 225; presence in Egypt, 293, 304; trade, 189
Assyrian Colonies Period. *See* Old Assyrian State
Astarte (goddess of fertility), 100, 178
Aswan Dam (Egypt), 292
Ataturk, 106, 145, 174
Athena (Greek deity), 87, 88, 89, 110; Temple of Athena (Delphi), 99; (Pergamum), 121, 122
Athens (Greece), 83–94, 95, 101, 109, 121
Athos, Mount, 227
Atlantis, 93
Aton (Egyptian deity), 293–296
Attalids, 120–22
Auditoire de Calvin, 34, 364–66
Augustus, Emperor; and Caesarea (Judea), 218; imperial palace, 55; imperial forum, 65; island of Capri, 77–78; rebuilding of Corinth, 102; religious role, 54; successor of Caesar, 76; Temple of Jupiter (Baalbek)191;Temple of (Ephesus), 115
Augustine, 366
Azhar-al, 287, 290–91

Baal (Canaanite deity), 100, 178, 182, 217, 226
Baalbek (Lebanon), 135, 191–92; International Festival, 192
Bab, the, 218
Bab-es-Siq. *See* Siq
Babylon, 137, 225; *akitu* ceremony, 157–58; civilization, 182; Hanging Gardens, 111, 374; and Hittites, 150; Ishtar Gate, 137; Israelite exile, 265; siege of Jerusalem, 252
Baha'i, 217, 218–19
Baha'u'llah, 218–19
Balaam, 185
Balak, King of Moab185
Baldwin I, King of Jerusalem, 223, 274
Baptistery (Pisa), 48
Baptistery of St. John (Florence), 43, 46, 371–72
Bar Kokhba, 248
Barnabas, 166
Basil of Caesarea, Saint, 159, 161
Basilica of Holy Sion (Jerusalem). *See* Holy Sion, Basilica of
Battle of Marathon. *See* Marathon
bazaar, 146, 188–89, 261–62, 280–81, 290; Great Covered Bazaar, 131, 143
beatitudes. *See* Sermon on the Mount
Bedouin, 188, 193–94, 201, 202, 205, 207, 209, 211, 212, 261, 286
Beersheba (Israel), 212, 265
Begin, Menachim, 286
Beirut (Lebanon), 191
Bekaa Valley (Lebanon), 191
Bellarmine, Cardinal. *See* Urban VIII, Pope
Benedict XIV, Pope, 50

Subject/Name Index 399

Bergama (Turkey), 116, 119
Bernini, 58, 62
Berrett, LaMar, 191
Bethlehem (West Bank, Palestine), 273
Berry, Thomas, 317–18
Bet Alfa Synagogue, 186
Bet Shean (Israel), 227
Beza, Theodore, 363, 365
Bible; and Canaanite religions, 179; and geocentricism, 49; land of, 226, 250; and Mount Tabor, 226; Near Eastern cultural parallels, 184–85; and Shechem (Nablus), 228; and the Transfiguration, 226–27
Birth of Venus (Botticelli), 45–46
Blood Brothers (Chacour), 215–16
Blue Grotto (Capri), 73, 78
Blue Mosque (Istanbul), 132, 135–36
Bogazkale (Bogaskoy), 148, 153, 158
Book of the Dead, 307, 310
Bosporus Strait, 127, 132, 144, 149
Botticelli, 43, 45
Bourbons, 73
Brindisi (Italy), 74, 78–79
British Mandate Rule, 215
British Museum, 89, 90
Bronze Age, 148, 175, 252, 327–28
Brown, Dan, 63
Brunelleschi, Filippo, 372–73
Buddha, 2, 219
Burkhardt, Johann, 203
burial practices; in Anatolia, 147; in Egypt, 297, 299, 301, 306–8
Burning Bush, Chapel of the (Sinai), 205, 206
Buyukkale (Hattusa), 153, 155–56
Byron, Lord George, 62, 66, 73
Byzantines; Arab-Byzantine wars, 160; aristocracy, 129; architecture and art, 130, 134–35, 140, 160–62, 199–200; and Cappadocia, 160; and Constantinople, 127, 132; and Corinth, 101; coronation of emperors, 135; desecration of pagan sanctuaries, 89, 113–14, 123; and Ephesus, 111; and Jerusalem, 236–37; and Madaba, 199–200; and Petra, 202–3; and Seljuk Turks, 106, 160; Turkish conquest of Constantinople, 134. *See also* Justinian
Byzantium, 128, 163, 236, 237

Cabala, 224
Caesarea (Israel), 218
Caesarea (Turkey). *See* Kayseri
Cahill, Thomas, 211, 244–45
Cairo (Egypt), 206, 283, 287–92, 298–99, 304, 310, 312; pollution, 291–92
Caligula, Emperor, 57, 69
caliph, 132
caliphate, 106, 183
Callicrates, 87
Callixtus, Saint, 68
Calvary, 270, 271–80
Calvin, John, 34, 362–68; Academy (*see* Auditoire de Calvin);
Calvinism, 366–68
Campbell, Joseph, xvii, 1
Camp David Accords, 203, 286
Campo dei Miracoli (Pisa), 47–48
Canaanites, 175; Abrahamic Covenant, 228; Akko, 218, 223; Hazor, 225; religion of, 178–79, 226; and Sea Peoples, 151; southern boundary of, 286; Treaty of Kadesh, 151; Ugarit, 178; Warren's Shaft, 254
Capitoline Hill (Rome), 53
Cappadocia (Turkey), 159–62
Capri (Italy), 73, 77–78
Cardo (Jerusalem), 254
Carmel, Mount (Israel), 217, 218, 219, 226
Carmelites, 217
carpet shopping, 116–18
Carter, Jimmy, President, 180, 258 n. 7
Caruso, Enrico, 73
caryatids, 89–90
Castel Sant' Angelo, 63

Subject/Name Index

Castor and Pollux, Temple of (Rome), 54
catacombs, 67–69
Catal Huyuk (Turkey), 146–47
cathedra. *See* Peter, Saint, Throne of
Catherine, Saint, Monastery. *See* Saint Catherine's Monastery
Catholicon, 275, 276, 277
Catholicism. *See* Roman Catholicism
Cellini, Benvenuto, 43, 44
Celtic, 145
Center, the, xvii–xviii, 1–2, 8–12, 16. *See also omphalos*
Chacour, Elias, 215–17
Chagall, Marc, 243–44
Chalcolithic Age, 147–48, 327
Champollion, 288
Chartres Cathedral, 11–12
Cheops, Pharaoh. *See* Khufu
Chephren, Pharaoh. *See* Khafre
Chichén Itzá (Mexico), 5–6
Christ. *See* Jesus Christ
Christendom, 57, 275, 276, 372
Christians; early Jewish Christians, 249; and ecumenism, 35, 36, 37, 138; in Galatia, 145; and Islam, 139; and Jerusalem, xi–xii, 7–9, 199–200, 262, 264, 271–80; and Jewish views of the New Testament, 220–22; and Jews and Palestinians, 217; in Madaba, 199–200; and martyrdom, 57; and mysticism, 319–20; understanding of the sacrifice of Isaac, 265
Christianity; and Antioch (Syria), 166–67, 168; and conversion of Franks, 163; and Corinth, 103–4; and Constantinople, 128; and Damascus, 182, 189–90; and Ephesus, 111; and fundamentalism, 315–16; and Greece, 107; and Islam, 173; and liturgy, 175; and pagan temples, 114, 192; and Pax Romana, 79; and Petra, 202–3; and the sacramental dimension, 318–19; and science, 317–18; and the Transfiguration, 226–27; understanding of God, 316. *See also* Orthodoxy, Eastern; Protestantism; Reformation, Protestant; Reformed Christianity; Roman Catholicism
chronos, 36, 321
church councils, 111, 129
Church of the Holy Sepulcher. *See* Holy Sepulcher, Church of
Church of St. Savior in Chora. *See* Kariye Museum
Cilicia (Turkey), 151, 166
Cilician Gates, 149, 166
City of David. *See* Ophel
City of the Dead (Cairo), 291
Cleopatra, Queen, 122, 223, 293
codex, 122
Coliseum, 55, 64, 65–66
colonialism, 314
Copernicus and heliocentrism, 49–50
Conservative Judaism. *See* Jews, Conservative
Constantine, Emperor; and Constantinople, 128, 130; conversion to Christianity, 182, 273; and Ephesus 113; and Jerusalem, 273–74, 276; and sacred geography, 231; and St. Peter's Basilica, 57, 69
Constantinople, 111; aqueducts of, 128–29; conquest by Ottomans, 131, 139; founding of, 128; under Justinian, 129–30; Latin invasion and rule, 131; statue of Athena, 89
Constantius II, Emperor, 130
Coptic, 40, 272, 275, 289
Corinth (Greece), 97, 100–104
Corpus Juris Civilis, 129
cosmic symbolism, 232–34
covenant, 228
creeds, 367
Crete (Greece), 92–93, 104, 109
Croesus, King, 95, 96, 112

Crusades; and Acre, 222–24; and
Antakya, 168; castles and
citadels, 222; causes of, 164;
and the Church of the Holy
Sepulcher, 274–75, 276; and
Corinth, 101; and Damascus,
182; and Emmaus (el-Qubeiba),
251; First, 223; Fourth, 131;
and Petra, 203; and Saladin,
189, 223; Second, 223; and
St. George, 160; and Temple
Mount, 262, 264, 268; Third,
223
Cybele (Anatolian deity), 76, 108–9,
111, 186–87
cycling; Holland, 25; Switzerland, 30;
Turkey, 162; United States, xv,
16
Cyprus, 151
Cyrus, King, 96

Damascus (Syria), 166, 168, 173, 179,
180, 188–90, 192; antiquity
of, 179; historical overview,
181–83; house of Ananias, 190;
Umayyad Mosque, 189
Damascus Gate (Jerusalem), 229, 250,
262
Dante Alighieri, 43, 61, 372
Dardanelles, 127, 149
Darius III, King, 167
Dark Ages, 314, 315
David (Michelangelo), 44, 46–47, 64
David, King of Israel, 182, 196, 250;
defeat of Philistines, 184, 285;
and Jerusalem, 7, 225, 229, 238,
239, 253, 254; and Temple site,
231–32; tomb of, 255
da Vinci, Leonardo, 43
Day, Dorothy, 210
Dead Sea, 199, 200
Dead Sea Scrolls, 249–50
Debir. *See* Holy of Holies
Decalogue. *See* Mosaic Covenant
Decapolis, 198
Deir el-Bahri, 306, 308, 309
Delian League, 86–87

Delos (Greece), 104
Delphi (Greece), 4, 8, 9, 84, 96–100, 191
Delphic oracle, 8, 95–96
Demeter (Greek deity), 161,
186; Temple of Demeter
(Pergamum), 122
democracy, 81, 83
dervishes. *See* Mevlevi Dervishes
desert (wilderness), 211
Deuteronomy, Book of, 151
Diana, goddess. *See* Artemis
Diaspora, 195
Diocletian, Emperor, 161
Diolkos, 102
Dionysus, 76–77, 90, 109, 187
divination, 185
Divine Comedy, 61
divine right of kings, 128
Doges' Palace (Venice), 40–41
Dome of the Rock (Jerusalem), 232,
236–38, 264, 268–69
Domitian, Emperor, 62; Temple of
(Ephesus), 115–16
Dort. *See* Synod of Dort
Duomo (Florence), 43, 46, 372–73;
Piazza del Duomo (Florence),
370–73; (Pisa), 48
Dura-Europos, 185–87

Easter, 277
Eastern Orthodoxy. *See* Orthodoxy
Ebal, Mount, 228
Ecce Homo Arch (Jerusalem), 375
Eden, Garden of, 8, 181, 233, 237, 238
Edicule, 276, 277
Edom(ites), 201, 202
Egypt, 194, 200, 203, 283; ancient
Thebes, 182, 304; and Acre,
332; art of, 294–97; deities
of, 304–5; and funerary cult,
297, 307–8; hieroglyphics,
184; history of, 292–93; and
Hyksos, 225; Battle of Kadesh,
150; Treaty of Kadesh, 136, 151,
156; Lower, 292, 302; Mount
Sinai, 205–9; and Nabateans,
202; New Kingdom, 297, 306;

Egypt – continued
  Saint Onophrius, 161–62; Sinai
  Peninsula, 204, 211, 285–86;
  sphinxes, 155; Suez Canal,
  285, 286, 287; Upper, 292,
  302, 306, 307; Via Maris, 224;
  visit to, 285–311; West Bank
  temples and tombs, 307–9. *See
  also* Cairo; Egyptian Museum;
  pyramids
Egyptian Museum, 283, 290, 293–97
Eilat (Israel), 203, 206, 212
El (Canaanite deity), 178
El Arish (Egypt). *See* Arish, el- (Egypt)
Eliade, Mircea, 6–7
Elijah, 206, 208, 211, 217, 219, 227
Emmaus (Israel), 250–51
engineering. *See* Romans, engineering
Enlightenment, the, 314
Ephesus (Turkey), 104, 106, 107–8, 136;
  and Book of Revelation, 119;
  ruins of, 114–16, 199, 378. *See
  also* Artemis, Temple of
Erechtheum, 89–90
Esquiline Hill (Rome), 64
Essenes, 249–50
etrog, 186
Etruria (Etruscans), 6, 53, 67
Eumenes II, King, 90, 120, 122
Euphrates River, 182, 184, 293
Euripides, 82, 90
Eusebius, Bishop, 272, 274
Exodus, 136
Ezra, 252

Fackenheim, Emil, 246–47
faith journey, 320–21
Farel, William, 366–63
Fatah, 257, 258
Fertile Crescent, 175, 225
Fire. *See* Holy Fire
First Temple. *See* Temple of Solomon
Florence (Italy), 42–47, 49, 369–73
Forum (Rome), 41, 53–55, 65, 66
Fox, Matthew, 313
Franciscan, 226, 251, 255, 270, 275, 276
Francis of Assisi, 210, 217
Franks, 130, 163

French, 167, 180, 288
Freud, Sigmund, 4
Friesland (Netherlands), 22, 23
Frisian, 22, 23
fundamentalism, 221, 314–15

Gaia (Greek deity), 123
Galatians, 123, 145, 149
Galatians, Epistle to the, 145
Galen, 124
Galilee, 103, 186, 214, 215, 224–27; Sea
  of, 220, 223, 224, 226, 227
Galileo, 43, 47, 48–50
Galleria dell' Accademia (Florence),
  46–47
Galleria degli Uffizi (Florence), 45
Garden Tomb, 271–72
Gaul(s), 113, 130
Gaza (Palestine), 184, 194, 195, 197,
  202, 213, 235, 258, 285
Genesis, Book of, 61
Geneva (Switzerland), xi, 27, 31–37,
  311, 362–66, 367; Old Town,
  33–34
George, Saint; and the Dragon, 160–61
George, Saint, Church. *See* Saint
  George's Church (Istanbul)
Gerizim, Mount, 228, 229
Geschichte, 322
Gethsemane, 255
Gezer Calendar, 136–37
ghetto, Jewish (Rome), 56
Ghiberti, Lorenzo, 371–72
Gibeah (West Bank, Palestine), 250
Gibeon (West Bank, Palestine), 250,
  251
Gifts of the Jews (Cahill), 211, 244–45
Gihon, Spring of, 233, 239–42, 252–53
Gilboa, Mount, 227
Giza, pyramids, 287, 298, 299–302, 374.
  See also pyramids (Egypt)
God (Yahweh); in Baha'i belief, 219; in
  Christian belief, 277, 316–21;
  in Jewish belief, legend, and
  practice, 231–34, 244–45, 263;
  and the Holy Spirit, 322; and
  the Jewish Holocaust, 246,
  260; and Mount Sinai, 207–9,

Subject/Name Index   403

211; and Mount Tabor, 226; in Muslim belief and worship, 9–10, 234–35; in St. Paul's preaching, 86; and science, 316–17, 319
Golan Heights, 179, 213–14, 224
Golden Gate (Jerusalem), 269
Golden Horn (Istanbul), 127, 132, 136
Golgotha. *See* Calvary
Good Friday, 66, 131, 271
Gordion, 145, 146
Gordon, Charles, 271–72
Goreme (Turkey), 160, 161, 162
Goths, 111
Grand Canal (Venice), 39, 42
Greco-Roman paganism. *See* paganism
Great Covered Bazaar (Istanbul). *See* bazaar.
Great Revolt, 248, 254
Great Sphinx (Egypt), 299, 300, 301–2
Great Temple (Hattusa), 154
Great Theater (Ephesus), 114–15
Greece, 80–105, 106, 182, 202; the Acropolis and the age of Pericles, 86–91; and art, 91–94, 377; and civilization, 98, 123, 128, 148; Corinth in New Testament times, 103–4; crossing the Aegean Sea, 104–5; and gods, 122–24; heritage, 81–82; and language, 184; and Turks, 107; visit to Athens, 84–94; visit to Corinth, 100–104; visit to Delphi, 96–100. *See* The National Archaeological Museum
Great Mother. *See* Cybele
Gregorian University (Rome), 51, 52
Gregory the Great, Pope, 63

Habiru, 184–85, 296
Hadad (Canaanite deity), 137, 182; Temple of (Damascus), 182
Hadassah Hospital (Jerusalem), 243, 252
Hadrian, Emperor, 53, 55, 63, 85, 195, 270, 272

Hagia Sophia, 131, 132, 135, 140; construction under Justinian, 130; conversion to mosque, 134, 140; description, 134–35; original building, 130; and Temple of Artemis, 114, 135; and Temple of Jupiter (Baalbek), 135; visit to, 142
Haifa (Israel), 215, 217, 218–19, 222, 224
Hajj, 9–10
Halicarnassus (ancient Greek city), 136, 374
Halys River (Turkey), 96, 150
Hamas, 197, 258
Hammurabi, King, 150
Hannibal, 109
Haram al-Sharif, 264
Haran, 185
Hatay, 167
Hathor (Egyptian deity), 305, 308 n. 3
Hatshepsut, Queen (Pharaoh), 304, 306, 308–9
Hatti, 150
Hattusa, 146, 150, 153–58, 379
Haught, John F., 317–18
Hazor (Israel), 224–26
Hebrew (language), 260
Hebrew Scriptures. *See* Bible
Hebrew University, 216, 225, 248
Hebrews, 184, 185
Hebron, 224
Hekhal, 267
Helena, Queen (mother of Constantine), 205, 273; Chapel of, 276, 376
Helen of Troy, 110
Heliopolis. *See* Baalbek
Heliopolis (Egypt), 57, 287, 305
Helios (sun god), 186
Hellenes, 81
Hellenism, 152; and ancient Greece, 81; and Athens, 90; and Christianity, 222; and Ephesus, 114; Hellenistic art, 186–87; and Pergamum, 120–23
Hepat (Hittite deity), 157

Hephaestus, Temple of (Athens), 85
Hera, Temple of (Samos), 111
Herculaneum (Italy), 75
hermeneutics, 220–22
Hermes, Temple of (Ephesus), 115
Hermon, Mount, 182, 226, 227
Herod Antipas, 189
Herod Atticus, 84, 90
Herodotus, 95, 300
Herod the Great, 218, 223, 265–66
hero's adventure, 1–2, 281
Hezekiah, King of Judah, 240
Hezekiah's Tunnel, 136, 239–42, 252
hierarchy of needs, 3, 358
hijrah, 235
Hinnom Valley (Jerusalem), 238
Hippocrates of Cos, 124
Historie, 322
Hitler, Adolf, 246
Hittites, 182; and art, 146, 155–58; and Adana (Turkey), 167; and Ankara (Turkey), 145; history of, 149–52; religion of, 149–52; treaties, 151; Treaty of Kadesh, 136, 151, 156. *See also* Hattusa
Holland. *See* Netherlands
Holocaust, 245–47, 258, 260
Holocaust Museum (Jerusalem). *See* Yad Vashem
Holy Fire, 13, 277–80
Holy of Holies, 237, 269
Holy Land; and Crusades, 222–23; and Constantine, 273–74; and Madaba Map, 231; and ultra-Orthodox Jews, 260
Holy Land: An Oxford Archaeological Guide, 272
Holy Roman Empire, 369
Holy Saturday, 277–80
Holy Sepulcher Church, 9, 200, 236, 270, 271–80, 376, 382
Holy Sion, Basilica, 237
Holy Spirit, 58, 237, 255, 323
Holy Trinity, 208
Holy Week, 270
Homer, 82, 93, 119, 152, 304
Horns of Hattin, 189, 223, 227
Horus (Egyptian deity), 305

Hospitalers. *See* Knights of St. John
House of Livia (Rome), 55
House of the Vettii (Pompeii), 75
Hulda Gates, 263–64
humanism, 366, 369
human rights, 194–97, 214, 215, 258
Huns, 165
Hurva Synagogue (Jerusalem), 262
Hussein, King, 194, 203
Hygeia (Greek deity), 90
Hyksos, 225

icon, 227, 275, 277
iconoclastic, 34
iconostasis, 275
Iconium. *See* Konya (Turkey)
Ictinus, 87
Iliad (Homer), 82, 93, 152, 304
illumination, xviii, 2, 12, 281
immanence, 316
imperial cult, 116
incarnation, 221
Index of Prohibited Books, 50
Indiana Jones and the Last Crusade (film), 200
individualism, 365–66
Industrial Revolution, 314
Inquisition, 49–50
Institutes of the Christian Religion (Calvin), 362, 364
Interlaken (Switzerland), 27–30; Balmer's Hostel, 27–30
Intifada, 194, 197, 256–58, 265
Ionians, 80 n. 1, 106, 111, 122
Iraq, 180, 184, 235
Iron Age, 252, 329
Isaac, 186, 265
Ishtar. *See* Shaushga
Ishtar Gate (Babylon), 137
Isis (Egyptian deity), 76
Islam, xii; architecture of, 236–38, 289; art of, 186; hermeneutics of, 222; and Istanbul, 134; and Jerusalem, 234–38; and non-Muslims, 142; and "People of the Book," 139, 173; and relics, 133; and Rumi, 164–65; Seljuk Turks and Byzantium,

Subject/Name Index 405

160, 163–66; and Temple Mount, 189, 264–65, 268; and Turkey, 107; Umayyad Mosque (Damascus), 182–83, 189. *See also* Arab-Israeli conflict; sacred geography; *tawaf*
Islamic Jihad, 213
Ismail the Magnificent, 288
Israel, 182; ancient Israelite society, 184–85; archaeology of, 247–50; David, King, 184; Golan Heights, 179; stele, 294; tribal confederacy, 228; visit to, 212–81, 283. *See also* Arab-Israeli conflict; Israel Museum; Jebel Musa; Jerusalem; Mea Shearim; Promised Land; West Bank (Palestine)
Israel Museum (Jerusalem), 247–50
Israel Stone. *See* Merneptah, Pharaoh
Issus, Battle of, 167
Istanbul (Turkey), 127–43, 198; aqueduct system, 128–29; and Constantine, 128; description, 127; and ecumenical councils, 129; and Justinian, 114, 129–30; sack by Crusaders, 131; visit to, 127, 131–43. *See also* Istanbul Archaeological Museum; Constantinople; Hagia Sophia; Orthodoxy, Eastern; Topkapi Palace
Istanbul Archaeological Museum, 136–37
Ithaca (Greece), 82
Izmir. *See* Smyrna (Turkey)

Jacob, patriarch, 173, 175, 225, 229, 244
Jaffa Gate (Jerusalem), 239, 243, 261
Janiculum Hill (Rome), 52
janissary guards, 131, 132
Jebel Musa. *See* Sinai, Mount
Jebusite, 232, 238, 240, 253
Jerash, Gerasa (Jordan), 199
Jericho (Israel), 200, 248
Jericho Road, 239
Jeroboam, King of Israel, 228

Jerusalem (Israel), 4, 7, 137, 175, 225, 229, 230–81; Armenian Quarter, 238, 380; in Christian lore, 9, 331–44; Christian Quarter, 238, 269–80, 380; Crusades, 223; Hezekiah's Tunnel, 136, 239–42; history of, 230–31; Islamic expansion, 235–38; in Jewish lore, 8–9, 231–34; Jewish Quarter, 238, 252, 254, 262–63, 380; Madaba map of, 200, 231; model of, 248; mosques in, 182, 236–38; in Muslim lore, 234–35; Muslim Quarter, 229, 238, 270, 380; Old City of, 238–39, 252–54, 269–70, 380; pilgrimage to, 10–12, 163, 223; walls of, 238–39; West Jerusalem, 243–44. *See also* Aelia Capitolina; Church of the Holy Sepulcher; Israel Museum; Mea Shearim; Temple Mount; Yad Vashem
Jesus Christ, 2, 270, 277; in art, 61, 140, 275, 372; and Baha'i, 219; deity of, 366; and Isaac, 265; and Jerusalem, 7, 255, 264, 270–71; and John the Baptist, 189; and Judaism, 220–22; and Nabatean Arabs, 201, 202; resurrection of, 210. *See also* Emmaus; Sermon on the Mount; Transfiguration; Via Dolorosa
Jezreel Valley (Israel), 223
Jews, xii, 7, 79, 235; art of, 185–87, 243–44; and Christians, 220–22; Conservative, 259; and early Hebrew society, 184–85; in Holland, 20; and Islam, 139; Israelis, 213–14; and Palestinians, 194–97; Reform, 259; and Rome, 104; Sephardic, 224; slaves, 67, 103; wars, 67, 103, 248, 254, 256, 285–86. *See also* Arab-Israeli conflict; *Gifts of the Jews*; Holocaust; Israel Museum; Jerusalem; Judaica, Yad Vashem

jihad, 234
John Chrysostom, Saint, 142
John Paul II, Pope, 35, 50, 57 n. 2, 71, 247
John the Baptist, 182, 189, 371
Jordan (nation), 33, 193–204, 231
Jordan River, 197
Joseph, 225
Josephus, 254
Joshua, 228
Judah, 286
Judaica, 248
Judas, 210
Judea, 198
Judges (Israelite period), 226
Julius Caesar, 54, 55, 65, 76, 102, 122
Julian the Apostate, Emperor, 109
Julius II, Pope, 47, 60–61, 63, 64
Jung, Carl, xi, 4
Jupiter (Roman deity), 75, 182; Temple of Jupiter (Baalbek), 135, 191
Justinian, Emperor, 129–31; Hagia Sophia, 130, 134–35; and Jerusalem, 236, 237; Nike Revolt, 130; and St. Catherine's Monastery (Sinai), 205–6; plunder of the Temple of Artemis, 114. *See also* Corpus Juris Civilis
Juvenal, 304

Kaaba, 9–10, 237–38
Kadesh, Battle of, 150; Treaty of, 136, 151, 156
kairos, 36, 322
Karain Cave (Turkey), 146
Karnak (Egypt), 396, 307, 309, 383
Kariye Museum (Istanbul), 140
karum, 149
Kayseri (Turkey), 149, 159
Kay-Qubad, Ala al-din. *See* Keykubat
Kemal, Mustafa. *See* Ataturk
Kerak (Jordan), 199
Keykubat, 164
Khafre, Pharaoh, 299, 301, 302
Khalil, al-, Sultan, 223
Khan el-Khalili (Egypt), 290

Khazneh, el (the Treasury), 200–201
Khnum (Egyptian deity), 305
Khufu, Emperor, 299–302
kibbutz, 213
Kidron Valley (Jerusalem), 238, 239, 253, 266
Kingdom of Heaven, 11
King's Gate (Hattusa), 155
King's Highway, 198, 199
Kirshub (Hittite deity), 157
Knesset, 248
Knights of St. John, 223
Knox, John, 34, 364
Konya (Turkey), 146, 164
Kotel. *See* Western Wall
Kreeft, Peter, 13
Krepp, E.C., 157
Kukulkan (Meso-American deity), 5–6
Kultepe (Turkey), 149, 150
Kurds, 117, 167
Kusadasi (Turkey), 105, 107, 114
Kuttab, Jonathan, 258

labyrinth, xvii, 10–12, 269, 275–77
Lachish (Israel), 248
Last Day; Last Judgment, 140, 235, 238, 260, 269, 372
Last Judgment (Michaelangelo), 59, 61
Last Supper, 255
Latakia (Syria), 178, 179
Latin Rule, 131, 164; Latin Kingdom of Jerusalem, 189
Lawrence, T.E., 203
League of Nations, 33, 34
Lebanon, 167, 175, 180, 190–92, 222, 224
Leo IV, Pope, 57
Leto, goddess, 110
Levant, 175
Lewis, C.S., xvi–xvii
Library of Celsus (Ephesus), 115, 122
Likud, 196
Lion Gate (Hattusa), 155
lions, symbolic use, 155
Lithostrotos, 270, 375
Loggia dei Lanzi (Florence), 44
Lombards, 131

Subject/Name Index   407

Lord's Prayer, 273
Lot, 181
lulav, 186
Luther, Martin, 366
Luxor (Egypt), 305, 306, 310, 383
Lybia, 177
Lycurgus, 84, 95
Lydians, 95, 112, 120, 145, 152
Lysimachus, General, 120

Maccabees, 249
Macedonia, 80, 101, 113, 120
Machiavelli, 43
Madaba (Jordan), 199–200, 231
Magna Mater. See Cybele
Mahfouz, Naguib, 290
Mamluk, 239, 287
Man and Nature (Nasr), 314
Manzikert, Battle of, 160, 163, 166
Marathon, 98
Marco Polo, 224
Marduk (Babylonian deity), 137, 187
Mar Elias College, 217
Mari, 184–85, 187
Mark, Saint, 40–41; Basilica (Venice), 41–42; Square (Venice), 39–42
Marmara, Sea of, 127, 132, 133
Marmaria (Delphi), 99
Mars (Roman deity), 46, 85
Mars' Hill. See Areopagus
Martyrion. See Church of the Holy Sepulcher
Mary. See Virgin Mary
Masada (Israel), 89, 249
Maslow, Abraham, 3, 358–61
matriarchal civilization, 108–11, 147, 161–62
Mausolus, Tomb of, 111, 136, 374
Mea Shearim (Jerusalem), 259–60
Mecca, 4, 7, 9–10, 136, 165, 182, 202, 234, 237, 238
Medicis, 43, 370; Grand Duke Cosimo, 49; Lorenzo, 43, 46
Medina (Saudi Arabia), 182
Medinet Habu, 306, 308
Medjugorje (Bosnia-Herzegovina), 29–30

Medusa, 44, 161
Megiddo (Israel), 248
Mehmed II, Sultan, 139, 142
Melkite Greek Catholic Church, 215
Memphis (Egypt), 287, 304, 305
Menkaure, Pharaoh, 299
menorah, 67, 186, 267
Merneptah, Pharaoh, 294
Mesopotamia, 148–49, 161, 173, 184
messiah, 220, 260, 269
metopes, 88–89
Mevlevi Dervishes, 167
Michelangelo, 43, 44, 46–47, 53, 58, 59–61, 63–64
Midak Alley (Mahfouz), 290
Midas, King, 145
Middle Bronze Age, 148, 225, 254, 328
Middle East peace. See peace, Middle East
mihrab, 255
Miletus (Greece), 106, 107, 152
millet, 139
Minoan civilization, 93, 184
miracles, 231, 277–80
mithraeum, 185
Mithras (Persian deity), 76
monasticism, 159, 227
Mongols, 163, 164, 165, 182
monotheism, 244, 293, 315
Monteverdi, Claudio, 41–42
Montreux (Switzerland), 31
Moriah, Mount, 265, 269
Moses, 2, 136, 199, 244; in art, 64, 244; and Baha'i, 219; Mosaic Covenant, 151; and Transfiguration, 227. See also Sinai, Mount
Moses (Michelangelo), 63, 64–65
Mot (Canaanite deity), 178
Mother Earth. See Gaia
Mother Goddess, 108–11, 147–48, 173
Mother Teresa, 71
Mount Athos. See Athos
Mouw, Richard, 280
Muhammad, 2, 7, 9, 131, 133, 206, 211, 219, 234–35, 236, 237, 264; Night Journey, 235, 268

Subject/Name Index

Muhammad Ali, Pasha, 288
Muslims. *See* Islam
Mycenae, 104
Mycenaean civilization, 93–94, 184
Mycerinus. *See* Menkaure, Pharaoh
mysticism, 227, 328. *See also* Sufism
mythology, myth, xvii, 1–5, 88–89, 92, 123–24, 233, 305

Nabatean, 200–202
Nablus (West Bank, Palestine), 228–29
Nachmanides, 262
Naples (Italy), 72–74, 78, 131
Napoleon, 218, 287–88
Nasr, Seyyed, 314
National Archaeological Museum (Athens), 91–94
National Museum (Damascus), 178, 183–87
Nativity, Church of the (Bethlehem), 273
NATO, 174
naturalism, 314
navel (of the world). *See omphalos*
Navona, Piazza (Rome), 62
Nazareth (West Bank, Palestine), 226, 227, 273
Nazis, 20–21
Nea Church (Jerusalem), 237
Nebo, Mount, 199, 200
Nebuchadnezzar, King, 137, 265
Nefertiti, Queen, 296–97
Nehemiah, 252
Nemrut Dagi (Turkey), 162
Neolithic Age, 146–47, 326–27
Nero, Emperor, 55, 66, 103
Netanya (Israel), 213, 217
Netherlands, 16, 17–26, 366–68
New Kingdom (Egypt), 297, 306, 307
New Testament, 220–22
Newton, Sir Isaac, 49, 317
New Year Festival, 157
Nicholas III, Pope, 63
Night Journey. *See* Muhammad
Nika Revolt, 130

Nile River, 62, 225, 287, 289, 292, 293, 300, 304, 305, 306, 307, 309, 374, 383
Nobles, Tombs of (West Bank, Egypt), 306, 307
Notre Dame Cathedral, 306
Nuweiba (Egypt), 204

O'Connor, Jerome Murphy-, 272
Odeon of Herod Atticus, 90
Odeon of Pericles, 90
Odysseus, xvi, 82
Odyssey (Homer), 82
Oedipus, King, 95, 97. 99
Oedipus Rex (Sophocles), 97, 99
Oikoumene, 37
oil, 286, 287
Old Assyrian State, 149, 150
Olives, Mount of, 237, 240, 273
Olympia, 99, 104; Olympian gods, 123; Olympics, 81, 84–85, 99
Omphalos, 8–9, 100, 158, 232, 277. *See also* the Center; the sacred; sacred places
Onophrios, Saint, 161–62
Ophel (Jerusalem), 230, 239, 240, 252, 254, 263
Ophel Archaeological Garden, 261, 263–64
Ordonnances, 364
Orthodox Judaism, 259–60
Orthodoxy, Eastern, xi, 40, 85; art of, 140; Church of the Holy Sepulcher, 275–80; definition, 138; Mount Tabor, 226–27; and Ottomans, 139; Patriarch of Constantinople, 129. *See also* Geneva, Ecumenical Center; Kariye Museum; St. Catherine's Monastery; St. George's Church (Istanbul)
Osiris (Egyptian deity), 76, 308 n. 3
Otto, Rudolph, xvi
Ottomans; and Aqaba (Jordan), 203; defeat during WWI, 139, 142, 167; and Germany, 123; invasion of Europe, 164; and Istanbul, 127, 131, 135, 139;

Subject/Name Index   409

rule in Egypt, 298; rule in
   Greece, 85; rule in Turkey, 106,
   166. *See also* Topkapi Palace
Ozymandias (Shelley), 306

paganism, 182, 192
Palais des Nations (Geneva), 34–35
Palatine Hill (Rome), 55, 65, 67
Palazzo della Signoria (Florence), 370
Palazzo Vecchio (Florence), 44
Paleolithic Age, 146, 325–26
Palestinians, 198; Liberation
   Organization (PLO), 257;
   Nablus, 228; nationalism, 180,
   228, 256–58; Philistines, 184;
   refugees, 194–97; West Bank
   and Gaza, 184, 195, 196, 204,
   213, 227, 228, 256–258. *See also*
   Arab-Israeli Christian; Elias
   Chacour; Gaza (Palestine);
   West Bank (Palestine)
Palmyra, 184, 187
Panathenaea, 88, 90
Panhellenic Games, 104
Pantheon (Rome), 53, 57, 58, 124
Papacy, 44
papyrus, 122, 303
parchment, 122
Parnassus, Mount (Greece), 95, 97
Parthenon (Athens), 85, 87–89, 111
Pascal, Blaise, 13
Passover, 220
Patras (Greece), 80, 82
Patriarch (Orthodox), 129, 139, 141,
   275, 277–80
Patriarchal Church. *See* Saint George's
   Church
Paul, Saint; at the Areopagus (Athens),
   86; in art, 64; at Corinth,
   103–4; at Damascus, 183, 190;
   imprisonment in Caesarea
   (Judea), 218; journeys of, 105,
   166; and Orthodoxy, Eastern,
   138
Paul IV, Pope, 56
Paul VI, Pope, 70; Audience Hall, 71
Pausanias, 145

Pax Romana, 79
peace, Middle East, 194–97, 258
Peloponnese, 82, 93, 100, 102, 103, 104
   Peloponnesian League, 101–2;
   Peloponnesian War, 101
Pensées (Pascal), 13
Pentecost; Pentecostals, 222, 225, 368
Pergamum (Turkey), 90, 106, 119–26;
   library of, 120, 122; Museum,
   Berlin, 123–24
Periander, 102
Pericles, 87
Persephone (goddess), 186
Perseus (Cellini), 44
Persians, 182, 186; and Ankara
   (Turkey), 145; and Arabs, 235,
   236; and Baha'is, 218; defeat by
   Alexander the Great, 143; defeat
   of Egypt, 293; defeat by Greece,
   86, 101; Delphic oracle, 96;
   Jerusalem occupation, 236; and
   Madaba, 199; and Pergamum,
   120
Persian Gulf War, 180
Peter, Saint, 68, 227; Basilica (Vatican),
   52, 56, 57–58; grave of, 57,
   69–70; Square (Vatican), 52, 57,
   58; Throne of, 58
Petra (Jordan), 198, 200–203
Petrarch, 43
Pharisees, 249
Phidias, 87, 89
Philadelphia. *See* Amman (Jordan)
Philetairos, 120
Philip of Macedon, 98
Philistines, 136, 184, 285
Philo of Byzantium, 374
Phoenicians, 184, 191, 218
Phrygia(n), 108–9, 145, 149, 151, 152
Piaget, Jean, 32
Piazza di Spagna (Rome). *See* Spanish
   Steps
Pietà (Michelangelo), 58, 64
Pilate, 220, 270, 375
pilgrimage, xi, xvii, 5, 9–12, 163, 209,
   231, 263, 273, 283, 321
pillarization, 24

Subject/Name Index

Piraeus (Greece), 104
Pisa (Italy), 42, 47–48, 223, 270, 372;
    Leaning Tower, 47–48
Pius XII, Pope, 69–70
Pliny, 113
Plutarch, 95, 113
Polycarp, Bishop, 119
Pompeii (Italy), 72–77, 199
Ponte Vecchio (Florence), 45
Pontifex Maximus, 54
Pontius Pilate. *See* Pilate
Pope; definition, 72
Porta Appia (Rome), 68
Port Said (Egypt), 286
predestination, 366, 367
Presbyterian, 34
Priam, King, 110
Priene (Turkey), 107
Primavera (Botticelli), 45
Prisca (Priscilla), 104
Promised Land, 181, 199, 228
prophecy, prophet, 185, 189, 195
Protestantism, 29, 137, 138, 277; and
    Garden Tomb, 272; in Geneva
    (Switzerland), 32–34, 362–66;
    in Holland, 24, 25; Stations of
    the Cross, 270. *See also* Synod
    of Dort
Ptolemy (ancient astronomer), 49
Ptolemy, King, 122
Punic War, Second, 109
purgation, 12
pyramids (Egypt), 111, 114. *See also*
    Giza, pyramids
Pythagoras, 88, 95
Pythia (Delphic oracle), 95–96, 99
Pythian Games, 99, 100

Qaddafi, Muammar al, 177
qiblah, 234
Qubeiba, el. *See* Emmaus
quest, xvii–xviii, 1–5
Quetzalcoatl. *See* Kukulkan
Quirinal Hill (Rome), 55
Qumran (Israel), 243, 249–50
Qur'an, 9, 10, 133, 236, 265, 290–91

rabbi, 266
Rafah (Palestinian city), 285, 286
Ramban Synagogue, 262
Ramesseum, 306, 308
Ramses II, Pharaoh, 150–51, 306,
    307–8
Ramses III, Pharaoh, 293, 306, 308, 309
Rape of a Sabine Woman
    (Giambologna,), 44
Rape of Europa, 77
Raphael, 57, 60
Ras Shamra, 178
Re (Egyptian deity), 305
Red Sea, 203, 288
Reformation, Protestant, 206, 365–66
Reformed Christianity, xi, 34, 362–68
Reform Judaism. *See* Jews, Reform
relics, 273, 277
religion, 37, 211, 219, 221, 222, 318–20
Rembrandt van Rijn, 26
Remonstrance, Remonstrants, 366–67
Renaissance, 41, 43–46, 140, 365,
    369–73
resurrection, 210, 221, 227, 270, 371, 372
return(ing), xviii, 12
Revelation, Book of, 119

Rhodes (Greece), 104, 111, 374
Rialto Bridge (Venice), 40
Rijksmuseum, 26
rites of passage, 3
Robinson, Edward, 241
Rockefeller Archaeological Museum,
    248
Roman Catholicism, xi, 9, 24–25, 49–
    50, 51–52, 56, 57, 66, 105, 137,
    138, 270, 362
Roman Empire. *See* Romans
Romanesque. *See* architecture,
    Romanesque
Roman Forum. *See* Forum (Rome)
Romans, xi, 4, 6, 98, 108, 109, 128,
    198; and Anatolia, 152, 164;
    and Asia Minor (province),
    111, 119, 145, 152; and Baalbek
    (Heliopolis), 191–92; cities, 187,
    199, 254; and Constantinople,

Subject/Name Index   411

127–29; and Corinth, 102; decline and fall of, 74, 113, 130–31, 185; and Dura-Europos, 185; engineering, 53–55, 65–66, 114–16, 128–29, 182, 187, 191–92, 198, 199, 201, 254; and Jerusalem, 273, 278; and Jewish revolt, 67, 266; Justinian, 130–31; law, 67–68; religions, 75–77, 109, 191–92; and Petra, 200–202; and Pompeii, 74; sea trade, 102; visit to, 51–72
Romanticism, 314
Romulus and Remus, 55
Romulus Augustus, Emperor, 74
Rosetta Stone, 288
Rousseau, Jean-Jacques, 32
Rowling, J.K., xvii
Rumi, Jalal al-Din, 164–65

Sabazios, 76
Sabbath, 198, 216, 220, 243, 250
sacramental sense of reality, 318–20
sacred, the, xv–xviii, 219, 232–34. *See also* the Center; *omphalos*
sacred journey, xvii–xviii, 1–13. *See also* quest; pilgrimage
sacred places, 4–12, 95, 224, 229, 230–31, 234–35, 295, 301. *See also* the sacred
Sadat, Anwar, 286
Sadducees, 249
Safed (Israel), 224
Saint Catherine's Monastery (Sinai), 200, 205–07, 208
Saint George's Church (Istanbul), 131, 139, 140–42
Saint-Pierre Cathedral (Geneva), 34
Saladin, Sultan, 189, 223, 287
Salamis, Battle of, 98
Samaria, 248
Samaritan, 216, 228–29, 249
Samos (Greece), 104, 111
Samuel, 250
Samuel, First Book of, 328
Samuel, Second Book of, 328
San Carlo Opera House (Naples), 73, 74

San Pietro in Vincoli (Rome), 63–65
Santa Trinità dei Monti (Rome), 62
Santorini (Greece), 92, 104; frescoes, 92–93
Sarah, 181
Saronic Gulf (Greece), 102
Sassanids, 185
Satan, 235
Saturn, Temple of (Rome), 54
Saul, King of Israel, 250, 252
Savonarola, 44–45
Savoy, House of, 73
Schliemann, Heinrich, 93
schul, 260
Sea Peoples, 136, 151, 178, 184, 308
Second Commandment, 186
Second Temple, 248, 249, 262–65, 271
Selcuk (Turkey), 108, 116, 119
Seleucia (Turkey), 167
Seleucus, King, 120
self-actualization (Maslow), 3, 358–61
Seljuk Turks, 119, 145, 160, 163–67
Semitic, 150, 167, 175, 182, 185, 225
Sennacherib, King of Assyria, 240
Sephardic Judaism, 224
Septuagint, 221
seraglio. *See* Topkapi Palace
Serapis. *See* Osiris (Egyptian deity)
Sermon on the Mount, 216
Serpent Church (Goreme), 160, 161
serpents, 160–61
Seth (Egyptian deity), 182
Seven Hills of Rome, 56
Seven Wonders of the Ancient World, 111, 113, 114, 136, 299, 374
Shakespeare, William, 323
Sharm el-Sheikh (Egypt), 204
Sharon, Ariel, 257
Sharon, Plain of, 217
Shaushga (Hittite deity), 156–57
Shechem (Israel), 175, 228, 229
Shelley, Percy, 62, 306
Shiloh (Israel), 229
Shrine of the Book, 243, 248, 249
Sibylline Books, 109
Siena (Italy), 43, 369–70, 372
Signoria, Piazza della (Florence), 43–45

412 Subject/Name Index

Silk Route, 187
Siloam Channel, 240
Siloam Inscription, 136, 240
Siloam Pool, 240, 242, 252
Sinai, Mount, 4, 7, 64, 205–11
Sinai (peninsula), 198, 204–11, 285–86
Sinan, 136
Sion (Jerusalem), 254–55
Siq (Petra), 200
Sisera, 226
Sistine Chapel (Vatican), 47, 59–61
Six Day War, 256, 261, 262, 265, 286
Sixtus IV, Pope, 59, 60
Sixtus V, Pope, 55
Slavs, 131
Smith, Huston, 138–39, 312
Smyrna, 106, 119
Sneek (Netherlands), 22
Sobek (Egyptian deity), 305
Socinianism, 366
Socrates, 91
Solomon, King of Israel, 182, 212, 263
Solomon, Temple of (Jerusalem), 7, 8; and Dome of the Rock, 237; and Hagia Sophia, 135; and Jewish lore, 231–34; and Muslim lore, 234–35; and Samaritans, 225; and Sistine Chapel, 59; and St. Peter's Basilica, 58; and Temple Mount, 264–69
Solon, 95
Sophocles, 81, 82, 90, 97, 99
Sorrento (Italy), 77
souk, 261–62, 280, 290
Spanish Steps (Piazza di Spagna), 62
Sparta (Greece), 94, 101
Sphinx (Thebes), 97; riddle of, 97
sphinxes, 155. *See also* Great Sphinx (Egypt)
Sphinx Gate (Hattusa), 155
Spice Route (Arabia), 202
Stables of Solomon (Temple Mount), 268
stages of adventure, xviii, 2, 12
Starry Messenger (Galileo), 49
Stations of the Cross (Jerusalem), 270, 275, 375–76

Stoa of Eumenes, 90
Stonehenge, 4, 302
Storm God (Hittite deity), 154, 156
Strabo, 100–101
Straight Street (Damascus), 189
Strasbourg (France), 362, 364
Suez (Egypt), 286
Suez Canal, 285–87, 288
Sufism, 164–65
Suleiman the Magnificent, 136, 239, 255, 268
Suleymaniye Mosque (Istanbul), 136, 142
Sultanahmet Square (Istanbul), 131, 140, 141
Sumer(ian), 136, 158, 184
Sun God (Hittite deity), 157
Sun Goddess (Hittite deity), 154
Sunnis, 163
Suzerainty Treaty. *See* Hittite treaties
Switzerland, 27–37; Swiss Alps, 27–30
Sword God (Hittite deity), 157
synagogue, 185–87, 260
Synod of Dort, 366–68
Syntagma Square (Athens), 84
Syria, 166–69, 171, 173, 174, 193, 200; Antakya, 166–68; Cybele, 109; Hatay, 167; Islamic expansion to, 236; Levant (Canaan), 175; Nabatean Arabs, 202; Seleucids, 120; Via Maris, 224; visit to, 177–92. *See also* Damascus

Tabor, Mount, 206, 226–27
Tahrir Square (Cairo), 289, 293
Talmud, 216, 265, 268
Tarsus (Turkey), 104, 152, 166
Taurus Mountains, 149, 166, 167
tawaf, 9–10, 237
tawhid, 234, 237–38
Teacher of Righteousness, 249–50
tel, tell, 146, 178, 224, 225, 226
Tel Aviv (Israel), 212, 213, 217, 256
Tempietto, 52
Temple of Solomon. *See* Solomon, Temple of (Jerusalem)

Subject/Name Index 413

Temple Mount (Jerusalem), 189, 231–38, 252, 261–69, 381
Ten Commandments, 64, 205. *See also* Second Commandment
terrorism, 213–14
Teshub (Hittite deity), 156, 157, 182
Theater of Marcellus (Rome), 56
Thebes (Greece), 95, 97, 101
Thebes (Egypt), 283, 304–6
theocracy, 236, 364
Theodora, Empress, 129
Theodore, Saint, 160–61
Thera. *See* Santorini
Theseus, King, 88
Theseus and the Minotaur, 77
thin places, xv–xvii, 8, 9, 158, 322
Third Ecumenical Council (Ephesus), 111
Tholos (Delphi), 99
Thomas, Saint, 161
Thoth (Egyptian deity), 305
Thucydides, 87
Thutmose II, Pharaoh, 309
Thutmose III, Pharaoh, 293, 308
Tiberius, Emperor, 55, 77–78
Tiberius (Israel), 224
tin, 148
Tintoretto, 40
Titus, Emperor, 65; Arch of, 55, 67
Tomb of Mausolus. *See* Mausolus, Tomb of
Tombs of the Nobles. *See* Nobles, Tombs of (West Bank, Egypt)
Topkapi (film), 133
Topkapi Palace, 131, 132–34, 136; harem, 134
Torah, 9, 186, 208, 216, 228, 247, 255
Trajan, Emperor, 54, 65, 191; Column of, 55; Forum of, 41, 55; Temple of (Pergamum), 122
transcendence, 316
Transfiguration, 207, 226–27
Transfiguration, Church of the (Sinai), 206, 207
Trastavere (Rome), 56
Treaty of Kadesh, 136, 151, 156
treaty pattern, 151

Trevi Fountain, 52
tribal confederacy, 228
Trinity. *See* Holy Trinity
Trojan War, 89, 93, 110
Troy, 93, 135, 136, 152
True Cross, 273, 274
TULIP, 367
Tulkarm (Palestine, West Bank), 213, 214 n. 1
Turkey, Turks, 105, 165–67, 182, 278; and Acre, 223; in Ankara, 144, 145; and Acropolis (Athens), 89; and Baha'u'llah, 218; and Corinth, 101; and Greeks, 107, 160; Hagia Sophia, preservation of, 134–35; nationalism, 142, 167; origins of, 163; and Smyrna, conquest of, 119; visit to, 106–174. *See also* Ataturk; Hatay; Ottomans; Seljuk Turks
Tuscany (Italy), 42
Tutankhamon, Pharaoh, 295, 297
Twelve, the (Hittite deities), 157

Ugarit, 152, 175, 178–79, 184
Ulysses. *See* Odysseus
Umar, Caliph, 236
Umayyad, 182, 189; Mosque, 182, 189
ummah, 235
union. *See* return
Unitarianism, 366
United Nations, 32, 34–35, 197, 285
United States' Middle Eastern policy, 180
Upper Room (Jerusalem), 237, 255
Ur, 185
Urban VIII, Pope, 49, 58
Uris, Leon, 231
utopia, 315
Utrecht (Netherlands), 18, 23–25; Union of, 24
Valens, Emperor, 128–29
Valley of the Kings (West Bank, Egypt), 297, 306–10
Valley of the Queens (West Bank, Egypt), 306
Van Gogh Museum, 26

Subject/Name Index

vaporetto, 39, 42
Vatican City, 56–59; audience with the Pope, 71; Castel Sant'Angelo, 63. *See also* Sistine Chapel; St. Peter's Basilica; Vatican Grottoes; Vatican Museums
Vatican Grottoes, 69–70
Vatican museums, 59, 61
Vatican Hill, 56
Venezia, Piazza (Rome), 63, 65
Venice (Italy), 26, 38–42, 58, 223
Venus, Temple of (Jerusalem), 273
Veronese, 40
Vesta, Temple of (Rome), 54
Vespasian, Emperor, 65, 103
Vesuvius, Mount, 72, 74, 77
Via dei Fori Imperiali (Rome), 65
Via Dolorosa (Jerusalem), 270–71, 275, 375–76
Via Maris (Canaan), 224
Via Sacra (Rome), 55
Victor Emmanuel II, King of Italy, 53
Villa dei Misteri (Pompeii), 74, 75
Villa Jovis (Capri), 78
Viracocha. *See* Kukulkan
Virgil, 152
Virgin Birth, 220, 221
Virgin Mary, 109, 128, 140, 276
Voltaire, 32
Vulgate, 64

Warren, Charles, 240
Warren's Shaft (Jerusalem), 240, 241, 252–54
Water Gate (Jerusalem), 252
Weather God. *See* Storm God (Hittite deity)
Wesley, John, 364
West Bank (Egypt), 307–10
West Bank (Palestine), 195–97, 226, 227–28, 256–58
Westminster Assembly, 368
Western Wall (Jerusalem), 230, 255, 261, 262, 263, 266, 267, 270
Wiesel, Elie, 246
wilderness. *See* desert
William II, German emperor, 192

World Council of Churches, 32, 35; Ecumenical Center (Geneva), 35–36
World's Religions (Smith), 312

Yadin, Yigael, 225
Yad Vashem (Jerusalem), 243, 245–47
Yahweh. *See* God
Yam (Temple Mount, Jerusalem), 267
Yazilikaya (Hattusa), 156–58
Yerkapi (Hattusa), 154
yeshiva, 260
Yiddish, 260
Yom Kippur War, 286

Zealots, 249
Zeus, 8, 76, 109, 122–23, 182; Altar of (Pergamum), 122–24; Great Statue (Olympia), 111, 374; Temple of (Pergamum), 120; Temple of Olympian Zeus (Athens), 85
Zion (Jerusalem), 8, 231, 233, 238, 254
Zionist, 260
zodiac, 186
Zoroaster, 219

www.ingramcontent.com/pod-product-compliance
Lightning Source LLC
Chambersburg PA
CBHW071226290426
44108CB00013B/1310